KOREA

OSPREY
PUBLISHING

Thus, we see that war is not only a political act, but a true instrument of politics, a continuation of politics by other means.
Carl von Clausewitz, *On War*

He, therefore, who desires peace, should prepare for war. He who aspires to victory, should spare no pains to train his soldiers. And he who hopes for success, should fight on principle, not chance. No one dares to offend or insult a power of known superiority in action.
Vegetius, *Military Institutions of the Romans*

RICHARD DANNATT & ROBERT LYMAN

KOREA
WAR WITHOUT END

OSPREY PUBLISHING
Bloomsbury Publishing Plc
Kemp House, Chawley Park, Cumnor Hill, Oxford OX2 9PH, UK
Bloomsbury Publishing Ireland Limited,
29 Earlsfort Terrace, Dublin 2, D02 AY28, Ireland
1385 Broadway, 5th Floor, New York, NY 10018, USA
E-mail: info@ospreypublishing.com
www.ospreypublishing.com

OSPREY is a trademark of Osprey Publishing Ltd

First published in Great Britain in 2025

A catalogue record for this book is available from the British Library

ISBN: HB 9781472869753; PB 9781472869746; eBook 9781472869739; ePDF 9781472869784;
XML 9781472869777; Audio 9781472869760

25 26 27 28 29   10 9 8 7 6 5 4 3 2 1

Plate section image credits are given in full in the List of Illustrations and Maps (pp. 10–13).
Maps by www.bounford.com

Index by Fionbar Lyons

Typeset by Deanta Global Publishing Services, Chennai, India
Printed and bound in Great Britain by Clays Ltd, Elcograf S.p.A.

Imperial War Museums Collections
Many of the photos in this book come from the huge collections of IWM (Imperial War Museums)
which cover all aspects of conflict involving Britain and the Commonwealth since the start
of the twentieth century. These rich resources are available online to search, browse and buy at
www.iwm.org.uk/collections. Imperial War Museums www.iwm.org.uk

Osprey Publishing supports the Woodland Trust, the UK's leading woodland conservation charity.

MIX
Paper | Supporting
responsible forestry
FSC
www.fsc.org   FSC® C018072

To find out more about our authors and books visit www.ospreypublishing.com. Here you will find
extracts, author interviews, details of forthcoming events and the option to sign up for our newsletter.

For product safety related questions contact productsafety@bloomsbury.com

DEDICATION

In memory of the men, women and children of Korea who died in this most devastating of wars, without knowing why; and for those who also fought, both for the Republic of Korea and their allies across the United Nations, not always knowing the answer to 'Why Korea?', except that they were resisting untrammelled aggression, and doing their duty.

Contents

Notes to the Reader

To make unit designations between the various UN, ROK, North Korean Peoples' Army (NKPA) and Chinese formations fighting in Korea distinguishable from each other, those of the NKPA (known as the *In Mun Gun*) and of China are in *italics*.

For British readers, Korean (both North and South) and American divisions comprised three regiments ideally (two when the division was under-manned), the equivalent in the British Army of a brigade. Each regiment (or 'brigade' in British parlance) ideally comprised three battalions, each of between 600 and 800 men, although all too often in Korea two battalions was the norm.

Given the International Date Line, times and dates are those that pertain to the countries in which events occurred.

The spelling of Korean names and places are those commonly adopted by Western commentators at the time. Likewise, the names of North Korean and Chinese leaders and military commanders are those most commonly used during the war, using the Romanised form of spelling.

The authors have tried to streamline the narrative and for this reason have kept citations to an absolute minimum. All uncited references are from books listed in the bibliography.

List of Illustrations and Maps

The war was dominated by artillery, North Korea and Chinese as
much as American and British, by the time the lines had been
allowed to solidify after July 1951. During June and July 1952,
the expenditure of artillery had become astonishing: in less than
60 days the communists fired over 700,000 rounds at the UN
positions (nearly 12,000 per day), while the UN troops fired
back over 4.7 million (nearly 80,000 per day). Not much seemed
to have changed in positional warfare since 1916. (Photo
© Hulton-Deutsch Collection/Corbis via Getty Images)

American troops of the 35th Infantry Regiment observe smoke shells
striking enemy positions on 1 February 1951. At the Imjin River
in April 1951, the guns supporting a single British battalion fired
24,000 rounds during the three-day battle, an average of 1,000
rounds per gun. (US Army)

A detachment of the 16th New Zealand Field Artillery Regiment firing
in support of the 1st Battalion, Argyll and Sutherland Highlanders,
all part of 27th Commonwealth Brigade. (© IWM BF 364)

Napalm being dropped on an enemy position forward of US Marines
as they withdraw from the Changjin (Chosin) reservoir in
November 1950. Napalm, a petroleum-based explosive, was used
extensively by UN forces. (US Army)

US troops digging in on a hilltop position in 1952. This type of
positional combat characterised the two-year period from July
1951 to the end of the war in July 1953. (Photo by MPI/Hulton
Archive/Getty Images)

US Marines duck for cover as an enemy 82mm shell explodes above
their position on 11 April 1952. Artillery played a significant role
in the fighting, especially that of the static warfare conducted in
the two years following July 1951. (Photo by Keystone/Getty
Images)

The UN enjoyed supremacy at sea for most of the war, a situation that
allowed MacArthur to achieve success at Inchon. Here, the 16in.
guns of the USS *Missouri* fire on land targets off North Korea.
(US Navy)

Men of C and D Companies of the 1st Battalion, The Gloucestershire
Regiment, 29th Brigade, having captured Hill 327 south of
Seoul in February 1951, wait for the next phase of the attack. It
was the Glosters' first battle in Korea. The one for which they

would receive well-deserved renown would follow two months later at the Imjin River. (© IWM BF 377)

Men of 1st Battalion, Royal Ulster Rifles and Centurion tanks of the 8th Hussars. (© IWM BF 510)

A wounded Chinese soldier being tended by a soldier of 1st Glosters. (© IWM BF 379)

A Vickers medium machine-gun team of the 3rd Battalion, Royal Australian Regiment. (© IWM BF 423)

Men of 3rd Battalion, Royal Australian Regiment prepare barbed wire in front of their positions. Note the nature of the terrain. (© IWM MH 31535)

Five weeks after the battle of the Imjin River, the British were back. Here, a soldier of the 1st Battalion, The Gloucestershire Regiment stands on the old A Company position, pointing to the main supply route through the Imjin River valley as seen from there. The ridge on the left is the route the Chinese used to attack D Company in the famous battle in April 1951. (© IWM BF 10277)

In a piece of theatre, not required by the terms of the armistice, Kim Il-sung signs the Korean Armistice Agreement at Pyongyang, assisted by General Nam Il. (Photo by Hulton Archive/Getty Images)

MAPS

Chronology

1950

The first war for Korea

25 Jun	North Korean People's Army (NKPA) crosses the 38th Parallel into the Republic of Korea (ROK), beginning the first Korean War.
25 Jun	The United Nations drafts UN Security Council Resolution 82, calling for the cessation of hostilities and withdrawal of North Korean forces from the ROK.
27 Jun	UN Security Council passes Resolution 83, which allows the United Nations to act militarily to support the ROK.
28 Jun	Fall of Seoul.
30 Jun	President Harry S. Truman orders US ground forces into Korea from Japan.
2 Jul	Task Force Smith disembarks at Pusan.
5 Jul	Task Force Smith goes into action at Osan.
7 Jul	UN creates United Nations Command, under commander appointed by USA.
5 Jul–4 Aug	UN forces fight delaying action across South Korea.
4 Aug	Establishment of the Pusan Perimeter by Eighth Army.
5–19 Aug	First battle of the 'Naktong Bulge'.
27 Aug – 15 Sept	Perimeter battles, heaviest fighting of war.

1–5 Sep	NKPA Naktong offensive.
15 Sep	UN forces land at Inchon.
17 Sep	UN forces begin breakout from the Pusan Perimeter and drive towards Seoul.
19 Sep–1 Oct	UN pursuit and exploitation.
26 Sep	First recapture of Seoul.
1 Oct	ROK forces pursue NKPA forces across the 38th Parallel and into North Korea.

The second war for Korea

7 Oct	UN agrees to an attack into North Korea and the reunification of the country.
9 Oct	The first UN Forces cross 38th Parallel, the effective start of the second Korean War.
12 Oct	The first Chinese troops enter Korea undetected by UN forces.
15 Oct	Truman and General Douglas MacArthur meet at Wake Island.
19 Oct	Pyongyang captured by 1st ROK and 8th Cavalry Divisions.
25 Oct	ROK II Corps defeated in a four-day battle at Onjong.
26 Oct	X Corps lands at Wonsan and Iwon.
1 Nov	Chinese ambush 1st Cavalry Division at Unsan.
10–26 Nov	X Corps continues its advance towards Yalu in east, Eighth Army in west.
21 Nov	First elements of 7th Infantry Division reach the Yalu.
24 Nov	Start of MacArthur's 'final offensive'.
25 Nov	Chinese strike Eighth Army along Ch'ongch'on River in west.
27 Nov	Chinese strike 1st Marine and 7th Infantry Divisions at Changjin (Chosin) reservoir in east.
26 Nov–1 Dec	US 2nd and 25th Divisions defeated along Ch'ongch'on in west. Retreat.
26 Nov–13 Dec	US 1st Marine Division and British 41 Royal Marine Commando fight at the Changjin reservoir, then withdraw to Hungnam and Wonsan. Marines retreat from Koto-ri.

28 Nov	MacArthur is refused permission to extend the war into China by means of B-29 bombing and a naval blockade.
22 Dec	General Walton Walker killed in road accident; Matthew Ridgway appointed to command Eighth Army.
24 Dec	X Corps completes the evacuation from Hungnam.

1951

1–4 Jan	27th Commonwealth Brigade fights at Uijongbu, allowing Eighth Army to withdraw beyond Seoul.
4 Jan	Chinese capture Seoul.
11 Jan	UN terms for a ceasefire rejected by China and North Korea.
14 Jan	UN lines rest along 37th parallel in South Korea.
15 Jan	Eighth Army's Operation *Wolfhound*.
20–22 Jan	New Zealand 16th Field Regiment joins 27th Commonwealth Brigade.
25 Jan	UN reassumes offensive with Operation *Thunderbolt*.
1 Feb	UN votes to end Korean conflict by 'peaceful means'.
10 Feb	Eighth Army's Operation *Roundup*.
14 Feb	Chinese counteroffensive; Chinese turned back at Chipyong-ni.
17 Feb–17 Mar	UN continues offensive; Operation *Killer* moves north.
7 Mar	Eighth Army's Operation *Ripper*.
18 Mar	Second recapture of Seoul.
22 Mar	Eighth Army's Operation *Courageous*.
5 Apr	Eighth Army's Operation *Rugged*.
11 Apr	Eighth Army's Operation *Dauntless*.
11 Apr	MacArthur recalled; General Matthew Ridgway assumes command at FECOM (Far East Command).
14 Apr	Lieutenant General James A. Van Fleet takes over Eighth Army.
22–24 Apr	Chinese offensive begins; the 'Glorious Glosters' hold on at the Imjin River and 3 RAR at Kapyong. Chinese attack

is halted. The 27th Brigade leaves Korea soon after as fresh British and Canadian units begin to arrive.

30 Apr	Chinese break contact.
16–22 May	US forces halt the Soyang offensive. May Massacre.
23 May–1 Jun	UN drives north.
13 Jun	UN on 38th Parallel.
23 Jun	Soviet Union proposes truce talks at UN.
10 Jul	Truce talks begin at Kaesong.
28 Jul	1st Commonwealth Division formed.
1 Aug–31 Oct	UN launches limited attacks to straighten lines: battles of Bloody Ridge and Heartbreak Ridge.
12 Nov	UN offensive is called off by General Ridgway. Static phase begins.
27 Nov	Truce talks resume at Panmunjom; ceasefire line agreed upon, at line of contact.

1952

2 Apr	Screening of UN POWs begins; Koje-do riots commence.
7 May	General Francis Dodd captured by communist POWs at Koje-do.
12 May	General Mark Clark takes over command of UN forces from General Ridgway.
12 May–12 Jun	General Haydon Boatner quells disturbances on Koje-do.
Jun–Oct	Stalemate along battlefront while truce talks deadlocked on POW repatriation question. Hill battles rage on Baldy, Whitehorse, elsewhere.
8 Oct	Truce talks recessed at Panmunjom; complete deadlock.
Oct–Nov	Heavy pressure on ROK in centre of line.
Nov	Indian proposal on POWs in UN.
Dec	President-elect Dwight D. Eisenhower comes to Korea; intensification of UN psychological warfare.

1953

11 Feb	General Maxwell Taylor replaces Lieutenant General James A. Van Fleet at Eighth Army.
22 Feb	UN proposes exchange of sick and wounded POWs.
5 Mar	Death of Stalin.
28 Mar	Chinese agree to POW exchange proposed by UN.
30 Mar	Chou En-Lai indicates communists will accept Indian UN proposal of November 1952. Resumption of truce talks at Panmunjom.
16–18 Apr	Battle for Pork Chop Hill.
20–26 Apr	Exchange of sick and wounded POWs at Panmunjom.
27 Apr	Resumption of plenary sessions at Panmunjom.
May	Savage fighting along stalemated line while details of truce ironed out at Panmunjom.
4 Jun	Chinese agree to all UN truce proposals.
25 Jun	Walter Robertson begins 'Little Truce Talks' with Syngman Rhee to secure ROK acceptance of armistice; Chinese launch massive attacks against ROK divisions.
7 Jul	ROK agrees to truce terms.
27 Jul	Ceasefire signed at Panmunjom. Fighting ends.
4 Sep	Screening and repatriation of POWs begins at Freedom Village, Panmunjom.

Introduction

The war that smashed into the Korean peninsula in 1950 is commonly described by many in the West as a forgotten war. This is certainly true. It remains largely forgotten today, even for those members of the United Nations who sent their soldiers, sailors and airmen to fight. Few in the USA, the UK, Turkey, Thailand, the Philippines, Colombia, Australia, or any of the other countries which answered the call of this new international body in 1950, remember the war or the reasons for their countries sending troops to fight, other than perhaps to 'fight back against international communism'.* One might suggest that it is a forgotten war precisely because it was a war that few have wanted to remember. It certainly was never forgotten by those who fought there, though in the UK it was such an insignificant war in social memory that it didn't even make its way onto the village memorials that dot the country, visible signs of the savage impact made on every community in the land after the two world wars. In the writing of this book one of the authors undertook an admittedly not very scientific survey of pedestrians in a shopping precinct in Bracknell, Berkshire. Not a single person asked, of all ages, had ever heard of the Korean War. A memorial statue was only unveiled in London in 2014, itself the gift of the government of the Republic of Korea, ROK. It may well be, of

*Troops from the USA, Australia, Belgium, Canada, Colombia, Ethiopia, France, Greece, Luxembourg, the Netherlands, New Zealand, the Philippines, Thailand, Turkey and the UK fought alongside the ROK Army. Eight of those countries sent naval forces and five sent air forces. Eight countries provided logistical support, including Norway, and seven countries provided medical units, including Denmark, India, Italy and Sweden.

course, that the combatants were all too happy to forget a war that was unexpected in its arrival, inglorious in its execution and unresolved in its ending.

But the war is certainly not forgotten in Korea, or in China. In China, the Korean War continues to be referred to as the War to Resist America and Aid Korea, and is presented entirely as a defensive response to a threatened American invasion. It's a reminder today that China and the United States have been at war before; and the Chinese remember it, even if Americans don't. In both North Korea and the ROK, memories remain visceral of the moment when the simmering tensions between both parts of the artificially divided peninsula erupted in devasting violence on 25 June 1950, leading directly to the deaths of as many as 3 million people, most of whom were guilty of nothing more than being caught up in a country at war.*

The fighting was to last just over three years, but the hostility between the two sides, and between North Korea and the West in general, has remained a festering sore not merely in the region, which lives day-by-day under the continuing bellicosity of the regime in Pyongyang, but in the world. For although an armistice was signed in mid-1953 to bring the fighting to an end, a peace treaty has never subsequently been agreed, and the state of war that erupted when Kim Il-sung sent his 'Peoples' Army' across the 38th Parallel into the Republic of Korea persists. This remains a purposive determination of North Korean policy. The so-called Democratic People's Republic of Korea (DPRK) does not want to accept that its war with democracy is over; and that it lost the first and hopefully last round. And so North Korea remains at war with the world. It is also at war with itself, running a repressive, totalitarian state that has one purpose: to maintain in power the familial dictators of the Kim family, existing under a banner of communism that has never been much more than a cloak for a brand of violent autarchy. It is now 75 years since the start of this war, and as long as North Korea wishes the war to continue in its present form, no resolution remains.

---

*Best estimates suggest that the ROK lost 1 million civilians and 415,000 soldiers from a population of 20 million. This is 7.5 per cent of its population. The North lost 1.5 million from a population of 9 million, or over 16 per cent of its population.

On 11 June 2024, to pick a random day during the writing of this book, the BBC reported the following:

South Korean soldiers fired warning shots after North Korean troops crossed the border by mistake, Seoul's military said on Tuesday.

The incident at the Demilitarised Zone (DMZ) on Sunday comes as tensions continue to rise between the two Koreas. A small group of North Korean soldiers carrying field tools including pickaxes entered South Korea at 12:30 local time (05:30 GMT), Seoul's military said. They were among 20 who were in the border area at that time. They retreated immediately after the South Koreans fired the warning shots.

In recent weeks, the North has flown hundreds of rubbish-filled balloons to border towns in the South.

Seoul has responded by broadcasting propaganda and K-pop music to the North using loudspeakers. Activists have also flown propaganda balloons into the North. There was no notable movement from the North in the DMZ after its troops retreated on Sunday, Seoul's military said.

'Inside [the border area] the vegetation is overgrown, and the border markers are hidden. There are no paths, and they were wading through the overgrowth,' it said.

On Monday, North Korean leader Kim Jong Un's sister, Kim Yo Jong, threatened the South with 'new counteractions' if it continues loudspeaker broadcasts and does not stop activists from sending balloons. Last December, Mr Kim ended all efforts at a peaceful unification with the South, accusing Seoul of 'hostility' towards the North.

Since then, the North demolished a highly symbolic unification monument in Pyongyang and ended all communication with the South.

Earlier this month, South Korea suspended what remained of its 2018 military agreement with the North, which will allow it to resume drills and propaganda activities such as loudspeaker broadcasts.

South Korea had partially suspended the agreement last November, following the North's launch of a spy satellite.

In recent months, Seoul detected North Korean soldiers planting landmines along the border and disconnecting railways to the South. North Korean soldiers were also seen installing guard posts within the DMZ.

These events were followed by the State Visit of President Vladimir Putin in mid-June 2024, the Russian president eager to cement ties with any country willing to provide him with ammunition and manpower to sustain a war of diminishing returns in Ukraine. North Korea continues its bizarre marriage of convenience with Russia, the successor state to the USSR, itself the successor to the Tsarist Russia which had long held Manchurian and Yellow Sea ambitions. In 1950 North Korea was a pseudo-state, recognised only by the Soviet Union and its friends, serving as one of the national buffers that a neurotic Stalin was erecting around the periphery of the home country, presumably to prevent another Hitlerian-like *Barbarossa*. Korea is truly a war that had deep origins, and which has never ended.

But if it has been forgotten, at least outside its borders, the war appears to the authors to have been more *misunderstood* than forgotten, then as now. This is because it was in actuality two wars, not one: one that was legally sanctioned (by the UN) and with a logical premise (to reverse an injustice), and the second, a follow-on war, an attempt by the USA to squeeze an additional political outcome from the military victory that it had achieved at the conclusion of the first. In this it failed, because in expanding beyond its original remit (the ejection of North Korea from the South, and the defeat of the North's invasion), it decided to invade North Korea and to unite the peninsula by force. This was not the initial political purpose of military intervention in Korea, and it failed. By invading the North, the USA and the UN widened the war, because this action invited such massive Chinese retaliation and intervention that the entire UN effort in turning back the North Korean invasion was very nearly negated. If the *first* war for Korea was a response by the United Nations to the attack by the North on 25 June 1950 based on the principles of newly established law and to restore the *status quo ante bellum* (or at least a defensive position along the rough line of the 38th Parallel), then the *second* war for Korea, which began with the United Nations' own invasion of North Korea in mid-October 1950, precipitating the Chinese counter-reaction, was based on exactly the same premise as Kim Il-sung's initial land grab. Thus, the United Nations' invasion of North Korea suffered from precisely the same form of aggrandisement with which it had charged North Korea in its initial invasion. Even though, unlike North Korea, the UN could claim legality (the invasion of the North was authorised by the UN in response to the North's illegal act of aggression and therefore technically legal), the question was whether it was proportionate, practically possible and politically rational.* The United Nations could not have it both ways and secure from a position of raw power that which it had denied to North Korea earlier in the year. It is also important to acknowledge, especially in relation to the second war for Korea, that although fought under the auspices of a compliant UN, Korea was always an American war, with its friends and allies following along, sometimes shakily but in the main faithfully, in the American vortex.

The attack by UN forces into North Korea also opened itself up to the law of unintended consequence, the bane of any strategist, for whom prediction and analysis are often finely balanced, based on assumptions and intelligence about what *might* happen (or, more accurately, what they would like to happen), not real events. Unintended consequences, of course, can only be assessed after the event. But they can be predicted, if done so carefully and honestly. In dismissing the possibility of Chinese intervention in June 1950, the UN – led by the USA – was guilty of the same grotesque miscalculation made earlier in the year by Kim Il-sung when he assumed that the United States would have no interest in getting involved in his war. One would have thought that the UN and the USA would have learned that lesson; but in the excitement of victory in October 1950, the purpose and consequences of an invasion of North Korea were not as rationally considered as they ought to have been. Hubris can afflict every politician in war, as well as every careless soldier, no matter what uniform they wear. Real events, in this case, proved to be very different from those imagined by President Harry Truman and General Douglas MacArthur when they determined to follow through their defeat of the North Koreans in mid-October 1950 with the wholesale subjugation of the entire country. For the UN, therefore, the first war for Korea was a war fought for a righteous cause and was a war first of defensive and then offensive manoeuvre, designed to correct a manifest injustice. The second war for Korea was a war first

*The issue of whether North Korea's invasion was illegal depends on a determination as to whether North and South Korea were a single state or two separate legal entities. Most opinion agrees with that of the distinguished US jurist of war, Michael Walzer. The US took the issue to the UN, which judged that the North's invasion did constitute illegality. The very fact of the 38th Parallel's existence constituted a legal line between what was fast becoming two states, a position that the UN accepted, and logic upholds.

of conquest, followed by one of defensive attrition and the resultant political jockeying necessary to bring an unwinnable imbroglio to an acceptable end. That the ultimate end to this war was roughly the *status quo ante bellum* – i.e., the position of both parties as they stood before the invasion of 25 June 1950 – constitutes the essential tragedy of this conflict. It is not hard to see, in the decision during the Vietnam War not to transgress the border of North Vietnam (while nevertheless bombing its territory intensively), and the 1990 decision not to invade Iraq following the successful ejection of Iraqi forces from the country, the shadow of a different decision being made in October 1950.

The war was thus both intra-national and international, a war within a country and a war between countries. It has been variously portrayed as a civil war, a war between global communism and the West, and a limited war in which East and West worked out a *modus vivendi* to ensure that the scraps and squabbles of both sides never escalated to the point of nuclear exchange. None of these, on their own, seem to the authors to be entirely satisfactory descriptions of the war. It certainly was, at least in part, a civil war between two competing elements of Korea, crudely (and cruelly, many thought) divided at the end of the Second World War in order to facilitate the disarming of Japan. But thinking of it only as a civil war was an early deceit by communist propaganda, which asserted that as the war was an internal matter, all foreign troops (meaning, UN troops supporting the ROK) needed to leave Korea. It was certainly also a war between differing ideological conceptions of domestic and global polity, most notably post-colonial capitalism on the US model in the South and that of Soviet-inspired communism in the North. Certainly, this was how it was seen in the West. But, in addition to these twin causes, it must be remembered that it was also a war for domestic (i.e. intra-Korean) *power*, and it is this endless human quest for familial, social, political and economic dominance that most assessments of the war ignore.

The war has for many years been seen by military theorists as the archetypal limited war, one in which both sides deliberately determined to ensure that the fighting took place within the geographical confines of the Korean peninsula and was limited to conventional weapons. This idea traditionally – well, in the post-war period at least – formed the triumvirate of British military doctrine's view of the spectrum of war, from nuclear war at one end, to insurgency (e.g., Malaya), limited conventional war (e.g., Korea), general conventional war (e.g., the Second World War) and nuclear war (not yet...). This definition works, but it does have its difficulties. The idea that wars could be limited – politically, geographically and so on – was a concept developed as a response to the creeping totalisation of war in the First and the Second World Wars. The word 'limited' was applied to any war that didn't lead to atomic catastrophe or was fought within the political constraints provided by the threat of what theorists came to describe as Mutually Assured Destruction (MAD). Apart from this broad concept, we need to understand how the war might have been limited. It wasn't limited in terms of combatants. At its peak UN and ROK forces numbered just under 1 million men; China and the DPRK just over 1.7 million – a total of nearly 3 million men fighting for battlefield mastery in Korea at the high point of the fighting. During the three years of war, over 6 million fought as combatants on both sides. The idea that future war can be fought without large numbers of combatants is a chimera. Likewise, it certainly wasn't limited for the large number of civilians, for example, who were not asked whether they wished to die as the result of conventional bombs or atomic ones. The war was certainly limited by political purpose (President Harry Truman, for example, refused to call it a war, but rather a 'police action' or a 'conflict', which hints of Putin calling his invasion of Ukraine in 2022 a 'Special Military Operation'), limited to specific battlefield geographies, and did not entail the use of nuclear weapons. In all other respects, however, the battlefield remained unlimited in terms of the determination of both sides to win, or the vast scale of the munitions both armies deployed against each other, or the savage intensity of the fighting, especially that of the fixed lines which developed between 1951 and 1953. But one understands the point the theorists are attempting to make. It was a war deliberately limited by the ambition of both sides and their sponsors. The UN sought to defeat a war of aggression in Korea by fighting the war on its own terms, not by expanding it to become a Third World War, or a war beyond the confines of where it had begun (i.e., the Korean peninsula), and where it belonged. In other words, the Korean War was the military equivalent of the children's game of 'whack-a-mole'. When and wherever the communist enemy reared its head, it was attacked there, and there alone. The USSR and the USA would thus fight each other by proxy, but not directly, as that of course might have precipitated the slide to a nuclear Armageddon: it was this possibility that both sides in the Cold War for the most part attempted to avoid.*

Not everyone in Seoul, Tokyo or Washington was enthusiastic about the idea of the deliberate self-limitation of war. Some, certainly, had brought with them into the modern age the total war legacy of the Second World War: the idea that wars had to be won, and victory achieved, and that the means to do that must be unlimited. In Tokyo, the US military governor of Japan – General Douglas MacArthur – could not conceive of why the USA, fighting the insidious scourge of communism that was seeking to dominate the world, didn't simply use the 369 atomic bombs it had in its arsenal to remove the threat entirely, regardless of the consequences to the millions of innocents who would die as a result.† In total war, he reasoned, these considerations of human loss did not apply because there could never be a substitute for victory. War was a zero-sum game: you either won or you lost; there were no in-betweens. He said as much to Congress in a speech on 19 April 1951 (after Truman had removed him from his post as Commander-in-Chief, Far East Command), arguing that 'once war is forced upon us, there is no alternative than to apply every available means to bring it to a swift end... War's very object is victory, not prolonged indecision. In war there is no substitute for victory.' MacArthur's inability to think beyond the zero-sum conditions of unconditional victory for one combatant and unconditional defeat and surrender for the other – the inheritance of 1945 – in a new world in which such a stratagem would force protagonists into mutually assured destruction – or atomic Armageddon – was a remarkable deficiency in a man initially given strategic oversight for the design and conduct of the war. Likewise in Seoul, the idea of negotiating a ceasefire to end the war that deliberately resulted in the dismemberment of its country was anathema to many, not least the party of the president, Syngman Rhee, who saw the war as an opportunity to achieve what had been impossible in peace. In

*The Cuban missile crisis in 1962 was arguably the precipice into which both sides looked at the fires of a nuclear holocaust and walked back from the brink of global catastrophe.
†General Douglas MacArthur was appointed Supreme Commander for the Allied Powers (SCAP), Commander-in-Chief of US Army Forces Far East (FECOM). Both made him de facto military governor for the social, political and economic rebuilding of Japan. It was a unique role in history for an American serviceman.

Washington, to many, limiting the war was a sin akin to appeasement, typical of the namby-pamby liberals who always struggled to put the American national interest first.

The problem with these arguments is that none considered the possibility of unintended consequences. How could 'total war' be achieved in a nuclear world without blowing up the planet in the process? It is in this respect – that of defining what 'victory' actually means – that in our view the concept of limited war in Korea has the greatest utility. The UN, under what we might call the Truman Doctrine of Limited War, was to achieve a political peace by means of a military victory that did not expand beyond the benighted country in which the war was being fought. Victory meant the achievement of peace on acceptable terms, not the zero-sum concept – espoused publicly by MacArthur after his dismissal in 1951 – that victory could only mean the absolute military defeat of one's enemy and the military triumph of one's own. This lack of clarity about the nature of victory in October 1950 caused the USA and the UN to step into the second war for Korea on the back of battlefield victory without fully determining what the nature of that victory should be. It was to take at least a further year of pointless, grinding war for the UN to recognise that victory could be achieved for all parties on the basis of acceptable terms. The Korean War demonstrated, therefore, that political victory could be achieved without securing the entire destruction of the enemy and its people. This must be an enduring lesson for modern strategists of war, political and military. If war is regarded as a zero-sum game, outside of the sort of crusade waged against German Nazism and Japanese militarism in the Second World War, the world will need to prepare for the consequence of a return to total war, with all that that entails.

In this respect, the war in Korea was a war that had to be won and victory achieved but could not be – in the sense of securing ultimate victory – by either side. The only alternative to this obvious conundrum was stalemate. To solve this problem, a cessation of fighting was eventually agreed, after much bloodshed. Nevertheless, this cessation of fighting has never been accompanied by acceptance by North Korea that the war is over, and hence that one side has won and the other has not. The war, therefore, remains in limbo, the embers of hostility stoked by a regime determined never to accept that it was in the wrong, that it had failed in its objectives and that it was forced to live with failure. That humiliation has clearly been a painful burden for Pyongyang to bear, even though over seven decades have passed since the guns fell silent along the 38th Parallel.

All wars occur within a context, which often has a varying mix of domestic and geopolitical influences. In the case of Korea in 1950, not all of these contexts seemed properly to be understood by the protagonists. For the West in general – and the USA in particular – the invasion of what constituted the legal (and UN-recognised) country of South Korea came at precisely the wrong time for anyone in a Western capital to dismiss it as merely a domestic squabble between Koreans. Both North and South had made no attempt to hide their desire to unite the country again under a single structure of governance, returning the country to the unity it had once enjoyed as an independent state prior to the arrival of the Japanese in 1910. For the North, this was Kim Il-sung's version of a 'people's republic', anathema of course to the more capitalistic inclinations of the Republic of Korea, led by a returned exile, Syngman Rhee. But there were greater, global geo-political imperatives that neither man – certainly not Kim Il-sung* – could fully appreciate at the time. This was the rapidly developing fear in Western capitals, beginning as early as the death of President Franklin Roosevelt in 1944, that the USSR was behind a deliberate programme to promote a brand of communism across the world subservient to Moscow's interests. As the decade progressed, the evidence for this accumulated rapidly. This extended from political subterfuge in Poland, to the organised capture of instruments of state in Czechoslovakia, the manipulation of indigenous communist parties in France and Italy, to revolution in Greece and China, military insurgency in Malaya and now, in 1950, outright war in Korea. The North Atlantic Treaty Organization (NATO) had been established in Europe in 1949 to provide the collective military security the West felt it needed to stand up to the threat of direct military

---

*This was a nom de guerre. His real name was Kim Sung-ju. Kim had joined the Chinese Communist Party in China in 1930 and had fought as a guerrilla against the Japanese in the 1930s. Sent to Moscow for military training in 1941, he returned to Korea in Soviet uniform in 1945. Carefully groomed by the Soviets, he was appointed to chair the 'Interim People's Committee' – what was effectively the interim Soviet-dominated government – in February 1946.

aggrandisement by the Soviet Union. Many in the West now regarded the Soviet Union, on the basis of its aggressive, intimidatory behaviour, to be the inheritor of the mantle of Nazism as the new 'Global Enemy Number 1'; so, when war began in Korea, the old crusade against Nazi terror was easily transferred to the threat from global communism. People generally didn't need persuading that the 'commies' were the bad guys. The Cold War had begun.

The purpose of this book is to examine the peculiar circumstances of a war that was both *forgotten* and *misunderstood*. In some respects it was also *unnecessary*, at least in its fullest incarnation, given that the second phase of the war, the invasion by UN forces in mid-October 1950, directly incited a massive counter-response by China, and achieved nothing that had not already been achieved by the recovery of South Korea following the Inchon landings. Likewise, how much of the war from the air was truly necessary to persuade the North to acquiesce in the UN's strategy to bring the war to a close? We have set out to trace both its military path and to understand something of its importance for our own times. For the West at least, the first war for Korea was unexpected and unwelcome. In Seoul, capital of the South, no preparations had been made to counter an attack from its sworn enemy, despite the fact that the communists were attempting to create a competing state in the northern half of the country above the 38th Parallel. That both North and South had a vision of a united Korea under their own governance and control, a full-scale war between them or a war initiated by one on the other should not, on reflection, have been the surprise it turned out to be. If people inside Korea had no inkling of the sudden, overwhelming attack that opened against the South on Sunday 25 June 1950, those outside the country, in the international community – and in the West certainly – had even less idea of what was about to happen. It was only five years since the defeat of the Nazi menace in Europe and Japanese militarism in the Far East. The world was just settling down to the new global order and a long-hoped-for period of peace. It was assumed by most in the West that the era of bullies forcing themselves on their neighbours was now a thing of the ignorant past, a time when ideological 'crazies' like Hitler were able to cause war with impunity for their own vainglorious ends. Victory for the Allies, and now, the creation of the United Nations, the world working in concert, would make that history.

When war came in 1950 it did so quickly. A new international political structure now existed – the United Nations – to order global affairs and hopefully to prevent war. This organisation was quickly employed to organise a response to North Korea's illegal aggression, led by the United States, whose geopolitical interests in the region seemed to be most directly affected. To these geopolitical imperatives were quickly added another compelling issue. For countries that might otherwise have felt that Korea was a long way away, with a people of whom they knew – or cared – little, came precisely the same challenge that Britain had faced at Munich in 1938. In refusing to counter naked aggression against a neighbour, and thereby upholding the principle that sovereignty was inviolable, an aggressor would be allowed to flourish. For British Labour Party prime minister Clement Attlee, being accused of being a 'Tory appeaser' would be a slur too far. He needed to act, and he did so with alacrity. Britain quickly found itself in alliance with the United States, although not all their political imperatives were aligned. For much of the war Britain was concerned that the new regime in Peking might act against Hong Kong. It had reinforced the colony with an infantry brigade on the communist victory in October 1949 and had recognised the new government in January 1950. In any case, the UK was always the junior partner, and its influence in the decisions that were to take place with respect to the war in the years that followed can be exaggerated. But it held its course through the trials and tribulations that lay ahead, and the effectiveness of a partnership seeded by Churchill and Roosevelt at the Atlantic Conference in 1941 was demonstrated in that the UK and USA created the basis for a long-lasting relationship as partners in NATO.

Scholars approaching this subject are immediately confronted with a vast library of material – primary sources from US and British archives (and others), a large collection of memoirs and secondary sources, and a plethora of articles and papers on aspects of a war. In taking on this task, we have been reminded that no history of this complex war can be comprehensive, but that a number of very good attempts have been made in the past to capture the subject and to distill it into an essential theme. It is also apparent that the Korean War remains contested in scholarship, with debates about origins and perspectives – especially that of the atrocities perpetrated by both sides, and the USAF (US Air Force) bombing campaign – receiving much needed analysis and honest assessment, as well as considerable politically partisan commentary. It is also clear that, in English at least, the Korean side of the story is only just beginning to be told. For purposes of scope, the authors have deliberately restricted this book to the areas of the study of war which best suit their technical expertise: namely, the planning for and conduct of war. We do not pretend to be able to investigate every aspect of this war, which reached into virtually every Korean home, North and South, and our use of Korean sources has been limited to those freely available in English. For this reason, many aspects of the war – such as treatment of POWs and the current South Korean Truth and Reconciliation process – have been left to other commentators.

Our purpose in writing this book has been to offer a new analysis of this war from the perspective of professional practitioners of the military art three generations removed from the decision-makers and soldiers who fought in Korea between 1950 and 1953. Our lens is the Official Histories – all excellent works – published by (in chronological order), the USA, the ROK and the UK. Reasons of space and time have precluded detailed analysis of the military contributions of every participant in the UN war, such as that of Australia, or the naval campaigns, or indeed a detailed appraisal of the air war. We offer our conclusions in Reflections, but at this point wish to make one thing clear. For all its mistakes, the war was a necessary one in the context of the world as it existed in 1950, in which the Cold War split the globe into two armed camps. To those who question whether the war was worth fighting, one need only point out the desperate state of North Korea today. The so-called hermit-kingdom is a one-man hereditary dictatorship. South Korea, for all its faults and history of oligarchical influences, is not. The ROK is a fully functioning democracy with representative institutions and voter-determined civic governance. Without the war, and the resistance of the UN to Kim Il-sung's aggression in 1950, the entire peninsula might today be enslaved in the madness of what the people of North Korea are forced to endure at the hands of the Kim family. This does not excuse the way in which the war was fought, especially with regard to the indiscriminate slaughter of innocent civilians in bombing attacks which flattened most of North Korea's cities, a process of moral anaesthesia that does not redound well to the credit of the USA. There is no excuse at all for allowing the deliberate deaths of innocents in any plan of war, or in its execution. Nor does it excuse the indefensible strategic mistake of failing to insist on restoring the *status quo ante bellum*, and only this, once the 38th Parallel had been reached by UN forces in mid-October 1950.

———

Our argument is that the Korean War has certainly been *forgotten*, as well as *misunderstood*. But even more importantly, part of it was *unnecessary*. Kim Il-sung's miscalculation in initiating the war started the ball rolling in a war the North could never win in the context of the rapidly evolving Cold War. Then, the US miscalculation in extending the war beyond the *status quo ante bellum* on 16 October 1950 compounded the disaster. It was absolutely necessary for the UN to respond to the North's aggression as it did – war does have utility in certain circumstances – but in its conduct of the war the USA led the UN into a situation which unnecessarily extended the pain beyond that which was necessary to correct the initial injustice, namely to end the war and bring about a sustainable and negotiated peace. In attempting to make use of the North's humiliation and thus achieve a new set of war aims – the conquest of the North and the unification of Korea by force, which is what Kim Il-sung had attempted to do in the first instance, and the entire rationale of why he was being opposed by the UN in the first place – the UN extended the fighting for two and a half additional years at huge cost in lives and treasure, many of these being those of innocent Koreans, with no practical material, physical or political gain. The war started and ended on the 38th Parallel. That it could have ended much earlier than it did, with the same political outcome, was the war's greatest tragedy.

PART I

The First War for Korea

Prologue

Sergeant Collins' Baptism of Fire at Pyeongtaek

Sergeant First Class (SFC) Roy Collins looked out across the valley below him. The day was gently fading into the brief dusk that preceded the fall of pitch darkness, which came on suddenly at this time of year. It was the evening of 5 July 1950. The cloudy sky allowed no ambient light to penetrate the darkness. Despite it being summer, the temperature was unseasonably cold. The men of Collins' new platoon, fresh from Sasebo, their garrison town in Japan, shivered in their cotton uniforms. The location of their discomfort was the left hand of two grass-covered hills two miles north of the town of Pyeongtaek, where a bridge crossed the main arterial highway between Seoul 40 miles to the north and the town of Ch'osan 18 miles south. The port of Pusan, whence they had arrived in this country two days before, lay far to the southeast. When darkness came it also started to rain, exacerbating the men's discomfort, the rain falling gently at first and then heavily, seemingly without remission throughout the night. Without raingear it proved impossible for the men to stay dry, so after they had dug their new trenches in the red earth of the grassy knoll they huddled miserably together, in clumps. They had brought two days of combat – 'C' – rations with them, but, with no means of heating the food, the men ate them cold.

The men of 1st Battalion, 34th Infantry Regiment – part of Major General William 'Bill' Dean's 24th Division – had been in Pyeongtaek since about 5 a.m. that morning. The new commanding officer of the battalion had joined the men at Taejon as they travelled north. Lieutenant Colonel Harold Ayres was a veteran of the hard fighting in Italy six years before and boasted a distinguished combat record, but he was new to the 34th Infantry Regiment, and the men were new to him. Likewise, Sergeant Collins was new to his platoon, arriving to join Able Company of 1st Battalion, 34th Infantry the day they marched to this new position.* He was in a minority as an experienced combat veteran, being one of about 10 per cent of the battalion who had fought in the Second World War. Half of the 1,981 men of the 34th Infantry Regiment were here; the remainder – Lieutenant Colonel David Smith's 3rd Battalion – were 12 miles to the south at the small town of Ansong. Lieutenant Colonel Jay Lovless, the regiment's commander, had set up his HQ between the two, on the main road and rail line six miles south of Pyeongtaek at a hamlet called Songhwan-ni.

The 140 men of Captain Leroy Osburn's Able Company, of which Collins' platoon formed a part, occupied the hill to the left of the road, with a small group forming a block on the crowded road, while Baker Company was on the hill to the right. The distance between the two companies was about three-quarters of a mile, with rice paddies, the railroad and the narrow dirt road separating the two. The railway and road ran atop an embankment that for most of the way through the valley sat about ten feet above the paddy fields. Charlie Company was in Pyeongtaek in reserve, collocated with Ayres' battalion HQ. Normally, the battalion would have an additional rifle company and a further one with the heavy weapons, such as the 4.2-inch mortars and anti-tank recoilless rifles. But not now. The peacetime Eighth Army in Japan was too short of men to justify the luxury of having an

---

*Infantry companies in US infantry regiments were numbered alphabetically in sequence across the regiment as a whole, using the phonetic alphabet employed by the USA between 1941 and 1956. Hence, with four companies to each battalion, the first company in the 1st Battalion would be Able Company; the first company in the 2nd Battalion would be Easy Company, and the first company in the 3rd Battalion would be Item Company. Thus, George Company would be the third company in the 2nd Battalion, and Love Company would be the fourth company in the 3rd Battalion.

organisation structured for combat. The war was over, the thinking went: now was time to win the peace. A small number of 60mm mortars were held at company level, and although the battalion had brought with them some 75mm recoilless rifles, they had no ammunition for them.

When Collins' men arrived on their grassy hillocks, they and the rest of the company had started digging, grumbling at first. They didn't know why, if they were here for a 'police action', they needed to dig in. Equally, the ground was hard and there weren't enough entrenching tools to go around. But slowly, as the evening progressed, the first trenches appeared across the two hills, tell-tale spoils of red earth lying to the side of each trench. Both companies were dug in on the forward slope, because this afforded them perfect views over the valley and the road to the north. In the area between the Able Company position and the road, the roadblock team of 17 men of the 1st Platoon under the command of Lieutenant Herman Driskell prepared to dig in. Driskell had an eight-man machine-gun team together with three bazookas from the Weapons Platoon. The troops who had to dig their two-man trenches out towards the road embankment along the paddy fields were shocked to discover the source of the awful smell that had accompanied them as they marched out of Pyeongtaek. It was suddenly apparent that the Koreans manured their fields with human excrement, mixed with ash. Piles of it could be found in the corners of each field. The smell was overpowering, several of the men gagging as they dug into the rich, heavily fertilised soil. 'What a shithole' was but one of the politer comments the soldiers made to their new and unexpected situation. The nauseating smell did nothing to endear the newcomers to the country they found themselves in, and in which they were expected to fight and perhaps die.

Unlike Sergeant Collins, the vast majority of the men digging in that day had not been trained for combat. Many had been rounded up from barracks, desks and stores across Japan to join this ad hoc expeditionary force, as the US Army had no force ready for emergencies such as the one that had just been thrust upon it. As Collins looked at his new, grumbling, disorganised charges, he considered that most of them simply did not see themselves as professional infantrymen. The bulk would have been recruited into the army by means of the selective draft and thus served largely unwillingly. The draft had the greatest impact on the poor, those who had failed to pass into university, those without young families, with those who boasted little influence in society, together with those from the ghettos, poor Hispanics and the poorest whites. Many struggled to assemble their rifle, let alone know how (and why) to keep it constantly clean, well-oiled and ready for action.

The battalion had been placed at Pyeongtaek because the otherwise dusty, straggling town offered what appeared to be a natural blocking position on the main road leading south from Seoul. The first battalion of the division – Task Force Smith – had arrived two days before, with instructions to drive from Pusan as far north towards Seoul as it could. Moving along this same road, it had formed a blocking position at a hamlet called Osan-ri 12 miles further on (and 12 miles south of Suwon). At Pyeongtaek, an estuary of the Yellow Sea on the left-hand side offered a perfect natural barrier to any enemy pushing south who might be tempted to flank the town to the west. To the south, at Ansong, where the 3rd Battalion now found itself, mountains closed up to the eastern edge of the town. It would be difficult, it was thought, for an enemy to outflank its way through the hills to the east. Roads, it was believed, were the essential arteries of an invader. Block them with determined troops and the North Korean offensive into the Republic of Korea would be defeated. Perhaps it is unsurprising that no one had undertaken an analysis of Imperial Japanese Army (IJA) tactics from 1941 and 1942, for the NKPA's plan looked suspiciously like the IJA's *Kirimomi Sakusen*, the 'driving charge' that had so discombobulated troops of the British commonwealth in Malaya and Burma. Those tactics had been remarkably simple. An armoured vanguard moved fast down the available roads, opening intense fire against any roadblocks they encountered. Accompanying infantry, brought up by captured trucks or bicycles, then worked their way around both flanks, some troops to attack the block from the rear but the others to continue on for several hundred yards to create their own block, behind the enemy's. It was enough to confuse the defenders, finding themselves attacked from front and rear, with their means of escape also denied to them. Ill-trained troops were often forced to escape into the jungle when their block fell to the enemy.

Lovless, Ayres and the nearly 2,000 men of the 34th could as well have been on Mars for all they knew of where they were and what they were supposed to be doing. A 'police action' (whatever that was) – using the phrase President Truman had used to the media, denying that this would be an all-out fighting war – was what most men had been briefed when they'd arrived by ship into the port at Pusan three days before. Ayres had been told, and so passed on this news to his men, that the North Korean soldiers were a ragtag army, poorly trained, only half of them with weapons. 'We won't be here long. As soon as the gooks see our US uniforms, they'll be scooting back off into the hills' was the prevailing opinion. 'There'll be no fighting. We'll be back in Japan in a few days' time.' This was just as well, as for all its time in Japan – coming on five years now – the regiment had never trained collectively for combat. It had no artillery, mines, tanks or anti-tank weapons beyond a handful of old 2.36-inch bazookas left over from the last war. Not, of course, that these would be needed to see off the North Korean Army. The soldiers had a mix of M1 (Garand) semi-automatic rifles and lighter M1 carbines, and in addition, each platoon had a 0.3-inch light machine gun and a single Browning Automatic Rifle, with 200 rounds of ammunition. It should be enough.

The whole of that day – 5 July 1950 – had been one of strange experiences for Collins' men, who only four days before had been living largely undemanding lives on garrison duty in peaceful Japan. The road which ran through Pyeongtaek had seen a never-ending stream of white-clad Korean civilians heading south, ox-driven carts piled high with possessions and the elderly, with women and children travelling on the cart if there was space. If not, they walked. There must have been tens of thousands of them. Refugees are always a sorry sight. In this case, a sense of panic accompanied the urgency of their retreat. If this was a police action, Collins thought, there were lots of refugees fleeing in front of the enemy. It was an enemy about whom the men had received no explanation, apart from the reassurance that they were up against a peasant rabble, and so had nothing to worry about. But the sight of the refugees raised the spectre in the minds of some of the men of a worrying thought. What if the North Koreans were inveigling themselves among the crowds of desperate refugees and retreating ROK Army soldiers? How could they be distinguished from one another? To be honest, Collins mused, they all looked the same. The pressure of crowds of refugees at guarded choke points (such as bridges) was to lead to this unanswered question having tragic consequences. There were undoubtedly occasions in the weeks ahead in which poor training, weak leadership and the consequences of combat-induced stress left soldiers unable to discriminate between friend and foe, and which allowed soldiers to believe they had no choice but to open fire on advancing crowds of civilians *in case* they contained groups of enemy troops making good use of the confusion on the roads to pretend to be what they were not. It didn't take long for soldiers to refer to all Koreans, friend or enemy alike, in this way.

But news was now beginning to trickle through. Collins was lucky enough to hear it directly from Lieutenant Robert Ridley, his platoon commander. He had been told that their compatriots in the 1st Battalion, 21st Infantry (also part of the 24th Division), the 403 men of Lieutenant Colonel Charles 'Brad' Smith – Task Force Smith – had encountered the enemy that same day further north at Osan. This weak battalion, accompanied by a field artillery battery, had been flown in by C-47 Skytrains to Pusan days earlier with orders to block the road. While accurate information about their fate was scarce, it appeared that the experience had not been a pleasant one. By all accounts the enemy advance had been led by a number of Soviet-supplied T-34 tanks, which had simply pushed aside the puny roadblock while infantry, brought up in trucks, had dismounted on either side of the road, clearing the American position by repeated frontal and flank attacks supported by large amounts of automatic fire. After a four-hour fight, the American force had been broken and forced to escape into the hills. The following day the battalion could only account for about 250 men, a loss of nearly 40 per cent. Major General George Barth, the divisional artillery regiment commander sent to the front as Dean's representative, and who was with the artillery battery behind Task Force Smith and saw the disaster unfold at Osan, rushed back to Pyeongtaek with the news that tanks were on their way. He had been shocked at the ease with which the tank-led North Korean advance had simply pushed aside Task Force Smith. As a result, he warned Ayres that tanks were expected in Pyeongtaek at any moment. He estimated the enemy had over 30 T-34s. He feared that they would be unstoppable with the troops and weapons Ayres' battalion had to hand at Pyeongtaek and – despite not knowing Dean's plans – advised him to withdraw the moment he believed himself to be in danger of being outflanked. The division, using Barth's reasoning, couldn't afford to lose a second major unit.

With the news that the first T-34s to punch through Osan had in fact reached a point about six miles forward of his position, Ayres sent a small group in trucks under Lieutenant Charles Payne armed with bazookas to see if they could find and destroy them. Ayres remained confident. On approaching the village of Sojong, Payne's men discovered tank tracks in the muddy road. A South Korean soldier on horseback galloped up and shouted at them in English, 'Tanks, tanks, go back!' It must have been something of a Wild West moment for Payne. He persevered, however, and by 4 p.m. found a single tank in the village. It appeared that this, and perhaps a few others, had simply punched through the Task Force Smith position and were now sitting waiting for their friends to turn up before they continued their advance. Inexperienced at tank hunting, however, Payne's bazooka men engaged the tank at too great a distance and caused no harm to the stationary leviathan. The men returned rather disconsolately to Pyeongtaek. They would have been even more disconsolate to hear that, the day before, a few miles up the road at Osan, Lieutenant Ollie Connor of Task Force Smith had fired 22 bazooka rockets against the sides of T-34s, one of which was only 15 yards' distance. None failed to penetrate. New 3.5-inch rockets had been developed in the USA but had not been manufactured in sufficient quantities to be deployed to the battlefield.

Ayres also ordered the destruction of the bridge crossing the river but, despite Barth's concerns, decided to keep his battalion where it was. He would assess for himself the scale of the threat when – and if – it arrived. He didn't want to be accused of scuttling to the rear on the basis of a single message which might, after all, prove to be wrong or exaggerated. His job was to block the enemy approach and that he would do, despite the self-evident weakness of the unit he had inherited, something he could see from watching them operate. With the large number of refugees clogging the road, blowing the bridge was not easy to achieve without inadvertently killing lots of civilians. Nevertheless, the demolition was successfully carried out at 3 a.m. on the morning of 6 July. Ayres' instructions from Barth were to hold the front if he could, but to withdraw to a new regimental position if he felt that he was in danger of being outflanked and cut off. At about the same time confirmation was received that Task Force Smith had indeed been destroyed at Osan. Smith and the remnants of his battalion – about 86 men, from a starting strength of just over 400 – had made their way cross-country to Lieutenant Colonel Lovless' position at Ansong. The position at Pyeongtaek was next.

At 4.30 a.m., as dawn arrived on the morning of 6 July, the rain had been replaced by a dense fog over the river valley. Collins despaired somewhat of his green soldiers. They hadn't wanted to climb into the two-man trenches they had dug because they had rapidly filled up with water. Instead, they had sat around getting increasingly wet and miserable as the night unfolded. He encouraged them to eat while they had the chance but, as with the previous night, they did so cold. Although the tide of refugees had reduced somewhat, the road remained thick with retreating ROK Army soldiers intermingled with civilian bullock carts jostling for space. As the first tendrils of light over the mountains indicated the arrival of dawn, a strange rumble could be heard in the distance. Collins, who the night before had sent out a two-man standing patrol in front of his position, was the first to identify the sound of heavy engines.

Looking out over the valley, he saw through the fog the shape of at least half a dozen tanks forced to halt at the demolished bridge about 600 yards to their front. The Americans quickly disabused themselves of the possibility that they were friendly. Sergeant Collins called back to his platoon commander, Lieutenant Robert Ridley, 'Sir, we've got company!' 'Could it be the remnants of the 21st Infantry?' Ridley asked him. 'Only if the 21st Infantry have got thirteen tanks,' came the reply. When the reality of their visitors became clear, the urgent call went across the position: 'Man your positions!' The men grabbed their rifles and equipment and plopped into their now water-filled foxholes. The North Korean *4th Division*, which had peremptorily disposed of Task Force Smith the day before – something about which the soldiers in the trenches had absolutely zero knowledge – had arrived. Lieutenant Colonel Ayres, who had been briefed during the night of the fate of Task Force Smith, turned up to visit Captain Osburn only a few minutes before the first tanks were sighted at the demolished bridge; he realised in a heartbeat that this was no ragtag army. The enemy looked organised and disciplined and appeared to be in considerable force. He immediately called up Able Company's 60mm mortars and ordered them to fire on the column. As the shells began to land, the North Korean tanks spotted the American positions on the forward slope of the hill to their right front, and returned fire with their main armament, huge 85mm High Explosive Anti-Tank (HEAT) rounds slamming with great spurts of dust and concussion against the side of the hill, inaccurate at first but improving with every shot. One of the first casualties on the Able Company position was the company mortar fire controller, sited in one of the forward trenches, who went into deep shock when the concussive blast from the second tank round landed near him. Without directions from this man, the mortars, firing from a baseplate to the rear of Able Company's position, were blind. Accordingly, they went silent.

All this had happened in what seemed a matter of moments. Roy Collins yelled to his men to get down in their trenches when he saw the T-34 turrets swivel in their direction. After the first 85mm tank shells had impacted in a cataclysm of punishing concussion, he poked his head above the lip of the trench and saw the enemy infantry spread out to their front in preparation for an attack. He then glanced at the two cowering men next to him. They were quivering with shock, mouths and eyes open wide. Only the previous evening they were being told that this was a police action, and they were unlikely to fire their rifles in anger. He didn't even know their names. 'Start firing!' he ordered them, curtly. 'You've got M1s. Start using them.' They didn't respond. Collins then looked hard to his front, trying to see what had happened to the two-man standing patrol he had placed 200 yards forward of the Able Company position the previous night. Through his binoculars he saw one of the men leap out of his trench and run in a zigzag back to the company position. The other man stayed where he was. He was never seen again.

Looking out from the Able Company position, Lieutenant Colonel Ayres saw the impossible reality of his position all too clearly. He counted at least a battalion – perhaps 600 men – lining up as though they were on a parade square, getting ready to assault the very spot on which he was crouching. There were more he could see on the road behind, marching along in columns of four. 'It looked like the entire city of New York moving against two little under-strength companies,' recalled one of the men afterwards. Already Ayres could hear the sharp crack of enemy mortars landing in some profusion to his right. Looking down on Lieutenant Driskell's roadblock, he saw a series of oily, black clouds of smoke burst across the position. Driskell was being mortared, heavily. Thankfully, the men had dug their trenches, despite the shit. That the enemy was good was a realisation that washed over him like a wave. The briefings he and the men had received had been nonsense. This was a real war, and like the nightmare of every western, the 24th Infantry Division had come to a gun fight with the wrong weapons. The division had been backfilled from a wide variety of other units in Japan to bring it up to strength for deployment. The men simply weren't equipped, mentally or materially, for combat. Few had any idea why they were in Korea in the first place.*

No sooner had the North Koreans been stopped on the road by the demolition than they had identified his troops' positions and were returning fire. Then, in another sudden moment of clarity, he realised that he had failed to cover the bridge demolition 600 yards to his front with sufficient fire. His own 4.2-inch mortars seemed to have stopped firing, and the enemy were seemingly free to begin their preparations for an assault unimpeded even by machine-gun, mortar or artillery fire. Of course, he didn't have many of the former and he had none of the latter. So that's why Brigadier General Barth had been so animated earlier that morning! No battalion of the 24th Infantry Division was equipped to deal with this enemy.

And now, following the tank fire, enemy artillery shells started peppering the position. So, the North Koreans had artillery as well! It was most likely self-propelled, he thought, accompanying the tanks. About 50 shells landed during the first 15 minutes. He didn't have anything with which to reply. The patter of rifle fire from his men seemed pathetic in response. It didn't seem as if all the troops were actually firing. Could they be cowering in their foxholes, he wondered? Probably, given what he had seen of the men so far. Those who were shooting were firing too early, in any case. It was the machine guns that should be firing at this stage, but he knew he didn't have enough BAR ammunition to ensure that the enemy could be harassed all the

*Of the 15,965 men who went to Korea, 2,108 were from other Japan-based units.

way from their forming-up point. Ayres now knew without any more persuasion that his weak battalion would not be able to hold back the oncoming tide. His roadblock had no mines and, apart from the bridge demolition, enemy tanks could drive past unhindered once they had found a crossing point over the river. That wouldn't be difficult, as the river level was unusually low for this time of year. He had only a handful of rockets for the bazookas, and, in any case, he had been depressed to hear how pathetic these had proved to be in the engagement the previous day. He had had no time to dig reverse slope positions, so the company positions on the hillsides – on the forward slope, and in direct line of fire from the tank guns in the valley below – were vulnerable to direct attack. He had no barbed wire, no hand grenades, and the men had between 80 and 100 rounds of ammunition apiece, nowhere near enough to fight a prolonged battle against determined attackers in the numbers that the enemy appeared to enjoy. Accordingly, he decided to withdraw back to Ansong. He told Osburn to withdraw his company from the hill. There was no point, he concluded, in becoming another Task Force Smith. He then returned to his command post in a house on the forward edge of Pyeongtaek and telephoned Baker Company, on the other (eastern) side of the road to do likewise. The battalion would withdraw to a new position about 18 miles south near Ch'onan, which Brigadier Barth had gone back to prepare.

Captain Osburn had been ordered to provide covering fire for the withdrawal of Baker Company, on the other side of the valley, but when he ordered his men to provide rapid fire only a splutter from a handful of weapons came in response. Not getting any instructions from their mortar fire controller, the mortar section had evacuated their position and were making their way to the rear without further ado. Withdrawals in combat are one of the hardest operations of war to manage. With the state of training of the 24th Infantry Division, it is surprising that it went as well as it did. In Able Company men reacted differently to the order to disengage. Some did well. Others jumped out of their foxholes, leaving behind their fighting equipment; a few even left their rifles and ammunition. When an enemy machine gun managed to engage one of the withdrawing groups, several of the men simply ran away in panic. They had not joined the army for this sort of thing, and they were quite unprepared for the trauma of battle. Captain Osburn had successfully withdrawn the bulk of his men to a position ready to march back to behind Ayres' headquarters in Pyeongtaek, but the sight of these panic-stricken troops, many without helmets or weapons, unnerved the remainder and a general panic ensued. In the confusion, the order to withdraw had not been relayed to Lieutenant Driskell at the roadblock. Four of his men had attempted to leave their trenches but had already been cut down by enemy machine-gun fire. Driskell and the Weapons Platoon sergeant, Sergeant Williams, could see Baker Company to their right abandoning their positions, but as they had not received any orders they determined that they would stay. They waited for 30 minutes until with some consternation they saw North Koreans walking over the recently vacated Baker Company position. 'What do you think we should do now?' Driskell asked. 'Well, sir,' said Sergeant Williams, 'I don't know what you're going to do, but I'd like to get the hell out of here.'

When Driskell had determined that his platoon was in fact alone, he ordered that they withdraw to Pyeongtaek to receive further orders, pulling back in two groups – one under himself and the other under Sergeant Williams. They had pulled back to the base of the Able Company position when the group met some other withdrawing troops near some houses, who told Driskell that some of his platoon had been left behind, including some who were wounded. By this time, of course, the enemy were atop the now-vacated Able Company positions. News came back later that Driskell had been surrounded by North Korean soldiers and he and four men with him, attempting to surrender, had been shot dead.

By this time the panicked mob that had fled to Pyeongtaek had been organised into a semblance of order. It was only 9.30 a.m., about five hours after the North Korean tanks had been first sighted. About 40 men from the 140 who had been on the hills that morning were now unaccounted for. But of the remaining hundred, many were wounded, some with catastrophic shell shock. The mortar fire controller had been brought off the hill but remained in deep shock, his eyes rolling, moaning 'rain, rain, rain' over and over to himself, with self-evidently no knowledge of who or where he was. This individual psychiatric casualty depressed morale among the survivors, but the man's buddies were determined to get him back to safety. The rain had not abated, the tracks and main road thick with mud.

As Captain Osburn prepared to march his men along the road to Asong, Sergeant Collins pulled his men together to get them ready for a 12-mile forced march with all their kit, in the pouring rain. He still didn't know most of their names. Some of the men had complained that their rifles hadn't worked, and in any case Collins wanted to understand why the fusillade put up by his platoon that morning had been so pathetic. What he discovered horrified him. Of the 31 M1 rifles he inspected, 12 were broken, dirty or assembled incorrectly. Basic weapon husbandry was the first thing on the agenda for the retraining sessions he was already planning when he could get his troops out of the line.

Blowing the bridge in front of Pyeongtaek, Osburn wasted no more time and marched the remnants of the company down the road in two columns either side of the road. A few desultory shells followed their path, but on the whole the North Koreans seemed content to consolidate their gains, reorganise and proceed at their own pace. 'This was one time,' said one of Collins' colleagues later, 'when we didn't have to kick the men to get them to move. They kept going at a steady slow run.' It continued to rain until midday, when the weather changed and a heavy, oppressive heat developed. A few wisecracks among the men shared jokes about their sudden, unexpected predicament. 'I wonder when they're going to give me my police badge,' said one, observing that they were clearly in Korea on false pretences. But mostly they were quiet and just kept moving. Most of the inexperienced men had discarded their equipment as they left their defensive positions, and they were now without water bottles. Foolishly, some of the men now decided to drink from puddles, ditches and, extraordinarily, paddy fields. Some of the men, their boots giving them trouble, took them off and carried them, or discarded them by the side of the road. The great bulk of the company stores had also been discarded, which meant that the men had to go hungry until they managed to get to their destination south of the town of Ch'onan.

The three-hour non-stop march out of Pyeongtaek was broken by a ten-minute rest at midday, before the column resumed its near-silent journey. The road south was now increasingly littered with equipment and stores, showing that they were following in the path of other elements of the battalion. Most of the refugees had thankfully disappeared, though those who remained on the road were walking without carts. These had all gone on ahead. In the rear of the pitiful columns of civilians came the old and the weak, unable to keep up with their faster compatriots, most weighed down with enormous bundles of household goods and dragging exhausted children in their wake. Every now and then a single jeep or truck with ROK Army soldiers careered past on its way to safety. At a rest stop later in the afternoon the column was spotted by an American F-51 Mustang fighter plane overhead. Some men waved, while the others in their tiredness simply ignored it. Suddenly turning and banking hard, the plane screamed down on the column, opening fire with its six .50-calibre machine guns. The idea of what was known as a 'blue-on-blue' – friendly forces mistakenly firing on their own side – had not crossed the men's minds. Now they were forced to throw themselves into ditches alongside the road as this latest indignity was pressed upon them. One man was badly wounded. Morale slumped even more. It took about two hours for the long, strung-out columns to enter the town of Ch'onan that night, 18 miles from their start point that morning. There had been no sign of the North Koreans during the day, but there were no obstacles on the way, and the enemy tanks would surely be on them before long. They could see that the town of Ch'onan was in chaos. The population was intent on getting out, thousands of desperate people crowding the roads south. Certain that Ch'onan was indefensible, Brigadier General Barth had reconnoitred a defensive position for the two battalions of the 34th Infantry about two miles to the south of Ch'onan, and during the night the tired survivors of the day's battle and forced march were placed in their new positions, ready to receive another attack. Here they were joined by men of the 1st Battalion, 21st Infantry, remnants of the battalion that had not travelled north as part of Task Force Smith, who had arrived from Pusan that day by train.

The news by telephone from Lieutenant Colonel Lovless that the block at Pyeongtaek had been withdrawn was greeted with anger in his HQ in Taejon by Bill Dean. He had instructed Lovless and, through him, Ayres, to stop the North Korean advance. If he couldn't do it with a full infantry battalion equipped with mortars and bazookas, there was something dramatically wrong with his commanders, he thought. Not knowing anything of Brigadier General Barth's instructions to Ayres to bug out the moment he felt in danger of being outflanked, Dean was also ignorant of the challenge the poorly prepared battalion faced when opposed by the NKPA's *105th Tank Brigade* and the skilled troops of the *4th Division*'s vanguard. But at a stroke, the two blocks on the enemy advance – the first at Osan by Task Force Smith and the second at Pyeongtaek by Ayre's battalion – had disappeared. At first glance it wasn't good for the prestige of the United States Army and certainly no good at all for the reputation of the tall, crew-cut Bill Dean. There is no doubt that he felt anger at the news, disappointment and embarrassment in equal measure, in all likelihood. So, it was an uncomfortable conversation that took place on the night of 6 July at Lieutenant Colonel Lovless' regimental headquarters at the Ch'osan position. Major General Dean demanded the name of the person who had authorised the withdrawal. He was minded to send the battalion straight back. No one told him that many men were now boot-less, lying exhausted on the bare earth in the rain not far from where he was conferring with his commanders. In little less than 24 hours, the battalion had become a spent force. An awkward silence prevailed until Lieutenant Colonel Ayres, realising that no one more senior was prepared to explain the situation that led to the withdrawal, accepted responsibility. He had been the man on the ground, and it had been his decision, within the overall context of the situation explained to him by Barth, to withdraw. Dean needed the enemy advance stopped: constant withdrawals without fighting would not succeed in achieving this. Sending the 1st Battalion back to Pyeongtaek in darkness was out of the question due to the risk of ambush, so he ordered Lovless to send a company back to Ch'onan to defend the town from an enemy incursion. Privately, he determined also to sack Lovless for failing to grip his regiment. He already had a replacement in mind.

In the meantime, the men who had withdrawn from Pyeongtaek awoke on the morning of 7 July to the task of digging in. They had no entrenching tools. Many had lost their boots. They only had the weapons and ammunition they carried. All had been soaked through the previous day by the heavy rain and, although the heat of the afternoon had dried them off, it was raining again. And there was no food. Some dug with cutlery, others with bayonets, while others went off to neighbouring farms to see if they could scrounge tools from the empty houses now that the occupants had fled. Some were able to return with food given by Koreans, who were leaving their homes for the road. Collins looked disconsolately at his men. This war was either going to be very short, he thought, if the North Koreans caught up with them, or it would be very long. Only time would tell.

A long way away, far across the Pacific Ocean, great decisions were being made on this very day. On 7 July the Security Council of the United Nations voted unanimously to ask the USA to create a unified command in Korea and to name its commander. On the following day, President Harry Truman issued a statement saying that the new Commander-in-Chief, United Nations Command Korea was to be General Douglas MacArthur, currently in Tokyo as Commander-in-Chief, Far Eastern Command. Across the United States a cheer went up. This man knew about war. More importantly, he knew about winning.

I

Who Started It, and Why?

Sitting down to their breakfast on the morning of 8 June 1950, North Korean workers about to go to their places of employment would have read in their daily newspapers a startling announcement. Twenty months before, Pyongyang had refused to allow a UN-supervised plebiscite to determine the future governance of the united peninsula to be conducted in the territory of North Korea. The elections had gone ahead without them and had resulted in the formal creation of the Republic of Korea, recognised by the UN as the legitimate government of a united Korea. In practical reality, because of North Korea's resolute unwillingness to join in a programme of elections that it could not hope to manipulate, the new ROK's remit only ran south of the 38th Parallel of latitude and not in the North. Not to be outdone, the Soviet-created client-state in the North declared itself to be the Democratic People's Republic of Korea, claiming authority over the entire peninsula. It was recognised only by the USSR and its lackeys across the Soviet bloc. Now, everyone in Pyongyang could read that the DPRK government had announced that elections would be held across the entirety of Korea on 15 August 1950. As the North had no jurisdiction in the ROK, this could only mean that the North intended, by that date, to have joined the two parts of the peninsula. For those able to interpret the signs, it meant war – an invasion, in fact, by North Korea of the Republic of Korea, as there were no plans for a political union. If the Pyongyang workers had given it any thought, perhaps in surprise at the boldness of the announcement, the West didn't. While a steady stream of alarming intelligence about the DPRK's preparations for war were flooding into Seoul and being despatched just as quickly to the American Far East Command in Tokyo, the pronouncement received no attention. Pyongyang had beaten the war drum before and would undoubtedly do it again. This, if it was considered at all, was dismissed simply as noise from a paranoid and self-obsessed government led by a man whom the people of the DPRK were encouraged to call the 'Eternal Leader'.

The first Korean War, which began when the forces of North Korea smashed across the 38th Parallel in a sudden explosion of terror, trauma and violence on 25 June 1950, came about because of miscalculation. This is often the way of war. Leaders intent on conflict often assume too much or too little about their enemy. Equally, many such leaders come to believe that the surprise that framed their attack, and which gave them their initial advantage, was a brilliant piece of strategy that underpinned their personal strategic brilliance. Instead, it is usually a short-lived starter's advantage which proves ephemeral when countered by robust opposition. Even with modern, sophisticated signals intelligence and electronic eavesdropping technology, decision-makers often get it badly wrong. At Munich in 1938 the British and French prime ministers assumed that Hitler's ambitions were limited to the absorption of the Sudetenland into the Reich following the remilitarisation of the Rhineland in 1936 and the Anschluss with Austria in 1938. In giving away a little, they hoped that Hitler would be content with these gains – and no more – as the German leader established his perfectly peaceful, progressive, beneficent (well, to Germans of the correct blood, at least) *Grossdeutschland*. In 1982 General Galtieri of Argentina assumed that a combination of extreme distance from the UK and the disapprobation of the USA (against a British military response) would result in the UK meekly giving in to a *fait accompli* in respect of a forcible occupation of the Falkland Islands. He had not reckoned on the response of the British prime minister, Margaret Thatcher, nor indeed of the view of President Ronald Reagan that the USA's relationship with the UK was far more important than that with Argentina. Again, in 2003, sustained by faulty intelligence – or, rather, faultily analysed intelligence – the West convinced itself that Iraq had access to weapons of mass destruction. What's more, it came to persuade itself that Saddam Hussein in Baghdad was ready to use them. Neither assumption was correct, and what followed was to have immense implications for the balance of power globally for a long time to come. In more recent times, Vladimir Putin invaded Ukraine in February 2022 after having persuaded himself that the government in Kyiv would quickly collapse. It didn't. Ukraine had the temerity to fight back against its hubristic tormentor, humiliating Russian arms and political ambition in the process.

So it was in Korea in 1950. The leader of North Korea, a pseudo-country created as a client state of the USSR in the great re-buffering that Stalin engineered at the end of the Second World War, did not believe that the USA would commit its blood and treasure to protect the southern half of the peninsula, the Republic of Korea ('South Korea'), from attack. He may have come to believe this because he misinterpreted a speech given on 12 January 1950 by Dean Acheson, the Secretary of State, at the National Press Club, which defined US Far Eastern policy as a front line from the Aleutians to Japan, the Ryukyus down to the Philippines. If any country was attacked, they would be expected to deal with it themselves first, before 'the commitment of the entire civilized world [operating] under the charter of the United Nations.' In fact, only two weeks later on 26 January 1950, the USA and the ROK signed a mutual security and military assistance agreement which obligated US involvement in the defence of the South. In any case, Kim Il-sung was confident that he could overwhelm the weak ROK forces in weeks, a month at the outset. But while Kim Il-sung may well have been right in his assumption as to how quickly he could subjugate the South (which itself was debateable, as a core assumption in the invasion plan was that over three-quarters of South Koreans would rise up in support of the invaders), he was spectacularly wrong about how the USA would respond. This miscalculation also demonstrated a failure to appreciate how most other Western countries, so soon after the end of the Second World War, would also respond to what they regarded as unprovoked aggression of a kind that the United Nations had made illegal. The result of unalloyed military aggression against a neighbour, especially one which was a ward of the United States, and with which it had a defence pact, immediately determined the direction of Washington's foreign policy. Pyongyang's move smacked of Tokyo's extraordinary ignorance of the possible American reaction to the surprise assault on Pearl Harbor back in December 1941. It was Kim Il-sung's misfortune that his political horizon was so limited to Pyongyang and its immediate environs that he could not appreciate this geo-political reality. He was to learn quickly.

———

The USSR had worked assiduously from 1944 to build a post-war settlement that favoured Soviet interest, and where Stalin could he did it subtly, in the face of Western naivety about the ruthless and uncompromising nature of his regime in remaking eastern Europe in the Soviet image. In the countries of eastern Europe which they now occupied – Poland, Hungary, Romania and the Baltic states, and by means of a coup d'état Czechoslovakia in February 1948 – the chaos of the post-war world was ruthlessly exploited to impose communist ruling parties, making them all client states of Moscow. In the jostling for power following the German surrender, the jostler-in-chief was the wartime hero of the alliance, 'Uncle Joe' himself. The Soviet gloves were now off, and visible to all. Communists attempted to seize Trieste in 1945, Greece in 1946, and Moscow resolutely refused to reach a settlement with the Western Allies on the future of Germany and its capital city, Berlin, which led to the start of its blockade in June 1948. The Cold War was now a serious confrontation between East and West. In Britain the threat was perceived to be a global one, with the Malayan Communist Party beginning its terrorist campaign for an independent communist Malaya in June 1948. Soviet intransigence had the perverse (and probably unintended) effect of slowly fuelling reluctant Western governments to organise themselves into a defensive alliance. The Berlin Blockade saw the arrival at British airfields for the first time of nuclear-armed American aircraft of the Strategic Air Command. For the first time in its history, Britain signed a treaty to create a binding collective commitment to the continent of Europe, first with the Western European Union in 1948 and then with the North Atlantic Treaty Organization in April 1949. If this was radical in terms of the long-term reluctance of Britain to make any form of European commitment for its armed forces, this was equally true for the United States, which decisively turned its back on the strident isolationism of its past. The United States Congress passed the Mutual Defense Assistance Act in direct recognition of the Soviet threat. With the detonating of the first Soviet atomic bomb in August, followed by Mao Tse Tung's victory in China in October, Western fears seemed not at all exaggerated or hubristic.

NATO built on the collective premise that also lay at the heart of the United Nations, which had been created at the end of the war in October 1945. Where, to paraphrase Winston Churchill, 'jaw, jaw' failed, 'war, war' would be authorised against malefactors by the UN on the basis of six clauses in the Charter. These include Articles 42 and 43 of Chapter VII, which *inter alia* authorised the Security Council to 'take such action by air, sea, or land forces as may be necessary to maintain or restore international peace and security' and obliged all members 'to make available ... armed forces, assistance, and facilities, including rights of passage, necessary for maintaining international peace and security.' The creation of the UN heralded for a generation of men and women, sick to death of the relentless wars of their lifetimes, an opportunity to embrace international peace on a new legal footing, backed by the commitment of its members to act together rather than, as in the past, in isolation. Self-interest was being redefined as collective interest, for reasons of international stability and the quest for peace, with an organisation that had none of the weakness of its predecessor, the League of Nations. The British prime minister Clement Attlee captured this view in a speech in January 1946:

> The United Nations Organisation must become the overriding factor in foreign policy. After the First World War there was a tendency to regard the League Of Nations as something outside the ordinary range of foreign policy. Governments continued on the old lines, pursuing individual aims and following the path of power politics, not understanding that the world has passed into a new epoch... Looking back on past years we can trace the origins of the late war to acts of aggression, the significance of which was not realised at the time. Failure to deal with the Japanese adventure in the Far East and with the acts of aggression of the Fascist rulers of Germany and Italy led inevitably to the breakdown of the rule of law and to the Second World War. In the last five years the aggression of Hitler in Europe drew eventually into the contest men from all the continents

and from the islands of the sea. It should make us all realise that the welfare of every one of us is bound up with the welfare of the world as a whole, and that we are all members one of another.*

The Korean War came about as the result of years of mischief-making by the USSR and its acolytes, which in turn had been established by the machinations of Moscow, determined to push the advantage of the communist bloc and its interests over those of all others. Exploiting the profound naivety of many in the West who believed that the creation of the UN automatically made the world a safer place, Stalin worked to ensure that the interests of the USSR always came first. It was only as year ran into year after the war that American policymakers became profoundly aware of, and worried about, the implications for American interests of the new bloc that Stalin had so assiduously been building in Europe.

So, when the leader of North Korea launched his invasion of the South on Sunday 25 June 1950, the instant response of the United States was to defend the *status quo ante*. That America would do so instinctively was the key issue lost on Kim Il-sung. The vehicle through which it decided to respond was, quite naturally, the UN. After all, the organisation existed precisely for this purpose. If the USA did not immediately respond to aggression against one of its close allies or, in this case, one of its wards, the entire credibility of the USA's collective defence commitments to its friends, not least of all that of the newly established NATO, was jeopardised. It mattered little if that country appeared to have little or no strategic significance to the defence of the USA. What was important was the USA's obligation to support its commitments to the collective defence of its friends and allies. Indeed, in the context of the commitment to the UN, it involved the collective defence of *any* country unjustly invaded. Using the form of words provided in Article 42, the UN Security Council promptly asked that members 'furnish such assistance to the Republic of Korea as may be necessary to repel the armed attack and

---

*C. R. Attlee, *As It Happened* (Heinemann, 1954), 198–99.

to restore international peace and security in the area.' In truth, the UN was only able to play the role it did in Korea because the USSR was at that point in time boycotting the Security Council over its refusal to allow the new People's Republic of China to take the seat up until then occupied by Chiang Kai-shek's Kuomintang, now in forced exile on Formosa (Taiwan). In turn, the UN invited the USA to take the lead in preparing a military response to North Korea's aggression and to provide the military leadership necessary to counter Kim Il-sung's egregious assault on the sovereignty of its neighbour. The UN was dependent on US military leadership throughout the war and, because of this, the UN response to the war became a thinly disguised mantle for American national interest, though one in which most other contributors were content to acquiesce.

The USA did not respond to North Korean aggression *because* it happened to be engaged in a Cold War interplay at the time with the USSR, although it is true that the USA – and most countries in the West for that matter – saw Moscow's hand behind Kim Il-sung's actions. With everything else going on in Europe it seemed clear that an attempted communist takeover of the world, orchestrated from Moscow, was under way. There was another reason why the USA regarded the UN to be the right organisation to lead the world's response. The UN had been attempting to bring the two parts of the now divided Korea together since 1947. The United Nations Temporary Commission on Korea – UNCOK – had attempted to act as the neutral party that would oversee the unification of the country. It had failed spectacularly, because the USSR had shown no interest in letting go of its new pseudo-state in the North. Both states, therefore, one *de jure* and the other *de facto*, secured only by the protection afforded it by Moscow, were born in the teeth of each other's determination to be the rightful heirs of the ancient kingdom of Korea that the Japanese had so cruelly subjugated in 1910.

When Kim Il-sung began his invasion on Sunday 25 June 1950, he had not considered the state of crisis underlying East–West relations, and certainly had not considered that his attack might be thought by the West an assault by global communism on the free world, as one of the incremental 'land grabs' of which Greece, Czechoslovakia and Poland had already been exemplars. He hadn't considered how the loss of neighbouring China, for so long an American-supported bulwark against the Japanese, would affect American considerations of the threat to its hegemony or interests in the region. Korea was, therefore, a multi-faceted war. In the first place it was a war between two competing visions of how a united Korea should be governed. It was, in this sense, a civil war between Koreans. But it was also a war of inter-state aggression of the type that had allowed Nazi Germany to bully its way through Europe two decades before and which had precipitated a global war and killed as many as 75 million of its inhabitants. Aggression of this sort needed to be resisted, preferably by the collective action of allies. In the West it was also seen as a proto-communist war, in which the USSR attempted to spread communism and destabilise the Western democracies. The Americans (and the British to a lesser degree) saw intervention in Korea as a war against communist expansion in the developing world. In his memoirs Clement Attlee described his exasperation that 'the Korean attack was not an isolated episode', noting that the attack demonstrated 'that Communist forces were prepared ... to resort to war.' He and Winston Churchill, the Leader of the Opposition, were united in agreement that 'it was Britain's duty to give full support to the United Nations..."* The egregious assault on national sovereignty so evident in Europe during the 1930s must not be allowed to be repeated even though there was some dispute as to what half of the Korean Peninsula enjoyed sovereignty over the whole.

The immediate backdrop to the conflict which burst into war in June 1950 was the dismantling by the victorious Allies of the extensive Japanese security infrastructure in Korea, the military corollary of the Japanese civil infrastructure and administrative fabric that had embedded itself in Korea since the occupation had begun in 1910. Japanese involvement in Korea has a very long and unhappy history indeed, but for the purposes of painting the context in this account we need to restrict ourselves to the period immediately following the defeat of Japan in August 1945. In early August 1945, before the dropping of the atomic bombs on Hiroshima and Nagasaki, Stalin had undertaken what Roosevelt had asked him to do at Yalta and

*Attlee, *As It Happened*, 231.

joined the war against Japan. The price for his involvement was steep. It included the Kurile Islands, the lower Sakhalin peninsula, together with long leases on the warm water ports of Port Arthur and Dairen and the Manchurian railways. On 9 August 1945 Soviet armies totalling 1.7 million troops flooded into Manchuria, Korea, Sakhalin and the Kurile Islands. On 10 August Colonel General Ivan Chistyakov's 25th Army entered Korea and occupied the country down to Pyongyang. At very little cost the Soviets benefited dramatically by Roosevelt's ill-fated invitation to participate in the reduction of the Japanese empire. They made the most of it. A worried Truman – Roosevelt's successor as president – tried to secure some limitation on Soviet ambitions. The Americans suggested that they undertake the work to dismantle the IJA below an arbitrary line drawn along the 38th Parallel, while the Soviets undertake that required above this line. Moscow agreed without demur. They had got what they wanted. Stalin found himself the unheralded heir of the Tsarist strategy to conquer Manchuria denied to Russia by the Japanese 40 years before. Not only had he redeemed Russia and magnified its glory, but he had placed himself on the neck of the Korean peninsula, forever limiting the ability of the USA to intervene on Russia's new Manchurian flank.

But Allied plans to remove the estimated 700,000 Japanese in Korea and hand back Korea to the Koreans – in 1943 the British had mooted a form of international trusteeship for the country while it found its feet after so long a slave of Japanese imperialism – was faced with two problems. The first was that there was no single publicly mandated Korean government-in-exile awaiting the Japanese departure, but a variety of noisy, fractious and squabbling groups all claiming the right to rule. The second was that the process of occupying the country and removing the Japanese was undertaken without any consideration for the deep political, social and economic undercurrents within the country. Indeed, the extent of this colonial enterprise was not at all understood by outsiders. Korea's identity and culture had been erased by the Japanese. Civic administration, education, and law and order were all run by the Japanese, in Japanese. Koreans were forced to adapt to their new Japanese overlords, or rebel. Some did, especially those with Marxist leanings. Many decided to live with the new regime, hopeful that one day they could recover their country, but in the meantime kept their heads down. The communists dismissed these as 'collaborators'.

Many Koreans were the product of 19th-century American missionizing, and were devoutly Christian, for the most part content to seek God's kingdom in the next world, rather than trying to fight for it in this. Those Koreans who had fled the harshness of the Japanese regime, a proto-'Asia for the (Japanese) Asians' – to the USA were, on the whole, Christians and opposed to the communist guerrillas who had tended to stay behind. The leader of one of these exile groups was Yi Sung-man, known as Syngman Rhee (the latter name a pseudonym he originally adopted to hide from the Japanese secret police and then retained thereafter). During the Second World War, Japan exploited Korea ruthlessly, pressing over 5 million Koreans into forced labour, in which one in ten died, sending 40,000 of its young men into its army, and forcing many tens of thousands of women to be prostitutes for the Imperial Japanese Army. Yet more Korean exiles served the Chinese, in either the Kuomintang or Mao Tse Tung's 8th Route Army in China, and others yet still fled to the USSR.

A month after the Soviets' arrival, Lieutenant General John Hodge's XXIV Corps disembarked at Inchon harbour on 8 September 1945. The job of the Americans in the southern zone and the Soviets in the north was to disarm and repatriate the Japanese, not to create a new country or countries. But from the outset the Soviets determined to model a client state from that piece of the country they possessed, separating it from the remainder of Korea. It perfectly suited Stalin's interests to have a client pseudo-state sandwiching Soviet Siberia and China. A wave of repression followed the Soviet arrival, provoking an exodus of refugees for the south. In the absence of effective government, many towns and villages across the country – north and south of the 38th Parallel – set up their own self-appointed committees to govern themselves. In many of these, communist sympathisers took control. When the central government attempted to reassert itself in coming years, self-governing committees were immensely popular and often opposed the new administrators imposed on them. Some looked to the communists in the North for leadership, rejecting that of the US military government or its successor in Seoul.

Bizarrely, one of the first things Hodge did was to ban the 'Korean People's Republic', formed more or less spontaneously on the Japanese surrender, and before the arrival of the Americans, from a wide range of nationalist factions which at least shared a common will to unite the country.* It included in its ranks many of the exiles who had returned to Korea from Russia, China, America and several countries of Europe on the defeat of the Japanese. The Korean People's Republic nursed hopes that it would be recognised by the new occupying power and had already set up its own regional governments. Paradoxically, those in North Korea were dominated by the centrist parties, while those in the South were mainly from the extreme left. It was hardly surprising that Koreans of goodwill and political moderation were frustrated by the arrival of an occupier ignorant of the political fabric of the country and who snatched from them a very real chance of unification. Hodge did not believe that he was there to nation-build. But he brought with him no sense of what he needed to do to bring about a calm and peaceful accession to power of Koreans who could fill the void left by the Japanese, and at the same time overcome the local power of organised communists determined to pull the South into the North's political orbit.

This failure allowed something of a politically fractious milieu to develop in the South, with a variety of groups competing for the available political oxygen. Not so in the North, where a disciplined single party, albeit demonstrating a modicum of public representation, was imposed by Stalin's Korean henchmen, led by Kim Il-sung and enabled by the presence of Colonel General Chistyakov's 25th Army. Of course, in the South, one of the many political voices competing for attention was the one sponsored and supported by the communist North, for it was in Kim Il-sung's interest to win over the South, by political means if possible. By means of fomenting political discord and supporting indigenous Marxist groups, the North did much to destabilise the South in the years that followed. For their part, the Americans, keen to return home, struggled to understand what was happening around them. They wanted merely to establish order and move on, assuming that the benighted people of Korea, now free of the shackles of a repressive imperialism, would rise up as one body to create a new, united future for themselves. This, of course, was spectacularly naive, especially with a regime in the North assiduously

*There are resonances here to the disbanding of the Iraqi Army and the Ba'ath Party in 2003, the two institutions that could have held Iraq together after the departure of Saddam Hussein.

working against the democratic will of the people having any form of free expression. Establishing order in the South entailed reappointing the only people who had experience of such things: namely those who had previously worked for the Japanese. While this probably could not have been avoided, the animosity it generated undid much of the goodwill the USA was trying to engender by being a neutral party. All this time massive population flows, mirroring those in Europe at the end of the war, kept society in a state of constant flux. By mid-1946, 435,000 Japanese civilians and 180,000 soldiers had been repatriated, but Japanese civilians were still crossing the 38th Parallel from the North in 1947. Some 2 million Koreans returned home to both North and South following the Japanese surrender. By 1948, 3 million Koreans migrated from the communist North to the non-communist South, voting with their feet against the new totalitarianism of the supposed Eternal Leader. This led the North to prohibit the voluntary movement of civilians to the South, forbidding both free movement and trade.

The communist government in the North had quickly established the active mechanisms of central power. These entailed the central clique (the North Korean Labour Party, led by carefully vetted functionaries endorsed by Moscow), in charge of making decisions and ordering affairs; another allowed the people to believe that they held a share of 'people's' power. This was in accordance with the standard Soviet playbook. Christians, landowners, shopkeepers and those who had been in the employ of the Japanese were designated class traitors and jailed or executed. Land was redistributed to the 'people', which meant in effect the new communist state, with the peasants invited to work their newly 'owned' land. At the start they did so eagerly, believing the nonsense that they were the same as 'the people' they heard about in the communist dictionary. Only time and the horror of collectivisation would disabuse them of this notion and reveal the reality that they were, to all intents and purposes, slaves. Society and the instruments of civil government were ordered and disciplined. But the purpose of this pseudo-state – it had no international recognition outside of the Soviet bloc and had no legal status outside of the appropriation of actual, physical power – was to offer subservience to the USSR, its birthparent. It had no intention of unifying with the South on terms other than its own, and it actively opposed the efforts of the UN Commission on

Korea to reunify the country. Indeed, it worked assiduously through the years to 1950 to weaken and undermine the South, sponsoring insurrection, local rebellions and security force mutinies, attempting to do by nefarious means what it could never achieve by political persuasion alone. It became impossible for the US military government to work with the Soviets, so they ceased trying. In June 1947 the Americans transferred administrative responsibility for the South to the South Korean Interim Government, tacitly acknowledging the impracticability of securing a united country despite the commitment to trusteeship. This coincided with the rapidly growing realisation in the USA that the USSR was actively conspiring against US interests and had been doing so since the Second World War. With this came a fear of Soviet expansionism, building on Winston Churchill's warning in a speech at Fulton, Missouri, in 1946 that an 'iron curtain' was descending over Europe. Not just in Europe, concluded many in the USA, including Truman, whose declaration of what was dubbed the 'Truman Doctrine' in March 1947 committed US aid to any country attempting to resist communist aggression. In September 1947 the USA presented the problem of Korea to the United Nations. The failure of dialogue with the USSR over the previous two years to reach agreement on establishing a single government for a united Korea had led the USA to recommend that the UN support a nationwide election in early 1948, with the occupying powers withdrawing their forces on the establishment of a new, united Korean national government. The artificial line across the peninsula represented by the 38th Parallel became, day by day, solidified, the direct result of Soviet policy and purpose. It was Soviet determination to keep the country divided so that it could achieve its own strategic objectives through establishing a client state in the North, resulting in the permanent division of the peninsula. The political animosity between the two new countries – one legal and internationally recognised and the other a pseudo-state, built and sustained by the USSR for its own purposes – led, in 1950, to war.

By 1948 communist-inspired guerrilla warfare was rampant in the southern provinces of South Korea in what was effectively a civil war. The government responded by launching anti-guerrilla operations and imposing martial law. The rebellion on the island of Cheju in April 1948 was the first major flashpoint in this increasingly savage war. The trigger for much of the fighting was a refusal to accept the moves under way by the USA and the UN to recognise the independent republic of Korea as the *de jure* government of Korea as a whole. This was bitterly opposed by those who desired unification of the country under the communist government of the North. Armed rebellion in the South was therefore regarded by Seoul to be an attack on the nascent ROK, and thus a challenge to the survival of an independent Korea, free of communist interference. Accordingly, the uprising on Cheju was met with a savage response. By the time it was suppressed a year later, as many as 60,000 people – one in five of the island's population – had been killed. A rebellion in the army then threatened to strangle the ROK at birth. The 14th Regiment was ordered to go to Cheju. Instead, on 19 October 1948 it seized the southern city of Yosu and executed some 500 police, soldiers, government officials and civilians. Neighbouring Sunch'on also caught the fever, and it too fell to the rebels. Meanwhile, Pyongyang radio continually called for rebellion. The South Korean government responded toughly, sending in 5,000 loyal troops who surrounded both cities and crushed the mutiny in a week, the USA providing military support. In putting down these brushfire rebellions, however, extreme brutality was often used, forever staining the reputation of Korean democracy and leaving a lasting bitterness on the psyche of the nation. All the while, in an attempt to place pressure on the South in its efforts fighting guerrillas and suppressing rebellions, even if ineptly, the North launched as many as ten cross-border raids into the South in 1949 by as many as 2,400 North Korean guerrilla fighters.

By the time the uprising petered out, 8,000 members of the Security Forces had been killed and perhaps as many as 90,000 civilians – some insurgent but many not – had died. But South Korea was safe from dismemberment at the hands of the North, at least for the time being. The ROK was formed in August 1948 as the UN-recognised government of the whole of Korea following UN-supervised elections in the South (the USSR, of course, refused permission for them in the North). True to form, the North formed the Democratic People's Republic of Korea in September. Syngman Rhee's success was regarded in Pyongyang, however, as a red rag to a bull; Kim Il-sung's strategy to so weaken the South that it would fall into his lap by default had failed. Throughout, he laboured under the misapprehension that people in both North and South wanted communism. The evidence – by refugee flows alone, some 3 million during the years of UN trusteeship

– suggested otherwise. There was only one other recourse available to him to achieve his ends: war.

These rebellions and the blatant interference of the North in the affairs of the South forced Rhee to expand his security forces. In November 1948 the Armed Forces Organisation Act created a 100,000-man army and a 10,000-man navy. The National Police Force was increased to 50,000, but the great deficiency of the ROK was that it did not have an effective air force.

With the departure of US troops from the ROK in 1949 (most Soviet forces left the DPRK late in 1948), the circumstances seemed to Kim Il-sung perfect for a rapid subjugation of the South. He knew just how weak the ROK Army was and how stretched it was fighting the various insurgencies he himself had helped instigate. He began making the arrangements for a blitzkrieg-type thrust into the South, designed first to capture Seoul, before driving southeast to Pusan, cutting the country in two from north to south. In early 1949, when Kim Il-sung had attempted to persuade Stalin to support an attack on the South, he had been rebuffed. Stalin did not want war with the USA, certainly not one over a country as strategically insignificant as Korea. In the view of the Soviet leader, it would have been better to encourage Syngman Rhee to invade the North first: that would provide the perfect *casus belli* for a war of self-defence. A year later, when the two met again in Moscow on 30 March 1950, the situation had changed sufficiently for Stalin to be persuaded, grudgingly, to give an attack his qualified support. His condition was that Mao Tse Tung had to agree. Kim Il-sung dutifully secured agreement from Mao on 15 May. Mao also promised the Koreans that if the USA became involved, China would respond. Kim Il-sung airily dismissed the possibility. 'The USA didn't attack China when the Nationalists were beaten,' Stalin's generals had told him. 'There is no way they'd bother with Korea.' This, too, was Kim's view.

By 1950 Kim Il-sung had prepared the North Korean People's Army for an impending war of conquest. It had inherited substantial quantities of surplus Soviet materiel left over from the war, including 242 of the T-34 tanks that had helped the USSR to fight its battles all the way to Berlin, and a formidable air force of 210 ex-Soviet Ilyushin Il-10 twin-seat ground attack planes and single-seat, single-engine Yak-9 fighters. The NKPA had 76mm self-propelled artillery (the SU-76) and the much larger and formidable 122mm field guns. The army was formed around cadres of men with operational experience in the Red Army. Pilots and technicians were trained in the USSR. About 2,000 Soviet military advisers were retained for technical and training purposes. The NKPA was built on Soviet lines, with Soviet doctrine, weapons and training. In addition, Kim Il-sung secured agreement with Mao Tse Tung's China that 50,000 Korean veterans of the Chinese Communist Army and the USSR would be repatriated to North Korea, to form the backbone of the NKPA. By 1950, this meant that a third of the NKPA were combat-experienced veterans. By the time of the invasion, the NKPA comprised 198,380 troops. The assault force would comprise 111,000 men in ten divisions, an independent infantry regiment, a motorcycle reconnaissance regiment, an armoured brigade and five brigades of border troops with an additional 15,000 men.

The attack was to have five principles, and had to be over in a month, certainly before the seasonal heavy rains began in July. First, Seoul would be captured quickly by means of a swift armour-led drive on the capital using the main roads from Pyongyang. At the same time, the population of the South would be encouraged to rise up in armed rebellion against their imperialist oppressors and their running-dogs in the ROK government and armed forces. This would enable a unified communist government to be established across the country, in accordance with the newspaper announcement, by 15 August, the fifth anniversary of liberation from Japan.

The plan was that the invasion would comprise two corps comprising five divisions each. The 53,000 men of *1st Corps* (Lieutenant General Kim Ung) would constitute the main attacking force, charged with driving on Seoul from the north. Its major attacking units were the *3rd* and *4th Divisions*, with support from elements of *105th Armoured Regiment*, the *6th Division* and the *1st Division*. Meanwhile the 54,000 men of *2nd Corps* under Lieutenant General Kim Kwang Hyop would undertake a wide turning movement and attack Seoul from the east. Its primary attack force were the *2nd* and *12th Divisions*. The *5th Division* would attack in the Kangnung–Samch'ok area, while the *766th* and *549th Independent Infantry Regiments* would carry out landing ops in Chongdongjin and Imwonjin on the eastern coast. After Seoul had been secured, the *1st Corps* would head south to the Mokp'o-Yosu area while the *2nd Corps* would drive on Pusan.

Throughout, the North concocted mischievous stories of Southern aggression and malicious intent as a cover for its own war planning. The excuse for the attack was self-defence. Kim's delusion was such that he believed that once Seoul had been captured the population would rise up in support of the invasion, the country would quickly surrender, and the whole war would be over in three days.

In contrast to the NKPA, the ROK Army was weak and entirely unconfigured to defend the country from invasion. This was partly the product of a failure by the United States in leaving the country without adequate defences against a known predatory neighbour, and partly due to the fact that the ROK security forces were busy fighting an active, DPRK-inspired insurgency. The army of the ROK began as an armed constabulary in the years following the end of the war, the US unwilling to sponsor the creation of an army while the country's long-term status remained uncertain. Training had focused on the maintenance of public security, not preparation for combat. Nine regiments were established in 1946 and an additional six in May 1948, with a total strength of 50,000. With the establishment of the Republic of Korea on 15 August 1948, this constabulary became the ROK Army. By March 1949 the strength of the ROK Armed Forces had reached 104,000: 65,000 in the army, 4,000 in the navy and 35,000 in the police force. A few months later, following mass recruitment, the army stood at 100,000 men, none of whom had been trained for combat or were equal to withstanding the onslaught that was to come. The Americans, concerned not to leave too much military equipment in the ROK lest Syngman Rhee used it to fuel his own attack on North Korea, had few heavy weapons, and no tanks or modern anti-tank weapons. The only artillery it had were 91 old American M3 105mm howitzers which boasted a range of only 6,500 yards. Modern artillery of this calibre had more than twice this range.

By June 1950, certain that the NKPA were intent on invasion, the army had eight divisions, divided into front-line and rear formations. In the front line the 1st Division was in Kaesong; the 7th Division at Chorwon; the 6th Division at Ch'unch'on; the 8th Division on the right wing, and the 17th Regiment on the Ongjin peninsula.

The role of these troops was to deny the enemy lines of advance along the forward positions on the 38th Parallel, destroying roads and bridges, while the 2nd, 3rd and 5th Divisions assembled. If the enemy broke through, an alternate line was to be constructed to the rear. However, no significant defensive works had been built along the 38th Parallel by the time of the invasion. There were no anti-tank obstacles and no anti-tank mines. Some open trenches, made of concrete or logs, had been constructed with barbed wire, though there were no facilities to protect forward troops from indirect fire. Positions lacked depth and there were no anti-tank measures.

At the same time there were lots of indications of a build-up by the North Koreans. The intelligence flooding into Seoul told Syngman Rhee all he needed to know about North Korea's intentions. Border guards had been replaced by army units, civilians had been evacuated from the frontier area, and there were unmistakeable signs of a massive forward loading of munitions, fuel and military stores on the railway. All this intelligence was dutifully fed to the US Far East Command in Japan, which blithely dismissed it as ROK scaremongering. As General Matthew Ridgway was later to observe: 'Our national mind was made up to liquidate this embarrassing military commitment and we closed our ears to the clashing of arms that sounded along the border as our last troops were taking ship for home.'

2

From a Clear Blue Sky

SHOCK ON THE GROUND

It was 4 a.m. on the morning of 25 June 1950. The early monsoon rain drizzled across the mountains through which the 38th Parallel cut a dramatic, straight, artificial line, crossing high ground, rivers, wide tapestries of green paddy and occasional human habitation, with no respect for topography. It was Sunday morning, and many of those in the garrisons guarding the ROK frontier were on home leave for the weekend. The only people truly on alert that morning were the nearly 90,000 men of the *1st* and *2nd Corps* of General Chai Ung Jun's NKPA Army, the *In Mun Gun*, ready to storm across the frontier in what their Soviet advisers had planned to be a rapid, decisive storm of conquest. The troops had been told that they were on exercise, although this fiction had now been revealed for what it was when orders – initially in Russian and written in Cyrillic, before being translated into Korean – had been transmitted and disseminated for the attack. Speed and shock action were to be the hallmarks of this assault. The few roads leading to Seoul, following the Uijongbu corridor from the north, would form the axis of advance for the NKPA *1st Corps* (*1st, 3rd, 4th* and part of the *6th Divisions*), whose advance would cover the 40 miles between Kaesong in the west and Chorwon in the east. T-34 tanks and combat engineer vehicles would lead the charge to smash through any barriers, supported by self-propelled 76mm artillery guns and 122mm towed howitzers of Soviet origin, to push opposition aside and to allow it to be mopped up by following troops. Their orders were not to stop for

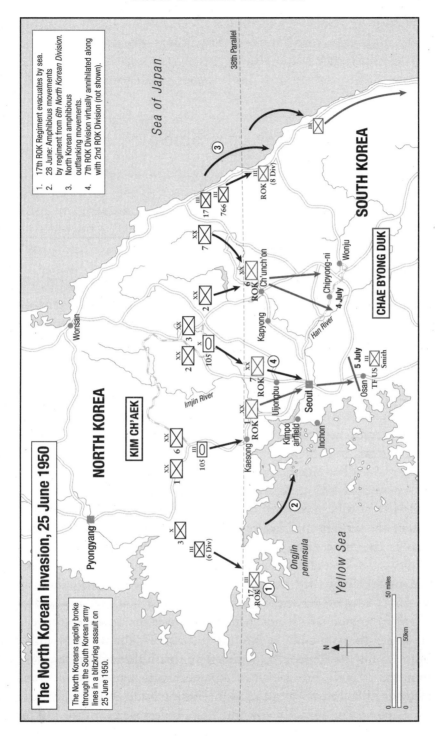

anything, but to advance in armoured columns as quickly as possible, capturing bridges, road junctions, villages and towns, and overwhelming any defenders they found. The Soviet advisers knew only too well the power of armour to entirely discombobulate an enemy unprepared to face the onslaught of heavy metal. The objective was the rapid capture of Seoul, followed by the more leisurely occupation of the ROK. Seoul would fall in a few days; the whole of South Korea within a month. Kim Il-sung knew that the only way he could remove Syngman Rhee's government was by a rapid, decisive attack, preferably on a weekend or public holiday, that would achieve victory before the Americans – the only foreigners, now that the Japanese had gone, with any interest in the country – might respond. If indeed they were interested. He doubted this. His strategy was to knock in a goal while the referee wasn't looking. It very nearly worked.

Facing the NKPA's *1st Corps* were four divisions of the ROK Army, garrisoning the frontier, with the 17th Regiment garrisoning the Ongjin peninsula, a topographical anomaly thrown up by the 38th Parallel, on the west coast, northwest of Seoul.

An hour later, Captain Joseph Darrigo of the US Army's Korean Military Advisory Group (KMAG), serving as an adviser with Colonel Chun Sung Ho's 12th Regiment, part of the ROK Army's 1st Division, was fast asleep in his house on the southern slopes of the vast, T-shaped mountain known to soldiers as Hill 475 and to the locals as Songak-san. It was Sunday, and he wasn't expecting anything unusual to happen this day. When he had gone to bed the previous night he had anticipated a day of rest on the morrow. Indeed, the recent proscription on weekend passes had been lifted, and about half of the regiment were away from their posts. There was annual weeding to do at this time of year on the family farms, and the men valued the opportunity of going home to help with this tedious but essential chore. The 1st Division had responsibility for the defence of this westernmost part of the 210-mile-long border with North Korea. Hill 475 dominates Kaesong, the ancient capital of Korea, which lay two miles to the south. It was about 5 a.m. on Sunday 25 June 1950. Suddenly, the concussive boom of incoming artillery shells, preceded by their distinctive whine, woke him with a start, tiny pieces of shrapnel soon peppering the house. Grabbing his clothes, he rushed out into the wet, early dawn light. The noise was tremendous. Clearly, a serious attack was under way. Jumping into his jeep, he rushed down otherwise empty roads into the town. In the centre he stopped the vehicle with a jolt and watched, astonished to see a train, the engine still puffing smoke, disgorging hundreds of troops. As he gaped, he saw soldiers running into the town, rifles and bayonets levelled. He didn't need to be told that the North Korean People's Army had arrived. He estimated a regiment of them – perhaps 3,000 men – had simply steamed across the border as though they were on a day excursion, and were now attacking the town, still deep in its slumbers.* It would have now been about 5.15 a.m. Stepping on the jeep's accelerator, bullets landing around him, the startled Darrigo sped south to cross the railway bridge at the Imjin River, carrying this astonishing information. At 7 a.m. the commander of the 1st Division, 29-year-old Colonel Paik Sun Yup – temporarily seconded to a course in the capital – sleepily picked up his telephone at the side of his bed in Seoul to hear the news brought by Darrigo. By 9.30 a.m. Kaesong was firmly in NKPA hands. It seemed that the bulk of Paik's 12th Regiment had been lost. It was war.†

As clocks struck 4 a.m., the first North Korean artillery salvoes began to fall on the depleted ROK positions along the whole length of the frontier. Half an hour later, under the covering fire of the artillery, infantry moved out of their hiding places and began to cross the frontier at designated crossing points. About a third of the NKPA comprised veterans with considerable experience of the last war. The ROK 17th Regiment, defending the Ongjin Peninsula, was quickly cut off (as was anticipated in the ROK Army's contingency plan for an invasion) and the survivors taken off by sea the following day. This area was never defensible. Nor was Kaesong, sitting on the main Seoul–Pyongyang highway and railroad. Two battalions of the 12th Regiment, ROK 1st Division, held positions just north of the town. The other battalion of the regiment was at Yonan, the centre of a rich rice-growing area some 20 miles westward. The 13th Regiment held Korangp'o-ri, 15 air miles

---

*The *13th* and *15th Regiments* of the NKPA's *6th Division* delivered the attack on Kaesong. Many of these men were experienced Korean veterans of the Chinese Civil War.
†Paik had been commissioned into the Japanese Manchukuo Army, where he had fought Chinese communists during the war. Many ROK officers had been previously employed in this army. This was less common in the NKPA, but it was a feature of the Chinese Army that invaded Korea in October 1950, soldiers swapping their allegiances at the end of the Second World War.

east of Kaesong above the Imjin River, and the river crossing below the city. The 11th Regiment, in reserve, and divisional headquarters were at Suisak, a small village a few miles north of Seoul. Lieutenant Colonel Lloyd H. Rockwell, senior adviser to the ROK 1st Division, and its youthful commander, Colonel Paik, had decided some time earlier that the only defence line the division could hold in case of attack was south of the Imjin River.

Within hours, Colonel Paik and his staff had arrived at his forward headquarters in a school at Munsan-ni. On a normal day he could see all the way beyond the Imjin River to Kaesong. Today was different, however, as billowing smoke from extensive enemy artillery obscured the entire front. With the remnants of his 12th Regiment retiring from Kaesong towards the Imjin River bridge, his remaining 11th and 13th Regiments occupied prepared positions between Munsan-ni and Korangp'o-ri. Almost at once they were both engaged in bitter fighting with the NKPA's *1st Division* and tanks of the *105th Armoured Regiment*. Paik's soldiers had nothing with which to oppose the enemy's T-34s. No soldiers, Paik recalled, had ever seen a tank. With remarkable courage, the men resisted with everything they had. The battalion's anti-tank weapons – 57mm anti-tank guns and 2.36-inch bazookas – made no difference to these leviathans. Some soldiers resorted to hurling themselves underneath the tanks with explosives in suicide attacks, while others attempted to get grenades in through the closed-down hatches. The division's 15 105mm howitzers managed to fire at the tanks and made it difficult for them to traverse. But soon their ammunition was all gone. Remarkably, some tanks were destroyed by these efforts. Even more remarkably, the men of the 11th and 12th Regiments managed to hold Korangp'o-ri for three days before they were outflanked on the right in the Uijongbu corridor and were forced to withdraw back to the Han River. To the left, however, the Imjin River bridge had not been destroyed as planned, and the enemy used this route to flood south towards Seoul. Even worse was the new disease of 'T-34-itis', which gripped the ROK Army. Whenever soldiers now heard the rumble of tank tracks it sent them in paroxysms of despair.

While Colonel Paik was trying to deal with the developing situation on the left of the ROK Army, the main enemy thrust – by the NKPA *3rd* and *4th Divisions*, accompanied by the remaining two regiments of the *105th Armoured Regiment* (with 80 T-34s) – came down the two roads that converged on Uijongbu, only 20 miles north of Seoul, through the area defended by the ROK 7th Division, commanded by General Yu Jai Hyung. The *107th Tank Battalion* with about 40 T-34 tanks supported the *4th Division* on the Tongduch'on-ni Road, while another 40 tanks of the *109th Tank Battalion* supported the *3rd Division* on the P'och'on Road. These two armour-led columns smashed their way to Uijongbu by the end of the day, allowing the residents of Seoul that night their first sound of distant artillery fire. They had already had their first sight of battle that day, as North Korean Yak fighters zoomed over the city, striking Kimpo airfield and the city's main street. Another distressing feature of the day's fighting was the sudden appearance on the roads of thousands of terrified refugees. From the start, unmanageable crowds of white-clad peasants on the roads, hauling carts, mattresses, cooking utensils and other goods hurriedly stripped from homes in the battlefront, clogged the roads, made the movement of military units extraordinarily difficult, and brought about the inevitability of civilian casualties, caught in exchanges of fire between both sides and, when foreign troops arrived, making it impossible to determine friend from foe.

The enemy pressure during 25 June was relentless, and by the morning of 26 June the troops on the right-hand road from P'och'on had pulled back to Uijongbu. On the left, despite suffering heavy losses, the NKPA's *4th Division* captured Tongduch'on-ni by the evening of the 25th and kept going, their T-34s carrying enough fuel for 180 miles. The morning of the 26th was critical, therefore. Paik's division was holding firm on the left, but the right – the front – was now under threat. The army commander – Major General Chae Byong Duk, as a result of his bulk universally known across the army as 'Fat Chae'* – decided to turn back the entire NKPA offensive at Uijongbu by launching a counterattack against enemy columns crowding both routes. Troops were pulled together by rail from as far as Taejon, 90 miles below Seoul (the 2nd Division), Kwangju (the 5th Division) and Taegu (elements of the 3rd Division). Most were en route north by the end of Sunday, the 25th, which, given the surprise of the enemy attack, was no mean feat. By the morning of 26 June, a counterattack

---

*He was 245 pounds in weight, the equivalent of 111 kilos or 17.5 stone.

was launched, with the 7th Division attacking on the left along the Tongduch'on-ni Road out of Uijongbu, and with the 2nd Division on the right on the P'och'on Road. However, although the attack by the 7th Division had considerable success, that by the 2nd Division didn't even start. The enemy armoured column punched through P'och'on during the night, and the next morning, driving through ineffective artillery fire, entered Uijongbu. The newly arrived battalions of the 2nd Division – entirely unprepared for battle – broke and fled into the hills. This in turn prejudiced the 7th Division attack on the left, causing it to abandon its own attack. By the evening of 26 June, the *3rd* and *4th* NKPA Divisions were in Uijongbu. Although it was no consolation, both NKPA divisions suffered irreplaceable casualties from their ranks of experienced veterans, incurring about 1,500 casualties. The ROK 7th Division caused the NKPA *4th Division* a total of 1,112 casualties. When well-prepared and well-led, the ROK Army had demonstrated that it was a match for anything the NKPA could throw at it, even columns of seemingly invincible T-34s. As Colonel Paik was to conclude from his experience of this battle, it was ignorance of tanks that was the primary problem with untrained troops. Once the psychological battle had been won, tanks were relatively easy to stop, even without dedicated anti-tank weapons. They would, of course, have been very useful, but in their absence artillery fire could slow down advancing tanks by forcing the crews to close up; infantry could then get in close and attack them by hand.

Meanwhile, Paik's gallant 1st Division, holding the line on the left, was now threatened with being outflanked. Paik had been annoyed to see his senior divisional KMAG adviser hold out his hand to shake it farewell, with the news that he had been ordered not to fight, and to withdraw to Seoul. In fact, that day Tokyo decided that the KMAG should be immediately evacuated, 700 men and their families being taken by sea from Inchon on Monday 26 June. So much for friends, Paik thought to himself. The ROK was on its own. There were now no troops between Uijongbu and Seoul, only 20 miles away. Disaster beckoned.

By nightfall on the second day of war, confusion wafted through Seoul. What was happening? The country's parliament debated what to do, inconclusively. To flee or not to flee? Part of the government machinery, including Syngman Rhee, decided to relocate south, to

Taejon. He escaped the city in his armoured train on 28 June. The danger of being caught in the capital, with NKPA artillery booming less than two dozen miles away, concentrated minds. By dawn the following morning – 27 June – fear was palpable. The US ambassador John Muccio left, and large numbers of Seoul residents, who, in the absence of precise instructions, flooded the crowded roads. It was suddenly looking like Belgium 1940 all over again, and the perennial problem of refugees disrupting military plans had still not been solved. General Chae took his army HQ south across the Han River but was persuaded to return to Seoul later that afternoon by the senior KMAG officer in the city. Meanwhile, the NKPA made its presence felt, ratcheting up the sense of doom as the hours passed. Yak fighters buzzed the sky and, as well as a few bombs, they dropped leaflets urging the city to surrender. The radio in Pyongyang went on the offensive too, urging the people to rise up against their capitalistic oppressors. Meanwhile, in Uijongbu the weak defences began to crumble. Bridges were not prepared for demolition, there were no mines or anti-tank weapons to stop the tanks, and many troops were demoralised. On the left flank, held by the 1st Division, however, a column of 25 T-34s could not penetrate the concentrated fire of artillery, together with a new weapon wielded by Colonel Paik's troops: blocks of TNT explosive fastened around a hand grenade. Thrusting them under a moving tank was a suicide mission, but a number of ROK soldiers gallantly threw themselves at the T-34s with nothing more than these makeshift weapons and their own raw courage. On the Imjin River, men of Paik's 1st Division destroyed 11 T-34s using such desperate measures. It was insufficient to stop the inevitable, however. By the evening of 27 June, the first NKPA troops reached the outskirts of Seoul. For the government and ROK Army, confusion reigned. Were the ROK to defend Seoul or withdraw over the Han River to form another defence line further south? The authorities – civilian and military had long since ceased to operate together – started to collide. During the early hours of the following morning, 28 June, the massive bridge over the Han River, carrying a road and three railway lines and providing the only route to safety for the divisions fighting in the north – which now comprised all or parts of the 1st, 2nd, 3rd, 5th and 7th Divisions – was destroyed to prevent it falling into enemy hands. The instructions to blow the bridge seem to have come from a senior civil servant in the Ministry of Defence, rather than the military chain of command.

The blowing of the Han River bridge was, apart from the terrible loss of life, a catastrophic mistake and the crisis point of the campaign, equalling the disaster on the Sittang which had led to the loss of Rangoon – and thence Burma – nine years before. Not only were many hundreds of soldiers and refugees killed, perhaps as many as 800, when the bridge was demolished, but the only withdrawal route for the army north of Seoul was removed. The bulk of the ROK Army was now north of the river, with no means of recovering its fighting strength south of Seoul to create a new set of defensive positions to halt the NKPA offensive.

During the morning of 28 June, Colonel Paik began to realise the extent of his predicament, with the remnants of his division holding strong defensive positions northwest of Seoul, but ammunition for his artillery, the backbone of his defence, exhausted. The trucks he had sent back, loaded with casualties, to collect ammunition were returning from Seoul empty. Then suddenly, to the east, he spotted a group of about 50 NKPA soldiers on Mongolian ponies making their way nonchalantly through the hills, heading south. He had been outflanked to his right! It must mean that the 7th Division had given way. A running fight followed. But something else then happened. The sound of aircraft filled the sky. So far, the only aircraft he and his men had seen were NKPA Yak fighters, swooping over the battlefield, exulting in their impunity. Looking up, he saw American F-51 Mustangs roaring overhead. The Americans had arrived! He had thought that they had been abandoned, but now, it appeared, the Americans were here to fight alongside them. Perhaps. The next moment the aircraft had turned and dived on Paik and his men, spraying 0.5-inch bullets over the ROK troops standing in the open, waving at their saviours. Several were killed and many wounded. Paik didn't mind. The American pilot clearly thought that they were the enemy, he rationalised to himself. It was an easy mistake to make. But at least they were here: that was the main thing, he told his shocked troops. 'You did not think the Americans would help us,' he told the men around him. 'Now you know better.' There was still hope! He didn't yet know that the ROK Army had withdrawn from Seoul, that NKPA troops were already on the outskirts of the capital to his south, and that his only escape route across the Han River had been destroyed. When he discovered this, standing forlornly on the banks of the wide, swiftly flowing Han River near Kimpo airfield, 12 air miles northwest of Seoul the following day – 29 June – he was to admit to shedding bitter tears, conscious of the accusing eyes of the refugees on him, 'the bitter ignominy of the soldier in retreat'. Only about half of his remaining division – 5,000 men – were able to cross on makeshift rafts, and without any of the division's 150 vehicles, artillery pieces or other heavy equipment, which had to be left on the northern bank. The men brought with them their crew-served and personal weapons, however. Although he didn't regard it as such, this was something of a triumph. Colonel Paik's personal leadership and the professionalism of his troops meant that the 1st Division retained its fighting integrity throughout the challenging months to follow. The destruction of the Han River bridge meant that what troops could cross the river did so as best they could, but in a disorganised state, without heavy equipment or, in many cases, weapons or ammunition. Groups of troops banded together with what leaders they had, making their own decisions about what to do next. Most opted simply to head south. There would be an opportunity to regroup at some stage, they reasoned.

The NKPA *3rd* and *4th Divisions* fought their way into Seoul on the afternoon of 28 June. By evening the city was in communist hands. Wasting no time, they began arresting their enemies: rounding up remaining ROK troops, police, and those South Korean government officials who had not escaped. The British diplomatic representative in Seoul, Captain Vyvyan Holt, managed to burn his ciphers before he was taken prisoner along with his staff. The First Secretary was George Blake, head of station of MI6, the Secret Intelligence Service. Some measure of the animosity of the North Korean regime to those with whom they disagreed was the rounding up of Korean clergy and nuns, none of whom were ever seen again.

On the eastern flank of the 38th Parallel, the *In Mun Gun's 2nd Corps* was defended by the 6th and 8th Divisions. As in the west, two North Korean assault divisions struck on the morning of Sunday 25 June at Ch'unch'on, an important road junction on the Pukhan River and the gateway to the best communication and transport net leading south through the mountains in the central part of Korea. Here the ROK 6th Division – for whom no weekend passes had been issued – fought the invaders to a standstill from their prepared positions in the hills. Reserves quickly arrived from Wonju to the south. The following day the NKPA

7th Division moved around Ch'unch'on to the east, threating to cut off the defenders of the town. Reluctantly, the 6th Division withdrew on 28 June, but in good order and with all its equipment. Nine T-34 tanks led the way into the town as the South Koreans marched out. The 6th Division were annoyed by this need to withdraw to conform with what was happening elsewhere on the line, but they had given the attacking NKPA divisions a very bloody nose. Subsequent reports told of 50 per cent casualties in the attacking troops and 76mm Soviet self-propelled guns, many caused by accurate ROK artillery fire. Dug-in with well-prepared concrete bunkers and alert troops, the defence of Ch'unch'on suggested a model for what might have been possible across the remainder of the South Korean defence line had it been as thoroughly prepared. As the division moved back, disconsolate but in good order along the roads to Hangchon and then Wonju, its progress was impeded by crowds of white-clad refugees.

By the end of 29 June only about 1,200 men of the ROK 7th Division and four machine guns, all that was left of the division, had crossed the Han River on boats and rafts to join those of Colonel Paik. The ROK Army had started the battle four days before with 98,000 men in uniform. After the Han River disaster, it could account for 54,000, many of these in the largely intact 6th and 8th Divisions that had withdrawn in good order on the eastern side of the country. With 45 per cent of its troops gone and with perhaps 70 percent of its personal weapons, the ROK Army was in a poor place to counter the inevitable NKPA offensive across the Han River when it came.

But, and it was a small 'but', the NKPA had not removed Syngman Rhee. Nor had it completely destroyed the ROK Army. But there was only one way in which the ROK Army could survive, and that was with the support of the USA, together with any other of Korea's international friends who might wish to lend their support.

SHOCK IN THE CAPITALS

The surprise attack across the border between North Korea and the ROK on Sunday 25 June 1950 came from a clear blue sky. Although indications of an attack had been mounting over recent weeks, as ROK agents in the North had been repeatedly telling Seoul, the government had not expected a full-blown war. People had ignored the ROK head of intelligence who had warned only weeks before, 'North Korean movements are abnormal. An attack is possible.' A large 'rice raid', as they were called, was possible, perhaps, but not war. American CIA analysts believed that North Korean strategy would be limited to continuing support for communist insurgency across the South, allowing the ROK to come undone at the seams. Those who thought an invasion might occur nevertheless believed that the ROK Army would be able to contain it. There were two principal factors at play at the time. The first was consistent over-assessments of the capability of the ROK Army by the USA's KMAG. The second factor, the primary problem in Tokyo, headquarters of the US Far Eastern Command, ultimate guarantors of South Korean security, was one of *imagination*. Because it didn't want it to happen, Tokyo had persuaded itself that it wouldn't, ignoring any evidence that pointed in any other direction. It wasn't just Tokyo, though. Most analysts and observers in Washington thought similarly. Only weeks before it happened, Dean Rusk, Assistant Secretary of State for Far Eastern Affairs, said that he saw no likelihood of war in Korea. Although there was clear evidence of North Korean offensive preparations, and the difference between the North's military capabilities and those of the South was clear for anyone to see, the idea that Kim Il-sung would be foolish enough to resort to war to unite the two now quite separate countries was considered preposterous. Those strategists in Washington and elsewhere who believed that decision-making was always undertaken on a rational basis were horrified at the apparent foolishness of this move, such that they immediately assumed that the nefarious hand of Kim Il-sung's big brother in Moscow was behind it all. The wishful thinking of those in power in Seoul and Tokyo – that the North would not resort to war – overrode the clear factual evidence that it could.

The United States had ended the Second World War with a frenzy of defence cuts to secure its long-awaited peace dividend. The country wanted the boys to come home and Congress was all too keen to get them off the payroll. With over half a million casualties sustained during the fighting against Germany, Italy and Japan, the country wanted to put the war behind it. The 85 divisions with which the US Army had ended the war had been reduced to ten by 1950. But numbers only told part of the story. The greatest war in the history of mankind was over, and war, it was hopefully inferred, would not trouble mankind again for a long time to come. Very little effort was made to prepare those new recruits now joining the army for the unique demands of combat. To compound matters, the US Army had no deployable expeditionary capability. This means that it wasn't able to bring together and despatch to a war zone a military force ready and able to fight immediately in defence of US national interests. The country, in other words, was simply not ready for war.

News of the invasion exploded like a thunderclap in Washington and London, and quickly reverberated around the world. Seoul is 13 hours ahead of Washington, across the international date line. President Truman was having a busy weekend at home in Independence, Missouri, when he received a call on Saturday evening from his Secretary of State, Dean Acheson. 'Mr President,' Acheson said, 'I have very serious news. The North Koreans have invaded South Korea.'

When the news arrived for Acheson from Ambassador John Muccio on the afternoon of Saturday the 24th, Acheson returned to his office and informed Dean Rusk, his Assistant Secretary of State for Far Eastern Affairs. Ambassador Muccio asked that the USA immediately provide the ROK with a list of urgently required military equipment, weapons and munitions. He asked his staff to contact Trygve Lie, the Secretary General of the United Nations, requesting an emergency meeting of the Security Council the following day, Sunday 25 June. On hearing the news, Lie didn't need any encouragement. The Secretary General was from Norway, a country that had lived under the Nazi jackboot for five years: he wasn't going to waste any time wondering whether or not to condemn the North for this blatant aggression. It was what the United Nations had been formed for. He acted immediately, using his executive authority as Secretary General to activate the United Nations from its slumbers and place it, and its members, on a war footing.

Only after doing these things did Acheson then ring President Truman, a couple of hours after the first attacks took place across the 38th Parallel. Acheson made a series of critical decisions, acting on behalf of the executive authority of the president; that is, without invoking Congressional approval or consulting the Joint Chiefs of Staff. For Acheson, speed was essential, the challenge existential. Following his conversation with Truman, Acheson presented a written resolution to Trygve Lie to be debated the following day: it demanded a cessation of hostilities and the withdrawal of North Korean troops back to the 38th Parallel. Acheson also authorised the aid to the ROK that had been requested by Ambassador John Muccio in his first telegram warning of the invasion,* directing the commander of Far East Command in Tokyo, General Douglas MacArthur – previously the Supreme Commander of the Allied Forces in the South West Pacific Area during the Second World War – to deploy the USAF's Far East Air Force to protect the evacuation of US personnel from Seoul. He also instructed the Japan-based US Seventh Fleet to place itself between Formosa and China to discourage any attack on the island, just in case the aggression in Korea was part of a wider attack by the communist regimes against the West.† On news of the attack, and fearful that this was actually an attack on the USA and its direct interests, not merely on South Korea, the commander of the Seventh Fleet, with Pearl Harbor uppermost in his mind, immediately ordered all his vessels to leave their home port of Sasebo in Japan. This time the United States Navy wasn't going to be caught napping in its home ports. The following day – 25 June in Washington – a further message arrived from Muccio stating that in his view this was no rice raid, but something that constituted 'an all-out offensive against the Republic of Korea'.

Acheson's immediate flurry of frenetic activity exemplified the instinctive reaction of the Truman administration to news of the North Korean attack. It was almost as if this latest example of communist perfidy had been expected, and a great test of the USA awaited. The administration's automatic response was to wade into Korea in support of the suddenly beleaguered ROK government, whatever its faults, because this was quite obviously a clear-cut case of one country transgressing the sovereign rights and prerogatives of another. On the other hand, the USA was cognisant of the need to support the

---

*General MacArthur ordered Eighth Army to ship to Pusan at once 105,000 rounds of 105mm howitzer, 265,000 rounds of 81mm mortar, 89,000 rounds of 60mm mortar, and 2,480,000 rounds of .30-calibre ball ammunition.

†The Seventh Fleet comprised an aircraft carrier, the *Valley Forge*; one heavy cruiser; eight destroyers; a naval oiler; and three submarines. The Seventh Fleet was divided between Okinawa and the Philippines.

young UN, and to allow it to take the lead in upholding the rules of international law, especially in support of the prohibition against the violation of national sovereignty. The domestic US context for this reaction was a heightened sense of real fear that the USSR was attempting to subvert the world ideologically through its imposition of communist rule on occupied territories (such as eastern Europe), the propagation of Marxism to developing countries, and practically through the assertion of its massive military strength. Whereas the USA had disarmed at the end of the war, the USSR had not. The Soviet Union was still very much a military state, spending a quarter of its GDP on defence, compared to America's 6 per cent. Defence spending in the UK was the same, at 6 per cent of GDP.* The mathematics of the military equation suddenly looked worrying. The Soviets had an army of 2.6 million; the USA, only 592,000, from an authorised strength of 630,000. The Soviets had 30 armoured divisions, whereas the USA had one. At the same time, the news was full of the insidious nature of communism's attack on democracy. The British atomic scientist Klaus Fuchs, a man who had worked at Los Alamos on the Manhattan Project to build the world's first atomic weapon, had been revealed to be a Soviet spy. Meanwhile, an otherwise unknown Wisconsin senator, Joseph McCarthy, had suddenly begun appearing at rallies waving a list of supposed 'commies' in the State Department. He started with 205 'known Communists', though the number fluctuated, on one occasion 57 and on another 81. The air in Washington during the early months of 1950 was thus filled with the fear of a range of new threats not merely to the American dream but to everything that had been achieved in the defeat of the Nazis and Japanese only five short years before.

Behind the Truman administration's response was a document that argued that the USA would need to back up the policy of containment (a concept developed by Dean Acheson, then Secretary of State, and George Marshall, the new Secretary of State, to use economic and military aid to prop up nations threatened by communism) by rebuilding its military strength, to act as an insurance against any

---

*In 1947 UK defence spending was 16 per cent of GDP but declined to 6 per cent by 1950. As a consequence of the Korean War, defence spending nearly doubled to over 11 percent in 1952. Thereafter, it declined through the rest of the 1950s to 7 per cent by 1959.

outbreak of communist-inspired lawlessness in the world. NATO had been established in Europe, binding together militarily the states that had benefited from the Marshall Plan, and the Berlin Airlift had demonstrated the West's resolve to resist Soviet bullying. But what happened if these measures short of war were insufficient, and *limited* military responses (i.e., non-nuclear) were required? A disarmed West was in no current state to counter the robust physical exuberance of the Soviet military machine. Accordingly, National Security Council Paper No. 68 ('United States Objectives and Programs for National Security', NSC-68) was presented to Truman on 7 April. It was blunt. The old policy of attempting to contain the USSR by diplomatic and political action alone needed to be reinforced by military power. What was needed were active measures to protect US interests, to deny the oxygen of communism and halt active subversion. If democracy was threatened by communist expansion, the USA had to be prepared to use force to counter it. But to use force entailed spending much more on defence than hitherto. This was politically and practically difficult. Truman, not a man to be rushed, put NSC-68 into his pending tray to ponder its arguments. He knew that acceptance of NSC-68 meant that if American interests were directly threatened by imperialising communism below the threshold of nuclear attack, the USA would be committed to war. As it turned out, 25 June 1950 forced his hand.

However, the idea of containment having an Asian dimension was never considered before China had fallen to the communists in 1949. This was a serious flaw in US conceptions of its security, all the more surprising given the weak spot it had had with Japan in 1940 and 1941. It was widely expected that Generalissimo Chiang Kai-shek, long propped up by US muscle, would win out against the communists. No thought had been given to the possibility of successful Soviet expansion in the region or of a communist victory. Pentagon war plans in 1949 considered two scenarios only: an attack on the continental USA and a thrust by the USSR into West Germany. The suggestion that China would fall and therefore a forward presence in Korea would retain some advantages for American security was never considered.

For Acheson, the arguments for rearming made perfect sense. A successful attack on South Korea by the North would lead to the unification of Korea under communist rule, something that would threaten the establishment of democracy in Japan (Korea was often described as 'a dagger pointing directly at the heart of Japan'), the Philippines and the rest of Asia struggling to emerge from the chaos and social and economic dislocation of the Second World War. In addition to conquering China, communism was threatening other parts of Asia as well, such as French Indochina and British Malaya. Not responding to overt aggression of the North Korean kind would demonstrate the weakness of the West. In other words, the issue for Acheson was existential. It wasn't necessarily existential to US security *per se* (though Truman was to claim that it was, in his 30 November 1950 off-the-cuff comment to the press that 'all' weapons in the American arsenal would be considered for use in the war, including the atomic bomb), but rather to the whole cause of global peace and security which had been the purpose of the establishment of the UN in the first place. While he expected any confrontation with the USSR to take place in Europe, the principle of resisting communist aggression wherever it might be found remained, even if that happened to be in a remote place such as Korea.

In this, Dean Acheson was not operating on a limb but was executing Truman's will, if not always his direct instructions. When he returned to Washington on Sunday 25 June, Truman retrospectively authorised the actions put in place by Acheson the night before. The president later commented that his visceral response to news of the North Korean attack was based on his understanding of the failure of international protocols to stop the descent of the world into the Second World War. He held that it was Western failure to respond to the Japanese takeover of Manchuria in 1931 and the 1938 Munich Conference that led directly to the Second World War. The failure to oppose the actions of aggressors had led to chaos and war. He had a track record of making tough decisions. He had made the decision in August 1945 to drop the atomic bombs in Japan. He had subsequently initiated the Marshall Plan and proclaimed the Truman Doctrine, the policy that offered material and military support to any country threatened by communist aggression. As he put it in his memoirs:

> In the final analysis, I did this for the United Nations. I believed in the League of Nations. It failed. Lots of people thought it failed because we weren't in it to back it up. O.K., now we've started the UN. It was our idea, and in its first big test we just couldn't let them down.

If a collective system under the UN can work, it must be made to work, and now is the time to call their bluff.

Some have suggested that America's military response to the North Korean invasion on the side of the ROK had nothing to do with the fact that the US was intrinsically concerned about Korea's security, but solely with American prestige. While it is true that America deployed force for its national interest rather than altruism, it is also clear that at this point in history the USA had decided that the only response to abuses of international stability by an assertive communism required military force. NSC-68 makes this point abundantly clear. The idea that the US response to North Korea's invasion of South Korea was for reasons other than (1) supporting a friend (2) meeting the terms of its defence obligations to the ROK, signed only months earlier (3) putting into practice a clear policy of armed containment against incidences of communist aggression (NSC-68) and (4) meeting its commitments to the United Nations to resist attacks on national sovereignty, is unconvincing. The truth is that the USA acted on the conviction that national sovereignty was worth defending, that friends were worth supporting, that the proscription against wars of aggrandisement was worth upholding. This was the reality of US national interest in 1950.

On Sunday 25 June the UN Security Council met in New York to debate a proposed resolution that called for collective action against North Korea for its 'unprovoked aggression'. The UK, France, Egypt, Norway and India wanted to understand why this should not be considered a classic case of civil war, as the many months of hostility across the border meant that it was hardly an 'unprovoked' attack, but the argument that one state had invaded another won the day. The resolution was passed unanimously. In the only time in its history, the Security Council enjoyed the unopposed passage of the American-drafted resolution. The Soviet representative, Jacob Malik, was at the time boycotting the Council because of its refusal to consider the appointment of the new Communist Republic of China to the table. The leader of the Kuomintang, now licking his wounds on Formosa, still held this seat.

Opinion in the US domestically was divided about how the USA should respond, if at all. Isolationists like Robert A. Taft, the powerful Republican leader in the Senate, rejected the idea that American blood should be spilt in this far-off place, but Taft was in a noisy and unpopular minority. For most others in Congress, the memory of Pearl Harbor remained too visceral to be ignored. Sudden, unprovoked attacks needed to be punished, even if they were on people in a faraway place about whom the USA did not know much. For General of the Army Omar Bradley, the Chairman of the Joint Chiefs of Staff, the biggest worry was somewhat more prosaic: he knew that the USA simply didn't have the troops available for the job. A war in Korea would place immediate pressure on virtually every aspect of armed forces that had been allowed to evaporate at the end of the war. For his part, Lieutenant General Hoyt Vandenberg, the Chief of the Air Staff, had a simple solution. Remembering how Japan had been brought to its knees by General Curtis LeMay's B-29s in 1945, he immediately proposed that North Korea should be flattened, and that Soviet air bases should be attacked with atomic weapons. He assumed, as did almost everyone in Washington, that behind Kim Il-sung lay the puppeteer-in-chief, 'Uncle Joe' Stalin. For his part, Truman was concerned that while the USA should respond robustly, it should not escalate the war any further than it needed to be. On 29 June, a series of explicit instructions were transmitted to the commander Far East Command – FECOM – a man whom he had never met, General Douglas MacArthur. With US aircraft already ranging widely over North Korea his instructions included the following injunctions:

- He was to use US troops to maintain communications and supply services for the ROK Army;
- He was to use US combat troops to enable the retention of an air and naval base at Pusan;
- He was to use air and naval forces against military targets in North Korea while staying away from Chinese and Russian territory, to avoid any accidental escalation;
- He was to ensure the defence of Formosa from any secondary invasion by China;
- He was to send supplies to the ROK Army, as they might be requested.

The 70-year-old Douglas MacArthur flew to Korea on Thursday 29 and Friday 30 June with some of his immediate staff – Major General

Edward 'Ned' Almond, his Chief of Staff, Major General Charles Willoughby, his head of intelligence, and General George Stratemeyer, commander of the Far East Air Forces – to assess the situation for himself.* He arrived in flamboyant mood, telling the press on touchdown: 'To give up any portion of South Korea to the aggression of the Chinese Communists would be the greatest defeat of the free world in recent times.' MacArthur seems to have arrived knowing precisely whom to blame: Communist China. It didn't really matter that the Chinese were not in the fight. The enemy was clearly the communists, and North Korean, Chinese or Soviet, that was all the same to him. MacArthur thanked Truman on 11 July for the appointment. 'I can only repeat the pledge of my complete personal loyalty to you as well as an absolute devotion to your monumental struggle for peace and good will throughout the world,' he wrote. 'I hope I will not fail you.'†

He was immediately worried about what he saw of the ROK Army. It had seemed to have disappeared. He watched some troops march down the road from Seoul, smiling at him happily as they passed. 'Well, nobody's fighting,' he observed succinctly to Almond. If anyone was to stop the North Koreans, it didn't seem that it would be the ROK Army. The NKPA had arrived in Seoul the previous day, Wednesday 28 June. With the collapse of the defence line 25 miles to the north, Seoul was effectively undefended, and by Tuesday the government had fled. British Communist Party journalist Alan Wittington, accredited to the *Daily Worker*, reported on Wednesday: 'Seoul, the capital of Korea, was completely liberated at 11:30 this morning Korean time. The majority of the puppet troops in the city were annihilated owing to the speed and power of the People's Army attack. Their fleeing remnants were pursued.' Wittington was in Peking, accurately citing North Korean communiqués. Close to the communist leadership, he was kept well informed. Refugee columns crowded the roads out of Seoul mixing

---

*In June 1950 the Far East Air Forces comprised nine groups with about 350 combat-ready planes. Of the 18 fighter squadrons, only four, those based on Kyushu in southern Japan, were within effective range of the combat zone in Korea. There were a light bomb wing and a troop carrier wing in Japan. The only medium bomb wing (B-29s) in the Far East was in Guam.
†Douglas MacArthur to Harry Truman, 11 July 1950, Korean War Folder, Truman Papers, Truman Library, http://www.trumanlibrary.org/whistlestop/study collections/koreanwar index.php

with bewildered ROK soldiers, separated from their units, knowing nothing more than to head south, if they could. Those Westerners who were going to get out, and avoid a long period of captivity, had done so from Kimpo airfield. The NKPA wasn't far away from where MacArthur stood south of the Han River. Advance units of the NKPA had reached the Han River and were preparing to cross. The problem was that if the USA were to provide troops, the nearest available were the shiny helmeted Eighth Army, undertaking occupation duties in Japan and in no shape for combat. Perhaps just a show of force would be sufficient to send the *In Mun Gun* back into North Korea? It was the only option available. MacArthur made up his mind on the flight back to Tokyo to tell Truman that he wanted to send an RCT, Regimental Combat Team (at three infantry battalions, or 2,000–3,000 men, the size of a British brigade) to help staunch the retreat of the ROK Army southward, perhaps even to stop the rot.

'The only assurance for the holding of the present line,' he told Truman when back at his desk in Tokyo on 30 June, 'and the ability to regain later the lost ground, is through the introduction of US ground combat forces into the Korean battle area.' He asked for permission to move an RCT immediately to Pusan, followed by a two-division corps if needed. Truman agreed without hesitation. The troops were not there to fight, cautioned Truman, merely to command the lines of communication (the key roads and railways). Yet American forces were already shooting down North Korean Yaks and bombing North Korean airfields. It was inconceivable that deployed military formations wouldn't end up fighting. On the same day, when pressed to say whether or not the USA was 'at war', Truman described the US military effort to be that in support of a police action. The decision to restrict the troops to support, rather than combatant, duties was quickly reversed, as MacArthur knew it would be. The Joint Chiefs of Staff also gave MacArthur permission to despatch all or any of the Eighth Army to Korea as he felt fit. A naval blockade of North Korea was authorised at the same time. The first US troops landed at the port of Pusan on 1 July. A month later, three divisions of the Eighth Army from Japan had arrived, totalling 47,000 men, under the command of Major General Walton 'Johnny' Walker.

Walker's Eighth Army of four divisions (the 1st Cavalry, operating as infantry, together with the 7th, 24th and 25th Divisions) could not in any way be described as combat ready. Though the men were of course soldiers, most of them had entered the army long after the last war had ended, and in the new pacific world order had no expectation that they would ever need to fire their rifles in anger. Their job in Japan was garrison-oriented, largely ceremonial and administrative. Recruitment into the US Army at the time as a whole was poor, as was the overall quality of troops in the army. To make matters worse, each of Walker's divisions was understrength, at 11,000 against an establishment of 12,500. Each division had six battalions rather than the normal nine. It had no deployable headquarters to command it on operations, and no formation training had been undertaken since the Second World War. At the same time the Seventh Fleet had been stripped back and the Far East Air Force was short of jet aircraft.

On 27 June the UN had met again to consider another US resolution, namely that member states 'furnish such [military] assistance to the Republic of Korea as may be necessary to repel the armed attack and to restore international peace and security in the area.' The resolution was passed without demur. A week later, on 4 July, the UN Security Council, still without its Soviet delegate, agreed to authorise the despatch of a military force to Korea, under the leadership of the USA. General MacArthur was put in command, reporting to the US president, who acted – supposedly – as the agent of the UN. The truth was that as soon as responsibility was transferred to the USA, it was never fully recovered. Politically, the UK instinctively wanted to help; militarily, it wondered just what it could do in the country's straitened circumstances. Attlee saw the issue in the same way as Truman. The governing Labour Party on the whole was united in the view that this was a war of naked aggression and that a collective response was required by the world to oppose a blatant act of lawlessness, made worse by the fact that it was again the communists that were causing the trouble. Giving in to the aggression was what the Tories had done with Hitler in 1938. Britain and the democracies needed to stand up to this sort of militarism and reject appeasement. It never worked with dictators. Indeed, it tended to encourage them. Attlee believed that if the UN was to have any more credibility than the League of Nations, it needed to act decisively against aggression of this kind. Likewise, the UK needed to be in the vanguard of the response. Britain had discredited itself when standing up to challenges to national sovereignty in the 1930s; it had learned its lesson. If Chamberlain, the Tory-appeaser, was the villain of this story, Attlee would be the protector of international law. But remaining in close step with its wartime ally, despite significant challenges to amity (such as the McMahon Act, which at a stroke removed the UK from involvement in the US atomic programme, something that Britain had helped with immeasurably by handing over its atomic research secrets to the Manhattan Project), was important to Attlee. The Conservative Party, in opposition under Winston Churchill, agreed with Attlee's instinctive reaction to news of the North Korean attack, and supported the government in what Churchill described as 'his inescapable duty'.

But the reality in 1950 was that Britain was bankrupt and exhausted, not merely from the exertions of the war that had just ended, but of the Great War which had preceded it. The armed forces were painfully stretched and couldn't offer much beyond the immediate use of elements of the Far East Fleet, then in Japanese waters. A carrier, two cruisers and some destroyers were provided. This was more in the way of a statement of solidarity between Allies rather than necessarily an offer of critical military capability. Australia and New Zealand immediately also offered their ships. It was much more difficult to find troops. In London the British Chiefs of Staff met on 3 July to discuss what resources it had to send to Korea. In a repeat of the situation with which Britain found itself in 1919, the British Army had no deployable military capability able to respond to urgent needs to defend Britain's national interest. As it had done precipitately in 1919, it had demobilised its forces after 1945 to the minimum necessary for the orderly management of its global obligations. The counterinsurgency in Malaya wasn't going well and was absorbing huge numbers of troops from an army that had rapidly diminished in size since the end of the Second World War. Then, with the triumph of the communists in the Chinese Civil War the previous year, the small garrison in Hong Kong had to be reinforced. This came on top of a range of existing military commitments in Germany, Austria, Trieste, Egypt and North Africa. The brand-new military alliance – NATO – was also hungry for troops. Accordingly, the Chiefs of Staff were reluctant to offer anything: the Joint Planners believed that it was militarily unsound to send any troops at all, given the massive commitments the UK already faced and the very real threat that was developing in Europe. No decision to send ground troops was made: a 'wait and see' posture was adopted. Three days later, however, following talks with the USA about the fact that the UK was naked against possible Soviet aggression, two USAF bomber groups and one fighter group were flown to new bases in Britain. If the attack in North Korea presaged a new round of communist aggression against the West, European defences needed immediate bolstering. This required a quid pro quo from Britain: troops of one kind or another would need to be found for Korea to demonstrate Britain's willingness to stand alongside its ally. In Washington the British military representative to the Joint Chiefs of Staff, Lord Tedder, visited General Bradley on 30 June with an offer to commit UK forces. Bradley observed that such a move would have an 'excellent political effect in sealing even more firmly our complete unity on this issue'. Complete unity? Perhaps not entirely. Britain would stand by its ally but would be a not uncritical partner. Throughout the Korean War the weight of commitment in Korea came from the USA, and Truman found himself unwilling to be overly influenced by very much a junior partner in the relationship.

However, the armed forces chiefs in London overcame their misgivings. On 24 July the Chief of the Imperial General Staff, Field Marshal Sir William 'Bill' Slim, told the Cabinet Defence Committee that the chiefs believed that 'although in their view it was still militarily unsound, they recognized the strong political arguments it would be wrong to send less than a Brigade Group.' The following day, the Cabinet endorsed the Defence Committee's decision: a land force would be sent to Korea.

3

Blitzkrieg, *In Mun Gun* Style

The North Korean People's Army retaught the United States a harsh lesson in the mountains of South Korea during the wet, humid summer of 1950. Combat is a hard business and is best mastered in peacetime before hot metal begins to fly. The sorry story of the period between June and September 1950 was one in which the consequences of profound unpreparedness for war were savagely rammed home to a country that had become complacent following victory in 1945.

The North Korean assault into the South was based on similar principles to many other successful advancing armies in history, demonstrated most recently in this part of the world by General Zhukov's Operational Manoeuvre Groups slicing through the Imperial Japanese Army in Manchuria in August 1945. Before that, the campaign which offers the greatest similarities to the tactics deployed by the *In Mun Gun* was the Wehrmacht's 'blitzkrieg' into Poland in September 1939 and France in May 1940. The primary characteristic of these operations was shock action against an unsuspecting foe, achieved in modern times by armoured columns working closely with mobile infantry, artillery and airpower, smashing through enemy weak points, outflanking fixed positions and driving hard for the enemy's rear. In these types of operations, moving and thinking faster than one's enemy – a feature known to soldiers as tempo – is key to removing the enemy's ability to respond appropriately to each move. This creates confusion among commanders and a sense among the fighting men that their commanders have lost control of events. When this occurs, morale often plummets. History has demonstrated repeatedly that the antidote to this challenge is hard, realistic training *before* actual fighting begins.

The plan drawn up by its Soviet military architects for the *In Mun Gun*'s capture of South Korea relied on a small number of very simple and well-practised Soviet Army operational principles. The first and most important principle was *operational shock*. A narrow vanguard of armoured troops would pierce the enemy defences on a small number of roads, the primary axes of advance, and shatter their coherence. Once an armoured thrust had broken through the crust of the ROK defences they would keep going, at speed, deep into the enemy's rear, there to sow confusion and dismay. Mobile artillery in the form of Soviet SU-76 (76mm) self-propelled guns would drop shells on enemy positions in coordination with the arrival of the tanks and infantry. When the tanks broke into a position, infantry, brought up behind the tanks in trucks, would envelop the enemy and place a strong block on the road to its rear, to prevent its successful withdrawal and to create the sense of being surrounded and of thus being helpless. The combination of all three – tanks, artillery and infantry – was designed to be psychologically overwhelming for untrained troops. It was the classic tactic of the roadblock practised to perfection against British troops in Malaya and Burma in 1942. The tanks would pause regularly to regroup and to allow the accompanying infantry to catch up, but their purpose was not primarily to fight, but to break the enemy's will to resist by means of relentless advance. Keeping the momentum of the advance going faster than the enemy could respond enabled the decision-making cycle to remain to the *In Mun Gun*'s advantage. Every time the defenders made a decision – such as to defend a particular location – it would be undone by the fact that the *In Mun Gun* had already pre-empted the ROK Army move. While vanguard units attacked frontally, others would bypass fixed defences entirely and infiltrate through and behind them to the rear, some to create blocks, others to attack less well-defended supporting and administrative units.

Such principles work well for short periods of time in circumstances when the enemy are simply not expecting an attack and are not mentally or physically disposed or deployed to respond to each enemy move. The utilisation of both strategic and operational surprise combines to make the enemy unable to respond in a timely fashion to each move, although well-trained and experienced troops can withstand such tactics if they are prepared for them. In this sense the plan was perfectly suited to the ambition to drive the ROK Army into the sea at Pusan. The first weakness of these tactics is that the pace of operations quickly exhausts the leading elements of the advance, as it requires amphetamine-like levels of energy to keep the pace of operations going, sometimes for weeks at a time – as the Wehrmacht found in France in 1940 and again in the Soviet Union in 1941. The second is the challenge of resupplying leading elements with fuel, food and ammunition during the advance. The Japanese, fighting the British in 1942 and 1943, always relied on refuelling themselves on captured British supplies, left behind in the haste to retreat or evacuate positions. They called these 'Churchill rations'. To deny these to an enemy, retreating armies have often resorted to a policy of 'scorched earth', burning and destroying supplies as they go, without discrimination between the local civilians caught up in the fighting and the army they are chasing, a policy adopted by the incoming American troops in the withdrawal to the Pusan perimeter that summer. The third challenge is to manage the potential for counterattacks from the air. For the Japanese in 1942, this did not prove to be a problem because they had command of the air, but for the *In Mun Gun* in Korea in 1950, it was to prove its Achilles heel as the USA's Far East Air Forces unleashed a savage aerial response to the NKPA offensive, first from its bases in Kyushu in southern Japan and later from airstrips in Korea itself.

———

The story of the relentless advance of the *In Mun Gun* against the ROK Army and the first troops of the US Army to arrive in Korea was one both of initial humiliation and rapid learning. An army which rested in the confidence gained by its great victory in the crusade against Nazism found itself being beaten by an enemy it had initially dismissed in a series of grindingly savage encounters all the way down the Korean peninsula between July and August 1950. The bitter experience of Task Force Smith at Osan was followed by the humiliation at Pyeongtaek. Unfortunately for the Eighth Army, these humiliations did not end there, being repeated by every new and unprepared formation sent to participate in the fighting. As the 34th Infantry Regiment's post-combat report concluded: 'early over-confidence changed suddenly to surprise, then to dismay, and finally to the grim realization that, of the two armies, the North Korean force was superior in size, equipment, training and fighting ability.'

The problem lay not merely in running down troop numbers and equipment following the Second World War. The US Eighth Army in Japan, which was to provide the first troops for the fray, was so unfit for service the US Official History of the war described it in uncompromising terms: 'command was flabby and soft, still hampered by an infectious lassitude, unready to respond swiftly and decisively to a full-scale military emergency." Equipment provision was poor. For instance, of the 226 recoilless rifles (RCL, anti-tank guns) it had on paper, only 21 were held by units; 55 per cent of the 18,000 jeeps and 4 × 4 trucks were unserviceable, as were 68 per cent of its 6 × 6 trucks. Nor did facilities exist to repair combat breakdowns. Supplies to fight a protracted campaign – fuel, rations and ammunition – simply did not exist. The problem was the underlying assumption among military planners that the next war would be the Third World War: atomic weapons had made smaller wars obsolete.

The advance north of Ch'onan, which Dean had hoped would halt the NKPA advance, quickly unravelled. While the 1st Battalion, 34th Infantry held positions on the hill to the east of the town on the main road that led south, the 3rd Battalion drove forward on the road by jeep and truck to create a defensive position blocking access down the road on the north side of the town. While they were doing this, they observed groups of men moving hurriedly across the hills on either side of the valley. The Americans, not sure who these men were, did nothing to investigate, assuming that they were simply ROK soldiers withdrawing south. In fact, two regiments of the NKPA's *4th Division* (the *16th* and *18th*) were infiltrating beyond and behind the Americans, aiming to envelope the town. It was at this point that the luckless Lieutenant Colonel Lovless was relieved and was replaced by the newly arrived Colonel Robert Martin. Out in front of the 3rd Battalion's new position, jeeps of the Intelligence and Reconnaissance Platoon were soon ambushed, the vehicles returning full of bullets: the enemy were clearly very close. The half-dug position then began receiving incoming

---

'James F. Schnabel, *United States Army in the Korean War, Policy and Direction: The First Year* (Center for Military History, 1992), 63–64.

small-arms rounds from the hills to the west. The troops were expecting an attack from the front, but none yet appeared, despite the bullets now whizzing through their position. Confusion and panic ensued. Mortars from the 3rd Battalion fired on its own troops, and before long, without having had any orders to do so, some of them began to withdraw back to Ch'osan. This unauthorised withdrawal was quickly reversed by the company commanders and battalion staff officers, and troops returned to their positions. On returning, they found their hastily vacated foxholes now occupied by the enemy. This time, the unplanned withdrawal became a rout, the men rushing back to Ch'osan in disorder, leaving their wounded behind, abandoning jeeps and mortars in their haste to escape. Many of those who were killed and wounded in this engagement were the officers who had been attempting to chivvy their reluctant men to fight. One wounded officer, who was subsequently to suffer three years of incarceration as a prisoner of war, watched in disbelief as his men hurried to escape, making no attempt to collect him or the other wounded.

An uneasy silence then settled over the battlefield until the evening, when columns of T-34s began to press the western edge of Ch'osan. Now in some semblance of order, but without many of its officers, the 3rd Battalion was reinforced by a battery of 105mm guns of the newly arrived 63rd Field Artillery Battalion, which Dean had sent up to help in the defence of the town. As the night proceeded, NKPA tanks of the *105th Armoured Division* and infantry broke into the town from the northwest, making their way through a minefield in which none of the mines detonated. Short of artillery ammunition and in danger of being cut off by an enemy envelopment, General Dean, 80 miles further south in Taejon, ordered Martin to withdraw his troops from the town the following morning, 8 July, and place them in a blocking position with the 3rd Battalion on the road to the east, where it made its way through the hills to Choch'iwon. Dean had now determined to conduct a fighting withdrawal all the way south to the Kum River, delaying the enemy as much as possible en route, buying time and causing damage to the enemy as it forced its way south. The Seoul–Pusan railroad crossed this river three miles due north of Taejon. Nine miles to the west the main highway crossed the river at the little village of Taep'yong-ni, 15 miles northwest of Taejon. At Konju, eight miles farther west from Taep'yong-ni and 20 miles northwest of Taejon, another highway crossed the Kum. Both crossings would need to be defended if the enemy were to be prevented from crossing the river, falling on Taejon and heading for Pusan along the primary artery.

To achieve this, the 34th Infantry would retire via the road to Konju while the 21st Infantry would make its way through the hills via Choch'iwon, following the railway line. The seriousness of the situation had hit home to Dean, who told MacArthur, 'I am convinced that the North Korean Army and the North Korean soldier and his status of training and equipment have been underestimated.' He asked on the same day for the expedited delivery of the new 3.5-inch bazookas, recently issued to the army, as the troops had lost confidence in the old 2.36-inch versions. They tended to fizzle out when hitting the sides of the T-34s and failed to penetrate, often even to explode. He also asked for HEAT rounds for the 105mm artillery pieces. MacArthur in turn had sent a cable to the Joint Chiefs of Staff in Washington to say that the situation in Korea had become critical, blaming the North Korean success on 'a combination of Soviet leadership and technical guidance with Chinese ground elements'. His message read:

His [North Korean] armored equip. is of the best and the service thereof, as reported by qualified veteran observers, as good as any seen at any time in the last war. They further state that the enemy's inf[antry] is of thoroughly first-class quality.

This force more and more assumes the aspect of a combination of Soviet leadership and technical guidance with Chinese Communist ground elements. While it serves under the flag of North Korea, it can no longer be considered as an indigenous N.K. mil[itary] effort.

I strongly urge that in add[ition] to those forces already requisitioned an army of at least four divisions, with all its component services, be dispatched to this area without delay and by every means of transportation available.

Some of MacArthur's comments were true, some not. There was no direct Soviet or Chinese role in the fighting at this stage. He was correct, however, in asserting that, despite his earlier sanguinity, the 'situation has developed into a major operation.' Although he didn't admit it, the ease with which the *In Mun Gun* had brushed aside elements of the 24th Division had been a shock to American commanders. Many who should have known better so shortly after the Pacific War had foolishly assumed the innate superiority of the Western fighting man. It smacked of the same ill-informed complacency rampant among Westerners in 1940 and 1941 about the Japanese and was just as deadly.

Dean was told that morning that the rest of the Eighth Army were being flown to join the fight in Korea. The Kum River – the largest river south of the Han, eight miles beyond which lay the key town of Taejon, was to be the place where the relentless march of the *In Mun Gun* would be stopped. If Taejon and its important railway lines fell to the NKPA the next defensive line would be the Naktong River, the last major physical obstacle ahead of Pusan. Dean accordingly ordered that the remnants of his battered 24th Division – the 21st and 34th Regiments, reinforced by the newly arrived 19th Regiment of the 21st Division – dig themselves in. The Kum River and Taejon had to be held at all costs.

It was a difficult task, however. The 24th Division was rapidly losing its confidence following the batterings it had received. It didn't have enough troops to defend the Kum River along its entire length, or in depth, and there were systemic problems within the division, such as the grievous lack of radios that prevented companies from communicating with their battalions, and battalions with regiments. Even worse, the Kum River dispositions could be easily bypassed and were a gift to even an amateur strategist. Because the river looped above Taejon, if the river line was to be defended forces would have to be disposed forward, leaving the flanks and rear soft and vulnerable. All the NKPA needed to do would be to attack from a flank underneath the foremost (northern) defences, cutting them off from Taejon, and thereafter block the main Seoul–Pusan Road to the east of the town, trapping ROK and American forces in a vast amphitheatre where they could then be defeated in detail. This was, as it turned out, the NKPA plan. Despite being battered by constant action and the attentions of the USAF, the *3rd* and *4th* NKPA Divisions had every advantage on the Kum River, and they planned to exploit it.

At the same time the nervous 3rd Battalion, 34th Infantry wasn't going to be given the opportunity to get out of Chonui cleanly, however, as the enemy had now comprehensively infiltrated into the town. During the darkness, illuminated by burning buildings, T-34s roamed the centre, firing on sites which they suspected of harbouring American troops. At 8 a.m. a lone T-34 rumbled up to a shed in which Colonel Martin and Sergeant Jerry Christenson were attempting to load a 2.36-inch bazooka. The tank fired just as the regimental commander was taking aim, cutting Martin in half. The explosion forced one of Christenson's eyes to pop out of its socket. Severely concussed, he nevertheless managed to force the eye back in place, shocked from the concussion and covered in the gore of his eviscerated regimental commander. Martin had commanded the 34th Infantry for only a couple of days and had been killed leading from the front, trying to set an example of combat to his green troops. Those of the 3rd Battalion who managed to escape from Ch'osan to their new positions to the east of the town did so by 10 a.m. As they made their way back, running, in small groups, and disorganised, Dean arrived at the hill south of the town, in time to watch the luckless survivors of the battalion, and of regimental HQ (which had been caught in the town and was now reduced to only 175 men) make their humiliating escape. All their mortars had been lost, along with many personal weapons. Morale was at rock bottom. Lieutenant Colonel David Smith, the commanding officer, was quietly evacuated with exhaustion and replaced by Lieutenant Colonel Robert Watlington.

Dean had little choice now but to order Colonel Charles Beauchamp, who had replaced Martin, to withdraw the 34th Infantry and to form new defensive positions further south on the Kum River at Konju. But as the dispirited men retreated south that day, enemy soldiers could again be seen moving fast high on the hills above them, as they had done the previous day. The Americans did not command the heights. The road was like glue, holding the vehicle-borne American infantry in its sticky grasp. The good news was that men of the 21st Infantry (Colonel Richard 'Dick' Stephens), who had arrived from Japan on 7 July, began moving up by train to meet the 34th Infantry at Choch'iwon, and deployed forward to provide two blocking points on the road out of Chonui. This, however, proved to be easier said than done. The South Korean locomotive drivers were not keen on going north, and were apt to abscond, taking their trains with them. Dean's plan, with the arrival of these welcome reinforcements, was that the 21st would hold at Choch'iwon (supported by a battery of 155mm howitzers), while the 34th would delay the enemy along the Konju Road.

Two companies of the newly arrived 1st Battalion, 21st Infantry accordingly moved into positions across the road at Chonui during the night of 8 July, and the remainder of the 3rd Battalion (Lieutenant Colonel Jensen) were a few miles further south.

The *In Mun Gun* began to move out of smoking Chonui on the road to Choch'iwon on 9 July in time-honoured fashion, with 11 tanks leading about 200 infantry in trucks and on foot. By this stage a Tactical Air Control (TAC) party (one of two now in Korea) had joined the 300 men stretched across the three-quarters-of-a-mile 21st Infantry Regiment block, and an airstrike by a flight of the versatile Mustang F-51 a few minutes later destroyed at least five of the T-34s. Until the TAC parties arrived, ground attack aircraft had made many embarrassing errors, shooting up their own side. The previous week four Mustangs of 77th Squadron, Royal Australian Air Force, based in Japan (part of the US Fifth Air Force) strafed the railway yards at Pyeongtaek in the mistaken belief that they were hiding Northern troops. Other attacks mistakenly targeted ROK Army units, it proving impossible apparently to distinguish them from NKPA. As a result of many errors in the early weeks of the campaign, strikes not directly targeted by TAC teams were abandoned.

Heavy mortars and 155mm howitzers pummelled the town, and air attacks further up the road to Pyeongtaek destroyed an estimated 100 vehicles. The men, watching Chonui burn that night, gained much pleasure in knowing that they had stopped the enemy advance. But their flanks remained wide open. The purpose of the tanks was to effect shock action to the front, holding the nose of the enemy while fighting columns enveloped from either side, some to attack, while other groups of enemy soldiers carried on to the rear. Through the early morning fog on the following morning (10 July), more tanks pushed through the block unseen, while infantry, creeping up overnight, attacked the American positions and overran their 4.2-inch mortar firing plates to the rear. Over the following few hours, relentless infantry assaults surrounded and destroyed each of the American positions in turn. Probing attacks began before 6 a.m., followed by mortar fire and massed infantry assaults at 9 a.m. A hilltop position on the extreme left was overrun two hours later, the men all dying in their foxholes. At the same time, an *In Mun Gun* encirclement on the right flank created panic, men running for the rear. In a now famous command,

Colonel Stephens yelled: 'Get those high-priced soldiers back into position! That's what they are paid for.' Some tried to restore order, but it wasn't enough to save the position, and at 12.05 p.m. Stephens gave the order to withdraw to the position held a mile to the rear by Lieutenant Colonel Jensen's 3rd Battalion. The men struggled to make their way through the wet paddy fields, carrying all their equipment. Twenty per cent of the defenders became casualties. Jensen launched a counterattack to retake the position but failed to take the hill on the left, south of the railway line. He found, instead, the bodies of six 21st Infantry soldiers, hands bound, each executed by a bullet through the back of the head.

At about the same time as the discovery of this unsettling scene, American superiority in the air was demonstrated to devastating effect. Flying from Japan, four squadrons of F-51 Mustang fighters from the Fifth Air Force supported the 24th Division on the ground soon after the start of the invasion. Indeed, as early as 28 June the Fifth Air Force flew 172 combat sorties in support of the ROK Army and continued this level of support in the days that followed. With the gradual development of airfields in South Korea, this number was to grow dramatically, especially as the versatile F-51 Mustang could operate easily from simple air strips. The problem in the early weeks of the war was that there simply weren't enough available aircraft or pilots, and only limited quantities of aviation fuel were available. When in the first week of July General Stratemeyer, commander of the Far East Air Force (FEAF), asked Washington for 164 F-80 Shooting Star jet fighters, he was told that the USAF only had 44 available. The large wartime stocks of the USA's first jet fighter had been allowed to become a maintenance problem.

There is no doubt that interdiction from the air caused the NKPA serious discomfiture. With ground forces constantly on the defensive, seeking new places to withdraw, American airpower proved to be the only means of counterattack available to the beleaguered US and ROK forces. On the same day as the Chonui block was broken, marauding F-80 Shooting Star jets spotted a large convoy on the road north of Pyeongtaek. The FEAF immediately sent every aircraft they had, with a massive airstrike by B-26 medium bombers, F-80 Shooting Stars and F-82 twin-Mustangs. Between them they destroyed as many as 45 armoured vehicles and over 100 trucks. The NKPA was hampered in its lack of air supremacy and its inability to support its ground troops in the advance, although Yak fighters provided limited and intermittent fighter ground attack capability. Colonel Paik and a colleague, Colonel Kim Paik, were caught in the open in a jeep in early July when they were attacked by a Yak diving behind them. They survived death by the narrowest of margins. But the *In Mun Gun* were quick learners, and very rapidly all movement on roads and tracks ceased during the hours of daylight. It became increasingly difficult for UN aircraft to spot moving NKPA units during the hours of daylight, as in time all movement by fighting troops and supply took place at night. This art was perfected in October and November with the arrival on the battlefield of the Chinese People's Liberation Army (PLA), but the *In Mun Gun* also quickly adapted to this new threat, no longer exposing its vehicles or troops during the hours of daylight. Now, the enemy generally remained quiet and camouflaged in orchards and buildings during the daytime, moving only at night and using village roads and tracks rather than main roads where they could. Even when they were forced to advance in daylight, they did so with as much camouflage as they could muster. Captain John Shipster recalled at this time near Pakch'on watching a long column of Chinese soldiers marching south about half a mile from his hidden position. 'I ordered everyone to keep still and not on any account give our position away,' he recalled. 'The Chinese were all heavily camouflaged, with what looked like natural vegetation.'*

———

Lieutenant Colonel Jensen began to pull back his battalion to its original positions (i.e., those occupied prior to attempting to recapture the defences east of Chonui), only to discover, in what was becoming something of a pattern, that enemy troops had already occupied some of their old trenches. There was no such thing as a linear defensive position on this battlefield, as NKPA units infiltrated behind and beyond any fixed defences they found. They did so in the main by keeping to the high ground, infiltrating along ridges while

*John Shipster, *Mist Over the Rice Fields* (Leo Cooper, 2000), 131.

the US troops kept to the roads. These enemy troops had to be prised from their positions by hard fighting, after which Jensen pulled his battalion back during the early hours of 11 July to positions just north of Choch'iwon. Dean signalled to Stephens: 'Hold in your new position and fight like hell.' They didn't have long to wait. At 6.30 a.m. the following morning (11 July) the NKPA tank-led advance struck at the 3rd Battalion (the 1st Battalion, now reinforced by the survivors of Task Force Smith, was two miles to the rear). In what the Official History of the United States Army in Korea records as 'one of the most perfectly co-ordinated assaults ever launched by North Koreans against American troops', the position was attacked by 1,000 infantry, supported by frontal assaults by tanks, heavy mortar and artillery concentrations, and enveloping attacks from both flanks. Lucky hits on ammunition stores and a depressing failure of the American units to be able to communicate with each other during the battle allowed the newly arrived NKPA *3rd Division* to overwhelm the 3rd Battalion, 21st Infantry. Lieutenant Colonel Jensen was killed along with many of his officers, and 60 per cent of the battalion destroyed. Ninety per cent of the survivors reached Choch'iwon without weapons; many had no shoes or helmets, so hasty was their flight. That night, the 1st Battalion, 21st Infantry, now holding the line at Choch'iwon, was struck hard. During the early morning of 12 July some 2,000 enemy infantry, supported by tanks and artillery, swept into the left of the line. Stephens, about to be swamped by overwhelming force, gave way at midday and began to withdraw his battered regiment to the Kum River, where the road crossed the river at Taep'yong-ni. The battered 34th Infantry, which had struggled down the road to the west, fighting off repeated attacks from the NKPA *4th Division*, crossed the Kum River into Konju on the same day. During this bitter period of fighting, the weak and unprepared 21st and 34th Regiments had received their baptism of fire in Korea. Many soldiers had behaved badly in combat, the result of poor training for the hard realities of war. The 21st Infantry was down to 325 men (only 64 of whom were left from the devastated 3rd Battalion), having already lost an astonishing 1,433 men in action. The strength of the entire division on 13 July was a mere 1,440 men. Facing it were the two divisions of the NKPA, one (the *4th*) chasing the 34th down the Konju Road to the west, the other (the *3rd*) chasing the 21st Regiment down the east to Taep'yong-ni.

The task of the battered 24th Division was to deny the river to the *In Mun Gun*. Dean placed the 34th Regiment on the left, under Konju; the 19th on the right at Taep'yong-ni, and the much depleted 21st Infantry in a reserve position southeast of Taejon. Thus, the division formed a two-regiment front, each regiment having one battalion on the line and the other in reserve. This was entirely insufficient to cover the entirety of the river. A large gap existed between the right hand of the 34th Infantry at Konju and the left hand of the 19th Infantry. The two regiments were forced by geography to fight two separate battles, an issue compounded by the fact that the division had few working radios and struggled to communicate internally. To their horror the forward observation officers found they could not call on their guns, and watched helplessly as enemy infantry crossed the river unopposed by the one weapon that could have stopped them. The infantry companies on the river also found that they couldn't communicate with their guns, making the artillery useless. Likewise, there was no reserve able to react quickly to any enemy breakthrough wherever it might occur.

The NKPA *4th Division*, now reduced to some 5,000 effectives after nearly three weeks of fighting, accompanied by 20 T-34s and 50 artillery pieces, both towed and self-propelled, butted up against the 24th Division's defences on the Kum River below Konju on the late evening of 11 July, reconnaissance troops attempting to ascertain the American defensive positions. The Americans had taken the precaution of clearing the river of boats for some miles downstream. The hard fighting of the previous two weeks, even despite the precipitate flight of both ROK and American troops, nevertheless had been unexpected and had worn down the North Korean advance. Even so, the *In Mun Gun* held a significant advantage over the Americans, not merely in respect of the number of troops fielded but being able to determine how best to engage and bypass the over-stretched defenders. The 34th Infantry had only three understrength companies' worth of men from the 1st Battalion on the river. The 105mm guns of the 63rd Artillery Battalion were two and a half miles to their rear, and the 3rd Battalion in reserve. The psychological state of the men of the 34th Infantry was, by this stage, a matter of grave concern. Some officers in the regimental HQ had been withdrawn because of combat fatigue, and on the night of 13 July, K Company, a composite group of about 40 men of the 3rd Battalion, were in such poor state of mental and physical health that they were withdrawn to Taejon for medical evacuation. The relentless pressure of the *In Mun Gun* was having its effect.

———

The Konju bridge was destroyed during the early morning of 13 July, but it wasn't until the following day that enemy tanks were heard on the far side of the river and widespread crossings by boat were reported. The NKPA crossings were supported by Yak fighters which drove off American artillery observation aircraft. The events which followed could be categorised as comedic were they not tragic for those concerned. Heavy artillery and mortar fire persuaded one of the 1st Battalion company commanders that his position was untenable so, without orders, he withdrew his men to the rear. A furious commanding officer threatened him with court martial, but the damage had been done. Three miles to the rear, the 63rd Artillery Battalion was supposed to be providing fire support but had no radio communication with its forward observers. When the North Koreans attacked, they were opposed by very little artillery or mortar fire and, surprisingly given the American air superiority, no fighter ground attack sorties seem to have been planned to destroy boats making the wide river crossing (air attacks had some effect on and after 15 July). All in all, the defence of the Kum River was a disaster both in planning and execution. With it Taejon would fall. While it is clear that by this stage both the Eighth Army and Tokyo had become thoroughly alarmed at the shocks being meted out to the unprepared 24th Division, none of these concerns was able to change the situation on the ground, where soldiers untrained and unprepared for the rigours of combat repeatedly made mistakes and errors of judgement that placed the continued ability to stop the *In Mun Gun* reaching Pusan in peril.

As NKPA reconnaissance had demonstrated, the Kum River defences were vulnerable to a wide outflanking move across the river to the west. Three miles to the rear of the 3rd Battalion defences, its left flank exposed to the Kum, the 63rd Artillery Battalion now found itself vulnerable to infantry attack. It was blissfully unaware of its predicament. It was a shock therefore when, at midday, the batteries were overrun by 400 men of the North Korean *16th Regiment*, accompanied by heavy mortar and machine-gun fire. Some men resisted bravely, though most fled without weapons or equipment at the first sight and sound of the screaming North Korean soldiers rushing their positions. Within 90 minutes all but one of the battalion's gun batteries had been overrun, losing ten guns with their ammunition, 80 vehicles and 130 men. An attempt by the 1st Battalion, 34th Regiment to recover the position later that evening failed, as with no artillery, tank or air support, the task was regarded to be impossible. An airstrike the following morning was Dean's only way of attempting to deny the captured howitzers and their ammunition, and the vast number of captured vehicles, to the enemy. The truth was that the entirety of the left flank of the 24th Division's defence on the Kum River had been undone in a matter of hours, its cause a poorly designed defensive position occupied by exhausted, poorly equipped and badly led soldiers.

Command of all US forces in Korea passed directly to General Walker of the Eighth Army on this day, 13 July, just as the 24th Division stretched itself across the Kum River. By this stage there were 18,000 US troops in Korea, operating alongside an estimated 58,000 troops of the ROK Army. The HQ moved from Taejon to Taegu. The task of Walker's army in Korea – and of the ROK for whom responsibility was transferred a week later – was to delay the enemy advance, secure the current defensive line, stabilise the military situation, and build up for future offensive operations. On the same day, fearful of the news from the land battle, MacArthur urged General Stratemeyer to deploy the greatest quantity of his newly arrived bomber force – 22 of the twin-engined B-26 Marauder and two groups of the giant four-engined B-29 Superfortress, able to carry 40 500lb bombs – against the enemy divisions marching south.

By the morning of 15 July, what remained of the 34th Infantry had withdrawn from Konju and occupied new positions just east of Nonsan. Its departure from the Kum River resulted in the left flank of the 24th Division being fatally breached, resulting in the exposure in turn of the 19th Infantry's left flank. The events of 14 July must have made it clear to General Dean that he could not long hold Taejon, but he gave no hint that he wasn't confident that his division could still hold off the *In Mun Gun* at Taejon. He was later to record that at this stage of the battle he had no idea of the wide flanking move the enemy were undertaking to surround the town and to cut off the main road to Pusan. Dean's plan was to congregate his whole division – the 34th, 19th and battered 21st – in this area to hold the road. He was to be beaten to it by the *In Mun Gun.*

The 19th Infantry, which had arrived on the Kum on 12 July, was forced to hold a line about 30 miles long, with the main regimental position astride the Seoul–Pusan highway where it crossed the Kum River at Taep'yong-ni. Considerable gaps existed in the line. Aerial strikes on the 14th failed to prevent the build-up of enemy armour on the north side of the Kum opposite Taep'yong-ni. The afternoon of 14 July brought the bad news of the collapse of the 34th Infantry at Konju.

The North Koreans began crossing in the 19th Division area on the morning of 15 July. On the same day the remnants of 21st Regiment – which now totalled 1,100 men – retired to take a position high in the hills at Okch'on, ten miles east of the city on the main Seoul–Pusan highway. All that day the *In Mun Gun's 3rd Division* prepared to cross the river, hampered by airstrikes. That night several attempts were made to rush the river, but it was at 3 a.m. the following morning – 16 July 1950 – that the major offensive began. The 19th Infantry's commanding officer – Colonel Stan Meloy – said the intensity of the bombardment equalled anything he had ever experienced in Europe during the war. Under this cover soldiers of the *In Mun Gun* waded, swam or crossed the river in hundreds of small boats brought up for the purpose. They were soon assaulting the widely separated American positions, as well as pushing hard for the rear, infiltrating through and between the defended positions. Fierce fights broke out right along the river line. Dawn brought the sight of hundreds more North Korean troops, in groups of 20 to 30 at a time, crossing the river and disappearing into the hills behind the US positions. Artillery and mortars did what they could, and in one case a fierce counterattack forced many North Koreans back into the river. But it was clear that the regiment would not hold forever. Although the regiment had done well to throw back many of the troops fighting to their front, they had no answer to those already in their rear. Reports soon came through to Colonel Meloy that a roadblock had been established on the main supply route three miles behind. It would need to be cleared if the regiment was to successfully withdraw that night to Taejon. Meanwhile, infiltrating *In Mun Gun* columns attacked the artillery battery positions to the rear. By mid-afternoon Major General Dean, fearful that the 19th Regiment was about to be cut off, ordered the now-wounded Meloy to withdraw as best he could, bypassing the roadblock. Enemy fire meanwhile was targeting American vehicles on the roads. Troops labouring back through the hills were doing so now in conditions of confusion and exhaustion: the intensity of the summer heat made climbing the jagged Korean hills a feat of significant physical endurance, made worse by the physical unpreparedness of most of the men. A clean withdrawal out of contact with the enemy proved not to be possible, enemy machine guns harrying withdrawing troops, splitting companies and platoons and sowing confusion and chaos. Some men fought bravely; many, too, sought the sanctuary of roadside ditches and determined to wait until the heat of the fighting died down before continuing their escape, while others threw away their weapons and ran. Attempts were made to remove the roadblock from the south, one using light tanks and four anti-aircraft artillery vehicles, two of them mounting quad .50-calibre machine guns and two mounting dual 40mm guns. But it failed to break the remarkable hold the NKPA had on the road, and all the vehicles were destroyed. Other troops tried to fight through the roadblock – which extended for at least a mile and a half – but also failed. The only other way the 50 men of the 19th Infantry held at the roadblock could retire on Taejon was to make their way across country. During that night – 16 July – many parties made their way through the darkness on compass bearings for safety to the south. Some took their wounded with them, many on litters. Others were left to an uncertain fate at the hands of the North Koreans.

The US Official History describes the battle of the Kum River on 16 July and the battle for the roadblock that followed to be 'a black day for the 19th Infantry Regiment'. Of the approximately 900 men in position along the river at the start of the battle, only 434 reported for duty in the Taejon area the next day, a loss of nearly 50 per cent in a single two-day action. The 1st Battalion lost 338 from 785 men, or 43 per cent, the 2nd Battalion, 86 from 777 men, or 11 per cent; and all attached units engaged in the action lost 650 men from 3,401, or 19 per cent. To all intents and purposes, the 24th Division was spent. The 21st had been smashed at Osan and Choch'iwon, the 34th at Pyeongtaek, and now the 19th on the Kum River. But much hard fighting was to follow. Dean's division had suffered repeated reverses. Its men were exhausted and demoralised, shocked at the proficiency of their enemy and overawed by the brutal horror of combat. Taejon would be difficult to hold.

The *In Mun Gun* assault on Taejon proved to be no different from previous attacks. A heavy frontal attack led by T-34s and artillery was accompanied by wide outflanking actions designed to cut off the defender's rear, preventing them from withdrawing in good order. It was a tactic those who had fought the Japanese in the last war knew well. It had also been a feature of Wehrmacht operations against the British and French armies in 1940, but it was a tactic largely outside the experience of US soldiers during the previous war, who in the heat of battle in 1950 struggled to conceive of a way to solve it. The problem of having the enemy deep in one's rear had been solved by the Fourteenth Army under Lieutenant General Bill Slim in India in 1944 and Burma in 1945, but to be effective it needed resourceful commanders, stalwart troops, air superiority and a means of aerial resupply.

When the T-34s smashed into Taejon on the morning of 20 July it was to a town full of refugees, confused ROK and American defenders and pillars of black smoke reaching high into the dawn sky. Regrettably, many troops appeared leaderless, some creating a sense of panic that was made worse when crowds of men then found the primary escape route from the city to the east – the road to Pusan – blocked by the NKPA. Many US accounts relate how NKPA soldiers infiltrated into the city to act as fifth columnists, a charge that was largely a figment of the imagination of men desperate to blame their battlefield performance on an enemy who didn't play by the rules.

Lieutenant Robert Herbert of the 19th Infantry watched four tanks approaching from the west, assuming, from the direction of approach, that they must be American. Few members of the 24th Division had ever received instruction in tank recognition. As he stood by the side of the road, the tanks drove past him, ignoring him completely. Only then did he recognise them as T-34s. Mouth agape, he had just shrunk into the cornfield when a party of four Americans came up behind, at the trot, carrying newly arrived 3.5-inch bazookas, a weapon that was far superior to its predecessor. He recognised one as the divisional commander. Major General Bill Dean was out hunting North Korean tanks. Another member of the 19th Infantry in the town, Sergeant First Class Joseph Szito, watched from a building in amazement as, in the early afternoon, a T-34 rumbled down his street, closely pursued by the unmistakeable sight of the divisional commander, carrying a bazooka. For the divisional commander to be doing a soldier's job – when so many others weren't – demonstrated the abject state of the town's defence.

An hour later the tanks returned from the city to Herbert's position and a fight ensued on the road. Herbert's position was stonked by artillery, with American 105mm guns finally stopping the T-34s. By this time, however, Herbert could see other US soldiers, presumably from the 34th Infantry, streaming away south from the city. To the southeast, he saw other men, clearly *In Mun Gun*, rushing to form a block to the rear of Taejon. NKPA troops and tanks were making their way into the city while Americans were trying desperately to escape. Those who managed to get out of the town on the road to the east found themselves caught up in a fierce fight for control of the road at the roadblock leading away to the east. General Dean also took to the hills, where he wandered for nearly a month before being captured.

The weeks that followed entailed attempts by the NKPA to break through into the southeastern corner of the country at Pusan from southeast (Hadong/Chinju), northwest (Taejon/Yongdong), north and northeast. At the same time, US and ROK forces rushed to form a series of defensive barriers to protect the pocket, known in time as the Pusan perimeter, an arc extending some 130 miles in length. Withdrawn from Taejon, what remained of the 24th Division was replaced at Yongdong – further along the road to Pusan southeast of Taejon – by the newly arrived infantry of the 1st Cavalry Division. The battered 24th Division was withdrawn to the south, being given responsibility for covering the entirety of the arc running from south of Chirye all the way down to the coast at Chinju. Twenty miles further north of Yongdong the 25th Division, fresh off the boat at Pusan, attempted to hold the road junction at Songju. Both divisions (the 1st Cavalry and the 25th) failed and were pushed back by the NKPA *2nd Division* (at Yongdong) and the *1st Division* at Songju. In both battles the American troops were outclassed by far superior enemy troops. At Chinju, far to the south, the two-battalion 29th Regiment, flown in from Okinawa but entirely without training and unprepared for combat, met the men of the advancing NKPA *6th Division* at Hadong on 25 July with rifles that had not yet been zeroed, machine guns still in their preserving oil and mortars that had not yet been test fired. The 3rd Battalion, 29th Infantry was immediately destroyed. It lost 300 men in the initial firefight and 100 ended up becoming prisoners. Some panicked men threw away their weapons and helmets in their haste to escape. In the days following, pressure from the *6th Division* pushed the men of the 19th and 29th Regiments back to Chinju, which the NKPA entered on 1 August. Enemy pressure was relentless, the 35th Regiment being forced back to positions at 'The Notch'* by 4 August, and the 27th and 5th Regiments pushed to the sea at Chingdong-ni, and the remnants of the 24th holding on at Chungni. The enemy were less than 20 miles from Pusan.

Further north, the 1st Cavalry Division, infantrymen despite their title, had been shocked by their defeat at Yongdong. They were now forced into a headlong retreat to Kumch'on. The divisional commander, Major General Hobart Gay – who had been Patton's Chief of Staff in Normandy – admitted that he didn't know how to organise a retreat. The circumstances of the division's arrival – untrained, under-equipped, unprepared to fight a tough, professional and uncompromising enemy in the heat and hills of Korea – immediately affected the men's confidence and morale. With no tactical preparation and little advice or training, they soon made all the mistakes of their 24th Division brethren three weeks before. Stuck to the roads, it appeared that every American formation on arrival in Korea had to go through the same bloody learning experience.

———

It was at this stage of the campaign that it became clear that, notwithstanding the battering being taken by Major General Dean's 24th Division, and the ROK Army as a whole, the Soviet-designed operational plan for the invasion of South Korea was fatally flawed. It no doubt made considerable sense at the start – an all-points-of-the-compass drive across the whole of Korea's landmass to squeeze the enemy like a lemon through the port of Pusan, leaving only the pips – but in its execution this plan proved in fact to be a mistake. The aim,

---

*A position at Masan, where US troops had repelled the NKPA two days previously.

it is presumed, was for the NKPA to so occupy the retreating ROK Army across the entirety of Korea's geography that they would become exhausted and demoralised. But battle exhaustion cuts two ways. The flaw in the plan was that it resulted in the dissipation of the *In Mun Gun's* effort across the entirety of the country and the dramatic elongation of its lines of communication back to Seoul and Pyongyang, vulnerable to interdiction from the air. In attempting to fight and win every battle, the NKPA lacked the advantage provided by concentration of force, and was unable to push through in a single, vital place, despite the weakness of the enemy facing it. What it ended up doing was pushing the defenders of South Korea into a single, concentrated position – Pusan – from which point they could be reinforced and at some future point execute a breakout. The NKPA failed to take into account the possibility that the USA might reinforce the ROK or despatch American troops to the fight. Nor did they consider that 16 other countries might send their forces to fight in defence of the ROK (a further four contributed medical contingents). Instead, NKPA planners chose to undertake a war of conquest, with the ambition of capturing the entirety of the South Korean land mass. As a result, the plan dispersed the *In Mun Gun's* effort across the entirety of the peninsula, rather than concentrating every effort in a rapid, single thrust to capture what was arguably the single most important target after Seoul. Pusan was a deep-water port with the ability to receive large quantities of men and stores, only a day's sailing from the west coast of Japan and two weeks from the USA, a vital gateway for the arrival of men and supplies. With Pusan in NKPA hands, the ROK defensive effort could not have been reinforced, and the war would have been over, a prospect which seems to have been discounted in the Soviet operational plan every bit as much as it had been dismissed by Kim Il-sung.

With the 24th Division battling the Seoul–Pusan Road, this should have been the North Korean main effort. Instead, it chose to engage in battle with the ROK Army in a wide arc covering the breadth of the country, from the west to east coast and the mountains in between. At the very least, a single main axis of advance should have been identified and pursued. The remainder of the country could have been cleared once the strategic prize of Pusan had been achieved. The NKPA found itself attacking across the mountainous grain of the country. In addition to the *3rd* and *4th Divisions* driving hard against the 24th Division on the Seoul–Pusan Road, the *6th Division* drove down the western side of the country aiming to attack Pusan from the southeast, at Chinju; the *2nd Division* took a northeasterly route to the *3rd* and *4th*, joining up at Kumch'on; the *15th Division* aimed for Songju; further east, the *1st Division* also headed for Songju; the *12th* and *8th Divisions* headed for Yech'on and Andong. And on the extreme right in the east, the *5th Division* drove from Pyonghae-ri to Yongdok. In addition, guerrilla bands were landed at Ulchin.

In fighting off each of these avenues of attack, the ROK divisions fought largely independent actions as they were pushed back to a general perimeter protecting the Pusan region in the first week of August.

In the first part of July, the ROK Army was generally spread west to east in the order of 17th Regiment, 2nd, Capital, 6th and 8th Divisions, and the 23rd Regiment of the 3rd Division. The NKPA did not have it all its own way during this fighting and suffered considerable casualties (manpower, tanks and vehicles) at the hands of the ROK and US airpower. Several battlefield reverses were inflicted on the *In Mun Gun*, including an ambush by Colonel Paik's 1st ROK Division and the 17th Regiment, together with one by the USA's all-black 24th Regiment at the Kallyong Pass on 23 July. The South Koreans rejoiced in the super-abundance of American 105mm and 155mm guns during these actions. The initial NKPA advance was commanded by Lieutenant General Kim Kwang Hyop. He was relieved from his position on 10 July because he wasn't making the progress demanded. The American intervention in the war, unexpected by Pyongyang, had dramatically affected the original plan, which could no longer run to its first, optimistic timetable. He was replaced by Lieutenant General Kim Mu Chong. Certainly, the advent of US air attacks came as an unwelcome surprise, as did US naval gun bombardments against members of the NKPA *5th Division* on the east coast. At the same time as the *3rd* and *4th Divisions* were crossing the Kum River in the West, the *5th Division* entered Pyonghae-ri, 22 miles above Yongdok and 50 miles from P'ohang-dong. It was a matter for some alarm in Walker's HQ that the NKPA was now knocking on the door to Pusan. So far, despite some localised and tactical success, the ROK and the Eighth Army had not yet demonstrated that they could stop the enemy's roller-coaster offensive.

4

The Pusan Perimeter

For the next three weeks the *In Mun Gun* attempted to smash its way into the Pusan pocket. It wanted to secure Taegu, the temporary home of Syngman Rhee and the ROK government, by 15 August, the date of the fifth anniversary of liberation from the Japanese in 1945. Equally as determinedly, the ROK and US forces fought to keep the North Koreans out. There was, arguably, nowhere for the UN to go if they failed, except an evacuation by sea. Failure presaged another Dunkirk or Bataan. It was an outcome that preyed on the minds of MacArthur's staff.

By this time, too, while the NKPA's offensive power was urging itself into a climactic assault on the Pusan perimeter, the results of deliberations made much further afield in London and other world capitals about the contribution of the members of the UN and its Security Council to the defence of the ROK were coming to fruition. The willingness of the UK to send troops to Korea in support of its membership of the UN and as a token of its commitment to an ongoing friendship with its great wartime partner – the USA – was never in doubt. Britain and the USA had a considerable recent history of partnership in adversity, and the depth and intensity of this relationship could not be easily dismissed. As Downing Street considered its options, the Cabinet Secretary, Norman Brook, observed that Korea was a rather distant obligation; the prime minister is said to have replied: 'Distant yes, but nonetheless an obligation.' Attlee was aware of at least two separate obligations. The first was to the new collective security arrangements embodied in the United Nations, arrangements which he had himself

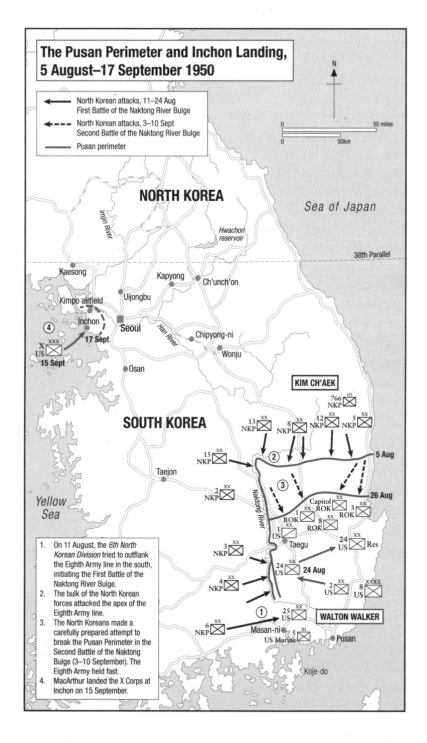

The Pusan Perimeter and Inchon Landing, 5 August–17 September 1950

N

◄──── North Korean attacks, 11–24 Aug
First Battle of the Naktong River Bulge

◄─ ─ ─ North Korean attacks, 3–10 Sept
Second Battle of the Naktong River Bulge

──── Pusan perimeter

0   50 miles

0   50km

NORTH KOREA

Sea of Japan

Imjin River

Hwachon
reservoir

38th Parallel

Kaesong

Kapyong   Ch'unch'on

Kimpo airfield   Uijongbu

Inchon   Seoul   Chipyong-ni

④   *Han River*

X   XXX
US   17 Sept   Wonju

15 Sept

Osan

KIM CH'AEK

766 III
NKP

SOUTH KOREA   13 XX   8 XX   12 XX   5 XX
                       NKP   NKP   NKP   NKP

15 XX
NKP   ②   5 Aug

Taejon

2 XX   ③   26 Aug
NKP

Yellow Sea   Capitol XX   3 XX
                                ROK   ROK
                    Naktong River   1 XX   8 XX
                              ROK   ROK
                              1 XX
                              US

3 XX   Taegu   24 XX   Res
NKP   US

24 XX   24 Aug
US

4 XX   2 XX   8 XXXX
NKP   US   US

1. On 11 August, the *6th North Korean Division* tried to outflank the Eighth Army line in the south, initiating the First Battle of the Naktong River Bulge.
2. The bulk of the North Korean forces attacked the apex of the Eighth Army line.
3. The North Koreans made a carefully prepared attempt to break the Pusan Perimeter in the Second Battle of the Naktong Bulge (3–10 September). The Eighth Army held fast.
4. MacArthur landed the X Corps at Inchon on 15 September.

①   25 XX   WALTON WALKER
         US

6 XX   Masan-ni   5 III
NKP   US Marine   Pusan

Koje-do

helped establish. This entailed responding actively around the world to attempts by predators to swallow up their smaller prey. The second was to the United States, Britain's greatest creditor. Britain was bankrupt and reliant on US loans for survival. The so-called 'special relationship' between the two countries of which Churchill spoke in his speech at Fulton, Missouri on 5 March 1946, in which he warned the world (which on the whole wasn't paying attention at the time) that an 'iron curtain' was descending on Europe, from Stettin to Trieste, referred as much to Britain's dependence on the USA for material sustenance as for its physical security against the threat of Soviet-orchestrated challenges to the free world. From the first loan from America in November 1945 under the $3.75bn Anglo-American Loan to the massive financial recovery plan initiated by the Secretary of State, George C. Marshall, and given his name when it came into being in 1947, in which the UK received more in US aid than any other country in Europe, Britain was irrevocably and utterly indebted to the USA.* It is possible to argue that financial indebtedness was accompanied by a degree of security indebtedness as well, as the USA began to commit substantial military forces to the protection of Europe through NATO. Britain's relationship with the USA was coloured by the reality that the two countries had recently successfully concluded a mighty crusade against totalitarianism (the presence within the Allied camp of a totalitarian state after June 1941 – the USSR – was a historic anomaly that existed alongside but was not part of the Anglo-American alliance), Britain expending half of its national wealth in the struggle to survive. While becoming indebted financially to the USA – hence this sense of obligation – the war also created a close bond between the people and armed forces of the two countries that would not easily be loosened. In the post-war world, this shared experience could not to be gainsaid. It is against this political, social, cultural, economic and strategic backdrop that Britain's response to the outbreak of hostilities in Korea needs to be seen.

In the period after 1935 Attlee had led the camp in the Labour Party arguing the case for peace between nations based on the threat of

*The Anglo-American Loan (finally repaid in 2006) and the Marshall Plan (a grant, and therefore not repaid) were over and above those received as part of the Lend Lease Act during the Second World War.

collective *military* action to deter and resist aggression. His view was that national armaments, such as those held by the UK, for instance, should be purposed not for selfish national ends but to support the collective enforcement of international law and the achievement thereby of global peace. The organisation existing at the time to achieve this purpose and to police international behaviour was the League of Nations. It had failed because there had been no willingness by its members to allow collective action to work. Now, in the post-war world, its successor needed all members to pull together and commit to collective military action when peace was threatened. The answer was not, as Attlee believed, the sort of Tory appeasement that had encouraged Hitler to further and greater acts of egregious violence against the peace of Europe during the 1930s. Peace needed to be protected against villains wheresoever they might appear. This included Korea.

These obligations did not mean that the two countries saw eye-to-eye on everything. Britain's relationship with the USA in the immediate post-war period was affected by significant disagreement over the issue of the League of Nations Mandate for Palestine, and the question of Jewish immigration to Palestine from the detritus of a shattered Europe. In another respect – nuclear energy – the relationship between Britain and the USA suffered from the American decision not to share nuclear secrets (and products) under the McMahon Act, despite receiving the benefit of British nuclear research at the inception of the Manhattan Project, which had created the world's first viable atomic weapons. As a result, Britain decided to go it alone and create its own independent nuclear programme. Another point of disagreement was the recognition of the Chinese Communist Party as the legitimate authority in China following the end of the civil war in October 1949. Britain was concerned about the security of Hong Kong with the new communist government in Peking. The USA remained fixedly supportive of Chiang Kai-shek and the rump of his Kuomintang, now in possession of Formosa. America was concerned that a communist-held Formosa would directly threaten American hegemony in the Pacific. But these issues were not allowed by Attlee to interfere with a clear-headed, unambiguous commitment to the United States in security matters. NATO, the agreement for which was signed in Washington on 4 April 1949, was the direct product of Attlee's determination to bring the USA into a close security embrace. When the need arose, the following year, to respond to US requests to bring an international coalition together to contribute military forces to repel the North Korean invasion of South Korea, there was no equivocation in Britain's response. Britain was determined that no matter its financial dependency on the USA, it was crucial that, in a time of a developing threat from international communism, they would remain close allies, whatever their various disagreements. Some things, Attlee considered, needed to rise above the prosaic: collective defence between Britain, the USA and their European allies was one of these. Another was Britain's commitment to the new instrument designed to bring about global peace and harmony: the UN.

Attlee had no doubt that responding to North Korean aggression by contributing forces to an international coalition corralled by the United Nations and led by the United States was the correct one for Britain. It reinforced Britain's (and Labour's) commitment to the role of the United Nations in creating a new world in which individual acts of aggression would be punished by a collective military response. The actions by North Korea, among other examples of communist aggression, demonstrated that communist powers were failing to abide by the rules they had themselves agreed to devise. But the Western democracies had responded to victory in 1945 by running down their armies in the expectation that these new rules would make the world a much safer place, such that major wars would become redundant. Significant rearmament was required, therefore, but with no spare money Britain was wholly dependent on 'assurances of American help, especially with regard to the availability of US dollars in an international currency environment in which exchange controls of sterling against the dollar severely constrained Britain's buying power.'[*]

The issue was the size of the force Britain was able to commit to the fight. The Second World War had accelerated the pace of decolonisation, and although by 1950 India had gone its own way (forming the separate countries of India and Pakistan), the British Army was managing an array of fragile security situations across its rapidly diminishing global empire. In particular, it had the equivalent of two infantry divisions (20,000 men) fighting communist insurgency in Malaya. A further brigade (the 27th Infantry Brigade, of two battalions – the 1st

[*]Attlee, *As it Happened*, 232.

Battalions of the Argyll and Sutherland Highlanders and the Middlesex Regiment) had been recently sent to Hong Kong to reinforce the colony on the victory of the Communist Party in China in October 1949. In the UK there was a so-called 'strategic reserve', the 29th Infantry and 16th Parachute Brigades, but it was hardly strategic and not much of a reserve, given the range of military tasks demanded of the country. The security situation in Europe wasn't in a good way, with Soviet sabre-rattling accelerating the creation of NATO. If the balloon went up in Europe (which was where the next fight was expected), the first call on this 'imperial reserve' would be at home. In other words, the cupboard was bare. The Chiefs of Staff in London were, understandably, reluctant to agree to yet another overseas commitment, especially if it involved warfighting. The 29th Infantry Brigade simply wasn't sufficiently manned or prepared for combat. A significant percentage of soldiers in the British Army at the time were conscripted under the National Service Act for a period of 18 months, but many of these were 18, and no conscript under the age of 19 could be sent to war. If the brigade were sent as it stood its combat effectiveness would be undermined by large numbers of troops ending their service during the period of deployment and others being drafted in to replace them. In order to send a fully prepared brigade from the UK, all its troops needed to be available for the entire period of the deployment, the brigade needed its full complement of combat support (artillery and engineers, for instance) and its combat service support, and they needed to be trained for combat. From a standing start of significant unpreparedness, this required time. It also required the calling up of men who still had unspent years of reserve service available. Men who had served during the Second World War and were still in the reserve now had call-up papers sent to them through the post, and a disgruntled bag of men who thought (and hoped) that their soldiering days were behind them began turning up at their regimental depots.

The challenge of what to do about Korea coincided with the need to make provision for military support to NATO. Britain's response was to accept the recommendation of the Chief of the Imperial General Staff (CIGS), Field Marshal Sir William Slim, that National Service be extended to two years' service. The country, which had experienced the cost of unpreparedness before, seemed content to accept these new realities and their financial implications for an economy struggling to rebuild itself after the war. The growth in defence expenditure this entailed amounted to an additional £4.7 billion over three years, with defence spending rising from 6 to 10 per cent of British GDP.

In the meantime, while the 29th Infantry Brigade* prepared to sail from the UK, and with the news from Korea becoming grimmer by the day, the War Office reluctantly agreed to despatch the weak two battalions of 27th Brigade from Hong Kong, 1,300 miles away. It was, after all, closest, and the brigade would at least be the first fruits of the promise of a larger commitment in due course. The 27th Infantry Brigade, however, had no stores for fighting a serious war. It had no artillery, heavy weapons, winter clothing or combat support troops, such as engineers or tanks, although it was accompanied to Korea by an anti-tank troop of the Royal Artillery equipped with 17-pounder anti-tank guns. The soldiers would have to arrive in Korea with their small arms only, the gaps in their ranks filled by volunteers from across the Hong Kong garrison, and rely on an already hard-pressed American logistic system for everything else, including their food and tentage. There was no doubt in anyone's minds that the commitment of the 27th Infantry Brigade was a political statement by Britain, not an act of war. The idea was that once the 29th Infantry Brigade had arrived from the UK, the 27th Brigade could return to its garrison responsibilities in Hong Kong. The two battalions of the 27th Brigade were a stopgap – a political message – nothing more.

The withdrawal into the Pusan pocket was, according to Brigadier General Paik Sun Yup, commanding the 1st ROK Division (he had been promoted in the field), 'the most painful period of the war'. Endless marching over long distances and long days, with the enemy snapping at their heels, drained men of physical energy and sapped morale. And yet,

*The 29th Brigade in fact resembled a US Army Regimental Combat Team, having within it embedded armour and artillery assets. The units were 1st Northumberland Fusiliers, 1st Gloucestershire Regiment and 1st Royal Ulster Rifles, supported by 45th Field Regiment Royal Artillery, the 8th King's Royal Irish Hussars (equipped with Centurion and Cromwell tanks), and the 41st Commando Royal Marines. It was commanded by the vastly experienced Brigadier Tom Brodie, who had led a Chindit column in Burma in 1944.

despite the privations of withdrawal, as many as 5,000 men lost in the earlier fighting made their way through the hills to rejoin Paik's division. It was, as he recalled, a minor miracle. During the withdrawal the division succeeded in shaking itself out, reorganising and even re-equipping while on the march through the central mountains. The 7,000 men of the division crossed the Naktong on 1 August and took up positions in the northwest of the pocket along a 25-mile front on the river running down to Waegwan. What became known as the Pusan box or pocket was 100 miles in width and 50 miles deep, at the base of which was the port of Pusan. Within the perimeter Walker had eight ROK and US divisions. South of the 1st ROK Division were three US divisions: the 1st Cavalry, the 24th (now at about 40 per cent strength, after collapsing across the Naktong on 4 August) and the 25th. To the east ran the four ROK divisions – the 3rd, 6th, 8th and Capital. Inside the Pusan pocket on 4 August Walker had 141,808 men, of whom 82,000 were South Korean and 47,000 American. Thousands of young Korean men were conscripted to join the US divisions as 'Korean Augmentation United States Army' (KATUSA) troops (as many as 5,000 Koreans for each US division), used in the main for porterage work, bringing up food, water and ammunition. In the first six weeks of war the USA had lost 6,000 men – dead, wounded and missing – the South Koreans a staggering 70,000. Such was the cost of unpreparedness. But the effect of this fighting was that the UN forces had been trading space for time. While their space on the Korean peninsula was fast running out, time wasn't on the side of the *In Mun Gun* as, although it still held the initiative, it was running out of men and supplies. Likewise, the withdrawing ROK divisions and the badly battered 24th Division had inflicted massive casualties on the NKPA. By now it had lost an estimated 60,000 men, most of them to the ROK divisions fighting their rearguard actions in the central mountains. Most of the North Korean divisions were now at half-strength, with perhaps a total of 70,000 men overall. Likewise, its tank strength had reduced to about 40 serviceable vehicles.

The four natural points of entry for an NKPA offensive went through the southwest towards the port of Masan; a further one followed the road and rail routes to Miryang; the third followed the hills to Taegu from the west, and the fourth led down the coastal valley to Konju. His troops spread thinly along the line, General Walker's plan was simple: while his eight divisions held what they could of the outer defensive line, Walker moved regiments to plug the gaps when they needed reinforcement in the battle.* It worked, just. The alternative would have been to hold Pusan in depth, allowing the enemy advance to wash around fixed defences, each resupplied by air, infiltrating enemy troops being targeted by mobile counterattack forces and air. The United States Army in 1950, however, was an army that was tactically and psychologically dependent on the idea of continuous battle lines.† The idea of defence in depth, in which the enemy were allowed the freedom to penetrate an area defence, thus making them vulnerable to counterattack, was experientially unknown. In Asia, during the war, the Japanese had repeatedly demonstrated the weakness of defensive lines that, once they had been penetrated, could be rolled up from the flanks or rear. The tactics deployed by the *In Mun Gun* at Pusan contained a strange mixture of the successful tactics of infiltration that were a hallmark of the Japanese, together with the ignorant battering of fixed, heavily defended positions that were characteristic of poorly trained and ineptly led troops.

Despite its losses, the NKPA, three times superior in number and ten times in weaponry, began crossing operations immediately, with the aim of seizing Taegu by 15 August. Paik observed that his men were confident of holding off the NKPA when they had the advantage of US air cover, but it was a different matter at night when it was simply impossible to cover all 25 miles of their front. The *In Mun Gun* attempted first simply to force its way across the river in human waves, causing itself huge casualties. The North Koreans were content, however, to expend the lives of their men, many of whom were Southerners conscripted in the previous weeks (so-called 'Volunteer Army' troops) and thrust into the fighting with next to no training. Working at night to avoid the attentions of the US Air Force, by 4 August they had crossed the river by building underwater bridges – jerry-rigged constructions that lay just under the surface, so they couldn't be detected by aircraft during the day, an old Soviet trick – and on 8 August the first T-34s were trundling across. The defence of the Naktong line was made more difficult by the large numbers of civilian refugees trying to flee to safety, unaware of

*Walker's remit was extended to all ROK troops on 17 July.
†T. R. Fehrenbach, *This Kind of War* (Macmillan, 1963), 108.

122

the sweep of the battle and attempting to cross the river in the midst of the fighting. The problem of identifying friend from foe was already apparent to journalists reporting the fighting. The *Time* correspondent John Osborne was horrified by what he saw of the battlefield, describing it as 'ugly', 'sorrowful', 'sickening' and 'terrible.' He reported on the savagery of combat but also on the 'savagery in detail – the blotting out of villages where the enemy *may* be hiding; the shooting and shelling of refugees who *may* include North Koreans in the anonymous white clothing of the Korean countryside, or who *may* be screening an enemy march upon our positions.'*

As the *In Mun Gun* pressed up against the Naktong, the Eighth Army defenders now sought out the ground in these precipitous hills that would give them the best positions with which to meet and repel an enemy offensive. Supporting them, the US and ROK enjoyed a massive preponderance of firepower: 105mm and 155mm guns (although ammunition wasn't limitless), together with complete supremacy in the air. Control of the air helped saved it from disaster. Airpower in the pocket focused on supporting troops in the land battle. With a general paucity of artillery and artillery ammunition inside the pocket, the supply of close air support aircraft provided an effective substitute. Without the rocketing, strafing and napalming of as many as 40 sorties each day by fighter ground attack aircraft, it seems unlikely that the Pusan pocket would have survived. By sea came reinforcements of men, more ammunition and weapons and, off the east coast, naval gunfire support. By 19 August, for instance, there were 500 US light (Chaffee) and medium (Patton) tanks in the perimeter, compared to perhaps 100 NKPA. Those in Pusan were trapped only insofar as they imagined themselves to be so. In all other respects they held the advantage of 'interior lines', of being reinforced and fed from the sea, supported from the air by planes flying from Japan and Okinawa, and able – by constantly rearranging the defences – to absorb and defeat every heavy assault launched against them. At the same time the NKPA was fighting at the end of its very extended lines of communication, and casualties were mounting. It had successfully pushed back the ROK Army since

*John Osborne, 'Men at War: The Ugly War', *Time* magazine, 21 August 1950. https://time .com/archive/6615304/men-at-war-the-ugly-war/

the invasion began on 25 June and had defeated the US 24th Infantry Division in four bloody battles since early July. But in pushing the combined ROK and UN forces south, the UN were able, at last, to concentrate their forces and build up strength in Pusan.

The line prepared by the Eighth Army around the general perimeter of Pusan, denoted on the western side by the line of the Naktong River, was the 'X-Line'; that further behind, the final containment line 16 miles in front of Taegu, beyond which there was to be no retreat, was the 'Y-Line'. The division moved back to the Y-Line on 12 August. Morale began to improve as small numbers of the new American 3.5-inch bazooka were deployed among the ROK divisions, and T-34s began to brew up in satisfactory conflagrations: Brigadier General Paik's 1st ROK Division destroyed about ten, to the delight of all for whom the problem of 'T-34-itis' had proven a troubling disease during the retreat.

On the southeastern perimeter of the pocket the 7,000 men of the NKPA *4th Division*, now awarded the title 'Seoul' Division following its rapid capture of the South Korean capital weeks before, struck across the Naktong into the heart of territory held by the recovering 24th Infantry Division, commanded by Brigadier General John Church. Unable to outflank and then block their enemy – their tactic of choice during the advance – they reverted to the tactics of blunt assault. By 7 August they had captured Cloverleaf Hill and the Obong-ni Ridge, which dominated the roads to Yongsan, five miles further east. Further east still was the town of Miryang, on the road that ran north from Pusan to Taegu. It was along these ridges that the battle raged over ten days. The newly arrived and untrained US 9th Infantry, 2nd Division was rushed in to hold the line. The fierceness of the fighting – repeated bayonet charges which reminded many of the *banzai* assaults of the Imperial Japanese Army in the previous war, heavy use of mortars, SU-76 self-propelled guns and tanks – came as a profound shock to the green troops of the 2nd Division. But in many remarkable actions over those ten days it was the fortitude and combat leadership of a small number of war-experienced NCOs and officers who rallied their troops and held the ridges against repeated and often overwhelming assault. Although the *4th Division* couldn't break through a stubbornly held Cloverleaf and Obong-ni, Walker had no reserves until on 15 August the Provisional Marine Brigade arrived. Raised in double-quick time in the USA with large numbers of Pacific War reservists recalled to the flag, the moment they arrived they were thrown into battle. MacArthur had wanted the Marines for an amphibious counterstroke he was planning (more of which later), but they were desperately needed in the immediate battle. Walker immediately sent the 5,000 Marines to Church's assistance. On 17 August the Marines assaulted part of Obong-ni, known to Americans as 'No Name Ridge', following heavy artillery bombardment and attack by 18 Marine Corsairs flying from Navy Light Carriers. Determined, bloody assaults failed to capture the hills, which were swept by fire from surrounding enemy-held heights. Of the 240 Marines who were committed to the first attack, only 98 survived alive and unwounded. Courage alone could not remove the North Koreans from positions they were determined to hold. But the Marine attack had weakened the defenders, causing them 600 casualties. By this stage of the battle, the remarkably hardy *In Mun Gun* was showing signs of exhaustion and had begun to starve. With no resupplies arriving from the North along lines of communication heavily interdicted by US airpower, soldiers were forced onto starvation rations. The persistence and fortitude of these troops, starving and with limited supplies of ammunition and military stores, was remarkable. But the mathematics of attrition was relentless, especially with US artillery and airpower – and naval gunfire on the east coast from a fleet of UN cruisers and destroyers – repeatedly smashing NKPA assaults. A night attack by the NKPA defenders smashed into the Marine positions, repulsed only by the timely intervention of Corsairs reprising their role in the Pacific half a decade before. A bloody but determined struggle by the Marines resulted in the sight, on 18 August, of the survivors of the renowned *4th Division* streaming back across the Naktong. It had been an extraordinary battle, one in which desperation for victory led to the decimation of the NKPA division: some 1,200 corpses were buried by the Americans in this first, major defeat of the *In Mun Gun* on the Naktong line.

Elsewhere around the perimeter, the separate NKPA divisions continued the bloody struggle to break into the perimeter. At the same time, reinforcements continued to pour into the pocket. By the end of the month the UN had 180,000 men in Pusan, enjoyed complete air and naval superiority over and into the battlespace, and had a massive preponderance of artillery.

Despite the challenges of the retreat, the ROK fought strongly in the defence of Pusan and for what remained of their homeland. This is remarkable given the fact that in the first six weeks of the war, in which US losses amounted to 6,000 men, the ROK Army had lost 70,000. And yet those that remained fought on, with the desperation of those who knew that it was fight or die. New challenges arose – for example, recruits flooding into the depleted divisions had barely fired their rifles before – but it was sound defensive tactics and the massive superiority of UN firepower, combined with the bravery and courage of the individual fighting man, that was ultimately to blunt and then reverse the *In Mun Gun*'s offensive. In Paik's division, each regiment (11th, 12th and 13th) created a counterattack reserve, kept to attack any successful enemy penetrations of its long defensive line, snaking north from Waegwan along and across this steeply ridged terrain to Poksang-dong. US airpower was efficient and powerful, 40 or so ground attack missions being called in every day from Itazuke and Ashiya air bases in Japan, only 30 minutes' flying time from the Y-Line. USAF air-ground liaison teams were allocated to each division, identifying targets and calling in and coordinating each of the air attacks.

The NKPA, whose scattered advance had meant it was unable to concentrate at a single point, had nevertheless managed to amass its forces around the Pusan pocket, ready for a powerful punch at Taegu. If the Songju–Taegu line broke, there was nothing to stop the NKPA capturing Pusan. It would be the end of the pocket and perhaps of a free Korea. It would also constitute a considerable embarrassment not merely to the UN but to the great victor of 1945, the USA. The stakes were high, and both sides knew it. Brigadier General Paik admitted that if he'd known that his battered division had been faced by the *3rd, 13th* and *15th Divisions*, which 'had sufficient strength to gobble up Taegu and do it quickly... I would've been obliged to hide my fear, adding another burden to my load.' Driving hard at all points of the perimeter, the fighting was hard; the *In Mun Gun* infiltrated at night and attempted to overwhelm the defences by sheer weight of numbers. By 15 August, the day the NKPA was supposed to be safely in Taegu, Northern and Southern units grappled together in a fighting embrace so close that Paik described his 20-mile front as degenerating 'into a bloody, life-or-death struggle based chiefly on the exchange of hand grenades'. Many men, he recorded, developed painful, swollen shoulders from hurling hundreds of grenades. The desperation of the fight, which turned out to be the *In Mun Gun*'s primary offensive in the northeast – the battle of Tabu-dong – led to the reinforcement of the embattled 1st ROK Division by Colonel Michaelis' 27th Regimental Combat Team (the 'Wolfhounds'), 25th Infantry Division and the 10th Regiment, 8th ROK Division. This reinforcement was precipitated by the first use of strategic airpower on the Korean battlefield on 16 August, as five formations of B-29 Superfortresses from the 19th Bombardment Group, flying from Okinawa, laid waste several square miles of landscape at Waegwan. A total of 98 aircraft dropped more than 3,234 bombs, totalling more than 900 tons of explosive. North Korean manpower was matched by extraordinary and overwhelming American firepower. While this otherwise spectacular bombardment didn't cause large numbers of casualties, evidence from POWs suggested that the sight of this vast armada sailing with impunity through the skies, unleashing an extraordinary firepower display, dealt a devastating blow to the morale of the men of the NKPA's *3rd Division* who saw for the first time the enormity of military industrial muscle that was arrayed against them.

When Michaelis' 27th Regimental Combat Team (RCT)* arrived outside Tabu-dong on 18 August, he brought with him three infantry battalions, together with a cornucopia of hardware that made Paik, heretofore without any artillery, gasp with astonishment. Michaelis told him he had brought with him 'a 105mm artillery battalion with 18 howitzers, a tank company, a company of 155mm guns – six of the monsters – and all the ammunitions we can shoot.' They were instantly engaged, the NKPA divisions facing them relaunching the attack that had been momentarily stalled by the B-29 bombardment. In the Sangu–Taegu corridor, Michaelis' 27th RCT and Paik's division successfully halted attacks by the *3rd Division* down what became 'Bowling Alley', Paik's men holding the hills and channelling the *In Mun Gun* into the teeth of Michaelis' guns and tanks. The fighting was fierce and encompassed every unit along the line. Even Paik's divisional HQ was attacked by commando raiders on 19 August. Responding to this all-out attempt by

---

*An infantry regiment with embedded combat service components such as armour, artillery and combat engineers under command.

three NKPA divisions to drive to Taegu, Paik's division was reinforced again on 20 August at Tabu-dong by the US 23rd Infantry and the 10th ROK Regiment. Each night Michaelis' tanks repelled massed infantry and armoured attacks. Although the NKPA was forced to divert the *15th Division* to Yongch'on, the ferocity of the enemy assaults in front of Taegu did not let up. During one penetration of the line between Paik's 11th Regiment and the Wolfhounds, Paik personally led a counterattack to seize a ridge to the east of Tabu-dong the enemy had briefly seized. The climax for the struggle for Taegu was reached on 21 August, when an all-out assault was launched at Michaelis' regiment, which repulsed it in a five-hour fight, successfully halting the North Koreans' main armoured thrust towards Taegu. During this battle, the NKPA lost 5,690 men dead; the 1st ROK Division 2,300. But the line held; Taegu did not fall. In accordance with Walker's fire-brigade strategy, the Wolfhounds were then redeployed south to Masan, where they were needed next. The 1st ROK handed over the line to the 1st Cavalry Division and moved north to guard a seven-mile stretch of the line through precipitous gorges on the far northeastern corner of the perimeter.

With time against it, the *In Mun Gun* prepared one final offensive to break into Pusan on the night of 31 August. Gathering all of its strength – some 98,000 men in 13 infantry and one armoured division (100 new T-34s had arrived during the battle) – the attack was designed to be a double envelopment of Taegu from north and southwest, striking across the front in the hope that at least one weak point would break. The attack would target five areas:

1 In the southwest, the *6th* and *7th Divisions* would attack the US 25th Division;

2 In the west, opposite Yongsan and Miryang, what remained of the *2nd, 4th, 9th and 10th Divisions* would attack the US 2nd Division;

3 In the Sangu–Taegu corridor, the remnants of the *1st, 3rd* and *13th Divisions* would attack the 1st US Cavalry and the 1st ROK Division;

4 The *5th* and *8th Divisions* would strike against the 6th and 8th ROK Divisions defending Taegu from the North;

5 Finally, on the east coast the *5th* and *12th Divisions* would drive against the 3rd and Capital ROK Divisions.

The *In Mun Gun* attack began with the fury of a last ditcher. Large waves of North Koreans attacked known positions with their signature frontal assault, and the battle cry *Manzai! Manzai! Manzai!* In the darkness across all sectors of the front, large groups of North Koreans charged headlong against US and ROK positions, while others infiltrated through and between to penetrate far to the rear. This wasn't hard, given the wide distances that separated defended localities. On the US 2nd Division front the hard-won Obong-ni and Cloverleaf ridges were overcome and Yongsan fell into enemy hands. The NKPA succeeded in splitting the 2nd Division in two, creating a hole more than eight miles wide and six deep in the line. General Walker, ordering the 5th Marines, the 27th Wolfhounds and the remnants of the 19th Division, his only remaining reserve, to prepare to plug the gap, ordered the 2nd Division to stand or die. They did so. Counterattacks saw tank-on-tank battles at Yongsan, and heavy air and naval gunnery attacks fell across the battlefield. By nightfall the enemy had retired. Counterattacks on 4 September saw the North Koreans being forced back in this sector by three miles, passing scenes of utter destruction on their way, the results of American air and naval gunfire. The bloody see-saw battle continued for several more days, but the exhaustion of the NKPA troops was now evident on the battlefield. The NKPA offensive had managed to break into the UN perimeter, but despite the extraordinary commitment of its tough and aggressive soldiers, it simply didn't have the power to exploit any of the breakthroughs it managed to make. On the Songju–Tagu front, all the ground that had been defended earlier at such cost was lost, the 1st Cavalry Division retreating over six miles to Taegu. There were panicked conversations about creating a new line even closer to Pusan, but the battle by this time had reached its culminating point. Paik observed that although the enemy attacks remained relentless, they ran out of steam earlier than before. Reinforcements and ammunition weren't getting to the front. T-34s were running out of fuel and being abandoned. NKPA fervour remained seemingly high, but its energy was noticeably diminishing. They could see Taegu, but frustratingly their prize remained out of reach. Across the shattered battlefield North Korean dead lay thick on the ground. One account described the flies buzzing over the dead in the summer heat to be so thick they blotted out the sun. In the period up to the middle of September the struggle continued across the battlefield; American 105mm ammunition ran critically short; defensive positions were reduced by the fighting to handfuls of exhausted men. On 12 September, on the closest enemy positions to Taegu on Hill 134, the 1st Cavalry redeemed itself of its earlier withdrawal from Songju. As the battle died away, here and in other places, across the battlefield the UN troops found evidence of the serious mistreatment of POWs. In many places were found the bodies of men who had been bound before being shot or mutilated. By 12 September the *In Mun Gun,* reduced by perhaps 40,000 men, its tanks destroyed and its artillery without ammunition, was forced to withdraw to the hills west of the Naktong. It could no longer attack. Would it have the capacity to retreat? General Walker had fought a brilliant defensive battle in the most difficult of circumstances, encouraging and cajoling his battered divisions, moving men and equipment from one hot spot to another and insisting on rapid counterattack to retain the local tactical advantage. It was by these means, supported by air* and, in some places, naval gun fire, that ensured the ultimate survival of a very hard-pressed pocket.

It was into this inferno that the two battalions of the British 27th Infantry Brigade (1st Middlesex and 1st Argylls) landed in Pusan port from Hong Kong on 29 August 1950. Under the command of Brigadier Basil Aubrey Coad, the brigade had left the colony four days before; five days before that, the Argylls and Middlesex had been issued orders to proceed to war, an eventually not considered likely only a week before that. The time at sea was spent in rifle training, firing practice and physical training. The brigade, like its American compatriots, had spent no time in combat training. It would have to learn on the job, depending on the professionalism of its officers and NCOs and the sturdiness of its men, many of them National Service conscripts. Nevertheless, the nature of the engagement to which they were being sent was not fully appreciated by the troops. Captain John Shipster of the Middlesex, for instance, arrived in Pusan as part of the brigade advance party. 'I surprised some of the Americans by alighting from the

*Over 4,000 sorties were flown by the Fifth Air Force between 1 June and 15 September 1950.

aircraft with golf clubs and tennis racquet,' he recalled. Information in Hong Kong had been so sparse that he had convinced himself that the brigade would be going to a comfortable base somewhere in Japan. He was forced to abandon his sports gear on the side of the airfield.*

On arrival the brigade was moved to reserve positions behind Yongsang. Attached to the 1st Cavalry Division, on 3 September the battalions went into the line, taking over from the 8th Cavalry Brigade to the southwest of Taegu. The frontages were huge: the two British battalions, for example, covered a front of about 14 miles. But the weather was dry and the men, eminently adaptable and pragmatic in the tradition of British infantry regiments, settled down to make the best of their new circumstances. One of these was learning to live with one's neighbours. In the area of responsibility for D Company, 1st Middlesex, were two parties of South Korean police of about 140 men each. They were shockingly ill-equipped for the task required of them. On the first night, the commander of the larger unit presented the British company commander – Major John Willoughby, a tall, tough and imposing veteran – with an ultimatum: he and his men wouldn't stay in the line unless they were equipped with machine guns and received other tactical help from the newly arrived British. They felt abandoned by their own side, knew nothing of the tactics for defence and wanted to come under the comforting umbrella of the British unit. The police were spread along about two and a half miles of riverbank at intervals of about ten yards. Most of them were armed with old Japanese rifles with two or three rounds each. Unsurprised that they were concerned about their predicament, Willoughby promptly gave them a Bren gun and a box of ammunition, all he could afford at the time, given that the British brigade had arrived in Korea with light weapons only and he had little else to spare.

The next day, on hearing the story, the commanding officer (Lieutenant Colonel Andrew Man) seconded to the Koreans the Middlesex's sanitary corporal, Corporal Fields, and two others from the pioneer platoon, with instructions to help the Koreans in any way they could. The boost these two actions (the Bren gun and the secondment of three

---

*Subsequently, he was able to claim for their loss on his insurance. Shipster, *Mist Over the Rice Fields*, 119.

professional soldiers) gave to the Koreans was immeasurable and the results immediate. The Koreans now felt valued. Fields, who had been captured in Hong Kong by the Japanese in 1941, spoke a little of the language, having had Korean guards during the nearly four years of his captivity. He was a natural leader and soon took charge of the Korean dispositions and all other military and administrative functions of his new charges. One presumed this included sanitary arrangements. In short, he became their commander. Both the Korean police officers (a captain and a sergeant) were only too glad to take orders from Corporal Fields; they became his willing and trusty lieutenants in the fighting that followed. Willoughby, in a moment of levity, named Fields' two units Army Groups 'A' and 'B'. The titles stuck. Corporal Fields had, under command, 280 loyal Koreans, all suddenly energized by their new leadership and eager for the first time to confront the enemy, believing that with their new company commander and single Bren gun they had the means to do so. Corporal Fields now boasted many more troops than the other company commanders in the battalion and Lieutenant Colonel Man treated him as one of his company commanders.

5

The Masterstroke at Inchon

The operation that finally destroyed the *In Mun Gun* invasion of South Korea between June and September 1950 was the risk-laden amphibious counterstroke launched far to the rear of the North Korean armies at Inchon in late September 1950. Inchon was a brilliant piece of operational manoeuvre which, combined with the offensive out of the Pusan pocket by the Eighth Army, broke the NKPA in 1950 and brought Kim Il-sung's military adventure to a shuddering halt. It was a triumph for the Second World War generals who designed it and made it happen. It should, in fact, have ended the war, but by means of American (and UN) miscalculation and hubris, the battlefield victory brought about at the hands of this masterstroke was undone in the second war for Korea that followed.

From the earliest days of the *In Mun Gun* offensive, MacArthur had an eye for an amphibious counterstroke behind the advancing armies. It made no sense to him to attempt to reverse the penetration of the North Koreans into the South on the basis of a land-based counterattack. That would entail the hard slog of force-on-force confrontation which would promise only large numbers of casualties and a long, bruising fight. Better, he thought, to do what he had done in the South West Pacific during the war and seek a result at the operational, or campaign, level of war. 'Where,' he asked himself, 'was the enemy weakest? Where, if I struck him, would he be most likely to crumble?' He didn't want a long, hard struggle against heavy odds, but to exploit the opportunity provided both by geography and by his massive superiority in sea and airpower to achieve a decisive stroke against the enemy's weakest point: the *In Mun Gun*'s stretched line of communications. Standing at Suwon on 5 July, a quick perusal of a map gave him his answer. If he struck at Inchon on the west coast of the country close to Seoul, at a time when the bulk of the NKPA was far below this point charging headlong for Pusan, he would be able to cut the enemy in two, capture his lines of communication and isolate the enemy to the south. He had no idea at this stage that US and ROK forces would be pushed as far south as the Naktong River, placing Pusan in peril, although this eventuality made his counterstroke move even more imperative. Because there were no adequate roads to the coast, except for the coastal road on the other side of the mountains, the North Korean Army would be cut off. MacArthur had, of course, perfected the art of amphibious operations during the Pacific War, although the operation he planned for Korea had much in common with the concept for Anzio in Italy in 1944. This had been designed to cut off the Axis forces defending southern Italy from the Allies advancing north from their landings at Salerno the previous year. It is easy in hindsight to recognise the sheer brilliance and audacity of the plan and its execution; this, however, hides something of the chutzpah of MacArthur's proposal and strong opposition to the boldness of his plan at the time from the navy, Marines and even the Joint Chiefs of Staff. What we now recognise as brilliant wasn't seen the same way by everyone at the time. Indeed, some have subsequently scoffed at the Inchon landings, with the suggestion that it was made possible solely by US naval supremacy in the Yellow Sea. This is undeniably true, but the criticism is unfair, as it entirely ignores the extent of the immense physical challenges posed in mounting a successful landing at Inchon; the considerable military risks undertaken in the venture that came to be called Operation *Chromite* and the almost complete initial opposition to MacArthur's plans by the USN, the Marines and the Joint Chiefs of Staff. MacArthur had made his reputation in the Second World War not merely on the recovery of the Philippines ('I will return') but on a strategy in the South West Pacific in which some Japanese island positions were outflanked and ignored, allowing them to wither on the vine of isolation, exhaustion, starvation and slow obliteration, in favour of precise attacks on a carefully selected number of islands which offered stepping stones to the home islands of Japan.

The following day – 6 July – MacArthur told the Joint Chiefs of Staff in Washington that the first step was to halt the North's onslaught. To do this, he would need an Army of 30,000 to partner with the ROK to defend South Korea from the North's attack: at least two corps of four and a half infantry divisions, an airborne regimental combat team, and an armoured regiment of three medium tank battalions, together with integrated artillery and service support components. Once that was in place, and the NKPA onslaught halted, another army would be needed to provide a counterstroke. While he didn't specify his plan – it hadn't fully formed in his mind by that stage – the essence was clear. Once the NKPA had been fixed, he told Washington, 'it will be my purpose fully to exploit our air and sea control, and, by amphibious manoeuvre, strike him behind his mass of ground force.' The only place he was considering for amphibious action was Inchon. This strike from the sea would be coordinated with a land offensive from the army he had accumulated in the south, forming a decisive pincer movement against the NKPA. He was confident that this would smash his enemy.

One of the biggest problems MacArthur faced was finding enough trained men to do the job. America's cupboard was bare, made worse by the challenges of the coming weeks, as the *In Mun Gun* pressed hard against Pusan. MacArthur needed at least two divisions for the counterstroke: one to land at Inchon and capture Seoul, the other to drive eastwards to fight the battle for central Korea, seizing the enemy's rail and road lines of communication leading south. On 10 July he managed to persuade the Commander of the Pacific Fleet Marine Forces to give him the 1st Marine Division (Major General Oliver Smith, a hardened veteran of the Pacific War) for the first task, provided the Joint Chiefs of Staff agreed. If the order was given soon, it could be ready for operations in eight weeks' time – that is, in mid-September. This would entail recalling Marine reservists, men who hadn't fought since the great Pacific campaigns of 1944 and 1945 and, for some of them, earlier. The first Marine regiment to arrive in theatre – the 5th Regimental Combat Team – instead of being used to prepare for Inchon, was thrown into the fight at Pusan, so tough was the fight and so needful was Walker of experienced fighters in his struggle to hold back the NKPA tide on the Naktong. Meanwhile, the 1st and 7th RCTs were built up in Japan from reservists being recalled to the flag. Half of the Marine complement in X Corps were reservists. These were men who, on the whole, had considerable Pacific experience. The only other formation available to be the second major participant was the 7th Infantry Division in Japan, though its ranks were sorely depleted through the process of gifting its soldiers to other divisions going to Korea. In fact, it was only at half-strength, and most of its experienced officers and NCOs had already been seconded to the Eighth Army in Korea. The problem was that the more pressure the NKPA applied to Pusan, the more the troops allocated to the Inchon landings, such as the 2nd Infantry Division and the Provisional Marine Brigade (the 5th Marine RCT), were sucked into the fighting. Washington gave provisional approval to proceed, and planning for Operation *Chromite* got under way. Nearly 6,000 reinforcements from the USA flooded in, and Korean battle casualty replacements were hurriedly – though sketchily – trained.

From the outset MacArthur saw Operation *Chromite* to be an army-led operation, appointing his Chief of Staff, Major General Almond, as the new commander of X Corps.* The Marine division was to play the role of door-opener, rather than be responsible for the whole campaign. The planning team was taken from his own Joint Strategic Plans and Operations Group in Tokyo, in the former Dai Ichi insurance building, and included Admiral Arthur Struble, commander of the Seventh Fleet, who was to provide the covering forces, the close escorts, the bombardment forces, the air support and the amphibious lift. The latter, the 1st Amphibious Group, was commanded by veteran amphibian Rear Admiral James H. Doyle with his flag in USS *Mount McKinley*.

The plan for Operation *Chromite* hung on thin margins. In addition to the problem of finding enough trained soldiers in time, the navy no longer had the vast amphibious resources it had enjoyed just five years before. With the advent of the atomic bomb, amphibious operations of the kind that had dominated the Pacific War were regarded by most as irrelevant. The entire invasion fleet comprised 261 vessels of all types. A total of 47 Landing Ship Tanks were required for Operation *Chromite*, but the navy only had 17 LSTs remaining. Many had been transferred to the Japanese inter-island ferry service and were commanded

*i.e., 10th Corps. Many histories, unaware of military nomenclature, get this wrong. See the Order of Battle.

by ex-Imperial Japanese Navy officers. At least one at Inchon was commanded by an ex-battleship captain.

But the real problem with Inchon lay in its physical geography. Very little about Inchon favoured a seaborne assault, although MacArthur knew that the Japanese had made a successful landing here in 1905. There were much better places elsewhere, such as Kunsan, at Pusung-Myon near Osan to the south of Inchon and at Chinnamp'o, the port of the Northern capital Pyongyang. But despite all their physical advantages, none had the strategic advantage offered by Inchon, which was the only place where the NKPA lines of communication could be cut a short distance from the bridgehead. But strategic opportunity did not overcome the physical challenge. To approach Inchon, an invader had to confront a tidal rise and fall of about 32 feet up the Flying Fish and Salee River channels, a scattering of islands and rocks channelling the tidal flow, and both channels were easily mined. At low tide the beaching areas were unnavigable, acres of mud flats presenting themselves, far too soft to land men and vehicles. The precision required in getting landing craft and men onto shore at the right point in the flood tide was enormous. There were no natural landing places either. The landing points entailed a 16-foot-high seawall. Landings would have to occur at the highest point when the height of the sea allowed men to disembark; this was a window of two hours at the end of the day, just before dusk. Landing craft would have to arrive at exactly the right time and exit quickly to avoid stranding as the tide retreated rapidly at the end of the two-hour window. The best plan was to approach in darkness and assault at dawn, but this would require a set of tide combinations that occurred on only one day each month. The next were 15 September and 11 October. If the enemy knew these facts they could accurately determine the exact two-hour window in which a landing would take place. To make matters worse, an outcrop on Wolmi-Do Island – connected to the mainland by a causeway – dominated the harbour. Any successful landing would need to neutralise the defences on Wolmi-Do first, which therefore required a phased approach to the operation that would remove the element of surprise for the amphibious landings. All in all, it was a crazy venture. Strategically, it made perfect sense; physically, it was replete with impossibilities.

Six weeks later, on 23 August, when the Eighth Army was crammed into Pusan and fighting for its life, these impossibilities dominated the final planning session at MacArthur's headquarters. This meeting was to determine acceptance or not of the planning team's proposals. MacArthur sat at one end of the room, quietly puffing on his corn pipe, while the details were expounded. The room was crowded with representatives from the Joint Chiefs of Staff. One after the other criticisms and concerns were levelled at the plan. It was unworkable, too risky, a dangerous gamble. The USN believed it certainly impracticable – with its 32-foot-high tide and narrow approaches that could be easily mined – if not impossible. Although not in the room, General Omar Bradley, the Chairman of the Joint Chiefs of Staff, opposed it, believing that the era of large-scale combined amphibious operations was over. MacArthur allowed everyone to have a say, before calmly but passionately extolling the virtues of this strategic counterstroke, the only thing guaranteed to break the back of the enemy, but only if the USA was bold enough to embrace the risks and undertake the impossible: 'The very arguments you have made as to the impracticabilities involved will tend to ensure for me the element of surprise. For the enemy commander will reason that no one would be so brash as to make such an attempt.'*

After giving his captive audience a brief resumé of the impact of surprise in war – citing Wolfe's surprise landing at the inadequately guarded Anse du Foulon to take the Heights of Abraham and Quebec in 1759, another risky and seemingly impossible enterprise – he concluded by observing: 'I realize that Inchon is a 35,000 to 1 gamble but I am used to taking such odds.' Leaving no one in any doubt that the operation would proceed as planned, with the Joint Chiefs of Staff's approval, he said, 'We shall land at Inchon and I shall crush them!' Even though they opposed the plan, the USN and Marines knuckled down and undertook the task set for them. 'The Navy has never turned me down yet, and I know it will not now,' MacArthur commented. He was right. Like it or not, it was the navy and the newly formed X Corps that was responsible for execution of the agreed plan.

The genius of the Inchon landing lay in the risk that MacArthur was prepared to take. He knew he had the right men to do it, but everything else – the enormous tidal range being one of them – was extremely risky.

*David Rees, *Korea: The Limited War* (Macmillan, 1964), 82.

MacArthur knew that if he could pull this off, it would win him the war. Confident that a successful strike would be decisive militarily, it was a risk he was prepared to take. He knew he had to be bold. If the military side of the counterstroke failed, it would merely constitute a failed military operation. But, looking at it from the perspective of strategic opportunity, he knew that if successful, it was an operation that could win the war. With this supreme conviction burning in him, he persuaded even the most resistant members of his staff and the Joint Chiefs of Staff in Washington to accept his view. MacArthur's view – that the strategic opportunity was one too good to ignore – was correct, but the sort of risk only great commanders are able to make. At the operational level of war MacArthur was a master, and he knew it. Rather than seeing the immediate battle to be the source from which victory in the campaign would come, MacArthur knew that his strength lay in his ability to strike from the sea against the relatively unguarded enemy flank. Such an operation would be decisive in a way that a grinding infantry campaign on the Pusan battlefield could never be. MacArthur's genius lay not merely in his vision and in his imagining of what a strike at Inchon could achieve strategically, but in his ability to articulate clearly his argument above, sideways and below. There is no doubt that Inchon was the decisive masterstroke of the first Korean War, one that elevated US strengths while minimising its weaknesses, and it was entirely MacArthur's idea. MacArthur's subsequent failure lay not in the operational space, but in the military-political space, where he failed to comprehend the political and military ramifications of equating victory in Korea with the total annihilation of his enemy.

The plan comprised four elements, in which Inchon was to be captured in a pincer movement, from north and south:

1 Forty-five minutes after dawn on D-Day the 3rd Battalion Landing Team from 5th Marine RCT would capture the island of Wolmi-Do (known as Green Beach) at high tide;
2 The second phase would begin at the end of D-Day, with the return of the flood tide, when the remainder of the 5th Marine RCT would land on the seawall at Red Beach to the north of Inchon and the 1st Marine RCT on Blue Beach to the south;
3 The 1st Marine Division would then capture Kimpo airfield before advancing on Seoul;

4 The 7th Infantry Division would then follow to protect the right (southern) flank of the advance and link up with the Eighth Army advancing from the south at Osan.

The loss of surprise on D-Day could not be avoided. In any case, it was surmised that the enemy would be aware of what the UN was attempting to do, so strategic surprise wasn't achievable anyway. The plan was gossiped about so much in Tokyo that the press called it 'Operation Common Knowledge'. Offensive air and naval activity developed in line with the attempt to defeat the *In Mun Gun* finally on the Naktong. Inchon was attacked alongside other targets when offensive air operations were stepped up across Korea after 5 September. This coincided with commando landing actions (British, American and Korean) on both the east and west coasts, to divert attention from Inchon as a single place of interest. It was discovered during these raids that the North Korean Navy were deploying Russian magnetic mines.

The first element of the operation was undertaken with the assistance of Lieutenant Eugene Clark of the USN. Undertaking commando-like reconnaissance of Wolmi-Do, he ascertained that the entire region was weakly defended: a mere 500 North Koreans on Wolmi-Do, another 1,500 at Inchon and 500 at Kimpo airfield. Clark then personally undertook a reconnaissance by rowing a boat into the harbour at night to establish the height of the seawalls and the consistency of the mud, in order to confirm the essential parameters for the landing plan. He also landed on the small island of Palmi-Do at the junction of the Flying Fish and Salee River channels and realised that the lighthouse, extinguished by the North Koreans, could be relit to guide the invasion force on their final approach up the channels to the landing sites. He reported the lighthouse to be serviceable and confirmed by observation the Japanese tide charts. It was a remarkable effort, without which the landings would be even more hazardous.[*]

The renewed NKPA offensive against the Pusan pocket during early September added an additional hurdle to the plans for *Chromite*. The 5th Marine RCT had become indispensable to General Walker, and he was reluctant to release it from the fight. He complained to MacArthur

---

[*] Robert Debs Heinl, *Victory at High Tide. The Inchon Seoul Campaign* (Leo Cooper, 1972), 42.

that he would not be responsible for the safety of the pocket if it were removed. Without the 5th Marine RCT, however, the navy and Marines could not carry out the operation at Inchon. MacArthur, realising that the pressure on Walker would immediately dissipate at the moment of a successful landing at Inchon, told him to release the regiment. Walker did so, grudgingly.

With no choice but to land on 15 September (because of the auspicious tidal movement), the first of a complicated set of sea movements began off Japan on 5 September. This coincided with a near miss from a typhoon in the Sea of Japan, but the command ship, USS *Mount McKinley*, with MacArthur on board, successfully set sail from Japan on 13 September. Fascinatingly, it was the 191st anniversary of Quebec. Then, on D minus 2, naval and air attack struck hard at Wolmi-Do and its defenders, a bombardment so heavy that the North Koreans were left in no doubt that an assault was imminent. The bombardment continued through D minus 1. Indeed, the local NKPA commander sent a warning to Pyongyang that ships were standing off Inchon, suggesting that a landing was expected. It seems to have been ignored. A full-scale amphibious landing by 70,000 men at Inchon was not considered believable, especially when the Americans in Pusan were close to collapse. MacArthur was right. He had caught the enemy with their pants down, as he had hoped. As in most cases of surprise, the victim's self-delusion played an essential role in their failure. Remarkably naively, given that they knew well the dangerous nature of the neighbourhood in which they lived, the North Koreans left the back door open. They had discounted the possibility of an attack at Inchon despite the fact that most Koreans recognised this to be the obvious place for a counterstroke. In nearly three months of fighting, the NKPA had become dangerously dismissive of the USA's martial prowess. It was the same error the Japanese had made in 1941 and was one error they were never to forget.

The night before the 3rd Battalion, 5th Marine RCT landed at Wolmi-Do, accompanied by tanks, the redoubtable Lieutenant Clark again went ashore to switch on the lighthouse and thus provide guidance for the invasion force in the morning. This assault went ahead successfully on Green Beach after 5 a.m. on 15 September as planned, the 3rd Battalion securing the island in an hour and a half. Later that day, their comrades in the remainder of the 5th Marine RCT landed at precisely 5.33 p.m. on Red Beach to the north, and 1st Marine RCT on Blue Beach to the south of Inchon's built-up area. On Red Beach – the name a misnomer, as there was no beach – the assaulting troops climbed ladders to cross the wall and fall into Inchon, a task achieved in 20 minutes. Likewise at Blue Beach, itself a seawall, troops were in Inchon within minutes and soon cut the road to Seoul. Only darkness now impeded their onward movement. By midnight the 5th Marine RCT had established itself on the vital high ground in Inchon city and 1st Marine RCT had secured the hill feature overlooking the road to Seoul. The landing had succeeded for the loss of just over 20 killed and 174 wounded, many of these unfortunately hit by ill-disciplined gunfire from the LCTs.

On the 16th the Marine Division pressed inland, 1st Marine RCT on the right directed straight on Seoul, and 5th Marine RCT on the left towards Kimpo airfield, while 1st ROK Marine Brigade came ashore to mop up Inchon behind them. Two days later Kimpo airfield was captured, the same day that the 7th Infantry Division started coming ashore. The UN advance was not seriously opposed. Over 90 percent of the NKPA was in the south, and the *In Mun Gun*'s flanks were widely and deeply exposed. On 20 September the 5th Marine RCT crossed the Han River west of Seoul and developed an attack on the capital from the north, while at the same time the 1st Marine RCT developed a second pincer movement from the south. The North Koreans reinforced their garrison to 20,000 and put up a desperate fight. The 1st Marine Division's final component – the 7th RCT – arrived at Inchon on 21 September, and an airborne RCT was flown into Kimpo three days later. It was not until 28 September that Seoul was finally cleared. The following day MacArthur, at the height of his triumph, was able to welcome President Syngman Rhee back to his capital. 'On behalf of the United Nations Command,' a visibly emotional Commander-in-Chief intoned, 'I am happy to restore to you, Mr President, the seat of your government that from it you may better fulfil your constitutional responsibilities.'

A day after the initial landings at Inchon, General Walker at Pusan began the attack on the *In Mun Gun* besieging the perimeter. Savagely decimated, the NKPA nevertheless retained a ferocious determination to fight to its last soldier in its effort to smash a way through to Pusan. It was to no avail, despite fears in the perimeter in the weeks leading up to the breakout about the shortage of ammunition. On 20 September Walker's troops had penetrated the Naktong, and by the end of the month the hammer from the south had hit the anvil in the north. The counterstrike at Inchon and the counterattack by Eighth Army from Pusan had caught the hapless NKPA in between and crushed it. It was an amazing reversal of fortunes. The North Korean Army disintegrated. The seizure of the only road to the north involved the loss of almost all the *In Mun Gun*'s tanks, guns, vehicles and equipment. Many of its soldiers – perhaps 10,000 – disappeared into the countryside with their personal weapons to act as guerrillas. Only 25,000 managed to make their way through the mountains to rally north of the 38th Parallel. Furthermore, as the NKPA moved north, they took with them thousands of South Koreans as slaves, and many thousands were likewise left in shallow or mass graves as the North Koreans systematically slaughtered their political opponents in a last vicious act of revenge. At Taejon, the advancing UN forces found the bodies of 5,000 citizens in mass graves. Elements of the ROK Army displayed the same taste for vengeance, and captured communists found themselves likely to be shot in batches and thrown into mass graves.* According to one historian of the war, the 'ROK army and national police, for their part, showed little sympathy to any southern communists they found or suspected, and US aircraft attacked people and places with little restraint. As a result, the last two weeks of September saw atrocities rivalling those seen in Europe during the fratricidal Thirty Years War of the 17th century.'† For the cost of 3,500 casualties, the UN had inflicted some 20,000 casualties on the NKPA and had decisively worsted it strategically, with a further 135,000 taken prisoner. It was a blazing triumph for MacArthur, the more so because of the reversals suffered in the months following the invasion. The problem

---

*C. MacDonald (1991). '"So terrible a liberation" – The UN occupation of North Korea', *Bulletin of Concerned Asian Scholars*, 23(2), 3–19.
†Allan R. Millet, 'Korean War', https://www.britannica.com/event/Korean-War

was that its very success inflated MacArthur's ego to the extent that he began to believe the hype that he walked on water.

———

The breakout from Pusan had been the British 27th Infantry Brigade's baptism of fire in Korea. Two weeks of intensive patrolling and acclimatisation were followed by sudden instructions to advance across the Naktong as part of their parent US 24th Infantry Division. The Eighth Army breakout was centred on a strong thrust up the Taegu–Kumch'on–Taejon–Suwon axis by a new US-led corps, I Corps, commanded by Major General Frank Milburn.* D-Day was 16 September 1950, the day following the Inchon landings. Morale across the Eighth Army skyrocketed. In the 1st ROK Division, just to the north of Coad's brigade, Brigadier General Paik exulted that 'Now we finally get to kick some butt!' The task of Paik's division, and that of the 1st Cavalry, was to capture Songju. On the day of the attack, mist blanketed the Naktong River valley, accompanied by heavy rain. The initial assault encountered a very heavy counterattack, so that by the following day no progress was made until one of his regiments broke through a weakly defended area. To Paik's great joy, Milburn attached a considerable proportion of his corps artillery to the South Korean division. By now, there was general plenitude of 105mm ammunition, so that advancing units could always enjoy ample artillery support. Bypassing major points of resistance to avoid undertaking exhausting confrontational battles at this early stage of the offensive, Milburn encouraged Paik to infiltrate through and behind the NKPA divisions, attacking them in the rear, where they were weak, rather than in the front, where they were strong. It was gamekeeper-turned-poacher, successfully reusing North Korean tactics against them. It worked. By 19 September, Paik described seeing the results of battlefield victory. They weren't a pleasant sight. Four days after the start of the battle of the breakout:

> ... I stood north of Tabu-dong on the road to Kunwi... A solemn spectacle spread out before me. Countless enemy bodies were piled

---

*Comprising the 1st Cavalry Division, 24th Infantry Division, 1st ROK Division, 5th RCT and the British 27th Infantry Brigade, together with armoured, artillery and engineer units.

up at the bottom of every hill, and the bodies of horses and cows were scattered everywhere. The stench of putrefying flesh, human and animal, assaulted the nostrils. NKPA artillery pieces, T-34s, huge numbers of weapons, and ammunition were strewn all over the battlefield. I have no idea what the face of hell looks like, but it can't be more hideous than the battlefield at Tabu-dong. The NKPA 1st Division ... had defeated me ... on the Imjin, but here at the Naktong, the NKPA 1st had suffered not just defeat but utter destruction.*

While Paik's men streamed through the hills towards Songju, their tails high, rejoicing in a reborn fighting spirit that had been grievously damaged by the earlier defeats, the 5th RCT flanked Waegwan, stretching the NKPA *3rd Division* until it threatened to break, and by 21 September the 5th RCT had secured crossing points over the Naktong for the 24th Infantry Division and its junior partner, the British 27th Brigade. The brigade crossed the Naktong south of Waegwan, north of the ferry, with the task of climbing through the mountains to seize Songju some seven miles as the crow flies to the west. On 22 September the Middlesex attacked a hill – quickly dubbed Plum Pudding Hill – to the right of the Songju Road, together with its neighbour, Hill 325, subsequently called Middlesex Hill, later that day. NKPA artillery had covered the crossing over the ferry during the day but US artillery supported the Middlesex's second assault, as did fire from five American Sherman tanks on the Songju road. Both hills, strongly defended, were nevertheless captured by the Middlesex assaults. Meanwhile, to the left of the road, the Argylls attacked Hill 282, which they occupied at 6.30 a.m. the following morning after a stiff fight, interrupting the resident North Koreans at their breakfast. The mountains here are steep, covered with dwarf fir trees right to the summit, and the physical effort of climbing them prior to launching an assault was demanding in the extreme. The men climbed the features carrying personal weapons and extra ammunition, leaving packs and other equipment on the road far below. The enemy meanwhile was shelling the ferry crossing, and

*Sun Yup Paik, *From Pusan to Panmunjom* (Brassey's, 1992), 53.

the carriage forward of ammunition and stores was difficult during daylight hours. A company of Argylls now attempted to seize a second point – Hill 388 – to the southwest of Hill 282, but a range of difficulties faced the battalion. Heavy shelling and mortaring slowed the lead company down, and it was unable to be supported by the flat trajectory firing of the tanks on the road far below. At just this moment the US artillery in support was suddenly removed, without notice, just at a point when the battalion's own mortars were unable to get forward because of problems crossing the ferry. NKPA troops now began to advance from Hill 388 to counterattack Hill 288. Meanwhile, the two forward Argyll companies struggled to get their wounded down the slopes and ammunition back up to where it was required. This was alpine warfare, the men recognised, of the toughest sort. The battalion second-in-command, Major Kenneth Muir, went forward with resupplies of ammunition to Hill 288 to take control, evacuating the wounded and coordinating the defence of the hill. The enemy were now mortaring the hill heavily. Without any artillery support, the Argylls' commanding officer – Lieutenant Colonel George Neilson – asked for an American airstrike on Hill 388. Air recognition panels were laid out on Hill 282. Before long, three F-51 Mustang fighters of No. 2 Squadron, South African Air Force, circled the hills and attacked, at 12.15 p.m. It was a devastatingly effective strike, but it was on the wrong hill. Napalm engulfed Hill 282, and the Mustangs followed it up with a *coup de grace* of machine-gun fire. Heavy casualties were caused to the Argylls on the hill by what was to become known as a blue-on-blue, but Muir ensured that the survivors – five men and 35 soldiers – held on and prevented the enemy making the most of the disaster. The survivors, driven from the hilltop by the napalm, the flames and smoke of which billowed high into the sky, now re-charged the position to hold it still. Muir was killed in the struggle for the hill and was posthumously awarded the Victoria Cross for his gallantry. The Argylls lost 89 casualties in the fighting, a grievous blow for a unit in the field for only two weeks, and in its first battle – 13 men killed, 74 wounded and two missing. John Shipster of the Middlesex saw the action at first hand, and worried that such was the shock across the brigade that the Argylls might become inoperative because of it. He needn't have worried. Within a few days, he recalled, 'the Argylls, though depleted in strength, were once again in action and fighting hard with their usual good humour."* But the fighting, though tough, had demonstrated that the NKPA had lost much of its sting. Its losses had been grievous, morale was collapsing, and starvation was stalking the survivors: supplies hadn't been getting through to the front for weeks. Where they were encountered, however, as the Argylls discovered, the soldiers of the *In Mun Gun*, though severely depleted, continued to fight determinedly. Only a fool dismissed the *In Mun Gun*, even in defeat.

In the days that followed, Songju was taken, and Taejon on 28 September. On this day the 2nd Infantry Division struck across the peninsula 72 miles towards Chonju, on the west coast, cutting off and surprising the North Korean defenders and advancing so far the division ran out of fuel. Walker's Eighth Army advanced relentlessly northwards, there to meet, in the area of Osan, representatives of the 7th Infantry Division who had landed two weeks before at Inchon. The great UN pincer had closed shut on the hapless North Koreans as their army scattered to the hills, attempted to retreat to North Korea, or simply went into the bag. The misconceived NKPA attack on South Korea had been reversed, and the *In Mun Gun* destroyed. Collective defence had worked. The USA had come to the aid of its ally, and other countries, including the UK, joined the UN effort willingly though in much smaller numbers, to demonstrate the world's willingness to defend the principles upon which the UN had been founded. Truman, Attlee and others were unwilling to allow military aggrandisement to prosper, but the war, by virtue of unpreparedness and the flawed assumptions of peace, meant that once again it had been a close-run thing. But the fact was that just over three months to the day a surprise attack on South Korea had been launched, the UN had won a great victory. The principles of national sovereignty and collective defence had been restated. Military lessons had been re-learned – the hard way – but in time to prevent catastrophe. A triumphant counterstroke had been launched at Inchon, exploiting every advantage the UN enjoyed in its air and naval power, the experience and expertise of its troops in amphibious warfare. It demonstrated the experience and confidence of

*Shipster, *Mist Over the Rice Fields*, 122.

its most senior commanders – primarily MacArthur, the Commander-in-Chief – to plan and execute a counterstroke that would bring about the defeat of the enemy invasion, restore the *status quo ante bellum*, and end the war. It was an operation that transformed the prospects for South Korea from imminent defeat to definitive victory. The question now was: what would the future bring? Would a *military* victory in Korea lead to a *political* peace?

PART 2

The Second War for Korea

In October 1951, in response to the movement by UN troops into North Korea, China began feeding troops into North Korea, ready to repel the 'Wall Street imperialists' from its neighbour's soil. This intervention was largely unknown to the UN forces – or ignored by them as an inconvenient truth, as UN troops advanced into North Korea. Even after Chinese troops had been encountered in combat, a significant degree of cognitive dissonance existed in the UN Command, especially but not exclusively in Tokyo, about the presence in North Korea of the Chinese People's Liberation Army, and its purpose. What we are calling the 'second war for Korea' was initiated when the UN crossed the 38th Parallel with the aim of conquering North Korea, an act which prompted a significant Chinese counteraction and changed the entire nature and shape of the conflict. It was at this point that the first war for Korea ended, and a new and uncertain war faced the people of the Korean peninsula.

Prologue

Captain Muñoz and the Ambush of the 2nd Division Below Kunu-ri

On the night of 25 November 1950 US Army Captain Frank Muñoz, commanding George Company, 2nd Battalion of Colonel Sloane's 9th Infantry Regiment of Major General Laurence Keiser's 2nd 'Indian Head' Infantry Division, looked out over the Ch'ongch'on River and the wide river valley through which it flowed. The entire division was spread out higgledy-piggledy along about 15 miles of the river ready to begin its final drive towards the Yalu River, the border with Chinese Manchuria, and victory in the campaign.* This had begun a month before when forward elements of I Corps had closed up the river. The surprise arrival of groups of Chinese troops late in the month had forced a consolidation of the US-led armies from Pakch'on in the west to Pugwon on the Ch'ongch'on in the east. George Company of the 9th Infantry was in the steep hills overlooking the village of Kunu-ri. The advance – and subsequent operational pause – had been something of a mad rush over previous weeks for the whole of the Eighth Army, but current operations were the easiest the 2nd Division had faced since arriving in Pusan 90 days before and crossing the 38th Parallel on

---

*The 9th Infantry Regiment comprised only two of its usual three battalions: 1st and 2nd respectively. The 2nd Division, unusually for the time, comprised three infantry regiments, each of two battalions, the 9th, 23rd and 38th Infantry Regiments.

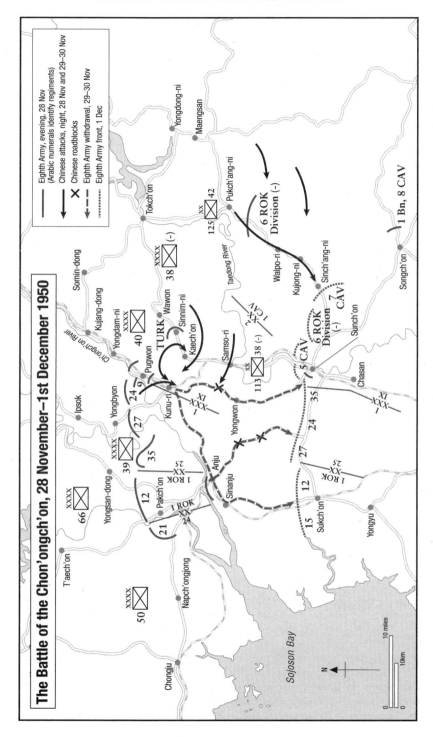

The Battle of the Chon'ongch'on, 28 November–1st December 1950

Eighth Army, evening, 28 Nov
(Arabic numerals identify regiments)

Chinese attacks, night, 28 Nov and 29–30 Nov

Chinese roadblocks

Eighth Army withdrawal, 29–30 Nov

Eighth Army front, 1 Dec

16 October.* The NKPA had disappeared into the hills and opposition had been light, even perfunctory, so much so that the men had grown complacent. Despite news of battles with Chinese troops across the Ch'ongch'on in recent weeks, the Chinese now seemed to have suffered a bloody nose and had disappeared as quickly as they had come. The men relaxed, visibly. The end of the war was in sight. They would all be home by Christmas, or so they were told. The Chinese in the hills were merely stragglers. The intelligence reports coming in to HQ Eighth Army did not suggest anything amiss. Accordingly, most men had discarded their helmets and bayonets. Few bothered to carry grenades or even to carry much ammunition for their rifles, light machine guns and BARs. Ammo was heavy, after all.

Only two days before the troops had celebrated Thanksgiving, complete with turkey, cranberry sauce and all the trimmings. The British soldiers of the Middlesex Regiment were astonished to be at the receiving end of American culinary largesse. 'Seldom in the history of war,' observed Captain John Shipster, 'can so much food have descended on front-line troops – turkey by the ton, prawn cocktail by the gallon, plum cake by the truck load, and tins of pumpkin pie by the gross – all to disappear down the throats of gastronomically bewildered … troops.'† This wasn't food they had at home, and didn't expect to see on the battlefield in Korea, but the times were strange and the men dismissed the novelty with a phlegmatic shrug. The army was always throwing surprises at them. At least this one, though odd, was pleasant.

The United States Army's 2nd Infantry Division, trucked and armoured, was crammed into the valleys of these steep, crazy mountains. There were no roads or tracks away from the few principal roads, no flat ground of any kind. It was, on paper, a powerful force. Comprising nearly 19,000 men, it boasted half-tracks carrying fearsome quadruple-mounted 0.5-inch Browning machine guns, M-26 Pershing heavy tanks, M-24 Chaffee light tanks and all the impedimenta and paraphernalia of a combined arms division in the advance, from policemen to medics,

---

*The Eighth Army comprised IX Corps (2nd and 25th US Infantry Divisions, plus the newly arrived Turkish Brigade) and I Corps (24th US Infantry Division and the ROK Army 1st Division). The British 27th Brigade was initially part of I Corps, but once the Chinese assault began on 25 November, was transferred to IX Corps.
†John Shipster (ed.), *The Diehards in Korea* (privately published, 1975), 31.

engineers, signallers and more. The men were convinced they would make mincemeat of the remaining NKPA – and any Chinese who dared to show their faces – between here and the Yalu.

But that night, everything changed. Frank Muñoz knew of course that there were – or at least, had been – lots of Chinese troops on the other side of the Ch'ongch'on. It was the presence of scattered groups of Chinese troops that had temporarily halted the rush to the Yalu a few weeks before. Indeed, the Brits had fought some spirited actions on the left flank of the army only a dozen miles to the west at Pakch'on. But there had been no suggestion that anything was amiss as the entire Eighth Army prepared to begin its final spurt to the Yalu; no news from army or corps intelligence to suggest anything other than a clear field for the final push. That night, however, all around the hills, the sound of small-arms fire and explosions split the night ear in a cacophony of noise, light and violence. Something was up: something unexpected, something big. Prompted by the noise and illumination provided by explosions and tracer rounds, the men of George Company leapt into their trenches, looking alert to their front, in increasing bewilderment as to what was going on. But whatever was happening around them that night passed them by. The early dawn of the following morning, however, revealed the source of the noise of the previous night. A long column of men was seen advancing unconcernedly towards the George Company position, obviously unaware of their presence. They were quickly identified as Chinese. Under Muñoz's orders, George Company waited until the entire column was in a kill zone beneath them, before opening fire with everything it had. An M-26 Pershing tank under George Company control opened fire into the flank of the column. Over 70 Chinese soldiers were killed and ten taken prisoner. Muñoz looked them over. Tall, fit-looking men, well dressed in mustard-coloured quilted jackets, they were equipped with rifles, entrenching tools, grenades and a great quantity of rice. Muñoz observed that they were dressed for the cold weather, some of them wearing fur-lined boots, whereas he and his men were still equipped with their cotton summer uniforms. They carried a weird mix of American, Soviet and Japanese weapons. There were even numbers of Thompson sub-machine guns, left over from American Lend-Lease supplies provided to the Kuomintang before and during the Second World War. According to Sergeant David Hackworth, a member of the 27th Infantry Regiment, the formidable 'Wolfhounds' that were part of the neighbouring 25th Infantry Division, many of the Chinese troops encountered that night didn't even have weapons, just bamboo poles with bayonets. Presumably they would equip themselves with weapons from either the fallen enemy or their fallen comrades. In any case, Hackworth and his buddy in their foxhole on the 27th Regiment's front west of the river that night had no problem chopping them down with hand grenades.

Muñoz's accidental ambush was one of few successes that night. All along the Ch'ongch'on and in the mountains to the north and far to the east large numbers of Chinese had crossed the river, smashing into American units. Some seemed to want to stay and fight; others bounced off defended American positions to disappear into the hills to the rear, as though making for some far-distant objective. Coordinated by bugles and whistles, the attack was entirely unexpected. Large numbers of Chinese troops had evidently been gathering in the mountains to the north over the previous month without anyone being aware of them. The news that filtered through to Muñoz in the hours that followed the arrival of dawn didn't get any better. Other companies in the 9th Infantry had been smashed, as had whole units from other parts of IX Corps. The 61st Artillery Battalion had lost an entire battery when it had been overrun, the artillerymen fleeing for their lives. In the days that followed, the Americans became aware that in the west the *Thirty-Ninth, Fiftieth* and *Sixty-Sixth Armies* of the People's Liberation Army were on the move.* This probably numbered in the region of 90,000 men. In the north and northeast the *Fortieth, Thirty-Eighth* and *Forty-Second Armies* were encircling the American Eighth Army. These amounted to another 90,000 men. So, it looked as though 180,000 Chinese troops were pressing down on the Americans from the north and west, determined to reverse the march to the Yalu. The shock in both Eighth Army and in Tokyo was profound. Unbeknown to the men on the Ch'ongch'on, the United States' X Corps on the eastern side of the Korean peninsula had also been struck hard. This was a Chinese offensive of unexpected power.

On the right of the division, Colonel George Peploe's 38th Infantry Regiment ('The Rock of the Marne') was attacked but held firm as large

---

*A Chinese army was the same size as an American corps, with three divisions each of about 10,000 men.

numbers of Chinese swept through and around their positions. Those onrushing enemy who weren't killed seemed to bounce off the American positions and just keep going. Peploe, a tough, uncompromising 50-year-old veteran of the campaign in Europe where he had served in XIII Corps, part of Simpson's Ninth Army, gathered his men together at dawn on 26 November and recovered the positions the regiment had lost in the night. Likewise, Colonel Sloane regrouped his battered 9th Infantry Regiment that first night two miles downstream on the Ch'ongch'on, determined to fight it out. The 9th Infantry was on the left side of the river; the 23rd held the right. The second night of the offensive – 26 November – a further Chinese attack fell across the 2nd Division's positions along the river. It was clear that many Chinese were now well behind them, to their rear. No one knew quite how many. Now, they were being attacked again, all across the line, again in huge numbers. This time the attack on the left-hand side of the river smashed through the 23rd Infantry Regiment, sweeping its two battalions away. Colonel Sloane, on the eastern side of the river, realising that his right flank was now exposed and that his entire position on the left-hand side of the river was about to be cut off by encircling Chinese, ordered the men of the 2nd Battalion, including Muñoz's George Company, to cross the river to take over the positions vacated by the 23rd.

But the moment the battalion began to move, it came under sustained attack. All hell was let loose around the George Company position. Unseen by the men, Chinese troops had crawled up in the darkness in silence to within 50 yards of their trenches. Suddenly the night was alive with the sound of machine-gun and rifle fire and the crump of grenades. Bugles and whistles blew, urging the Chinese troops in for the final assault. Two platoons of a neighbouring company disappeared under the onrush of men and bullets. In the melee, the men of George Company managed to congregate together around the trenches held by Muñoz. It became a magnet for enemy machine-gun and mortar fire as the night dragged on. The men were now regretting ditching all that extra ammunition and the stocks of seemingly redundant grenades. Successive assault waves attempted to overwhelm the defenders, but each time they were fought off, enemy bodies piling around the perimeter. During the early fighting, Hackworth observed, the enemy weren't sophisticated fighters, but they were in extraordinarily large numbers.

He described the assault as 'a wave – a human wave – of Chinese crashing over us'.*

But it couldn't go on forever. The rest of the 2nd Battalion had by now managed to re-cross the freezing four-foot-deep Ch'ongch'on, full of ice even at this time early in winter, to the eastern bank. Muñoz was cut off: he couldn't survive for long. He had run out of grenades; the tanks and the half-tracks with their powerful quadruple 0.50-inch Browning machine guns in the valley below couldn't provide any supporting fire in the darkness. In a matter of 20 minutes he had lost more than 70 men. In the chaos of battle Muñoz passed the order to withdraw from the hill to the waiting armoured vehicles below, and to re-cross the river. Under intense Chinese fire from the surrounding hills, the survivors managed to make their way across the river during the following hours. One of the supporting M-26 Pershing tanks was struck in the dark by some kind of anti-tank weapon, the fuel tank blowing up and lighting up the entire river valley. On the riverbank the 'Quad 0.50s' sprayed the hills the men had just vacated to hold the Chinese back, and two of the tanks repeatedly crossed the river with men clinging to the hulls. Others waded across the ice-filled river up to their chests to collapse, exhausted, on the eastern bank. Muñoz was to observe that everyone who crossed this way would become a cold-weather casualty. As the first rays of dawn filtered through the darkness, Muñoz hurried around his men. Only 20 remained. Looking down, he realised that his own trousers had been ripped apart by bullets. As the 9th Infantry reorganised itself that morning, the 2nd Battalion could now only muster nine officers and 200 men.

It had been a bad night for the entire Eighth Army. On the right of 2nd Division, the II ROK Corps had been smashed and were streaming south, opening up Major General Keiser's right flank. The 38th Regiment had been strung out on the road to the east of the Ch'ongch'on, the right-hand wing of the division. The 38th, too, had been hit hard by Chinese attacks on the night of 26 November, and confusion reigned across the front. Withdrawing ROK Army soldiers stumbled into American positions as they reeled from the onslaught. The fighting was confused; the battle was fought company by company and platoon by platoon.

*David Hackworth, *About Face* (Sidgwick & Jackson, 1989), 49.

It was clear that the Chinese were both infiltrating through and behind the American lines along the Ch'ongch'on, as well as assaulting hard any positions they found, seemingly without concern for casualties. The enemy plan looked simple enough: to break up the 2nd Division into its many separate components; surround and isolate them from their fellows in IX Corps and cut off any hope of retreat. Each surrounded element of the division could then be defeated in detail.

The Chinese plans progressed well, and probably better than they had expected. On the 2nd Division front Major General Keiser quickly lost contact with his units. Brigadier Coad of the British 27th Commonwealth Brigade, part of I Corps on the forward left of the Eighth Army, was told to move his three battalions to support IX Corps, the headquarters of which had moved south to Chasan.* Hysteria was rampant, Coad remembered. No one really knew what was going on, and commanders struggled to impose their will on the fighting. Colonel Peploe's 38th Regiment began pulling back from its exposed positions on the night of 28 November in constant contact with attacking Chinese. Slowly, chaotically, the 38th Regiment and the right wing of the 2nd Division contracted back to Kunu-ri. As this was happening, the 9th Infantry was being pushed back from the Ch'ongch'on. Far to the division's left, the 25th Infantry Division had also been knocked about and was withdrawing back to the road that runs east of the river between Anju and Kunu-ri. Chinese pressure on this part of the battlefield seemed to be focused on the 2nd Division at Kunu-ri itself. The Chinese were forcing Keiser's 2nd Division into one of two bottlenecks in the mountains south of Kunu-ri. Few men knew what was going on, apart from the need to keep fighting; keep repelling the Chinese. Little sense of the Chinese operation behind the division, in the mountains to the south, astride the road leading to Sunch'on, was understood. Decisions were being made by platoons and companies, finding themselves cut off from the rest of their units. Communications were difficult, as the radios didn't work in the mountains. The massive firepower enjoyed by the Americans was difficult to deploy, as the M-26 and M-24 tanks, half-track 'Quad o.50s' and artillery all found

---

*1st Battalion, Argyll & Sutherland Highlanders; 1st Battalion, Middlesex Regiment (the 'Die-Hards') and 3rd Battalion, Royal Australian Regiment.

itself tied to the handful of roads. Three roads ran south from Kunu-ri. One went directly east towards Kaech'on (where the newly arrived Turkish brigade was situated, at Sinnim-ni), before dropping south to Sunch'on. Another road ran directly through the steep mountains, through a high pass, to Sunch'on, following for part of it the general line of the railway, through the village of Yongwon-ni. A third ran back along the Ch'ongch'on to Anju, before it turned due south, reaching a point halfway between Sukch'on and Sunch'on. Anything with wheels or tracks would have to go by road. And as American soldiers were seemingly conditioned to move by vehicle, they too were tied to the road. In the meantime, the invading men of the People's Liberation Army moved along the ridges, from where they could dominate by fire anything happening in the valleys below.

On 29 November a message was sent to the companies along the Ch'ongch'on River front. Frank Muñoz received a note from his commanding officer, Lieutenant Colonel Barberis: 'we're starting an organised retrograde movement.' Muñoz smiled to himself. So that's what a retreat was now called? That night, fighting back to Kunu-ri in the darkness, lit only by the light from repeated explosions, Muñoz could see thousands of advancing mustard-coated Chinese troops swarming towards his retreating men. It was freezing cold: harsh Siberian winds whipped through the valleys, freezing everything. When his exhausted men got back to Kunu-ri it was at least minus ten degrees Celsius. The men, unable to light fires, fell on the ground and slept. All around them, the Chinese marched. The battle in which they were engaged has been described as the most decisive defeat American arms would suffer in the 20th century.* It was the start of what the soldiers quipped was 'the big bug out'.

For the duration of the battle along the Ch'ongch'on River, the road back from Kunu-ri to Sunch'on remained open. However, during the early dawn of 29 November, a convoy of supply trucks making its way to the Turkish brigade positioned in the hills to the east of Kunu-ri was ambushed. All the vehicles were set ablaze, and the men killed. Could the Chinese have entirely outflanked the Eighth Army and cut off its supply routes back to Pyongyang? A Military Police detachment sent to

*Fehrenbach, *This Kind of War*, 201.

investigate did not return. The road travelled through the hills, exiting before Sunch'on through a steep defile dominated by high ground on either side. The defile was substantial: it ran for a quarter of a mile, with the road cut between 50-foot-high rockfaces. If this were held by the enemy, any retreating army caught on the northern side of the gap, especially one tied to the road, could be defeated in detail. By this stage Major General Keiser was given permission to withdraw his division to Sunch'on. He'd been trying to hold his scattered division together for five days, in a battle he did not expect, against seemingly overwhelming odds. He was short of ammunition. Above all, he wanted to have the chance to consolidate his division on a defensive line. Having to fight confusing battles where the enemy swirled around, through and among the division was frustrating and exhausting. The area between Sukch'on on the left and Sunch'on on the right seemed ideal for such a line. That afternoon he undertook a reconnaissance in an L-5 spotter plane and thought the route to Sunch'on the right one to take. From his vantage point in the light plane, he saw large numbers of figures hurrying through the hills towards the south and the hills above the defile, but he did not for a moment think they might be Chinese. They must be refugees, he thought, or retreating ROK soldiers. He decided that on 30 November he would withdraw what remained of his division down this road to Sunch'on and create a new defensive line. It was a journey of perhaps 20 miles. The two weakened battalions of Colonel Sloane's 9th Infantry Regiment, supported by a platoon of M-26 Pershing tanks, would lead the advance, clearing any opposition as they proceeded, the tail following behind. The tail comprised everybody, wounded included. It was not disposed for fighting but was constructed simply as an ordinary convoy. 'Don't worry,' he was told, 'there can't be any more than a couple of Chinese companies on the road.' When they reached the defile, they were assured that the British 27th Commonwealth Brigade would have cleared the road from Sunch'on from the south and secured the pass.

Sloane's regiment proceeded the following day, down the main supply route as ordered. The 2nd Battalion marched on the left, the 3rd on the right. On the left with the 2nd Battalion was Frank Muñoz's George Company, or the couple of dozen men he had remaining. Starting out in the dark of the early morning, Muñoz hadn't made much distance out of Kunu-ri before he came under heavy fire. He was shocked.

The enemy weren't supposed to be here. The entire regiment formed a battle line and advanced, but when they got to the firing point near the village, they found it empty. The enemy had disappeared into the hills. The two battalions started off again. By mid-morning they hadn't encountered any more Chinese, so hopes began to rise that the withdrawal wouldn't be contested. Then, suddenly, all hell was let loose, machine-gun and mortar fire hitting the advancing troops on both sides of the road. The men dived to the ground, trying to identify the enemy firing points in the hills. Muñoz couldn't lift his head, the fire was so intense. It appeared that bullets were coming from both sides of the road. Men of the ROK Army, accompanying the 38th Regiment, mounted a counterattack, but such was the confusion of identifying friend from foe, the M-26 tanks accompanying the troops on the road fired on them instead of the enemy. As the attack broke up in confusion and tragedy, one thing was clear: the withdrawing men of the 2nd Division were not up against a simple roadblock. The hills ahead of them were swarming with Chinese. Keiser was then told that the tail of the divisional column, still in Kunu-ri, was also coming under Chinese attack. This looked like a planned envelopment, with Keiser caught in a trap constructed from Chinese ingenuity and American overconfidence. 'Push on,' ordered Keiser, who had come up to Muñoz's position at the front of the column to see what was causing the hold-up. There didn't seem to be much fire falling on the road, and now speed was of the essence. He had to have his division out of the valley by the time darkness fell that night. He remained under the misapprehension that the route ahead of him, down the main supply route through the defile and to Sunch'on, was relatively free of the enemy. He didn't know then that the PLA had already surrounded his position with an entire division. He was cut off and would have to fight his way out of this pocket if he were to survive. Equally, the British 27th Commonwealth Brigade had not reached Yongwon-ni, where it could help the 2nd Division through the defile, as it was fighting its own battle to advance north.

It was obvious now that the vast vehicle convoy in the valley was extremely vulnerable to Chinese fire from the surrounding hills. The convoy had not been constructed to enable it to fight but pulled together in line unit by unit. Tanks were, however, spread out across the length of the convoy to provide some protection for thin-skinned vehicles, but units weren't deployed for battle. Men from platoons and

The *In Mun Gun* attacked South Korea on 25 June 1950 in a blitzkrieg-type offensive led by Soviet-provided T-34s like these. (Getty Images)

General Douglas MacArthur and South Korean President Syngman Rhee. (Getty Images)

The war leaders. President Truman in a posed photograph with Prime Minister
Clement Attlee in Washington, December 1950. Secretary of State Dean Acheson
(left) and General George Marshall stand behind them. (Getty Images)

In a haunting photograph of the shock of combat for unprepared troops, a grief-
stricken American infantryman whose buddy has been killed in action is comforted
by another soldier in the Pusan Perimeter on 28 August 1950. (NARA)

A tragic feature of the war, like most others, were the mass flows of refugees. Here, refugees crowd the railway at Inchon in 1950 soon after the beginning of the North's invasion of the Republic of Korea at the start of the war. (NARA)

Refugees are seen coming from the battle area during actions in Sunch'on and Yongwon-ni. (© IWM BF 177)

Two wounded Korean girls limp past a dead South Korean (ROK) soldier during actions around Sunch'on and Yongwon-ni. (© IWM BF 188)

A soldier of the 1st Middlesex with a Chinese prisoner between Sunch'on and Yongwon-ni following the ambush of the US 2nd Infantry Division at Kunu-ri in the dying days of November 1950. (© IWM BF 174)

At Wake Island on 18 October 1950, US President Harry S. Truman met his Far Eastern Commander-in-Chief General Douglas MacArthur for the first time. (Getty Images)

Soldiers of the ROK Army withdrawing during one of the see-saw offensives of 1950. (© IWM BF 10227)

Boeing B-29 Superfortresses drop bombs during a raid on a chemical plant in Koman-dong on 14 August 1950. (Getty Images)

North Korean rolling stock under low-level fighter-bomber attack by napalm.
(US Army)

A railway bridge in North Korea, partially destroyed by Fairey Firefly aircraft of the
Fleet Air Arm operating from the carrier HMS *Theseus*. (© IWM KOR 640)

The cost of war is always counted in the lives of the innocent. This elderly woman
and her grandchild wander among the debris of their wrecked home in the aftermath
of an air raid by US planes over Pyongyang. (Getty Images)

Marines fighting in the streets of Seoul following the landings at Inchon,
20 September 1950. (NARA)

Three US Marines behind a barricade during street fighting in Seoul,
September 1950, following the landings at Inchon. (Getty Images)

The Korean War caused untold suffering to civilians in both North and South. An abandoned girl is shown crying in the streets of Inchon on 26 September 1950. (NARA)

During June and July 1952, the expenditure of artillery had become astonishing: in less than 60 days the communists fired over 700,000 rounds at the UN positions, while the UN troops fired back over 4.7 million. (Getty Images)

American troops of the 35th Infantry Regiment observe smoke shells striking enemy positions on 1 February 1951. (US Army)

A detachment of the 16th New Zealand Field Artillery Regiment firing in support of the 1st Battalion, Argyll and Sutherland Highlanders, all part of 27th Commonwealth Brigade. (© IWM BF 364)

Napalm being dropped on an enemy position forward of US Marines as they withdraw from the Changjin (Chosin) reservoir in November 1950. Napalm, a petroleum-based explosive, was used extensively by UN forces. (US Army)

US troops digging in on a hilltop position in 1952. This type of positional combat characterised the two-year period from July 1951 to the end of the war in July 1953. (Getty Images)

US Marines duck for cover as an enemy 82mm shell explodes above their position on 11 April 1952. (Getty Images)

Above. The UN enjoyed supremacy at sea for most of the war, a situation that allowed MacArthur to achieve success at Inchon. Here, the 16in. guns of the USS *Missouri* fire on land targets off North Korea. (US Navy)

Left. Men of C and D Companies of the 1st Battalion, The Gloucestershire Regiment, 29th Brigade, having captured Hill 327 south of Seoul in February 1951, wait for the next phase of the attack. (© IWM BF 377)

Men of 1st Battalion, Royal Ulster Rifles and Centurion tanks of the 8th Hussars. (© IWM BF 510)

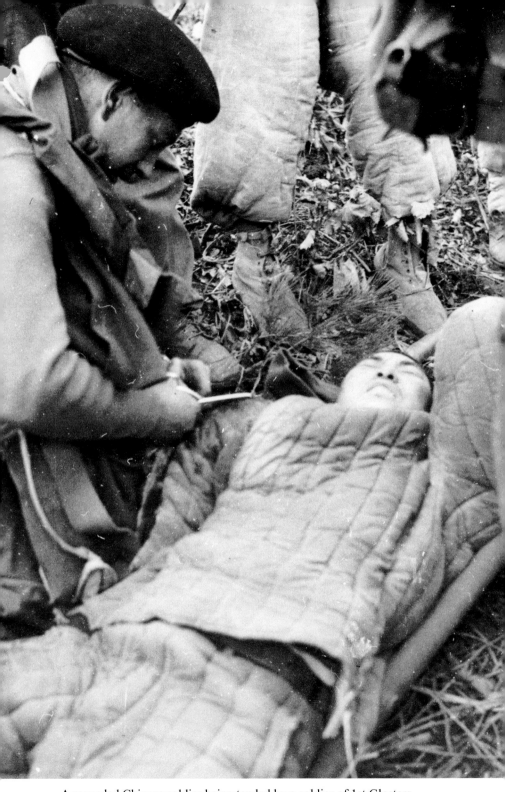

A wounded Chinese soldier being tended by a soldier of 1st Glosters.
(© IWM BF 379)

A Vickers medium machine-gun team of the 3rd Battalion,
Royal Australian Regiment. (© IWM BF 423)

Men of 3rd Battalion, Royal Australian Regiment prepare barbed wire in front of their positions. Note the nature of the terrain. (© IWM MH 31535)

Five weeks after the battle of the Imjin River, the British were back. Here, a soldier of the 1st Battalion, The Gloucestershire Regiment stands on the old A Company position, pointing to the main supply route through the Imjin River valley as seen from there. The ridge on the left is the route the Chinese used to attack D Company in the famous battle in April 1951. (© IWM BF 10277)

In a piece of theatre, not required by the terms of the armistice, Kim Il-sung signs the Korean Armistice Agreement at Pyongyang, assisted by General Nam Il. (Getty Images)

companies across the division were scattered across the convoy where they could find a lift. Once mounted, commanders lost all command and control of their units. It was every man for himself.

Captain Muñoz and George Company were still in the vanguard of the advance on the left-hand side of the road. The plan now was that a company of Turkish infantry, survivors of the brigade that had been surrounded and cut off at Sinnim-ni, would attack through George Company, supported by Pershing tanks firing from the road.* The Turkish attack succeeded in clearing the ridges, at which point the heavy tanks gunned their engines and picked up speed down the road, the vast column of soft-skinned vehicles following on behind. The lead tank was commanded by Lieutenant Mace. After two and a half miles, Mace, his tank peppered with machine-gun bullets fired from the hills, was forced to halt. Immediately ahead, blocking the road, were a damaged truck, tank and M-39 tracked carrier. The long, snake-like column immediately ground to a halt, vulnerable and exposed. A junior officer jumped out of Mace's tank to inspect the stricken vehicles and was immediately exposed to a hail of fire. Dead Turkish soldiers lay around the vehicles, evidence of an ambush much earlier in the day. With dawning understanding, Mace could see that they were in the midst of a well-constructed Chinese ambush, one that had been here for some time. The hills were full of mortars, machine guns and hundreds of Chinese, and held a position that ran in length for perhaps six miles. It was subsequently revealed that two Chinese regiments from the *113th Division* had inveigled their way into the hills, avoiding initial battle along the Ch'ongch'on for the purpose of establishing this ambush. A total of 40 machine guns ranged along the road from vantage points in the hills. The entire 2nd Infantry Division now found itself stretched out, unprotected, along the road between Kunu-ri and Yongwon-ni.

There was nothing for it now but to brazen it out. Lieutenant Mace's Pershing tank, having pushed the detritus from the road in front, started off again, and in another mile and a half – all the way under intense fire, bullets pinging off the armoured carapace – reached the opening to the defile. Smashing through some burned out vehicles littering

---

*The 5,000-strong Turkish Brigade arrived in October 1950 as part of Turkey's response to the United Nation's call for troops and became part of the US 25th Infantry Division.

the pass, Mace's tank burst out on the other side, into the welcoming arms of the 27th Commonwealth Brigade. It was the first and last tank to make it through the defile. At the British end of the defile, a stiff battle the previous day had removed a couple of Chinese platoons, and supported by five American tanks, the men of the Middlesex Regiment awaited the arrival of the 2nd Division. Waiting for it to arrive, they expected the division to advance with troops left and right of the road, dominating the ridges, clearing enemy positions as they advanced. Watching through binoculars, Captain Shipster was astonished to see, in the distance, the beginning of an endless column of vehicles stuck nose-to-tail to the ribbon of the road. It wasn't a fighting withdrawal as he expected but a rush to the rear, along the road.

With the Chinese trap now sprung, Keiser's division had no choice but to fight it out. The enormous weight of fire that smashed into the now stationary column, where Mace had been forced to stop to clear the road, began to cause serious casualties and brew up vehicles, which then added further blockages to the road. The entire column, along almost all of its length, was under fire. For vehicles to move forward, they had to push their burning compatriots out of the way and undertake their own, individual fight against the enemy in the hills and to make a path through the detritus along the road. This was made more difficult because, as the machine guns started slapping into the unprotected vehicles, men jumped out to burrow into the ground next to the road. It proved hard to remove them, either to fight their way out or to escape down the road. Tanks moved forward to clear blocking vehicles from the road, soldiers leaping on the back of the armour in an effort to escape, but the hulls of the tanks were as dangerous as staying in the ditch alongside the road. The only hope was that the Chinese firing into this mass of men and vehicles would run out of ammunition, such was the profligacy of their firing.

The one thing that significantly aided those who managed to escape from the Kunu-ri cauldron was American tactical airpower, which managed to strike the Chinese positions in the hills on both sides of the valley during the hours of daylight with bombs, bullets and napalm. For the troops on the ground, in the now stranded column, it was every man for himself. There was no unity of command, and certainly no control. Groups of men, officers and soldiers formed bands to get themselves out of the cauldron of fire. Many others simply waited where they were, some too shocked to move because of the intensity of the incoming fire, for some a sense of helplessness and for others because of wounds. Hundreds of vehicles lay burning and abandoned along the route, machine guns dancing their deadly tune from the hills on both sides of the stricken column. Tragedies were common. A group of 20 trucks carrying 180 wounded men were abandoned by their medical charges on the road. At dawn on 1 December, the column was struck by American fighter aircraft, thinking that the vehicles had been abandoned and were empty, in an attempt to deny their use to the enemy. Drums of napalm incinerated the vehicles and their helpless occupants.

Where men got out, it was by individual initiative. Some banded together to fight their way out. Some commandeered jeeps and trucks to push their way forward. Colonel Peploe of the 38th Infantry filled his jeep with wounded, and bounced and crashed his way through the defile to safety on the other side. The Chinese hold on the mountain pass was a genius of tactical aggression that succeeded precisely because the 2nd Division wasn't expecting it and had not prepared itself to conduct a fighting withdrawal. 'The American practice on withdrawal,' Captain Shipster noted later, 'was to disengage as quickly as possible and then take up new positions many miles back where they could be redeployed.'* This only worked when the enemy was not in a position to interrupt the withdrawal.

Captain Frank Muñoz managed to bring his small band of military refugees to the edge of the defile by about 3 p.m. The air was thick with bullets. He could see them dancing over the ground around him, little spirals of dust rising as they struck the ground. The ground was thick with bodies, mostly still, but some moving and groaning. He realised that the only hope of escape was to climb the ridge and to fight it out with the Chinese troops occupying the high ground. The defile itself was blocked with burning vehicles. Staying where they were would mean death, or surrender. With five men, Muñoz climbed the slope to his left, targeting the nearest Chinese machine gun. Others began doing the same. Lieutenant Tom Turner of the 38th Regimental Tank Company lay in a ditch about 25 yards from a Chinese machine gun

*Shipster, *The Diehards in Korea*, 36.

that was spraying the road. Looking about him at the other men lying in the ditch, he asked, 'Who'll join me in rushing that gun?' Few were interested. A couple of men told him to do it himself. He managed instead to gather about 30 ROK soldiers, and they swarmed over the gun. Meanwhile, with tactical air targeting each of the Chinese positions in turn, some semblance of order was returning to the chaos at the entrance to the defile. Major General Keiser had organised a number of rifle parties to stalk and assault the Chinese guns. Then, just as it was getting dark, two M-24 Chaffee light tanks were moved into the defile to act as bulldozers, pushing burning vehicles into the sides to create a route for vehicles to make their way through to the other side. Slowly the long column of stricken vehicles and men began moving again. The fire from the hills had noticeably slackened as counteraction by stalking infantrymen took a toll on the machine guns. This was just as well, as the advent of dusk meant a cessation of the air support that had so dramatically aided the column during the afternoon. By nightfall the greater part of the surviving elements of the 2nd Division had managed to exit the valley of death, making their way through the defile to safety. To the rear of the column, however, still back at Kunu-ri, the Chinese were closing in for the *coup de grace*. The rearguard had other ideas. They would abandon their heavy guns – the 8-inch howitzers, as it would be impossible to tow them through the mountain passes – but not before firing off all the remaining ammunition into the advancing Chinese. They would then retire not with the rest of the 2nd Division, but on the road running alongside the Ch'ongch'on to Anju. In a blistering bombardment, just before nightfall, the 15th Field Artillery Battalion fired 3,206 rounds at their persecutors in a 20-minute shoot. The Chinese attack stalled. The remaining troops evacuated Kunu-ri and succeeded in getting out through the road via Anju that night. All had to fight their way down the road, but what was left of the 2nd Division managed to escape.

It had, nevertheless, been smashed. Captain Shipster described those who managed to get out as 'bewildered and disillusioned'. The Middlesex loaded up their vehicles and, still under Chinese fire from the heights and laden down with 250 American casualties – as many as they could carry but by no means all – made their way back to Chasan. The 2nd Infantry Division had started the battle with 15,209 men in all units. By the morning of 1 December, it had 10,269. The fighting around Kunu-ri and the great ambush in the Sunch'on defile had cost it 4,940 men, a casualty rate of 32 per cent. Equipment losses were equally heavy. In addition to hundreds of trucks and trailers, most of its engineer equipment and half of its radios, the division lost 64 of its guns, many abandoned after having been spiked at Kunu-ri.

The day before, when the Middlesex had advanced north to the defile, they had been collocated with HQ IX Corps. Now, to their surprise, back in Chasan, they discovered that the corps headquarters had disappeared. It had bugged out south to Pyongyang without telling them. The roads to the south were crowded with military refugees, fleeing headlong from the fighting. The weather had closed in, winter wrapping its frozen tentacles around the thinly clad, shivering troops of the Eighth Army. The UN's drive to the Yalu had been spectacularly reversed. As Sergeant David Hackworth complained, 'MacArthur had said we'd be home for Christmas; I guess his supply people believed him, because the Chinese had caught us with our pants down and they were summer trousers… We were slowly freezing to death in the bitter below-zero weather while the Chinese, like Genghis Khan's mighty hordes, marched on, seemingly unstoppable.'*

---

*Hackworth, *About Face*, 52.

6

To the Yalu, or Bust

As Commander-in-Chief, MacArthur's operational brilliance – exhibited at Inchon – was countered by a profound inability to understand the political ramifications of war at the grand, or strategic, level. There were several aspects to this delusion. The first was his belief that ultimate victory for the UN could only be defined in terms of the utter destruction of the NKPA and of North Korea. For MacArthur, war was total in every respect, the only expectation of a beaten enemy being unconditional surrender. There could be no political or military half-measures to ensuring the complete annihilation of the enemy, using all the tools in one's armoury, as had been the case against Nazi Germany and militarist Japan. To MacArthur, these tools not only included the atomic bomb, but Chiang Kai-shek's anti-communist forces on Formosa as well. It made no sense, MacArthur argued, to pull one's punches. If that happened, war would erupt again in the future from the ashes of a negotiated settlement that lacked a definitive end. There was another problem, he thought. A negotiated peace, in which the enemy retained its armed forces and political dignity, was anathema because it did not bring justice to the victor. The enemy had to be utterly vanquished, punished indeed, for the crime of starting the war and bringing death to America and its friends. This led to another issue for MacArthur: the arrival in Asia of communism – demonstrated by the loss of China to Mao's revolutionary party in 1949 – and the threat this posed to US hegemony in the region and to the free world. For MacArthur, the purpose of the war in Korea quickly became one not merely of defeating the upstart North Koreans but of making 'the world safe for democracy; it must not be to rescue allies, but to destroy evil.'* That evil was transparently staring the world in the face. Communism must not be allowed to succeed here, or it would consume the world. The political ambition behind this military objective was the unification of Korea, placing it under the governance of the anti-communist ROK. The obvious threat to this assumption was that the new communist regime next door in China might regard the American conquest of its neighbour to be a threat to its own interests, and enter the fray.

Such an eventuality was repeatedly dismissed by MacArthur during the summer of 1950, though never with any basis other than his own opinion and the somewhat servile agreement of his military staff. The idea that China would not become involved in the war became an article of hubristic faith, an issue to be dismissed because it smacked of denying the USA the full fruits of its historic victory. Averell Harriman, recalled from his roving ambassadorial role in Europe to serve as one of Truman's wingmen in managing the new war in Korea, flew to Tokyo for discussions with MacArthur for a few days in early August.† He was accompanied by Lieutenant General Matthew Ridgway and General Lauris Norstad of the USAF.‡ On Harriman's return to Washington, he told Truman that the C-in-C had no concerns about the possibility of Chinese or Soviet intervention in the war. Harriman told Truman MacArthur's plan for Operation *Chromite*. All three men had been won over by MacArthur's detailed, two-and-a-half-hour presentation, his understanding of the strategic opportunity the counterstroke offered, his obvious command of the challenge he faced in Korea, and the solution he proposed. General Omar Bradley, a man Truman trusted more than many other military commanders, and chairman of the Joint Chiefs of Staff, was the least convinced of MacArthur's plan. Truman nevertheless gave MacArthur his backing and *Chromite* went ahead as planned. As MacArthur had promised, and Truman had trusted, the operation was an overwhelming success.

---

*Fehrenbach, *This Kind of War*, 181.
†Harriman had been Roosevelt's personal envoy to the UK during the Second World War.
‡Ridgway was the Deputy Chief of Staff of the US Army and had commanded the 82nd Airborne Division in Sicily, Italy and Normandy, and later the XVIII Airborne Corps.

The country exulted in a military victory few had expected, given the relentless barrage of bad news over the preceding three months. Truman was jubilant, telling MacArthur: 'I salute you all, and say to you from all of us at home, "Well and nobly done."'

But what was now to be done? Should the war end on the 38th Parallel where it had begun, in essence a return to the *status quo ante bellum*? In Washington, a number of senior policymakers advocated this view, such as George Keenan, the man who more than anyone else had prophesied the rise of Moscow-engineered aggression across the globe. But he and Paul Nitze, who had prepared NSC-68 – tabled to recommend a heavy increase in military funding to help contain the developing Soviet threat – were drowned out by the deafening cacophony of voices calling for retribution and pursuit. There is rarely anything as ugly as a population with its blood lust up: such was the state of popular emotion in the United States at the dramatic success of the forces in Korea that the overwhelming opinion was that the army should be told to occupy the North to smash North Korea and punish it for an unexpected, unrequired war. Press, politicians (Democrat and Republican), the Joint Chiefs of Staff and the huge bulk of the electorate all wanted one thing and one thing only: for the upstart North Korea to be sent back into the stone age. There was to be no mercy for a country that had egregiously brought the world back to war so soon after the end of the Second World War. In Seoul, President Syngman Rhee, newly returned to his country, argued the same strident, uncompromising view. Indeed, it seems certain that Rhee would have ordered his forces to continue into North Korea if the UN had decided not to do so. In the days following its capture Captain John Shipster of the Middlesex described Seoul as 'a city of the dead.' In a shocking revelation of the animosities behind this war, he watched 'a large number of men, women and children being marched along, tied together with ropes, escorted by South Korean soldiers... I suspected that they had been classed as collaborators and that in a few hours they would all be shot.'*

Under these circumstances it would have been difficult for the president to swim against the flow of popular and political opinion. In any case, Truman did not hesitate. He ordered MacArthur, as early as

*Shipster, *Mist Over the Rice Fields*, 123.

27 September, in a secret memorandum – NSC-81, written by Dean Rusk – long before any authorisation had been received from the UN – to cross the 38th Parallel into North Korea. His Secretary of Defense, the man who had been the US Army's Chief of Staff during the Second World War, General George C. Marshall, instructed MacArthur not to feel hampered 'tactically or strategically' in his new task, which was the destruction of North Korea's armed forces. His secondary mission was to unite the whole of Korea under Syngman Rhee. His only constraint was that he was to report any sign of intervention by Soviet or Chinese troops. He was equally forbidden from crossing the Manchurian or Soviet borders. If there were any Chinese intervention, MacArthur was ordered 'to continue the action as long as action by your forces offers a reasonable chance of success'. The responsibility for invading North Korea clearly sat with Truman and the Joint Chiefs of Staff, not MacArthur, but the task suited MacArthur – and his ego – perfectly. He had already determined that he needed a total victory: ending the war on the 38th Parallel constituted the incomplete destruction of the enemy, and most opinion in the USA agreed with him. Presumably he would then, as he had done in Japan, take on the role of phoenix, raising the vanquished state of North Korea from the ashes of defeat, personally leading it to the sunlit uplands of peace and prosperity within a united and democratic Korea. For his part, George Marshall agreed with the view that military victory allowed the opportunity to force a political settlement on Korea and was irritated at the talk of diplomacy by the UK, India and Communist China to bring the war to an immediate end. This, he considered, was akin to appeasement.

London's concern was not appeasement, however, but pragmatism. The UN operation to support the ROK in repelling the invader had been undertaken to right a wrong. Invading North Korea in return was tantamount to doing the same thing, in reverse. It was opportunistic: no thought had been given to the military tasks required of an offensive all the way to the Yalu River as the year came to an end, and winter beckoned. The use of military force to knock the two countries together under Syngman Rhee was utilitarian, but was it legal? Even if a legal case could be made for it, was it the right thing to do? There were certainly some fears for the consequences of an invasion of the North for the human rights of Rhee's political opponents. Enough reports existed of the bloody repression of political opponents in the years before the war in South Korea for London to worry about the bloodshed that would follow if Rhee got his hands on the whole country. Indeed, because of these fears, on 8 October the UN passed a resolution restricting the ROK's future jurisdiction in the North. Rhee was furious and did all he could to circumvent it.

Likewise, if the North could be criticised for using military means to secure a political objective, could not the same now be said for the UN, apparently making up its own rules? But the biggest worry in London was the response of Communist China. For those listening to Peking, the messages were unequivocal. On 1 October Mao Tse Tung could be heard on the radio stating, 'The Chinese people will not tolerate foreign aggression and will not stand aside if the imperialists wantonly invade the territory of their neighbour.' The Indian ambassador in Peking, K. M. Panikkar, had been told unequivocally by China's foreign minister, Chou En-Lai, that the Chinese were uneasy about the possibility of a US occupation of North Korea and reserved the right to respond as they felt fit. MacArthur dismissed such fears as bluff. The warning was repeated on Radio Peking on 10 October. If UN or US troops crossed the parallel, the Chinese People's Republic would send troops to aid the People's Republic of Korea. The warnings could not have been blunter, but in Washington, and Tokyo, no one was listening.

On 3 October Attlee received a report from the Foreign Office laying out in detail Chinese military preparations for war in North Korea. Some 400,000 troops were already massed on the Yalu, ready to cross into North Korea. Indeed, British reports from Mukden had reported the Chinese *Fourth Army* training actively in Manchuria since August. Convinced that Chinese involvement was impending, the Chiefs of Staff recommended that the UN be advised to halt on or close to the 38th Parallel. Despite the concerns of his Chiefs of Staff, Attlee made the decision to stand in solidarity with his American ally and, when the issue was finally debated in the UN during the first week of October, the UK voted to support the operation. The UN General Assembly announced on 7 October that MacArthur had been ordered to undertake the occupation of all of North Korea and to eliminate the NKPA.

Because MacArthur was determined to advance into North Korea in hot pursuit of the enemy remnants (as he thought), he was disinclined to consider any challenge to that aim. So it was that a range of indications that China was indeed planning to intervene in the war if the UN forces crossed the 38th Parallel were ignored, as not suiting MacArthur's views. He airily dismissed any suggestion of Chinese involvement, and his staff, most of whom were in awe of their god-like boss, aped this behaviour. With the dramatic success of Operation *Chromite*, MacArthur was now unchallengeable.

It was only at the end of the first week of October that the UN, under the pressure of a US *fait accompli* in Korea, backed Truman, Marshall and MacArthur, and authorised, by no means unanimously, to advance across the 38th Parallel and to bring the erring sheep back into the fold, after first destroying its army and humiliating its government and people. On 9 October MacArthur's troops crossed the 38th Parallel to occupy the town of Kaesong.

On 8 October Mao Tse Tung ordered his *Fourth Army*, under the command of General Lin Piao, to prepare to cross into North Korea. Mao had been reluctant to commit Chinese lives to the North Korean adventure, but Stalin had, on 29 September, asked him to do a favour for his puppet, Kim Il-sung, who had already pleaded to Mao for help. Mao's greatest concern was that Chinese intervention might cause a wider war: China was simply not ready for a confrontation with the USA, despite the violent political rhetoric he was willing to sling towards the great imperialist gangster in Washington. He preferred an attack on his old enemy, skulking away on Formosa. Stalin proved to be the architect behind the new stage of the war. He assured Mao that the war would not escalate, not in Asia anyway, and that the Soviet Union would provide a wide range of military assistance, including airpower for China to protect his air bases in Manchuria and his hydro-electric plants from US attack. Initially reluctant, Mao acquiesced, agreeing to a deployment to North Korea of nine divisions. Soon this number would increase dramatically, and Mao became more upbeat about the prospects of war.

Now that he had given authorisation to MacArthur to extend the war far beyond its original aims, President Truman arranged to meet his Far Eastern C-in-C, a man whom he had never met before (MacArthur had not returned to the USA for ten years), to determine his policy for bringing the war to a rapid and successful end. So far MacArthur had delivered what the White House wanted: a successful containment of the war and the dramatic recovery of UN military fortunes following North Korea's attack in June. The C-in-C had pulled Truman's irons from the fire, but the truth was that neither Truman nor Bradley, as Chairman of the Joint Chiefs of Staff, had any real control over MacArthur. This wasn't just MacArthur's fault. Big personality though he was, all military leaders require unequivocal terms of reference for the tasks their country requires of them. At no time had Truman made these clear to MacArthur. There were no written instructions, setting out explicitly the White House's objectives for the war. This left MacArthur free to make up his own, and to attempt to influence strategic policy as a result.

Truman's first mistake in meeting MacArthur was to appear a supplicant. He allowed MacArthur to pick the location for the meeting rather than recalling him to Washington. The meeting duly took place at Wake Island in the Pacific on Sunday 15 October. Flying 14,425 miles from Washington, Truman was accompanied by General Omar Bradley, Averell Harriman and Frank Pace, Secretary to the Army. Knowing something of the man he was travelling to meet, Truman wrote to a friend while he was on the plane: 'I've a whale of a job before me. Have to talk to God's right-hand man tomorrow'.* MacArthur had travelled the 4,000 miles from Tokyo with Joe Muccio, US ambassador to the ROK, and Admiral Arthur W. Radford, the USN's C-in-C Pacific Fleet. MacArthur – expansive, optimistic, persuasive, self-assured, in command and clearly enjoying it – greeted the president with a smile and a handshake rather than a salute. MacArthur self-evidently considered himself the equal of the president. MacArthur privately asked Harriman what the meeting was about. Harriman responded that it was to consider how political victory could be achieved in Korea, now that a military victory had been won. 'Good,' responded MacArthur, entirely misunderstanding Harriman's point that victory needed to be defined as a set of limited goals short of total war. 'The president wants my views.' In the discussions that followed MacArthur's optimistic assessments of the

---

*David McCullough, *Truman* (Simon & Schuster, 1992), 801.

situation dominated. There was no question of doubt or equivocation. Truman failed to impress on MacArthur the argument that any war above the 38th Parallel needed to be strictly limited, to avoid fanning the flames of regional instability, and to bring the war to a rapid political settlement. The meeting did the opposite, allowing MacArthur to think that he was in charge. Truman did not present the argument that the war had to be brought to an end. Dean Acheson, the Secretary of State and a strong proponent of halting along the 38th Parallel, had refused to accompany the presidential entourage to Wake Island. He thought that Truman needed to make the policy to end the war himself, and not be swayed by his arrogant plenipotentiary in Tokyo. 'While General MacArthur had many of the attributes of a foreign sovereign,' Acheson wrote, 'and was quite as difficult as any, it did not seem wise to recognise him as one'.* Acheson sent his assistant, Dean Rusk, along instead. He knew that MacArthur would do everything to get his own way, and in the debate between limiting the war and expanding it, Acheson knew exactly where MacArthur stood. He feared, correctly, that Truman would be outplayed.

The war would be over by 24 November – Thanksgiving – and the troops would all be home by Christmas, MacArthur confidently assured the president. The enemy rabble remaining in the South amounted to not many more than 15,000, MacArthur told him, and merely needed rounding up; in the North the number of remaining NKPA troops was perhaps 100,000, but they were clearly beaten. On the elephant in the room – the role of China – MacArthur was equally dismissive. There 'was no fear of Chinese intervention,' he assured his audience. 'The Chinese have 300,000 in Manchuria. Of these, no more than 100,000 to 125,000 are distributed along the Yalu River. They have no air force.' To be fair, the CIA hadn't been paying attention either, for it largely agreed with MacArthur's guesses. On 20 September the CIA concluded that Communist China, like the USSR, would not intervene, although individual North Koreans would enter the fighting, transferring from the Chinese to the NKPA. MacArthur assumed that if the Chinese had the temerity to enter the fray, US airpower – the same B-29s that had flattened Japanese cities

*Dean Acheson, *The Korean War* (W. W. Norton & Co., 1971), 456.

between March and August 1945 – would do likewise to the 'Chinese hordes'. MacArthur's head of intelligence – Major General Charles Willoughby – was an expert in writing reports that reflected the views of his chief. In analysis produced on 14 October, in time for the Wake Island conference, and, incidentally three days *after* Chinese troops of the *13th Army Group* had begun crossing the Yalu, Willoughby dismissed the threatening noise of Chinese intervention as nothing more than 'diplomatic blackmail'. MacArthur could not see that the NKPA were rushing north not to escape, but to be rescued by the Chinese. The cat was well and truly out of the bag. Truman, supinely, congratulated MacArthur for his achievements and, at the edge of the airfield before their respective planes took them home, pinned on his chest the Distinguished Service Medal. It was his fifth. Much as Dean Acheson had foreseen, Truman had been bulldozed. He had accepted MacArthur's military advice without demur or consideration for the consequences if China did commit itself to war. On his return, in a speech in Los Angeles, Truman referred to MacArthur as a man who had written a 'glorious new page' in the history of warfare. 'It is fortunate for the world that we had the right man for the purpose … General Douglas MacArthur.'

It wasn't long before he was bitterly to regret those words. The consequence of failing to understand the military costs of not bringing the war to a close when the opportunity provided soon become apparent. If that wasn't bad enough, MacArthur's plan for the invasion of North Korea was poor. The first mistake – to believe that an invasion of North Korea was the right and appropriate thing to do to bring the war to an end – was Truman's. His advisers, both civilian and military, including Averell Harriman and General of the Army Omar Bradley, were party to this decision. But the second mistake was MacArthur's alone. This was a failure to properly appreciate the military risks involved, and to prepare an effective and successful plan. MacArthur's nameless offensive into North Korea was the very definition of over-reach and was to be smashed on the rocks of hubris.

The problem was that, in crossing the 38th Parallel, MacArthur and his generals assumed that the NKPA was beaten and merely needed corralling into POW pens. He thought that all he needed to do was to occupy North Korea all the way up to the Yalu and undertake some perfunctory cleaning up in the process. After all, behind all his military muscle was the comforting power of the Fifth Air Force. If the Chinese became uppity, he'd bomb them to kingdom come.

MacArthur divided his forces for the pursuit into two parts. Both would operate independently and report directly to him, in Tokyo. There was to be no unified command in Korea because, thought MacArthur, the nature of the operation, and the ground, did not require it. The operation into North Korea was merely a pursuit against the detritus of a defeated enemy. On the left, the Eighth Army under Walker would drive north to Pyongyang, after which it would make for the Yalu in the west of the country. On the right, General Ned Almond's X Corps would be transferred by sea from Inchon to the east coast port of Wonsan, only 100 miles from the North Korean capital of Pyongyang, and would push into the northeast and to occupy the vast mountainous reaches of the country touching the Yalu in the north and Soviet Siberia in the far northeast. The way in which both MacArthur's and Willoughby's hands moved airily, when asked about the size and scale of the remaining NKPA enemy north of the 38th Parallel, perhaps indicated that both men thought that the advance to the Yalu would be akin to a grouse drive on a wide, open moorland. It wouldn't be particularly taxing. The talk was of 'liberating occupied territory', which of course wasn't true. North Korea was a de facto state in its own right. The primary task would be to collect up surrendered enemy personnel and put them into the bag for screening once the war was finally over. After that, MacArthur planned on sending the Eighth Army back to Japan, leaving the X Corps to maintain the peace across Korea, especially to supervise new elections. The ROK Army would be rebuilt and then the Americans would leave.

The plan broke several fundamental military rules. He divided his troops between both sides of the peninsula, decided not to appoint a single theatre commander to command both, and conducted what can only be described as a reckless pursuit to the Yalu. No attempt was made to secure high ground to anchor the advance in case of counterattack. He undertook the offensive in the face on an oncoming winter, the severity of which none of his troops were equipped or prepared for. It was made worse by the fact that MacArthur had never seen the ground over which he was instructing his soldiers to operate. Finally, MacArthur's plans for a pursuit – which required vast stores of fuel and supplies – were simply not matched by the logistics effort available. MacArthur had, against Walker's advice, decided to ship part of X Corps from Inchon to Wonsan, rather than allowing it to advance eastwards by road. This required a diversion of shipping from the task of bringing in the supplies into Inchon required to fuel the pursuit. As a result, the Eighth Army could only advance with one Corps 'up', rather than two. Likewise, the pressure on the logistics 'tail' to Eighth Army's advance was acute. Inchon was not ready to receive supplies by the time the operation was launched; the stock of fuel for tanks was so low that units in the advance could only rely on having fuel for a single day, and ammunition resupply struggled to get to the front. In terms of scale, on one day, 28 October, 1,037 tons of ammunition was carried from Kimpo airfield near Seoul north to Pyongyang. The Eighth Army 'needed 4,000 tons of supplies a day for offensive operations, and this level of supply was not achieved until 20 November.'* Trucks and vehicles of every kind, suffering from a general pre-war lack of maintenance, were smashed to bits on the poor Korean roads and failed at alarming rates. But for MacArthur and Walker, these logistical concerns were, though irritating, largely an irrelevance because, in their view, the war was all but over. These mistakes are only understandable in terms of MacArthur's core assumption: that this was a cattle round-up, not a fight. This mistake – a product of hubris – lay at the heart of the disaster that followed. If crossing the 38th Parallel was a *political* miscalculation – condemning Korea to two more years of bloodshed for no additional gain or purpose – the plan for the pursuit was a military miscalculation of the greatest magnitude, for whom the entire blame was MacArthur's.

An additional problem with all of this is that by the time MacArthur and Truman met at Wake Island, the nature of the UN intervention had changed out of all recognition from the original purpose, which was a military response to right a wrong on the basis of the principle of collective defence. By mid-October, with the NKPA thrown out of South Korea, the aim looked a bit more like US and ROK vengeance against the renegade country which was responsible for the original attack. Later, with the arrival of the Chinese, the war changed once more into one that appeared to be a straightforward fight between the

---

* Julian Thompson, *The Lifeblood of War: Logistics in Armed Conflict* (Brassey's, 1991), 120.

USA and China. If MacArthur had had his way, it would have been transformed even further into a total war – utilising all weapons at the USA's disposal – between America and all the forces of international communism, including the USSR. He undoubtedly had vociferous support from some political quarters in the USA for this idea, not least those which coalesced around anti-communist attack dog Senator Joe McCarthy. The second war for Korea was already exhibiting such characteristics. The danger for both the USA and the UN was that international support for the war would fade away.

The drive north of Seoul, undertaken in the period before MacArthur met Truman on Wake Island, in fact entailed a mix of hard fighting and turkey shoot or, rather, round-up. Brigadier Coad's 27th Brigade, joined now by the 3rd Battalion, Royal Australian Regiment – 3 RAR, sent from occupation duties in Japan – and dubbed by Coad the 27th Commonwealth Brigade, was flown forward from Taegu to Kimpo airfield by the USAF in preparation for the drive north. Milburn's I Corps was to drive to Pyongyang and thence to the Yalu. To its right II ROK Corps would advance north, in parallel with the US I Corps.

Pyongyang was occupied in a brilliant three-pronged attack by Brigadier General Paik's 1st ROK Division, accompanied by 50 Patton tanks, driving the defenders from their extensive defences in front of the city on 19 October. Plenty of NKPA troops had fight left in them and put up stiff resistance in places, although others were now simply surrendering to the thundering onslaught of the advancing Eighth Army. The chaos of the advance had its comedic moments. Captain John Shipster recalled the advance to Pyongyang to be 'one long traffic jam', as three divisions competed with each other to be the first to enter the city 'in noisy, dusty nose-to-tail columns. The flurry of competition caused an extraordinary situation in which friend and foe were alike elbowed aside by impatient formations. At one period it was even necessary to block the road with one of our anti-tank guns to allow us to take our designated place in the order of march.'* When the Argylls,

---

*Shipster, *Mist Over the Rice Fields*, 125.

accompanied by American Sherman tanks, reached the garrison town of Sariwon on 17 October, they quickly fought their way into the town, only to find it in confusion. Large numbers of North Koreans continued to move into the town from all directions, unaware of the presence of enemy troops. One of the consequences of the rapid collapse of the NKPA was a widespread failure of its command and control. Such was the confusion engendered by the brigade's rapid move into the town that some even thought the Argylls – wearing the British Army's distinctive 'cap comforter' on their heads – were Soviets, and greeted them with cries of 'Russki, Russki!' Large numbers of captives were taken as a result of the confusion. Now in the vanguard of the Eighth Army advance, the brigade passed through the North Korean capital on 21 October with instructions to keep heading northeast for the Yalu, 105 miles distant. On the same day, MacArthur visited Pyongyang, landing at the airport with Lieutenant General George Stratemeyer, confidently telling the troops that 'half of the remaining 300,000 North Korean troops – 150,000 men – would fall victim to the massive double envelopment, pounded on one flank by the US 187th Airborne Regiment and the ROK 1st Division and hit on the flank by the US 1st Cavalry Division. The war will soon be over.' Such was the poverty of MacArthur's intelligence and the extent of his hubris that he was unaware that as he spoke at least 120,000 of General Peng Te-Huai's Chinese troops of the *First Army* were already in North Korea, lying hidden in the Jongyuryong mountains. A month later this number would rise to 180,000, with a further 120,000 in the area centred on the Changjin reservoir. How was it that no one in FECOM had an idea of what was happening on the 'other side of the hill'? Perhaps the simple answer was that they didn't want to know. A massive Chinese infiltration into these mountains was so outside FECOM's expectation that even asking the question would have been regarded not merely as disloyalty to MacArthur, but a lack of faith in the prospect of ultimate victory. In response to his authorisation from the UN, MacArthur's initial plan was to clear all the way to the Yalu, but then to subsequently create what he shamelessly called the 'MacArthur Line', running from Chonju across the roof of the country to Hamhung on the east coast. He later moved this line further north, to run from Sunch'on to Sungjin.

Within days the 27th Commonwealth Brigade met up with the 4,000 men of the 187th Airborne Regimental Combat Team who had jumped into two drop zones some 30 miles north of Pyongyang, at Sukch'on and Sunch'on in an operation to cut the roads leading to the Yalu. It would also encircle large numbers of enemy troops thought to be withdrawing north and release many POWs. Fierce fighting took place along the road as the Commonwealth Brigade pressed north against the town of Yongy, valiantly held by the American paratroopers. North Korean troops put up a considerable fight. But the troops drove on, brushing aside resistance. They reached the Ch'ongch'on River on 24 October. That night they felt the foretaste of winter: a bitter wind blew down on them from the north. Lacking blankets or warm clothing, the troops felt the chill as the thermometer dropped below freezing for the first time. Crossing the river in small boats, the advance continued. As it did so, enemy opposition increased as the border area came closer, NKPA units attacking with T-34s, SU-76 guns and mortars. The town of Chongju was captured by the Australians of 3 RAR in a march of 31 miles over hilly terrain in 12 hours. The young commanding officer, 30-year-old Lieutenant Colonel Charles Green, was killed by artillery fire. The 27th Commonwealth Brigade had in two weeks travelled 160 miles, leading the Eighth Army's advance to within 40 miles of the Yalu River and the border with Chinese Manchuria. In an ominous sign that the shape of the battlefield was soon to turn, one of the prisoners brought to Brigadier Coad during the fighting was a Chinese, rather than North Korean, soldier. Paik and his men had been worried about an intervention by the Chinese communists since the start of the offensive across the 38th Parallel but on his own admission were so focused 'on winning total, unreserved victory that we put the Chinese out of our minds.'[*]

The offensive continued. On the I Corps front, on the western side of North Korea, the plan was for the US 24th Division to advance towards Uiju and the 27th Commonwealth Brigade to attack through Chongju and make for Sinuiju. Once these had been reached, the ROK 7th Division would pass through both formations and reach the Yalu. *Time* magazine reported in its edition of 6 November, 'ROK officers whose divisions were racing through northwest Korea jubilantly reported to

---

[*]Paik, *From Pusan to Panmunjom*, 84.

Eighth Army headquarters: "We will not stop until we bathe our sabres in the Yalu River."'

To the right in north-central Korea, the ROK II Corps was advancing to the right of Milburn's Corps. But as Paik's division advanced on Unsan, they noticed a distinct change in the human topography of the battlefield. No one was about. Previously, the roads had been clogged with disarmed NKPA soldiers attempting to get home. Now, the roads were quiet, the hills silent and the towns empty. Something was up, which would be revealed on 25 October 1950, when the advancing units of Paik's division were struck by a massive ambush in the Unsan valley, beyond the town. Mortar fire, anti-tank and artillery enveloped the troops advancing along the roads. The UN advance had not been undertaken in secret, or tactically. This was a race to the Yalu to demonstrate victory, nothing else. The publicity surrounding it was designed to frighten the remaining North Koreans – and the Chinese – into acceptance of a UN and US *fait accompli* in North Korea. This was, in effect, MacArthur's victory parade. Yet it was not to be. In the face of such a devastating wall of fire, burning tanks and trucks, Paik ordered an immediate withdrawal to Unsan, where the division created a defensive position, an action that saved the division from annihilation. An enemy soldier was captured. Again, he was Chinese, from Kwantung province. After rigorous questioning, it was obvious to Paik and Milburn that the Chinese were in the hills. They reported the same to Willoughby and MacArthur but were dismissed with the suggestion that the captured soldier was undoubtedly a Korean who had been a resident of China and who had volunteered to fight for his homeland. This was despite the fact that he was equipped and dressed as a soldier in the People's Liberation Army and admitted quite freely to being so. It is hard to open a mind that its owner has resolutely closed.

Far to the west, Almond's X Corps was moving north into a remote and mountainous terrain served by few roads. The further north the corps moved the more difficult the advance became. The Taebaek mountains run north–south, across which no east-west roads run until the Yalu itself is reached. The further north the troops marched, the fewer the roads and the tougher the terrain. For an army dependent on roads for its lines of communication, this was clearly a problem if the enemy was prepared to fight.

180

The planning assumption in Tokyo was that the *In Mun Gun* in these vast reaches was a spent force, and risks could be taken. And so they were. There was certainly a degree of Yalu-fever among Almond and his staff: it was as if reaching the border with Chinese Manchuria would demonstrate their martial virility, after which everyone could go home to enjoy Christmas with one's family. The port of Hungnam was occupied during the last week of October, and the advance had begun to seize the city of Hamhung and then to move through the mountains on which lay the great Changjin reservoir.* One hundred miles still further up the coast, the ROK Capital Division went ashore at Songjiang and also marched for the Yalu. The Eighth Army and X Corps were in no way able to provide each other with mutual support, given that some 50 miles separated the right of Walker's army and the left flank of Almond's corps. The terrain was mountainous, the roads nothing more than narrow gravel tracks, and winter was approaching, fast.

And the hills were full of the men of the Chinese *Fourth Army*. General Peng Te-Huai, given ultimate responsibility for the offensive, and his subordinate commanders were vastly experienced field commanders who had helped the Chinese Communist Party win the war in 1949. Professional soldiers, they had been at war all of their lives. They knew how to manage large peasant armies, equip, feed and train them, manage feats of prodigious physical endeavour and persuade them to fight with great strength and ferocious violence. They would be underestimated only by fools. Secretly they had infiltrated perhaps as many as 300,000 men across the Yalu in a matter of weeks, hiding them in the mountains in the vast hostile reaches of the country, hidden from the eyes of the Fifth Air Force, which found not a scrap of evidence of their presence.† Bridges across the Yalu and other rivers were built under the surface of the water; movement was conducted only at night, without lights, and during the day the remarkably disciplined Chinese *First Army* lay quiet in bivouacs that were hidden

---

*The lake's proper name is the Changjin reservoir, but, during Japan's annexation of Korea (1910–45), its name had been changed to Chosin, the Japanese name for Korea.
†The *13th Army Group* faced the Eighth Army, and the *9th Army Group* faced Almond's X Corps. The *13th Army Group* contained about 150,000 men in 18 Chinese Army divisions under six armies.

in forests and hilltops far from roads, without any revealing smoke from fires or movement that might give the game away. Sturdy, fit and disciplined, the soldiers walked hundreds of miles, marching 30 miles at night alone, to get into position.

The Unsan ambush against Paik's 1st ROK Division was coordinated with others across the Eighth Army front. To the east of Unsan the 3rd Battalion, 8th Cavalry Regiment, caught on the road, was ambushed and a block placed on its rear. Swarms of Chinese troops overran the surprised and entirely unprepared battalion: over 600 men were lost. Further to the right, the II ROK Corps – 6th, 7th and 8th Divisions – came under heavy attack, as was the 1st Marine Division moving into the hills towards the Koto-ri plateau on the X Corps front. Along the Ch'ongch'on River the Chinese smashed seven ROK and US regiments, suffering 8,000 casualties.

Yet, just as suddenly as the attacks began, the Chinese disappeared. The reason was simple. The UN advance was moving more rapidly than General Peng Te-Huai could get his men into North Korea, so he ordered what he described as a short, sharp 'First Phase Offensive' to bloody the enemy and slow down their rate of advance. Running between 25 October and 6 November, it worked. It also sowed surprise – discombobulation even – and up to 24 November resulted in 27,827 American casualties, over one-third of whom were killed or missing in action. It seems remarkable that the UN forces even had to ask who this enemy was. They interrogated the 100 or so prisoners they captured, wanting to believe that they were somehow North Koreans who had served in the Chinese Army and had now returned to fight for the NKPA, rather than actual members of the People's Liberation Army. FECOM's purposeful blindness during this period was profound, and disastrous. On the other hand, the Chinese rapidly formed a clear view about their enemy and waited to strike again.

On the ground in North Korea, Walton Walker immediately ordered his advance to halt. An experienced campaigner, he knew at once that his army was too widely separated to offer itself mutual support and could be picked off in detail. He realised that the drive to the Yalu must stop, especially if, as it appeared, a large force of Chinese was in the hills around him. The 24th Division and the ROK 7th Division were ordered to return to the Ch'ongch'on as part of a so-called 'tactical withdrawal' and he moved the 2nd Division up to the Ch'ongch'on. In the strange period of silence that followed the lifting of the Chinese attacks, the UN forces attempted to make sense of what had just happened. Was it merely a warning not to proceed any further?

As October ended and the early days of November ticked by, it became clear that Chinese troops were definitely in North Korea, despite FECOM's fervent wish that they weren't and public denials that the issue was serious. But there was now no denying it. Nevertheless, Willoughby resolutely refused to accept that there were any more than between 40,000 and 70,000 troops in the hills. Most likely, he argued, they were there to help the NKPA recover itself, or to protect the Yalu from attack by the UN. Any suggestion that a vast Chinese army might be in the hills awaiting the moment to counterattack was dismissed as alarmist. It was easy to deny that large numbers of Chinese were in North Korea by the simple expedient of calling the enemy 'Red'. As *Time* magazine reported on 13 November 1950, 'General MacArthur's headquarters estimated that the Reds were using twelve divisions and five independent brigades in North Korea. Some of these were probably remnants of North Korean forces defeated farther south, and others might be "ghost units," i.e., North Koreans held in reserve since the beginning of the war and never before met by UN forces.' This view gained traction during November, as the days grew shorter and the temperatures plummeted. How would an army survive in those mountains, anyway? This wishful view was widely held in Washington, too.

Meanwhile, on the eastern side of the peninsula Major General Ned Almond's X Corps, safely landed at the port of Wonsan, began to make its way north to the Yalu. The 1st Marine Division, however, undertook its progress into the increasingly cold and inhospitable mountains from Hungnam to Yudam-ni with caution, Major General Oliver Smith proceeding at a pace which allowed his division to remain concentrated, much to Almond's irritation. Almond demanded pace; Smith, unsure of the purpose of a race to the Yalu, wanted to protect his division from the possibility of counterattack when strung out in unfamiliar mountains, in winter, reliant on a single, poor, line of communication. Smith viewed the snowy mountains nervously: winter had arrived and would only get much, much worse, so he concentrated on building a strong base at Hagaru-ri which could form a strong anchor for subsequent operations if required. He was determined to do this first, before advancing further north. There was a vast gap between his left flank and the right flank of the Eighth Army, through which ran high mountains with few if any lateral routes for communication. He looked with concern at the Chinese First Phase Offensive against Eighth Army in the west, fearing for his own division should the Chinese fall on it from the north. The US 7th Division and the ROK Capital Division were meanwhile north and northeast of the Changjin reservoir (despite instructions from the Joint Chiefs to MacArthur not to use US troops in the march to the Yalu – Washington wanted the occupation of North Korea to be seen as an event undertaken by South Korean rather than American troops – an instruction he simply ignored), and the US 3rd Division remained at Wonsan. Smith improved his base at Hagaru-ri, including building an airstrip that would take C-47s. With the arrival of a fierce winter, 4,000 feet above sea level, it was the calm professionalism and soldierly preparations of Smith's division that enabled its survival. Smith, nervous about Almond's impetuous race to the Yalu, couldn't help worrying that advancing so high into these mountains, behind which trailed a single very poor track, was a trap. Nevertheless, two of his regimental combat teams, the 5th and the 7th, had been pushed 12 miles further into the mountains to Yudam-ni.

In London and other capitals in the UN alliance, MacArthur's belligerence was increasingly unsettling. The rush to the Yalu was quite clearly an unnecessary provocation to China, thought Britain, which had recognised the new government in Peking, rather than, as Attlee described in his memoirs, 'support[ing] the discredited Government of Marshal Chiang Kai-Shek.'* Driven by political realities rather than by ideology, Britain was desperate both to protect Hong Kong and to

---

*The USA did not recognise the People's Republic of China until 1979.

develop trade, to enable it to pay some of its eye-watering wartime debts to the USA. It was also anxious not to provoke a global war with communism, something Attlee averred in his memoirs was what some on the Republican right in the USA were keen to do. 'There was considerable support in America for an extension of the war,' he wrote. He almost certainly had MacArthur in mind, but others, too. 'Some people were anxious for a show-down with Russia.' Likewise, he and his Cabinet – and the Chiefs of Staff – were concerned that MacArthur appeared to wield far more power in political decision-making than was good for democracy. His hero status in both Japan and the USA wasn't helpful for him or the government, as it made him difficult to challenge. Although MacArthur assured Truman at Wake Island that he was not interested in running for political office, Attlee thought that Truman treated him with kid gloves precisely because he had prominent Republican views and was therefore politically dangerous. Whether this was correct or not, Attlee reflected on the 'curious relationship between Government and a General' that could result in MacArthur not being recalled 'back to America for discussions with the Administration'. The fact of the matter was that Truman was not in control of the relationship with his proconsul in Japan; MacArthur was. The British view was that under no circumstances should the Korean War be elevated to that of a conflict between the West and communism. That is precisely what an adventure across the 38th Parallel was likely to do and was fraught with danger not merely for the region but the whole world.

On 7 November Field Marshal William Slim, worried that the UN forces were currently overextended and unable to resist a Chinese counteroffensive, suggested that the UN forces withdraw to a line across the peninsula, and that the Chinese be invited in to North Korea in order to create their own *cordon sanitaire*. If MacArthur ever heard of this proposal he would have scoffed at it as the suggestion of a defeatist. As events were to prove, it was instead the suggestion of a pragmatist. But Britain had very little say in matters of which it was a very junior partner, perhaps an insignificant one. Marshal of the Royal Air Force Sir John Slessor described the British role in Korea as 'to tag along behind the United States with no previous consultation over policy and sometimes no advance notice of actions or decisions'. A Foreign Office paper concurred, complaining that 'British ministers and officials were continually being faced with *faits accomplis* and expected to fall in.'* Fascinatingly, voices in the USA were also making the same suggestion as the British CIGS. That month James 'Scotty' Reston in the *New York Times* suggested that Chinese intervention might have been forestalled had the UN, when Pyongyang had been captured, offered to establish a peace commission to 'take over a buffer zone on the Korean side of the Chinese frontier'.

In any case, the time for talking was drawing to a close. Meanwhile, MacArthur was talking about hot pursuit of North Korean aircraft into Manchuria, using US airpower to attack Chinese airfields, an issue of some acuteness following the arrival over the battlefield of Soviet-supplied and Soviet-piloted MiG-15s on 1 November (the pilots wearing North Korean uniforms). This had the effect of halting bombardment group activities for a week, until the arrival in theatre, from the USA, of a wing of the new F-86 Sabre fighters. The first bomber flight after the arrival of the Sabres was one supposedly to deny the Chinese a hiding place in the cities along the Yalu. This was an attack by 79 B-29s on the city of Sinuiju and its bridges on 7 November, flattening most of it in the process. The aircraft dropped 790 tons of high explosive on a defenceless city, so as to deny its habitation to the enemy. What about its 60,000 inhabitants? Guilty or innocent, civilians had long lost a say in the bombing of their homes from the air. Here in Korea was seen the first example of the area bombing policy, developed by General Curtis LeMay in Japan in March 1945, being transferred lock, stock and barrel to a North Korean city five years later. There was no consideration in the bombing decision made for the innocent civilians who would have to die as a consequence (though Stratemeyer bizarrely suggested that strenuous efforts had been made to avoid hitting any hospitals: area bombing had been adopted in March 1945 by the USAAF[†] precisely because precision bombing had proven impossible). Timing was important. In the months before the Chinese intervention, requests to bomb Sinuiju had been denied. MacArthur noted in his first report to the United Nations in September that: 'The problem of avoiding the killing of innocent civilians and damages to the civilian economy

---

*Sir Pierson Dixon, *Korea: Britain and the Korean War, 1950–51* (Foreign and Commonwealth Office Library and Records Department, Historical Branch; second edition, revised 1995), 9.
†The USAAF became the USAF in 1947.

is continually present and given my personal attention.' With the massive Chinese involvement in the war, such considerations were now ignored. The justification now was military utility. The city succoured the enemy; ergo, it could and should be destroyed, as it played a role in his war effort. This was total war, again. It was, of course, a preposterous argument, a 1950s example of Guernica, given policy legitimacy by the systematic firebombing of Japanese cities in 1945. The next logical step to dropping high explosive was to drop a few atomic weapons. What was the difference?

This captured MacArthur's view, of course. The enemy were the enemy, and no distinction in modern warfare could be made between those fighting at the front and those supporting them in the rear. And what was the difference between conventional explosive and atomic weapons? More people died in the firebombing of Tokyo, advocates of atomic bombs would argue, than were killed in either Hiroshima or Nagasaki. The difference was one didn't require all the effort of conventional weapons – hundreds of bombers, thousands of aircrew – to do what one bomber and its crew could achieve. Perhaps this was the message that MacArthur was attempting to send to China by bombing Sinuiju: that the USA had the power to unleash hell on anyone who opposed it. The problem here was that the towns and cities being bombed were in North Korea, not China, and had no impact on Chinese policy or its preparations for war. The B-29 attacks continued during the following weeks, destroying bridges over the Yalu and flattening every town north of the Ch'ongch'on River, protected now by USAF Sabre fighters. By undertaking a precipitate advance to the Yalu, and by undertaking its bombing campaign, America was increasingly alienating its allies but, weak as they were in terms of manpower on the ground in Korea, the allies could do little to influence the military decisions made in Tokyo and Washington. The Sinuiju attack almost certainly had the opposite effect on the North Koreans and Chinese, hardening their resolve to oppose what they considered to be the arbitrary brutality of US firepower.

———

By the third week of November Walker's Eighth Army had consolidated along the Ch'ongch'on, and two of Major General Oliver Smith's Marine regiments were close to the Changjin reservoir. The men of Eighth Army and X Corps had become more cautious. As *Time* magazine reported on 13 November:

> UN troops had abandoned the easy optimism of previous weeks. UN pilots who had long had the air almost to themselves were meeting increasing numbers of Yak fighters. Last week they had their first brushes with enemy jets coming from north of the Yalu – Soviet MiG-15s with swept-back wings and a speed of 600 miles an hour. Ground troops faced enemy units heavily equipped with tanks, automatic weapons, 76mm howitzers and multiple rocket launchers like the Russian 'Katushas' of World War II. The men who handled the weapons displayed skill and high morale. Said one GI last week: 'Those guys who hit us last night are the best we've run up against in Korea.'

Nevertheless, there was no suggestion of halting. Supplies continued to be landed in Pyongyang, although ammunition for the forward troops was estimated at only a day's firing, and fuel was limited. By now the 29th Brigade had reached Korea and had travelled north from Pusan with its new Centurion tanks. It was ordered into Eighth Army reserve. Walker's Eighth Army spread across 80 miles of tangled mountains divided by the Ch'ongch'on River, flowing westwards into the Yellow Sea. Milburn's I Corps was on the left, IX Corps in the centre and the ROK II Corps held the right. There was no link between the right flank of Eighth Army and the left flank of Almond's X Corps on the other side of the Taebaek mountains. But there seemed to be no further threat from the forces that had attacked them exactly a month before, so MacArthur ordered a renewed offensive to the Yalu. Men of the US 7th Division had reached the Yalu on 23 November, and Almond had used it as a photo opportunity. This demonstrated that it could and had to be done; winter was settling in and his forces could then provide a protective barrier along the border with Chinese Manchuria during the winter. It would also denote 'mission accomplished' and the opportunity to bring the boys home. In any case, if things got sticky, he still had the Fifth Air Force with which to bomb Manchuria.

On 23 November the men of the Eighth Army and X Corps ate their Thanksgiving meals. A day later, MacArthur's communiqué read:

The United Nations massive compression envelopment in North Korea against the new Red Armies operating there is now approaching its decisive effort. The isolating component of the pincer, our Air Forces of all types, have for the past three weeks, in a sustained attack of model coordination and effectiveness, successfully interdicted enemy lines of support from the North so that further reinforcement therefrom has been sharply curtailed and essential supplies markedly limited.

Words. None of them true, as General Peng Te-Huai well knew, but General MacArthur did not.

7

Cataclysm

The Chinese offensive that had slammed into Major General Keiser's 2nd Infantry Division – the Second Phase Offensive, described in the prologue to Part 2 – was part of a broad-based assault by the Chinese *First Army* to turn back and destroy MacArthur's ill-considered race to the Yalu. If it could, it would drive the 'Wall Street imperialists' back into the sea, finishing the job that the *In Mun Gun* had failed to do in September. The evidence had been mounting for some weeks that regular Chinese soldiers were fighting in North Korea but, as Paik averred, because none of these had been so far directed against US troops, the Americans ignored the warning signs. He thought that this was because Americans found it difficult to tell Koreans and Chinese apart, so they overlooked what was quite literally staring them in the face. Perhaps a more reasoned explanation for this blindness was that the presence in North Korea of a massive Chinese Army did not fit MacArthur's, Walker's or Almond's narrative about how the war was expected to end. The Eighth Army and X Corps, as MacArthur was repeatedly assuring anyone prepared to listen, was simply finishing off the task it had started at Inchon. It was tying up loose ends. There was a tendency not to listen to evidence that suggested anything was amiss with the plan. The Eighth Army was therefore rushing towards the Yalu, Paik observed, as though 'competing in a hundred yard dash'. The danger of this form of martial exuberance was two-fold. First, the Chinese Army had been consistently underestimated. Second, the US forces – with the exception of the 1st Marine Division – were not yet

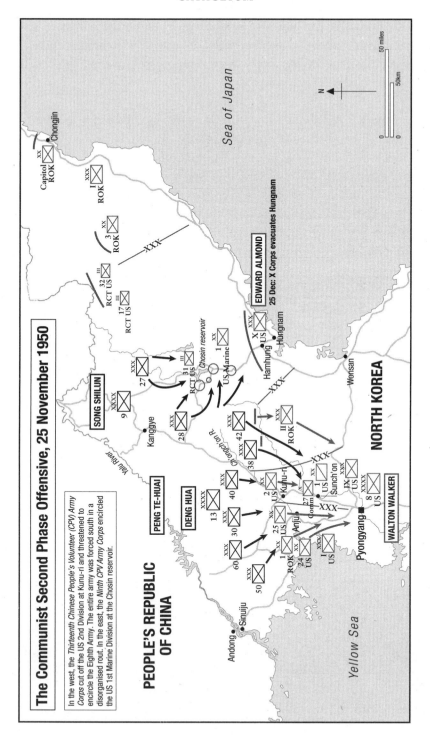

The Communist Second Phase Offensive, 25 November 1950

In the west, the *Thirteenth Chinese People's Volunteer (CPV) Army Corps* cut off the US 2nd Division at Kunu-ri and threatened to encircle the Eighth Army. The entire army was forced south in a disorganised rout. In the east, the *Ninth CPV Army Corps* encircled the US 1st Marine Division at the Chosin reservoir.

PEOPLE'S REPUBLIC
OF CHINA

PENG TE-HUAI

DENG HUA

SONG SHILUN

NORTH KOREA

Sea of Japan

Yellow Sea

EDWARD ALMOND
25 Dec: X Corps evacuates Hungnam

WALTON WALKER

Yalu River

Ch'ongch'on R.

Chosin reservoir

Andong
Sinuiju
Kanggye
Chongjin
Hamhung
Hungnam
Wonsan
Pyongyang
Anju
Kunu-ri
Sunch'on
Gomm

good enough at the basics of soldiering, let alone the complexities of what was effectively mountain warfare, against a tenacious enemy in the middle of an unforgiving winter. A report by General Peng Te-Huai observed of the Americans that:

> ... the US Army relies for its main power in combat on the shock effect of coordinated armour and artillery ... and their air-to-ground attack capability is exceptional. But their infantry is weak. Their men are afraid to die, and will neither press home a bold attack nor defend to the death... Their habit is to be active only during daylight hours. They are very weak at attacking or approaching an enemy at night... If their source of supply is cut, their fighting spirit suffers, and if you interdict their rear, they withdraw on their own.

In the West, the collapse in morale across the Eighth Army front as a result of the massive Chinese Second Phase Offensive was profound; much of the withdrawal that followed was conducted in conditions of what can only be described, for many units, as near panic. Troops who had been consistently told that they would be home for Christmas found themselves caught up in a confusing maelstrom of combat against a new and dangerous foe in which America's traditional strengths – copious amounts of air and artillery firepower – didn't seem to have much effect. Defeat and retreat are both so humiliating and disheartening that it can lead to a cycle of despair from which it is hard to recover. Rumours swirled everywhere. Some, such as 'the USA was abandoning Korea and retiring to Japan', were more debilitating than others, especially to South Korean soldiers. When one day he asked Lieutenant General Milburn about this rumour, Paik was assured that it was nonsense, and had his ear chewed off for even asking. Neither Milburn nor Paik knew that the crisis caused by the Chinese offensive had in fact forced both the United States and United Kingdom governments to consider evacuating Korea altogether. That it didn't come to this was because the Chinese offensive was itself an enormous undertaking with its own risks and miscalculations, combined with the terrible ferocity of a winter that was one of the worst in living memory. In that terrible period between late 1950 and early 1951 the UN forces in Korea were not merely fighting General Peng Te-Huai, but General Winter, too. The winter provided some of the most horrendous fighting conditions ever seen by American or British troops, made worse by the fact that in 1950, at least, they were entirely unprepared for the intense cold sweeping in from the north. Major David Wilson of the Argylls, a veteran of Kohima, was shocked at the fierceness of the cold. It was nothing like anything he had ever experienced. By the first week of November, he noted in his memoirs, 'the padi fields were frozen and there was a white rime on the roads and foliage. For those of us in 27 Brigade without proper winter clothing it was getting bloody cold. In those days the British Army's idea of a sleeping bag was two ordinary blankets fastened together with a bit of tape to tie yourself (and your shivering) in!'* Captain John Shipster recalled the 'cruelty of the Siberian winds' and was horrified one day when his lips froze momentarily to his mess tin, despite it being full of hot tea.[†]

On the right flank of the Eighth Army the headquarters of II ROK Corps dissolved, its division smashed and survivors forced to make for the south as best they could. Only Paik's 1st ROK Division retained its cohesion. On 3 December a decision was made to withdraw the Eighth Army to a line approximating the 38th Parallel, there to consolidate and draw breath. As the 1st ROK Division began its withdrawal to Pyongyang, through which it passed on 5 December, the city was already on fire as vast stocks of recently arrived stores and materiel, perhaps 10,000 tons' worth – including tanks, trucks and ammunition – were consigned to the flames. The sight of the army burning its own base in expectation of imminent capture by the enemy was profoundly disturbing to those who saw it. Bridges that had recently been rebuilt were being demolished again. There didn't seem to be any rhyme or reason to the great 'bug out', as it was being called. It wasn't a disciplined fighting withdrawal to a new defensive line. Instead, it seemed for many to be a hell-for-leather race to get as far south as possible. Some were even lying about the nearness of the enemy advance in order to get away. This was the view of the 27th Commonwealth Brigade. Its War Diary complained 'that so much ground was to be given up without a fight and at a time when there was no contact with the enemy'. The writer of the War Diary surmised a reason, or at least part of the reason

*David Wilson, *The Sum of Things* (Spellmount, 2001), 174.
†Shipster, *Mist Over the Rice Fields*, 127.

for the withdrawal: 'It is the opinion that certain units are giving false information in order to extract from commanders and staffs permission or even orders for premature and quite unjustifiable withdrawal. It was just this type of excitable dishonesty which caused some unnecessary and expensive withdrawals in France in 1940.' It was interesting language, the spectre of there being a Korean Dunkirk perhaps haunting the British contingent, determined to do what they could to prevent it.

Likewise, huge numbers of terrified civilians were on the move, crowding the few roads in their haste to flee, crossing frozen rivers, hundreds – perhaps thousands – dying from exposure, as the harsh winter blasts swept down from Siberia, encasing Korea in a frozen whiteness. This mass exodus of refugees from the North was mute testament, thought observers, of their terror of having to live once more under Kim Il-sung's repressive regime. Accordingly, they were now voting with their feet, in their tens of thousands. It made it even more difficult for the retreating Eighth Army, competing for space on the clogged roads with the frightened white-clad masses.

The only advantage for the retreating troops was that the 'big bug out' wasn't harried to the extent it could have been by the pursuing Chinese, advancing through the mountains on foot. Paik quipped bitterly that this was all down to 'the speed of our withdrawal'.

Major General Oliver Smith's caution in the east around the 30-mile-long Changjin reservoir was vindicated when, on 27 November, 100,000 Chinese swept from the north to cut the road between Hagaru-ri and Koto-ri, ten miles to the south. Hagaru-ri, on the southern edge of the Changjin reservoir, came under heavy attack on 28 November, as did a regiment of the 7th Infantry Division hunkered down on the northeastern shore of the reservoir. The following day it was the turn of the two RCTs at Yudam-ni – the 5th and the 7th – to be attacked and cut off. Heavy fighting took place across the mountains in conditions of extreme cold, the troops unable to dig trenches in the rock and ice. A bizarre event took place on 28 November, at the height of a fierce battle around the Changjin reservoir, that highlights something of the parallel universe inhabited by the corps commander, Major General Ned Almond. He dropped in on a unit of the 7th Infantry Division,

surrounded and fighting for its life, in his personal helicopter. In front
of Lieutenant Colonel Don Carlos Faith, commanding officer of 1st
Battalion, 32nd Infantry, he pulled out an envelope. 'Don,' he said to
Faith. 'I have three Silver Stars to give away. Choose two men to get
them with you.' Two astonished men – a wounded lieutenant who had
just happened to be in Faith's command post at that moment, and the
astonished headquarters mess sergeant, who'd also been passing the
command post – were ordered to stand to attention and receive
the United States' third highest military decoration for valour in
combat. Almond slapped Faith on the shoulder and said: 'Don't worry
Don. You're only fighting Chinese remnants fleeing north.' Nothing,
not even the truth about the enemy, was to be allowed to intrude
into the fantasy narrative about MacArthur's glorious crusade to the
Yalu. Watching the general's helicopter depart into the snow flurries
of a darkening, angry sky, the dumbstruck lieutenant colonel took
off the medal and threw it to the ground. With that sort of cognitive
dissonance by the corps commander, obviously believing a lie in the
face of overwhelming evidence to the contrary, what hope could there
be for the poor bloody infantry trying to make sense of the war – and
the presence of overwhelming numbers of Chinese soldiers in remote
North Korea – either? Almond was a commander with a well-known
reckless streak. He was also determined to follow his commander in
everything: thought, word and deed.* It's a *sine qua non* of successful
armies that those undertaking the fighting need to understand and
believe in the cause for which they are fighting and for which they
might be asked to sacrifice their lives. They also need to believe in the
professional competence of their leaders, their ability to understand the
battle and to construct and execute plans to defeat the enemy. In those
surreal moments on the northeastern shore of the infamous Changjin
reservoir, Almond demonstrated that he was not that man. Over the
following four days, the entire 32nd Infantry was smashed to pieces
in below-freezing conditions by large numbers of well-equipped and
motivated Chinese troops, these supposed 'remnants fleeing north'.
Lieutenant Colonel Faith was killed in the fighting, attempting to rally
his frozen men to escape an enemy envelopment and withdraw the

*Clay Blair, *The Forgotten War: America in Korea 1950–1953* (Doubleday, 1987).

survivors to Hagaru-ri. Only a handful of men – 200 from over 1,000 – made it out alive.

On 1 December, in order to conform with events in the west where Eighth Army was retreating in some turmoil, Smith was ordered to extract his division across the mountains from Hagaru-ri to meet up at Hamhung with the US 3rd Division, which would move up from Wonsan in support of the withdrawal. The fighting was severe in the appalling freezing weather, but the 1st Marine Division undertook a successful fighting withdrawal, carrying its wounded, beginning on 6 December, to Hamhung and thence to Hungnam. The reasons for the success of the staged withdrawal by the 1st Marine Division, as opposed to the unstructured flight of the Eighth Army in the west of the country, can be put down to several factors:

- First, the division determined not to withdraw exclusively down the main supply route – MSR – but across the mountains, fighting for the ridges, moving cross-country and attacking enemy columns in their flanks. This was unexpected, and proved very successful;
- Second, despite the cloud cover and freezing conditions, the withdrawing regimental combat teams were blessed with accurate and timely support from carrier-launched fighters at sea. Where roads had to be employed these aircraft, dropping bombs and napalm, cleared the way of roadblocks;
- Third, the Chinese, equally exhausted by the conditions in which they too were attempting both to fight and survive, could not actively follow up their victory at the Changjin reservoir.

It is clear that the superior leadership, training and morale of the 1st Marine Division was instrumental in enabling it to escape from the trap on the Changjin reservoir. The entirety of X Corps was now evacuated, along with scores of thousands of frightened civilians, from Wonsan to Pusan, by ship. By 15 December the remnants of the 7th Infantry Division, followed by the 1st Marine Division and the ROK I Corps, had been taken off – some 105,000 troops. In all, 193 ships transported the troops as well as 98,000 Korean civilians, 17,500 vehicles and 350,000 tons of stores to Pusan. In accordance with the policy of scorched earth, Hungnam and Wonsan were destroyed to keep them out of the hands of the Chinese, for a time at least. The Yalu adventure, in the east at least, was over.

Thoroughly frightened by this unexpected turn of events but equally not in control of the situation on the ground, on 28 November MacArthur told Washington that the Eighth Army was so hard pressed it could not be expected to hold its positions. Arguing without any sense of irony that Chinese intervention in North Korea was a criminal act, he demanded permission to bomb China with B-29s, and to institute a naval blockade of the country. For a while panic infused his messages home. 'We face an entirely new war,' he declared at the end of November. 'This command has done everything humanly possible within its capabilities but is now faced with conditions beyond its control and strength.' A lack of self-perception prevented him from recognising that the influx of Chinese was a direct result of his own rush to the Yalu. That morning was probably the moment when reality dawned on Truman. A shocked president told his personal staff in the White House: 'General Bradley called me at 6.15 this morning. He told me a terrible message had come from General MacArthur... The Chinese have come in with both feet.' He later wrote that this was the day 'when the bad news from Korea had changed from rumours of resistance into certainty of defeat.'

On 3 December MacArthur told the Joint Chiefs of Staff that the situation in Korea was 'increasingly critical' and demanded new 'political decisions and strategic plans ... adequate fully to meet the realities involved.' *Time* magazine, in its 18 December 1950 issue, sided, at least in inclination, with MacArthur. 'The policy of containment was dead,' it shrilled, gleefully announcing the failure of this pillar of Truman's foreign policy. 'There remained only the policy of retaliation and positive action by the US and its allies to damage Communist power at the sources from which aggression flowed,' it declared. Truman, finally demonstrating that he had balls in respect of his relationship with the vainglorious head in Tokyo – a man who was allowed to live as if he were a resurrected Roman proconsul, rebuilding Japanese society in his, and America's, image – refused the request and in so doing correctly denied the essence of *Time* magazine's argument. It simply wasn't true that the USA was suddenly under attack by the forces of international communism, engineered by Moscow and Peking. The advance by the Eighth Army and X Corps to the Yalu had unravelled, but this had been caused by MacArthur's failure to understand the nature of the political and military environment he was wading into, not a sudden determination by the East to go to war with the West.

For his part Truman, too, believed that the West was fighting a global communist conspiracy. He said so in a White House Press Conference on 30 November. Unfortunately, he also gave the impression that the USA had not ruled out the use of nuclear weapons to ensure it did not lose this fight. He told the press that the USA would use 'every weapon at its disposal'. Did that include atomic weapons? Truman repeated his point: 'every weapon…' The press didn't let up. 'Does that mean active consideration of the use of the atomic bomb?' Truman replied that there had always been active consideration of its use. In fact, the possibility of using nuclear weapons had been considered by the Joint Chiefs of Staff in July. The USAF had proposed launching B-29 raids against North Korean cities, though MacArthur's preference was to drop atomic bombs not on cities but on core transport infrastructure such as bridges and tunnels. No decision was made, though ten nuclear-capable B-29s were sent to Guam in case they were needed to respond to a Chinese attack on Formosa. On this occasion, however, it was both the right and the wrong answer. The next question allowed Truman to dig a bigger hole. 'Does that mean, Mr President, that atomic weapons would be used against military or civilian targets?' 'The selection of objectives or targets was a military decision,' Truman rather ineptly replied. In vain Truman and his staff struggled in the following days to emphasise that although it was theoretically true that the USA would never rule out the use of nuclear weapons, in the case of Korea the decision was one for the UN to make, but only if the president had first given authorisation. In any case, Truman was opposed to expanding the war by atomic bombs or any other means.

The task facing MacArthur was perhaps beyond him: in the face of cataclysm in the Philippines in 1942, he had staunchly demonstrated a resolve to return. Now, eight years later, he demonstrated an emotional fragility dangerous in high command. In a series of anxious telegrams from Tokyo to Washington, MacArthur asserted that the new circumstances faced in Korea entailed nothing less than an attempt by China to reunite Korea under communism, not merely a localised war with North Korea and its allies. But when permission to use the USAF B-29 bombardment groups to attack Manchuria was refused, MacArthur angrily attacked the strategy of limited war. It was absurd to suggest that the USA be asked to fight with one hand behind its back in the face of an onslaught such as it faced in Korea. He now believed that the best solution was that the USA should withdraw from Korea and leave the country to the communists. He even ordered plans to evacuate UN forces to Okinawa, mainland Japan and the Philippines, MacArthur working up a story that blamed the defeat not on his own hubris but on Truman's refusal to allow him to widen the war and to fight the commies with handcuffs off.* He blamed some of the Chinese gains on the constraints imposed on him by Washington, by limiting air and sea operations to South Korea. He even started falling out with the Joint Chiefs of Staff, who had long been reluctant to confront him directly. To concerns about the continuing divided command in Korea, MacArthur said that Eighth Army and X Corps would continue to report to him, with X Corps holding a presence in the northeast of the country. He was already out of touch with the fast-unravelling reality of the security situation. The Joint Chiefs, accepting that a withdrawal was required, suggested establishing a new defensive line across the waist of Korea, between Pyongyang and Wonsan. This made enormous sense. Although large numbers of Chinese troops were on the offensive, they were doing so on foot. The Eighth Army had the wherewithal, if well-led, to reposition itself, defend the gains it had made, and not undertake precipitate flight. But this is to assume that the troops in Korea had the moral wherewithal to stand firm. In any case MacArthur believed that the line proposed was too far north, and a withdrawal further south was necessary. The conversations at MacArthur's headquarters in Tokyo on 4 December demonstrated just how despairing FECOM had become. Walker was in favour of a 'deep retirement' far beyond Seoul, giving up all the ground won at Inchon in September and subsequently.

*Victor Davis Hanson, *Savior Generals* (Bloomsbury, 2013), 148.

Almond believed he should be allowed to stand at Hungnam indefinitely, but the decision was made to undertake a series of withdrawals towards Pusan. It looked very much like game over. Extraordinarily, MacArthur gave instructions to rebuild the defence lines on the Naktong River and instructed X Corps to withdraw in its entirety by means of a seaborne evacuation from Wonsan to Pusan. There were no conversations about fighting back, about undertaking a phased withdrawal in which the enemy advance was degraded successively through the winter, or about counterattacking the various Chinese thrusts. It was as if FECOM had simply given up and, in the new circumstances of Chinese involvement in the war, decided to limit UN losses.

In ten days, the Eighth Army bugged out, helter-skelter, a total of 120 miles, without putting up any fighting resistance to the slow-marching Chinese. On 5 December Pyongyang was evacuated and Walker ordered troops to move south of the 38th Parallel. At Pyongyang the newly arrived British 29th Infantry Brigade and the Centurion tanks of the 8th King's Royal Irish Hussars, arriving on 2 December into Eighth Army reserve, held the bridges over the Taedong River, seeing first-hand the exhausted men of both I US Corps and the IX ROK Corps trudge wearily southwards. They raised a special cheer for the three battalions of the 27th Commonwealth Brigade as they marched across the bridges in good order, the Britons still wearing their Hong Kong-issued uniforms. When these rearguards had departed, the engineers of the 29th Infantry Brigade blew the demolitions on the remaining bridges. The Taedong position, an ideal defensive position, was abandoned without a fight and the army withdrew in some disorder to the Imjin River, and the 38th Parallel. Here, the Eighth Army prepared to meet the advancing *13th Army Group*, which was falling on the west and centre of the line. The US I Corps (US 25th Division; ROK 1st Division, and the newly arrived Turkish Brigade) defended along the Imjin River; the US IX Corps north of Uijongbu (US 2nd Division and ROK 6th Division, with 27th Commonwealth Brigade in reserve) and the ROK I Corps (3rd and Capital Divisions) abutted the Sea of Japan on the extreme right of the line. Through the angry cold of the winter the Eighth Army dug in along the new line.

The cold was terrible. Entirely ill-prepared for the early arrival of the bitter weather, the men of the 27th Commonwealth Brigade were still in the temperate uniforms they had been wearing when they had left Hong Kong. It came as something of a shock to realise that the British Army had no arctic warfare expertise, clothing or equipment. It had no idea what clothes and equipment were required to live, operate and fight in this most unforgiving of environments. When the Siberian winds had first come whistling down on the shivering troops on 14 November, the temperature dropped overnight to minus 20 degrees centigrade. What had been rushing streams and rivers now froze solid; ice covered the roads and paddy fields. When it snowed great drifts would accumulate on tracks and roads, making travel hazardous. Water poured from a bottle froze into a long icicle before it even hit the ground. Water poured into a cold vehicle radiator froze immediately and would need a fire underneath it to bring it back to life. The oil in engines and for lubricating weapons also froze. On British Army oil-fired field cookers, it took one and a half hours to boil a kettle. Weapons, vehicles, rifles, razor blades all froze. Hands and fingers that were uncovered stuck to metal; blood froze, and simply staying alive became a matter of strict discipline. Fighting the Chinese was one thing; trying to fight and survive in this unforgiving climate was another matter entirely.

It was during this period that Lieutenant General Walton Walker, the tough fighting 'bulldog' who had held the Pusan perimeter together at the moment of its greatest danger, was killed in a head-on collision between his fast-travelling jeep and an ROK supply truck. There is some evidence that MacArthur was in the process of removing him from the command of the Eighth Army as the result of the bug-out fever that had gripped his army following the Chinese First Phase Offensive. None of that mattered now. Lieutenant General Matthew B. Ridgway, another experienced Second World War commander, serving as deputy Chief of Staff for operations at the Pentagon, was flown in to take his place. Whereas Walker had been a well-known figure across the command by virtue of his gruff, no-nonsense manners (Rhee called him 'ill-mannered'), his signature feature a helmet pushed back on the top of his head, Ridgway was a paratrooper, the famous commander of the 82nd Airborne Division that had played such a significant role in Operation *Overlord* in Normandy in June 1944. He was immediately identifiable by the pineapple-shaped hand grenade taped to one of his webbing straps and the First Field Dressing taped to the other. He always denied that this was for effect, but whatever the motive, it reflected Ridgway's persona as above all a fighting soldier. None of his soldiers missed the importance of this visual message. His nickname became 'Old iron tits'. He was happy to embrace it. Tragic though it was, Walker's death saved UN prospects in Korea, because it meant that Ridgway could be elevated to command the Eighth Army (and soon, X Corps) and pull the US's irons from the Korean fire. He was perhaps one of the only men in the US Army at the time who could do so. Ridgway's appointment followed shortly after Truman declared a national state of emergency, enabling him to authorise the call-up of reservists and the conscription of civilians for military training. This, only a few short weeks after the jubilation of Inchon, demonstrated just how quickly the fortunes of war had changed. At the same time, Mao Tse Tung took command of the NKPA. He was not merely helping a neighbour, however, but was responding, he said, to direct aggression by US transgression of Chinese airspace.

The briefing Ridgway received from MacArthur in Tokyo on Christmas Day 1950 suggested that any illusions the C-in-C might have previously held about the nature of his enemy had now gone. The Chinese were effective soldiers, he told Ridgway, and constituted 'a dangerous foe'. They used the hills, mountains and night to great effect, bypassing their road-bound enemy and striking at vulnerable locations when they were least expected. It was important that South Korea be held from as far forward as possible. Especially important was holding on to Seoul, for reasons of politics at home and civilian and military morale in South Korea. No mention was made of the importance of fighting communism as an existential enemy of the USA, or of occupying North Korea, or of reuniting the two halves of the peninsula. A new realism had appeared, or perhaps the pendulum had simply swung away from its early position of exuberant optimism. When Ridgway asked whether he had the Supreme Commander's backing for offensive action, MacArthur replied, '... the Eighth Army is yours, Matt. Do what you think is best.' Ridgway in fact was extremely well-briefed on the subject of Korea before he arrived in Tokyo. In his previous Pentagon role, he had made several journeys to Korea and had briefed the Joint Chiefs of Staff and President Truman on aspects of

the war.* He was also aware of, and had rejected, MacArthur's view that
the only way to win the war was to escalate the conflict. A few days later
MacArthur quietly allowed Ridgway to take command of both Eighth
Army and X Corps, his previous strident reasons for keeping the two
formations separate apparently no longer important. He had previously
insisted that the two formations – Eighth Army on the left and X Corps
on the right – be kept separate, the respective commanders reporting
directly to him. He now didn't seem to think that it mattered, and
Ridgeway didn't press him as to the rationale for his previous decision.
It was as though MacArthur was no longer interested in how to fight
and win the battle in Korea: that problem had now been handed to
Ridgway to solve. Perhaps it's not too much to suggest that MacArthur
believed that Korea was a lost cause, and that any blame for the loss of
the war could be pinned on the new theatre commander. Ridgway was
confident, however, that he could fight his way to success, and he set
out to do precisely this. He had at least three immediate tasks:

1 To halt the Chinese offensive without allowing for the collapse
   or defeat of UN forces;
2 To rebuild the morale and fighting spirit of UN forces;
3 To secure the best possible basis for a political negotiation to
   end the war.

The two Chinese offensives that had countered MacArthur's rush to
the Yalu were now paused, to allow the Chinese to follow up on their
retreating enemy and to prepare for their Third Offensive, which hit
with devastating effect, across the UN defensive line, on 31 December
1950. This line had been established in the west along the Imjin
River, with a backstop along the Han River. As many as 420,000
Chinese and North Korean troops were involved. The British 29th
Infantry Brigade came alongside Paik's 1st ROK Division on New
Year's Day, just as a sea of Chinese infantry washed across the front.
The Chinese had identified a weak spot east of Yulpo, which served

*Schnabel, *Policy and Direction*, 306.

as the boundary between Paik's division and the ROK 6th Division. Whereas the *In Mun Gun* had attacked with bugles, this time the Chinese, Paik noted, did so silently. Their assault units crept up to the UN line undetected, before pouring waves of infantry at the frozen UN positions. The ROK II Corps on the east of the Eighth Army flank gave way almost immediately. It had been severely shaken during the battles around Pyongyang a month earlier. Morale, already low before the onslaught, now collapsed. Ridgway noted in his memoirs that on taking command his first, overwhelming impression was that officers and men – US and ROK – 'were deficient in vigor, bravery, and fighting spirit.' Leaders at every level were unresponsive, surly and spiritless. 'The men I met along the road, those I stopped to talk to and to solicit gripes from – they too all conveyed to me a conviction that this was a bewildered army, not sure of itself or its leaders, not sure what they were doing there, wondering when they would hear the whistle of that home-bound transport.' Ridgway's first assessment was that the Eighth Army believed it had been defeated, though this attitude was psychological rather than physical. Defeatist attitudes prevailed across all ranks. Corps and division commanders and their staffs had little control over the battle, as they were too far from the front. Intelligence about the enemy was shockingly poor. Gaps between units allowed for extensive infiltration, and there was no offensive spirit or counteroffensive plans. Paik was to bitterly agree about the performance of his own men, soldiers of the most impressive ROK formation so far in the war. The Chinese offensive came as such a shock it psychologically shook the troops. Officers and men had begun to believe their own wishful thinking: that the NKPA had been destroyed, that the Chinese would not get involved, that the war had been won, that the present operation was nothing more than sweeping away the detritus of the enemy and, most importantly, that they'd all be home by Christmas. Ridgway immediately sited his headquarters alongside Milburn's I Corps near Seoul – up from Taegu, way back in the Pusan area – in order to demonstrate that commanders needed to lead from the front. He probably also did it to keep an eye on Milburn, a man who was an old friend but who he believed to be a mediocre tactician. Ridgway's new broom involved sweeping away corps and divisional commanders who simply weren't up to scratch on the demanding Korean battlefield. Many were in post as sinecures, as a gift for long and faithful service. Most had undoubtedly believed that they never needed to see action again, now that the Second World War was behind them and soldiering could revert to being a pleasant game.

On the night of New Year's Eve well-prepared Chinese assault troops rushed through great gaps in the ROK line over the frozen Imjin, which they had thoroughly reconnoitred. Paik recalled that he fell into the slough of despond, such was his shock – and shame – that the enemy had broken through his seasoned and hitherto accomplished formation. After all, his was the one ROK division that had held firm through the Pusan battles and that had distinguished itself in the pursuit north after the breakout. By the end of the second day of the offensive Paik found himself at the base of Pukhan Mountain, a stone's throw from Seoul. The attack had been so overwhelming that every ROK division had been pushed back, some with severe losses. Every Eighth Army unit was caught up in the fighting. Confusion reigned. No one seemed to know what to do with Brigadier Coad's 27th Commonwealth Brigade. It was finally tasked with joining IX Corps (Major General Breitling Coulter) as corps reserve at Uijongbu. On arrival Coad was shocked to hear open conversations at the corps HQ about pulling UN forces out of Korea entirely. 'Bug-out' fever had seemingly become contagious. A meeting with Ridgway, however, on 28 December provided Coad with assurance that the new Eighth Army commander was prepared to fight and was building a plan to do so.

Orders from IX Corps to fall back from the Imjin to the Han River initiated a chaotic and uncontrolled evacuation to the south, an out-of-control headlong rush to safety that so shocked Coad that he commented that 'this complete lack of control by higher headquarters was a feature of the American command.' One British veteran of the retreat from Burma in 1942 observed that in 1951 British troops witnessing this debacle were 'puzzled and ashamed of being involved in such a business: there were many Dunkirk veterans among them, as well as men who had been at Tobruk and Crete, Singapore and in the 1942 retreat out of Burma. But no one had ever experienced an operation like the recent withdrawal... The reservists had fought and beaten Germans and Japanese and were unconvinced that the Chinese were all that good.' But United States Army 'morale was at its lowest ebb: the retreat ... the gruesome winter, and the newly created myth of the invincibility of the Chinese combined to produce a disastrous mental attitude."* Ridgway clearly had his work cut out if this was to change. Meanwhile, the 29th Infantry Brigade, in its first exposure to fighting in Korea, found itself facing two entire Chinese armies to its front, north of Seoul, in defensive positions it had been preparing for a retiring ROK division which never arrived. The 29th occupied the position instead, fighting off all attempts by the *Thirty-Ninth* and *Fiftieth Armies* to surround and obliterate it. Early on 3 January the Chinese attacked, attempting to swamp the forward British positions. But the brigade stood firm, counterattacking with hastily created 'battle patrols' mounted in tracked weapons carriers and bringing down heavy artillery and 4.2-inch mortar concentrations on the attackers. Orders to disengage and withdraw south over the Han River that night – 4 January 1951 – were accompanied by ferocious attacks from the Chinese. It was at this time that the word 'horde' entered the lexicon of soldiers serving in Korea, as it accurately depicted the vast numbers of aggressive and fast-moving men the enemy threw at UN defensive positions. At Chunghung Dong, nicknamed 'Happy Valley' by the troops, the 29th Infantry Brigade held off the Chinese in vicious combat in which large numbers of attackers were killed – by Vickers machine guns, mortars, artillery and disciplined rifle fire – in unintelligent frontal attacks; it was in the orders to withdraw that most British casualties were caused. Not for nothing are withdrawals in combat the most difficult exercise of war. Although the Chinese offensive was rebuffed, one battalion of the brigade – the Ulster Rifles – suffered 208 casualties during the withdrawal, including ten tanks.

The refugee floodgates had opened again, and the thousands of men, women and children who had thought they were now safe in Seoul were evacuating again, further south. Great crowds of terrified humanity, many impoverished and hungry, crossed the frozen river on foot, carrying pathetic bundles of clothing and bedding with them.

Seoul fell, for the second time, on 4 January. Ridgway ordered a new line to be established south of the Han River. He quickly rescinded this order, instructing the Eighth Army to fall back even further. By the middle of January, a firm defensive line was established running

*Tim Carew, *The Korean War: The Story of the Fighting Commonwealth Regiments 1950–1953* (Pan Books, 1970), 167.

due east from Pyeongtaek to the east coast, 40 miles south of the 38th Parallel. Those, such as Paik, who had fought through the first dreadful campaign in June and July 1950, experienced this retreat as depressing déjà vu.

The biggest task Ridgway and his corps and divisional commanders had was to restore the broken morale of their armies, both US and ROK. But MacArthur and many parts of the Washington commentariat were themselves guilty of rampant defeatism. MacArthur's behaviour was driven by the embarrassment of being shown to be entirely wrong about Chinese motives and intentions, as well as constructing a poor offensive plan for his race to the Yalu that made Eighth Army and X Corps vulnerable to counterattack. With the failure of both, he was now prepared to throw Korea to the dogs. MacArthur wasn't the only one to be thoroughly fed up with the war. The commentariat in Washington was panicked about the see-saw nature of the war in Korea and about the seeming lack of certainly about a UN victory. They would support the war – and the continuing expenditure of American dollars and American blood – only if they saw a clear road to victory. Popular opinion, notoriously fickle when it comes to victory and defeat in wartime, likewise had lost heart. In opinion polls conducted in November 1950 and January 1951, a majority of Americans questioned declared they wanted the war to end. Half said it had been wrong to enter the war, and a majority (56 per cent) wanted nuclear bombs to be dropped on the communists to bring the war to a victorious end if truce talks failed.

While the military situation was bad, the US still retained considerable power in the region, which could be directed towards the war effort if only a decent plan to defeat the enemy offensive could be pulled together. The situation was redeemable, as Ridgway was shortly to demonstrate. In war, reverses need to be anticipated, and managed. The UN were saved in the bitter winter of early 1951 by several factors. First, the appointment of Ridgway turned out to be brilliant, as he, unlike MacArthur or Walker, as well as being a fine tactician also had a *strategic* brain. He knew that he could trade territory for time. He could drag the Chinese deep into Korea where it would be difficult for them to sustain large numbers of troops in the face of heavy US air interdiction against their extended lines of communication back to Manchuria. Ground was not important; defeating the enemy was, and American firepower could do this in time, especially with the enemy strung out over vast distances, which would make it hard to feed and sustain their advancing army. Ridgway's time in command of Eighth Army demonstrates convincingly the power wielded by the personal leadership of a charismatic, competent commander. It has been observed that:

> Successful generalship is concerned with inspiring soldiers to fight what might otherwise be unwinnable battles. It is about inspiration as well as perspiration, visible leadership as well as strategic sense, and above all it is about personal courage. It is what a general means to his soldiers that matters in the end, not the rhetoric, not the planning, nor the hangers-on, but the man. Soldiers will follow leaders whom they believe have their interests at heart, rather than their own self-advancement or glory.

This was Ridgway in a nutshell. Likewise:

> … it is not enough simply to be a good leader under fire, and to be a model of valour. As Socrates identified, generals must also be able to plan, and they must be able to understand and contribute to the strategic as well as the battlefield aspects of warfare. Effective command requires *strategic sense*. Higher commanders need to understand the broader picture and wider context in which their own military operations take place, and thus to structure, plan and mount operations that meet the requirements of this wider strategy. They may not themselves be involved in the construction of grand strategy, but it is paramount that they understand why these decisions are made so that they can make battlefield decisions intelligently.*

It was in this that the essential difference between MacArthur and Ridgway can be discerned.

Accordingly, Ridgway prepared the Eighth Army to withdraw as far back as Pyeongtaek – a place not remembered fondly by the men of the 24th Division – in order to stretch out the Chinese advance

*Robert Lyman, *The Generals* (Constable, 2008), 340–41.

while consolidating his own forces, repairing and resupplying his military capability through Pusan. In this his strategy was akin to then-Lieutenant General Bill Slim's drawing the Japanese 15th Army into Manipur in March 1944, there to destroy it when it was extended and vulnerable, counterattacking where and when the enemy was weakest. It worked. The Chinese Third Offensive was halted on 10 January 1951. Captured enemy soldiers spoke openly of exhaustion, starvation and frostbite. Their tactics of mass attack had caused devastating losses of men in their units. In April and May alone, General Peng Te-Huai lost 160,000 men. This level of attrition in an army in which people was its primary resource was unsustainable in the long term. It was a strategy for a quick war, not a sensible plan for a long one.

Second, unlike MacArthur, Ridgway did not allow his ego to interfere with the realities of what was required to be successful on the battlefield. A brilliant combat soldier, he knew how soldiers ticked, whether they were ROK, Turkish, British, American or any other nationality in the UN army of which he was C-in-C. He knew that soldiers needed to be fed before they could march, trained before they could fight, and led by officers whom they trusted. He understood that to recover from profound defeat, morale had to be rebuilt carefully and comprehensively. He met with Major General Paik on the day before the Chinese attack, interrogating him on his division, how it would fight and whether the enemy could cross the frozen Imjin. Paik later recalled:

Ridgway's greatest contribution to the war was helping his army overcome its loser psychology … he would appraise a unit's morale simply by jumping in a jeep and threading his way through the unit, watching to see whether the men saluted him. He would ask ordinary soldiers he encountered during these forays very detailed questions, hoping to uncover problems that had not come to his attention. Ridgway would ask the men whether they were receiving all the gloves and socks they needed, or whether they were getting hot meals, or even whether they had paper on which to write letters home.

He did this the moment he landed in Korea, jumping into an open jeep and for three days visiting as many troops of all nationalities as he could.

'I held to the old-fashioned idea that it helped the spirits of the men to see the Old Man up there in the snow and sleet,' he recalled, 'sharing the same cold miserable existence they had to endure.' There were limits, however. Until a kind-hearted major dug up a pile-lined cap and thick gloves for him, he 'damn near froze'. The theatre had a purpose, and it was effective. All soldiers, from PFC to general, were instructed in blunt, uncompromising language ('often impolite,' admitted Ridgway) that the role of the army was to fight, even if withdrawing. They were to get off the roads, control the high ground to deny it to the enemy, whatever the weather. When they halted, all ranks were to dig in and dig deep, creating positions with all-round defence capable of repelling enemy attacks by day and night. Too many men had been lost to poor defensive discipline, inadequate leadership and insufficient adherence to some of the basic principles of successful soldiering. This slackness had to stop or men would die unnecessarily. He had the old combat soldier's understanding that success in a fight was the only surefire way of raising men's morale. He, and his army, needed to engineer lots of small, local successes against their Chinese foe to defeat any myth of enemy invincibility and reboot the morale of an army conditioned to defeat, even in the face of seemingly overwhelming local superiority.

In his memoirs Ridgway recalled an incident during his first week in command.* Passing a unit of the 27th Commonwealth Brigade, at the time part of the Eighth Army reserve outside Pyongyang, a young British subaltern 'trotted down off a knoll to greet me when he spotted the insignia on my jeep. He saluted smartly and identified himself.' Ridgway knew that the British brigade had only a few men to cover a wide front, and that a Chinese attack was expected hourly. He asked the subaltern how he found the situation: 'Quite all right sir,' he replied quickly. Then he added with a pleasant smile, 'It is a bit draughty up here.' Quite, thought Ridgway, given that the snow was swirling thickly through the mountains and carpeting the country in a blanket of deep, frozen whiteness. 'Draughty was the word for it, with gaps in the line wide enough to march an army through.' But there remained the problem of how he could explain quickly and simply to

*Ridgway makes it clear that his comments related to the Eighth Army, not the 1st Marine Division of X Corps, which had joined Eighth Army on his assumption of command.

a British, American, or Turkish recruit for that matter, among recruits from many other nations, the reason why he was being asked to give up his life in Korea. In a masterpiece of logic, he sat down to draft a simple document that would explain this to his men. The final version, entitled 'Why we are here: What are we fighting for?', covered many different areas – legal, moral, political – but also appealed to the sense that they were fighting to withstand the assaults of the communist hordes on the borders of democratic civilisation and freedom.

The moment news of the Chinese Third Offensive came through, Ridgway rushed to the front at Uijongbu, seeing at first hand the rout of the US 25th and the ROK 6th Divisions. It was a salutary experience for any commander, especially one suddenly thrown into the maelstrom of a war with commanders whom he had only just met. One thing was apparent above all else: the virus of defeat had swept through the ranks of the Eighth Army. Ridgway immediately went to President Rhee and urged him to do more to inspire his soldiers to fight. He then accompanied Rhee to meet every one of the ROK divisions on the central front. He didn't just have an issue with South Korean commanders. He determined that many US commanders were not up to the job and would have to go. They weren't aggressive enough, sought safety and retreat rather than offensive action and, when they did withdraw, they didn't do it fighting, but running. Ridgway realised that his two corps commanders (Milburn and Coulter) and many of his divisional commanders had forgotten, in the panic of defeat and withdrawal, the essential principle that the best means of defence is attack. He was particularly appalled by the atmosphere in the Eighth Army's central command post in Daegu. The talk was about withdrawing from Korea entirely to avoid a potential Dunkirk. Ridgway visited I Corps and asked the senior operations officer, the G-3 – Colonel John A. Dabney – to brief him on its battle plans. Dabney responded by describing a series of withdrawals to 'successive positions'. 'But what are your attack plans?' Ridgway replied. Dabney hesitated. 'Sir – we are withdrawing.' Dabney was relieved of his position. It was a bit of theatre, and Dabney was the fall guy, but the message that there was a new broom in town, determined not to be driven by the enemy's agenda, went across

Eighth Army like wildfire, as it had been intended. In the months that followed he secured the removal of underperforming officers, with the agreement of General J. Lawton Collins, Army Chief of Staff, through the mechanism of a 'rotation' policy in which officers were quietly removed and placed on ships and flights bound for home postings. In one case, that of Major General Breitling Coulter of IX Corps, he managed it by means of upwards promotion. Coulter became his deputy, with responsibility for liaising with the ROK Army. Ridgway had determined that he had none of the offensive spirit he needed in his corps commanders. Ridgway's transformation of the morale of the Eighth Army in Korea, using robust measures, enabled it to turn defeat into victory in 1951.

Also, the Chinese over-reached themselves. Throwing their troops into operations based on mass human wave assaults in the middle of winter asked for massive levels of attrition from the cold, as well as from US firepower, despite the limitations that the bad weather placed on the use of airpower. Mao's determination to overwhelm UN forces and expedite their evacuation from Korea resulted in enormous casualties for the Chinese, especially in experienced and irreplaceable veterans. Ridgway realised this and built his plans for withdrawal on the creation of defensive positions that would not crumble when assaulted or surrounded by enemy attack and infiltration. Troops needed to relearn the basics of positional defence, something in which the US Army was inexperienced, while at the same time not removing their offensive spirit. The key was to degrade the Chinese offensive capability as vast numbers flooded south, using strong defensive positions as pivots of manoeuvre, while huge amounts of artillery and air-launched munitions accompanied resolute and determined infantry, dug in behind mines and wire. They could then counterattack when the attackers were themselves exhausted, stretched out and weak. To ensure that morale wouldn't collapse when positions were surrounded, he ordered that no units cut off were to be abandoned. To help blunt the next impending assault, he instructed Brigadier General Garrison H. Davidson to create a defensive line in depth, using thousands of South Korean labourers, south of the Han River. A wider problem, Ridgway realised, was that the US Army was not culturally inclined to understand how to create defences in depth: they hadn't had to understand or develop this aspect of warfare during the last war. Ridgway needed to teach his army how to create defensive positions that could absorb, degrade and ultimately repel large formations of enemy troops advancing in multiple thrusts. All the high ground would be dominated by friendly defences, to deny them to the enemy, the roads and bridges in the valleys below mined, and routes ambushed. The idea was that defensive positions would cause such casualties that the enemy would be forced to rethink their own tactics of mass assault. When the enemy attacked, their advance needed to be degraded by mines, wire and most importantly by artillery and airpower. When they attacked at night their approaches would be lit up by special artillery illumination rounds, and every attack was to be followed up by a counterattack by tanks, infantry, artillery and airpower. The aim was not merely to stop the quilt-jacketed 'hordes' but to make the casualties incurred so devastating they would become unacceptable even to Mao Tse Tung, a man who was, even at this stage, recognised to be unconcerned about committing scores of thousands of countrymen to the slaughter. With all the resonance of General Eric von Falkenhayn's 'bleeding the enemy white' at Verdun in 1917, this would become the UN's strategy to force China to the negotiating table.

As he had hoped, Ridgway's first counterattack found great gaps in the enemy advance. On 15 January Colonel John Michaelis' 'Wolfhounds' (27th Regiment, 25th Division) – upgraded to a regimental combat team by the addition of a tank battalion, three artillery battalions, combat engineer and close air support – swept through little opposition as far as Suwon, beyond that first infamous battlefield at Osan by Task Force Smith. In extraordinary scenes, Chinese troops were seen to run away from Michaelis' reconnaissance in force. On 22 January the US IX Corps advanced north and secured Yongin and Inchon against little opposition. It was clear that the enemy advance had run out of steam and was in disarray. Ridgway now mounted a full-scale offensive to recover territory all the way back to the Han River. Operation *Thunderbolt* was a dramatic success. Ridgway's plan was to undertake a methodical advance to the river, thus restoring the confidence of his army as the result of deliberate, purposeful action in which the troops could see the effect of battle-planning, discipline and massive firepower on the enemy. Ridgway's approach to battle was to advance while simultaneously building resilience into his army so that it could absorb any future Chinese attempt at counterattack. It was slow, but the manoeuvre worked. Units moved forward in phases, with plentiful artillery fire, coordinating their advance so that exhausted Chinese units were fixed in their positions by artillery, cut off by infantry and then assaulted by tanks and infantry. Fighter ground attack had been finely honed by early 1951, allowing infantry units to be sure of receiving support – such as 1,000-pound bombs or napalm – delivered from piston-driven or jet-powered aircraft within an hour of asking for it. Given the large number of Chinese killed during *Thunderbolt*, the men came to call it 'the meat grinder'. The journalist and writer René Cutforth of the BBC was astonished by the result on the morale of troops he had come to dismiss as irrecoverable. 'Exactly how and why the new army was transformed … from a mob of dispirited boobs … to a tough resilient force is still a matter for speculation and debate', he wrote.* Ridgway wasn't surprised: it had been what he had planned. The I US Corps (US 3rd and 25th Divisions and Paik's ROK 1st Division) reached the Han River on 10 February.

The Chinese counterattacked X Corps on 11 February, the Chinese believing they could achieve more in the mountains of the central area. They also knew that whereas in the west they faced the tank and artillery might of I US Corps, in the east they faced three ROK divisions equipped only with light weapons. A massive counteroffensive of four Chinese divisions and the refitted NKPA II and V Corps in what was the Chinese Fourth Phase offensive destroyed the ROK 8th Division at Hoengsong and severely damaged the ROK 3rd and 5th Divisions. The 8th Division lost 7,500 men; the 3rd and 5th 3,000 respectively. It was a devastating blow to the recovering morale and effectiveness of the ROK Army. The Chinese Army now drove inexorably to isolate the US 23rd Infantry Regiment, with an attached French battalion, at Chipyong-ni.

The five-day battle of Chipyong-ni has gone into the legend of war as a Custer's last stand, but one in which Custer and his men not only survived but triumphed. A more apposite equivalent is with the battle of the Admin Box in northern Arakan (Burma) in February 1944, when the 7th Indian Division was surrounded by a large Japanese force but,

---

*René Cutforth, *Korean Reporter* (Allan Wingate, 1952), 142.

unwilling to consider itself cut off, pulled itself into a series of self-contained defensive boxes, fought back and systematically destroyed the attackers. At Chipyong-ni the 23rd Infantry Regiment hunkered down in a circular defensive position and threw back every ferocious attack made upon it, repulsing the entire Chinese force. The regimental commander had first wished to retire, a move supported by Major General Almond. But Ridgway refused. He ordered the unit to stay and fight. It was a close-run thing, but the men did fight, and the advancing Chinese exhausted themselves against the defences, as Ridgway had hoped they would.

Colonel Paul Freeman's 23rd Infantry Regiment was supported by the 37th Field Artillery Battalion and a battery of the heavy 155mm guns from the 503rd Artillery Battalion. Having received Ridgway's order, Freeman told his three battalion commanders, two American and one French: 'We're going to stay here and fight it out.' They dug in as best they could in the frozen ground. The Chinese vanguard, having dispersed the remnants of the ROK at Hoengsong on 11 February, smashed into the waiting Americans and French two days later, expecting perhaps a similarly easy victory. They were to be disappointed. As each Chinese frontal assault thrust against the waiting defenders, their enemy proved immovable. Four separate attacks that first night were thrown back in the snowy darkness by bayonets and grenades. Dawn the following day was accompanied by devastatingly accurate rocket and napalm attacks on the Chinese forming up points from the air, while during the day cargo planes flew over 20 sorties to drop ammunition supplies to the isolated companies. The second night saw a repeat of the first, with mass assaults by Chinese infantry carrying pole and satchel charges to drop into the defender's trenches. The battle was fought from trench to trench, rapid counterattacks by American and French infantry ensuring the Chinese failed to gain any substantial footholds. The attacks that second night, however, weren't conducted in maniacal rushes, but rather by a stealthy creeping forward across the snow, followed by silent infiltration into the American and French positions. The American artillery fired repeatedly on their own positions to repel the interlopers, which comprised as many as 60,000 men. Gradually George Company (of the 2nd Battalion), which had borne the brunt of the Chinese assaults, gave way. Fierce counterattacks launched by the depleted battalion resulted in considerable American casualties, but as a result of their aggression the Chinese were unable to seize all of the George Company hill. By a whisker the position was saved. Throughout 15 February American artillery, tanks and air struck hard against the positions the Chinese did hold, and as a result of their prodigious efforts, the Chinese were now exhausted and had advanced far beyond their ammunition resupply. Late that day the Chinese attackers vanished into the countryside. In front of the George Company positions lay hundreds of dead Chinese. Although they weren't to know it then, the fourth Chinese offensive had been stopped. The defenders were relieved by tanks of the US 5th Cavalry. It was, arguably, the first tactical defeat experienced by the Chinese in 1951. More importantly, it was a turning point for American morale in Korea and a perfectly timed demonstration of what well-led and well-trained soldiers could do in even the most demanding of circumstances.

Shattered, the Chinese Fourth Phase Offensive (11–18 February 1951) collapsed. In General Peng Te-Huai's memoirs he admits that 'our units were acutely exhausted, and our supply lines had been severely attenuated, hurting resupply efforts badly. The drop in levels of non-combatants and combat soldiers alike had left our units at half strength.' As a result, he now accepted that 'A swift victory will not be possible in this war.' It remained to be seen whether Mao Tse Tung agreed. In any case, overreach by the Chinese in their Third and Fourth Phase Offensives exhibited the same miscalculation that MacArthur had exhibited in his race to the Yalu. The Chinese overestimated their ability to destroy the Americans. Their idea that massed human power would overcome American firepower was their undoing, as was their failure to recognise that US and UN forces were getting much better, very quickly. The National Emergency announced by Truman provided the legal conduit by which experienced combat veterans, now reservists, could be called back to the colours. The quality of ROK troops was gradually improving too. The Chinese made this mistake not once but twice. They underestimated the ability of America, specifically through the renewed leadership of Lieutenant General Ridgway, to counterattack at moments of their greatest weakness, especially with overwhelming artillery and air support, imagining that their *Kirimoni sakusen*-like*

---

*The Japanese tactic of 'driving charge', urging relentless pace to overwhelm the enemy's ability to respond to a fast-changing battlefield.

charge would be sufficient to drive the enemy into the sea. None of that happened in the face of a resourceful UN army commander willing to take the risk of accepting Chinese overreach and punishing that overreach with devastating counterattacks based on good tactics and overwhelming firepower.

Ridgway now ordered a counteroffensive across the entire front, to capitalise on Chinese exhaustion, prevent them from reorganising and to regain the 38th Parallel and Seoul. Operation *Killer* began on 21 February 1951 and succeeded with relative ease. During this operation the 1st Marine Division was employed for the first time since its fight at the Changjin reservoir. This successfully achieved, Operation *Ripper* then took the entire Eighth Army, some 150,000 men, beginning on 7 March, across the thawing Han River onto the 38th Parallel, again with relative ease, despite the spring mud. Huge quantities of US artillery were deployed for the attack. Much to his frustration, Major General Paik's 1st ROK Division was not involved, his division feinting towards Seoul to keep enemy troops in the city and preventing them from interfering with the western flank of the Eighth Army advance to Uijongbu. Ridgway hoped that with Seoul outflanked to the east, the enemy would evacuate the city without requiring a house-by-house clearance of the capital. This is precisely what happened, the Chinese evacuating Seoul on 14 March, the now ruined capital changing hands for the fourth time in nine months. Paik found the city in ruins, not a single building remaining unscathed from the fighting. The pre-war population of one and a half million had dwindled to 200,000 starving souls. Paik commented, on observing a population that had been psychologically crushed by war and occupation and on the verge of physical death, that they had not liberated a city, but 'had opened a grave'. Never again would Seoul be allowed to fall to the enemy. Fifty-four days after Ridgway had taken command the Chinese offensive had been repelled and UN forces were back across the 38th Parallel. Large numbers of Chinese and North Koreans had been killed. Ridgway's policy of fighting back against the enemy – rather than MacArthur's of demanding disproportionate escalation on the basis that UN troops couldn't defeat 'hordes' of Chinese – had been vindicated. 'The

American flag never flew over a prouder, tougher, more spirited, and more competent fighting force than was the Eighth Army as it drove north beyond the parallel', Ridgway wrote. It had been an astounding transformation in the fortunes of war.

Operation *Tomahawk* quickly followed. This entailed an airborne drop of the 187th Airborne Regimental Combat Team over Munsan-ni, with the ROK 1st Division, supported by a battalion of US tanks, pushing up from Seoul to meet the paratroopers, and thence to close the gap with the 3rd ROK Division at Uijongbu, trapping the greater part of the reformed NKPA *I Corps* in between. Most of the North Koreans escaped, however, but this operation placed the Eighth Army firmly along a defensive line approximate to the 38th Parallel, which Ridgway called the Kansas Line. Paik's 1st Division now found itself digging in along the Imjin River again, holding positions close to where the North Korean blitzkrieg had first fallen on 25 June 1950. In a period of just over two months, therefore, the great Chinese Second, Third and Fourth Offensives, despite their noise, ferocity and violence, had been halted. The Kansas Line was where, arguably, MacArthur's forces should have halted to rebuild the defensive line against North Korea following the Inchon landings the previous September, only six long months before. The defence line ran west to east across the peninsula, some six to 12 miles above the 38th Parallel. This was where the threat posed by a huge Chinese Army and the need to limit the fighting to this place, and nowhere else, had become real. It was time to fight the war to its end here, and without recourse to atomic weapons. The Kansas Line represented a deliberate doubling down by the USA and its allies in the UN on their ambitions for victory. That they were able to do so was largely because of the inspired leadership of Matthew Ridgway. General Omar Bradley agreed. 'His brilliant, driving, uncompromising leadership [turned] the tide of battle like no other general's in our military history.' Retorted a soldier, 'From now on there's a right way, a wrong way, and a Ridgway.'

Pressed by Mao Tse Tung, the Chinese launched their Fifth Phase Offensive, with the goal of recapturing Seoul, on 22 April 1951. On the same day, Ridgway issued Van Fleet explicit instructions to restrict

Eighth Army's offensive aspirations to a defensive position on the approximate line of the 38th Parallel. These were entirely in line with Washington's stated ambitions to de-escalate the war and to establish the basis for negotiations to proceed. Here, at last, was a Supreme Commander who was acting in accordance with the political Grand Strategy laid down in Washington. The author Clay Blair was right to describe this document as 'the Prevention of World War III'.* On 1 June 1951 came the final act in Ridgway's process of creating a solid defence line, Operation *Piledriver*, which reversed all the gains made by the Chinese Fifth Offensive. Truman's strategy, executed perfectly by Ridgway, was helped by the death of Joseph Stalin, the last hindrance in the communist bloc for agreeing to a ceasefire. Taking the cue, the USSR's representative to the UN, Jacob Malik, on 23 June called for an armistice. Two days later the USA accepted this Soviet proposal for a ceasefire as the basis for the start of armistice discussions.

*Blair, *The Forgotten War*, 816.

8

The End of the Proconsul

In 1950, General Douglas MacArthur stood tall in US history as an undisputed American legend. His star in the United States could not have shone more brightly as one of the titans who had overseen the strategy to defeat the Japanese in the South Pacific, engineered the Japanese surrender and subsequently superintended the rebirth of Japan as a democracy and an American ally. During the Korean War, however, glimpses of what might be described as operational genius were compromised by strategic ineptness of a kind which shattered his god-like status and consigned him to a degree of ignominy seldom seen in such stars. The problem with MacArthur was not merely that he considered the Korean War to be the necessary – perhaps even inevitable – catalyst for a righteous crusade by the Christian West against the ungodly forces of global communism; or that this war would necessitate the use of atomic weapons (so as to allow the West to overcome China's quantitative advantage in manpower), but that he thought it appropriate for a servant of the state publicly to pass judgement on the subject, especially in contradistinction to what the White House was saying. It was clear that in his role as de facto ruler of Japan since 1945, in which even the Emperor Hirohito sat in the palm of his hand, he had grown far too big for his boots, his time as Supreme Commander – not for nothing has he been described as a proconsul and, by one of his biographers, an 'American Caesar' – blurring the essential distinction between the construction of policy and its execution.

MacArthur suffered from several character flaws, by far and away the worst of which was vanity. To compound this problem, he had spent his entire career surrounding himself with sycophants, unwilling to bathe in anything less than constant adulation. According to General David Petraeus and Andrew Roberts, his 'highly self-curated reputation' concealed 'a monster of egotism'. They note that MacArthur put out scores of press releases covering his doings in minute detail. Of the 142 communiqués he sent from Corregidor during the Second World War, for example, 109 spotlighted himself.* Over time he seemed increasingly convinced of his military invincibility. The composition of his staff did not help. One historian described his headquarters as 'something like a princely court, which included a number of complaisant if competent time servers [who] had served him in many cases since before Pearl Harbor'.† The three key figures in MacArthur's entourage were Major General Edward 'Ned' Almond, the Chief of Staff, Major General Courtney Whitney, and Major General Charles Willoughby, the head of intelligence. This servile band's 'devotion to the master had turned them into flunkeys, anxious only to please the great man and tell him what they imagined he wished to hear.' Nowhere was this more disastrously demonstrated than in the provision of intelligence by Willoughby. In almost all respects the analysis (rather than the collection) of intelligence – much of the latter garnered by brave ROK agents – proved to be a disaster. Its principal defect was that Willoughby used the intelligence he was given to conform to his boss's military assumptions, rather than the other way round. In so doing it utterly failed to comprehend anything of the scale or nature of the military challenge facing the UN in 1950 or 1951. This was bad enough against the *In Mun Gun*; when it came to mis-appreciating the challenge posed by the People's Liberation Army, the consequences were catastrophic.

---

*General David Petraeus and Andrew Roberts, *Conflict: The Evolution of Warfare from 1945 to Ukraine* (William Collins, 2023), 24.
†Michael Hickey, *The Korean War: The West Confronts Communism* (The Overlook Press, 2000), 23.

The week following the launch of the Second Phase Offensive on 25 November 1950 saw MacArthur volubly nervous. His missives to the Joint Chiefs of Staff reeked of panic. How much of his argument for heavy attacks against the Chinese mainland was an emotional lash-out in response to the shock of being bettered on the battlefield remains unclear. Truman, to gain a clear sense of MacArthur's views, sent the Army Chief of Staff, Lawton Collins, to Tokyo. Collins returned to explain that MacArthur saw there to be three options for the UN. The first option was to continue to fight the war in Korea with the forces available, without the large-scale reinforcement of Korea or retaliation against China. The second was to escalate the war by bombing China, blockading the Chinese coast, and allowing Generalissimo Chiang Kai-shek to send his troops from Formosa to fight in Korea. The third was to enter into negotiations with China to restate the original border on the 38th Parallel and bring the war to a negotiated end, accepting that Korea would remain divided.

MacArthur considered the first option akin to surrender. Although he accepted the third option in principle, he found it difficult to imagine the circumstances in which China would voluntarily accede to a negotiated peace. He had lost any faith in the ability of the UN forces in Korea to defeat the enemy through battle. Truman and Collins were less pessimistic, judging that there was an Option 4, namely a combination of MacArthur's Options 1 and 3. They believed that China had to be fought to the negotiating table. Any other option threatened general war not merely with China, but also with the Soviet Union. Washington's view was that there was no geopolitical rationale for Option 2, and certainly many reasons for ensuring that the war did not escalate beyond that which was directly controllable.

This conversation between the president in Washington and the Commander-in-Chief in Tokyo should have rested there, Truman and his advisers allowed to determine what grand strategy would be pursued. MacArthur could not see this, however, and continued to press his views on a reluctant president. On 19 December he went so far as to request an additional four infantry divisions for the defence of Japan, the equivalent of 60,000 combat troops. He knew full well that these troops did not exist in the USA's arsenal (the only 'spare' division was the 82nd Airborne Division, in strategic reserve), so generating this number of troops would require mobilisation, something that was a political non-starter. What was MacArthur doing in making this suggestion? On the one hand, he was placing quite intolerable pressure on the president, to whom he was subordinate. At the same time, he was trumpeting his view that the only way to solve the problem of Korea was by a massive expansion of the war: his Option 2, in other words. The request was an unsubtle attempt to influence Washington and UN policy, and was bitterly resented by the president, who saw this quite outrageous political play for what it was: the interference by a soldier in grand strategic decision-making, for which he was not equipped or authorised. MacArthur's request for a massive increase in troop numbers was followed, ten days later, by a second request to blockade the Chinese coast and attack airfields in Chinese Manchuria. It appeared that MacArthur was not content to allow Truman and his government to determine war policy in Washington but was actively lobbying for the only option that to him made sense: escalation to general war. Truman tried one more time to get through to his irascible proconsul. On 9 January, a week after the Third Phase Offensive had begun across the frozen wastes of the North Korean winter, the Joint Chiefs of Staff sent Tokyo instructions, ordering him to fight to defend Korea. He was to withdraw only if he judged it essential.

These instructions triggered an angry response from MacArthur. He replied that he was being expected to fight with one hand behind his back* and that he could not be held responsible for the consequences. MacArthur believed that of the three options he had presented to General Joe Collins only one was rational. If there was a single feature of MacArthur's personality that let him down on occasions like this it was his inability to listen. Given his elevated status in America, Washington continued to treat MacArthur with kid gloves, desisting from providing him with direct, explicit and unequivocal instructions. The president sent a telegram to Tokyo on 13 January 1951 setting out the rationale

---

*He had, for example, been forbidden by the Joint Chiefs of Staff from attacking the Changjin reservoir and dam and other hydro-electric power complexes along the Yalu. MacArthur had argued that attacking these would so hurt China and the USSR – which both used power from these sources – that it would make them reluctant to intervene in Korea. The Joint Chiefs of Staff took the opposite view – that the positive strategic effects of the destruction of these sites for the UN were limited, while their potentially negative effects, such as encouraging further enemy involvement in the war, were considerable.

for Washington's thinking, and asking him to frame military plans in the light of these observations:

I want you to know that the situation in Korea is receiving the utmost attention here and that our efforts are concentrated upon finding the right decisions on this matter of the gravest importance to the future of America and to the survival of free peoples everywhere.

I wish in this telegram to let you have my views as to our basic national and international purposes in continuing the resistance to aggression in Korea. We need your judgment as to the maximum effort which could reasonably be expected from the United Nations forces under your command to support the resistance to aggression which we are trying rapidly to organize on a world-wide basis. This present telegram is not to be taken in any sense as a directive. Its purpose is to give you something of what is in our minds regarding the political factors.

1. A successful resistance in Korea would serve the following important purposes:

(a) To demonstrate that aggression will not be accepted by us or by the United Nations and to provide a rallying point around which the spirits and energies of the free world can be mobilized to meet the world-wide threat which the Soviet Union now poses.

(b) To deflate the dangerously exaggerated political and military prestige of Communist China which now threatens to undermine the resistance of non-Communist Asia and to consolidate the hold of Communism on China itself.

(c) To afford more time for and to give direct assistance to the organization of non-Communist resistance in Asia, both outside and inside China.

(d) To carry out our commitments of honor to the South Koreans and to demonstrate to the world that the friendship of the United States is of inestimable value in time of adversity.

(e) To make possible a far more satisfactory peace settlement for Japan and to contribute greatly to the post-treaty security position of Japan in relation to the continent.

(f) To lend resolution to many countries not only in Asia but also in Europe and the Middle East who are now living within the shadow of Communist power and to let them know that they need not now rush to come to terms with Communism on whatever terms they can get, meaning complete submission.

(g) To inspire those who may be called upon to fight against great odds if subjected to a sudden onslaught by the Soviet Union or by Communist China.

(h) To lend point and urgency to the rapid build-up of the defenses of the western world.

(i) To bring the United Nations through its first great effort on collective security and to produce a free-world coalition of incalculable value to the national security interests of the United States.

(j) To alert the peoples behind the Iron Curtain that their masters are bent upon wars of aggression and that this crime will be resisted by the free world.

2. Our course of action at this time should be such as to consolidate the great majority of the United Nations. This majority is not merely part of the organization but is also the nations whom we would desperately need to count on as allies in the event the Soviet Union moves against us. Further, pending the build-up of our national strength, we must act with great prudence in so far as extending the area of hostilities is concerned. Steps which might in themselves be fully justified and which might lend some assistance to the campaign in Korea would not be beneficial if they thereby involved Japan or Western Europe in large-scale hostilities.

3. We recognize, of course, that continued resistance might not be militarily possible with the limited forces with which you are being called upon to meet large Chinese armies. Further, in the present world situation, your forces must be preserved as an effective instrument for the defense of Japan and elsewhere. However, some of the important purposes mentioned above might be supported, if you should think it practicable, and advisable, by continued resistance from off-shore islands of Korea, particularly from Cheju-do, if it becomes impracticable to hold an important portion of Korea itself. In the worst case, it would be important that, if we must withdraw from Korea, it be clear to the world that that course is forced upon us by military necessity and that we shall not accept the result politically or militarily until the aggression has been rectified.

4. In reaching a final decision about Korea, I shall have to give constant thought to the main threat from the Soviet Union and to the need for a rapid expansion of our armed forces to meet this great danger.

5. I am encouraged to believe that the free world is getting a much clearer and realistic picture of the dangers before us and that the necessary courage and energy will be forthcoming. Recent proceedings in the United Nations have disclosed a certain amount of confusion and wishful thinking, but I believe that most members have been actuated by a desire to be absolutely sure that all possible avenues to peaceful settlement have been fully explored. I believe that the great majority is now rapidly consolidating and that the result will be an encouraging and formidable combination in defense of freedom.

6. The entire nation is grateful for your splendid leadership in the difficult struggle in Korea and for the superb performance of your forces under the most difficult circumstances.

Truman had no choice but to explain the de-escalatory US position to his powerful and influential proconsul in these detailed terms. MacArthur might disagree with it, but he could no longer be in any doubt about the reasons behind Washington's desire not to expand the war, as this would not secure peace in Korea and might inadvertently poke the Soviet bear.

Washington's position had also been influenced strongly by the extreme reluctance of America's allies to accept the arguments for expanding the war that had emanated from Tokyo, and that were unintentionally exacerbated by Truman's press conference on 30 November. The countries which had responded with such alacrity to the US crusade to resist North Korean aggression now refused to countenance escalation to general war, and possibly a nuclear one at that. There seemed insufficient reason in foreign capitals to go from supporting a righteous cause (the *first* Korean War) to supporting one that was less so (the *second* Korean War), especially when the reason for the second was arguably America's fault in the first place. In foreign capitals – such as London – the distinction between MacArthur publicly urging the bombing of Chinese Manchuria, and Truman's ill-advised comments about who had the authority to launch nuclear weapons, remained unclear. The UK and Europe more generally were dismayed to hear Truman talk so openly of atomic bombs. The USA, although it didn't much like it, at least now knew exactly what its allies in the free world thought of the issue of China. Attlee immediately made plans to travel to Washington to press Truman to rachet down the rhetoric. London was terrified for the security of Europe: a massive war in Asia would conceivably suck away resources from a potential confrontation with the USSR at home, already grievously under-protected. As Omar Bradley was to observe, a war in Korea against China in 1951 was 'the wrong war, in the wrong place, at the wrong time'. Quite. But what could be done to prevent it blowing up?

Britain had retained a close military relationship with the USA after the war. The Combined Chiefs of Staff, successful in coordinating the multiplicity of challenges between both countries during the war years, had been resurrected to manage the equally problematic difficulties of peace. The British representative, Air Chief Marshal Sir Arthur Tedder, previously the UK's Chief of the Air Staff, served simultaneously as Chairman of the British Joint Services Mission in Washington. The very public dispute in December 1950 between Tokyo and Washington panicked Western capitals, worried that the clear primacy of political control over the military had somehow been usurped by the over-mighty proconsul in Tokyo. Britain's interests also diverged very distinctly from those of the USA in respect of China. The problem in London was this: the Second World War had exacerbated the impoverishment of the country begun during the Great War. In the Second World War the United States had bankrolled Britain, but at a price, and now the debt was being called in. To raise sufficient income to pay both capital and interest on these debts required trade, and this included China. That China was now under communist rule was, to London, an uncomfortable irrelevance. In the British version of *realpolitik* this was insufficient grounds to stop making money from China, and vice versa. This clearly ran counter to the USA's more rigidly doctrinaire approach with respect to dealing with communist states: this was, after all, the early days of the McCarthyite era in America.

During the long struggle with MacArthur, the Chiefs of Staff Committee provided both Truman and the Joint Chiefs of Staff with support in opposing any attempt to widen the war. Attlee's visit to Washington was proclaimed by some in the Labour Party to have been instrumental in changing Truman's mind about the use of nuclear weapons. Claims such as this reflect a failure to understand the nature of the struggle taking place between Washington and Tokyo. At the time, Truman and MacArthur represented polarising views about how to manage the war: the issue for London was whose view would triumph. In reality, Washington would always win, but the discordant voices emanating from the USA were a worry in friendly capitals. Truman was already strongly opposed to expanding the war, and he was not inclined to use nuclear weapons on China, though he reserved the right to use any weapons the USA thought necessary. He certainly wasn't in the mood to be lectured to by the UK when the USA was bearing most of the burden to resisting the enemy in Korea. The best Attlee got from Truman was a promise that nuclear weapons would only ever be used in a response to a 'major military disaster' and that the UK would be informed when a decision was made to use them. But what really worried Attlee was that Truman seemed unable to control his C-in-C in Tokyo. London had been astonished at – and worried by – the Tokyo tail wagging the Washington dog. This is what he travelled to Washington to understand. It wasn't so much MacArthur's bellicosity which had so surprised London, but Tokyo's view that it was appropriate in a democracy to make policy in this way. In his memoirs Attlee was openly critical of MacArthur, but also implied criticism of Truman's failure to rein in his rebellious C-in-C, as the British prime minister wondered out loud why there had been 'insufficient control of his activities' by the US president. Was MacArthur simply too big to manage? Attlee wanted to find out.

For London, the MacArthur/Truman imbroglio demonstrated the essential requirement for civilian control of the military, for civilian leaders to provide unequivocal direction to military leaders, including any relevant military constraints and restraints on policy decisions. This, in the early months of the war, was lacking, and an unhelpful environment of ambiguity and challenge was allowed to develop between Truman and MacArthur. This wasn't in fact a vacuum: Truman's policy was clear. What occurred was a situation in which the country's military representative (MacArthur) held diametrically different views to those of the elected political leadership of the country. MacArthur struggled to understand that in a democracy his role was to execute policy, not dictate it. He could help develop policy, of course, through conversation and dialogue with the Joint Chiefs of Staff, his employers, but he didn't. His time as proconsul in Tokyo had made him believe that he had at least equivalent authority to that of the US government, and possibly superior authority – as he held an unchallenged political position in Japan – and the line between policy and execution had somehow, in his mind at least, become blurred.

If Washington ever assumed that Big Mac was now back in his box following Truman's explanatory telegram of 13 January, they were mistaken. On 20 March, Truman, Dean Acheson, General George Marshall, and the Joint Chiefs of Staff discussed the possibility of securing peace in Korea and determined that the policy of the USA (and therefore of the UN) was to seek peace via negotiation with China, and thus to restore the *status quo ante bellum*. They sent a message to MacArthur warning him of this policy determination:

> State Department planning a Presidential announcement shortly that with clearing of bulk of South Korea of aggressors, the United Nations now preparing to discuss conditions of settlement in Korea. United Nations feeling exists that further diplomatic efforts toward settlement should be made before any advance with major forces north of the 38th parallel. Time will be required to determine diplomatic reactions and permit new negotiations that may develop. Recognizing that parallel has no military significance, State has asked Joint Chiefs of Staff what authority you should have to permit sufficient freedom of action for next few weeks to provide security for United Nations forces and maintain contact with enemy. Your recommendation desired.

MacArthur responded to say that with the current restrictions on him he saw no chance of recovering North Korea for the UN, but he added no further comment.

The presidential announcement read:

> I make the following statement as Chief Executive of the Government requested by the United Nations to exercise the Unified Command in

Korea, and after full consultation with United Nations Governments contributing combat forces in support of the United Nations in Korea.

United Nations forces in Korea are engaged in repelling the aggressions committed against the Republic of Korea.

The aggressors have been driven back with heavy losses to the general vicinity from which the unlawful attack was first launched last June. There remains the problem of restoring international peace and security in the area in accordance with the terms of the Security Council resolution of June 27, 1950.

There is a basis for restoring peace and security in the area which should be acceptable to all nations which sincerely desire peace.

The Unified Command is prepared to enter into arrangements which would conclude the fighting... Such arrangements would open the way for a broader settlement for Korea, including the withdrawal of foreign forces.

The Korean people are entitled to peace. They are entitled to determine their political and other institutions by their own choice... What is needed is peace, in which the United Nations can use its resources in the creative tasks of reconstruction. A prompt settlement of the Korean problem would greatly reduce international tensions in the Far East and would open the way for the consideration of other problems.

Here, at long last, was a commitment by the USA that it would accept the limited war aims of a return to the *status quo ante bellum*. The policy determination to unite Korea as one under Syngman Rhee was now dead in the water, as was the idea, loudly advocated by MacArthur, of bombing China back to the stone age. The question for Washington was whether Peking (and, it believed correctly, Moscow) were also prepared to accept a purposive delimitation of the conflict. North Korea had attempted a coup de main attack on the ROK, precipitating the first Korean War, and had failed. The UN's initiation of the second Korean War, equally ill-advised, had also failed. Now, in Washington's view – and the many foreign capitals which had willingly followed the US's lead in the first war, but who were reluctant camp followers in the second – it was time to draw stumps and accept that it was in the interests of each side to bring the war to a negotiated close.

To the profound disappointment of Washington and London, it appeared that the leopard in Tokyo had not changed its spots during the intervening months. With the battlefield situation improving, thanks to Ridgway, Truman saw the opportunity of proposing a negotiated peace. But then, on 24 March 1951, without clearing it first with the Joint Chiefs of Staff, the Supreme Commander issued his own, supplementary statement to that of the president. He had spent the day with Ridgway in Korea, and he wanted the world to know:

Operations continue according to schedule and plan. We have now substantially cleared South Korea of organized Communist forces. It is becoming increasingly evident that the heavy destruction along the enemy's lines of supply, caused by our round-the-clock massive air and naval bombardment, has left his troops in the forward battle area deficient in requirements to sustain his operations.

Of even greater significance than our tactical successes has been the clear revelation that this new enemy, Red China, of such exaggerated and crucial vaunted military power, lacks the industrial capacity to provide ... items necessary to the conduct of modern war. He lacks the manufacturing base ... he cannot provide ... tanks, heavy artillery, and other refinements science has introduced into the conduct of military campaigns. Formerly his great numerical potential might well have filled this gap, but with the development of existing methods of mass destruction, numbers alone do not offset ... such deficiencies.

These military weaknesses have been clearly and definitely revealed since Red China entered upon its undeclared war in Korea. Even under the inhibitions which now restrict the activity of the United Nations forces and the corresponding military advantages which accrue to Red China, it has shown its complete inability to accomplish by force of arms the conquest of Korea. The enemy, therefore, must by now be painfully aware that a decision of the United Nations to depart from its tolerant effort to contain the war to the area of Korea, through an expansion of our military operations to its coastal areas and interior bases, would doom Red China to the risk of imminent military collapse. These basic facts being established, there should be no insuperable difficulty in arriving at decisions on the Korean problem if the issues are resolved on their own merits, without being burdened by extraneous matters not directly related to Korea.

The Korean nation and people, which have been so cruelly ravaged, must not be sacrificed. This is a paramount concern... Within the area of my authority as the military commander, however, it would be needless to say that I stand ready at any time to confer in the field with the commander in chief of the enemy forces ... to find ... [a] means whereby realization of the political objectives of the United Nations in Korea, to which no nation may justly take exceptions, might be accomplished without further bloodshed.

Later that day MacArthur made a further statement to the press to the effect that he had instructed Ridgway to take the Eighth Army back across the 38th Parallel 'if and when its security makes it tactically advisable.'

MacArthur seemed finally to have taken leave of his senses. The Supreme Commander's unilateral threat to China of 'the risk of imminent military collapse' and absurd demand that China publicly admit defeat – especially the veiled threat of the use of atomic weapons ('methods of massed destruction') – if it failed to accept the UN's line, was simply not his to make. He had already been instructed not to comment publicly on issues of military policy, or at least not before passing any pronouncements by the Joint Chiefs beforehand. Was he attempting to provoke China into precipitate action, thereby to justify a huge US counter-response? It was known that China had Soviet Ilyushin jet bombers. Attacking Seoul would be an easy undertaking. The government in Peking saw the threat for what it was and urged its people to resistance against America. In Washington, an astonished Truman wondered whether MacArthur was being deliberately provocative by challenging stated UN policy, or simply stupid. An immediate telegram to Tokyo instructed MacArthur to stay silent. It was too late to ask him to withdraw his announcement, as alarm bells were already ringing loudly across Western capitals, but he was to make no further comments of any kind. These instructions, however, were not interpreted by MacArthur as a warning to stop communicating his war-expansionist views in private. Innocent or not, the next scene in this *theatre macabre* was a letter he wrote to a friendly Republican senator, Joe Martin, who, perhaps unbeknownst to MacArthur, decided to read it out in full in the House of Representatives on 5 April 1951.

My views and recommendations with respect to the situation created by Red China's entry into war against us in Korea have been submitted to Washington in most complete detail. Generally, these views are well known and understood, as they follow the conventional pattern of meeting force with maximum counterforce as we have never failed to do in the past. Your view with respect to the utilization of the Chinese forces on Formosa is in conflict with neither logic nor this tradition.

It seems strangely difficult for some to realize that here in Asia is where the Communist conspirators have elected to make their play for global conquest, and that we have joined the issue thus raised on the battlefield; that here we fight Europe's war with arms while the diplomats there still fight it with words; that if we lose this war to Communism in Asia the fall of Europe is inevitable, win it and Europe most probably would avoid war and yet preserve freedom. As you point out, we must win. There is no substitute for victory.

The scale of the anger in Washington at the egregious temerity of this jumped-up plenipotentiary in Tokyo cannot be overstated. Ridgway's subsequent view was that MacArthur had 'cut the ground from under the President, enraged our allies, and put the Chinese in the position of suffering a severe loss of face if they so much as accepted a bid to negotiate.' In London, the perspicacious Chief of the Imperial General Staff thought he had his man bang to rights. Field Marshal Bill Slim expressed his views to his fellow Chiefs of Staff:

I may be evil-minded but I feel that MacArthur is playing his hand as he has done since the start of the war, to involve the United Nations in a real war against China. He has deliberately wrecked the attempt of the State Department and the Foreign Office to approach China to effect a truce. The State Department committed the error of telling him what they proposed. He jumped in, issued as his own half their message, and added a threat which was bound to make the approach worse than useless. He had added a bit of coat-trailing by 7th Fleet which could easily provoke an attack by a Chinese aircraft or two. He is now engaged in exaggerating the admittedly large Chinese build up, which may or not be intended for an offensive. He has also begun this insistence on the threat of a 'massive' Chinese air attack, to which the only answer is, he says, to bomb Manchuria, and if he does that he has achieved his object. America will then, in a state of hysteria, tear into a Chinese war with Chiang as an ally.*

It was the last straw for the president. He had probably waited too long to do it, but MacArthur had now provided all the rope necessary to hang himself. The sage and eloquent Dean Acheson observed that 'there was no doubt what General MacArthur deserved; the sole issue was the wisest way to administer it.' On Monday 9 April, Truman signed the order relieving MacArthur of his positions in Tokyo, ordering him to hand over his responsibilities to the man who over the previous 100 days had transformed UN military fortunes in Korea, Lieutenant General Matthew B. Ridgway. In getting rid of MacArthur, the USA appointed a brilliant soldier able to combine in his professional capacity and personality the perfect combination of tactician and strategist. Ridgway was, in respect of his ability to form an army capable of defeating a fearsome enemy, and motivate it to fight, the US equivalent of the British commander of the Fourteenth Army in the Second World War, Lieutenant General Bill Slim. Ridgway was replaced in Korea by Lieutenant General James Van Fleet.

Korea exemplifies the realities that generals are not immune from the curse of political stupidity or from military over-reach. MacArthur was brilliant at operational manoeuvre: that is, he was able to think and act superbly at the operational – or campaign – level of war. As for an understanding of the political ramifications of war in an age of nuclear weapons, however, he exhibited a childlike comprehension of the challenges of the post-war world. The Korean War was fought by Second World War generals with, in the main, Second World War equipment and tactics. Yet the shadow of the Second World War was that provided

---

*TNA, WO 216/837, CIGS letter to Chiefs of Staff on handling of war in Korea by Gen MacArthur, 1 May 1951.

by the mushroom cloud of the atomic bomb. Some generals made the switch to this fundamentally different environment well while others – MacArthur prime among them – did not. Generalship in the new world order needed to reflect the fundamental reality that escalating war threatened to open the door to Armageddon.

MacArthur wasn't removed for being outspoken, but for publicly articulating views contrary to US government policy, and for believing and acting as if his views were equal or superior to those of Washington or the president. That he also got things hopelessly wrong in his planning for and conduct of the second Korean War didn't help. His military plan for rushing to the Yalu was naive, failing utterly to consider the nature of the terrain through which his army would need to traverse – in the depths of winter – or of the possibility of significant Chinese intervention. His decision to undertake two advances into the north, one in the west by Eighth Army and one in the vastness of the east by X Corps, fatally split his available forces, reducing the logistical support required to allow one pincer to advance quickly and decisively with its base close to its fighting vanguard. Nor too were these two pincers in any way able to support each other as they proceeded to the Yalu. MacArthur had a remarkably incomplete understanding of the terrain above the 38th Parallel. He had never seen it, though he had once flown over the Yalu, in November 1950. His trips to Korea resembled Jove's descents from Olympus: fleeting and uncomprehending. Nor did he develop a subsequent plan to *fight* the rolling Chinese offensives – as did Ridgway, successfully – instead demanding immediate and potentially catastrophic escalation. All these factors demonstrated his weakness as a strategist. Although he got Inchon right, this battle was an *operational* success, not a *strategic* victory *per se*. It would only have been a strategic victory if UN forces had secured the original defence line along the 38th Parallel and ended the war. Invading North Korea on the basis of dangerously flawed assumptions in fact represented strategic failure, not genius. A man who was supposedly a military genius would not have miscalculated so spectacularly as did MacArthur in his disastrous determination to get to the Yalu, drink its healing properties, and get the boys home by Christmas. He repeatedly misinterpreted Washington's instructions, as much a feature perhaps of his psychological dissonance as his reluctance to appreciate an alternate view of reality. When Truman's long letter was read to him in Tokyo in

January 1951 MacArthur entirely misunderstood Truman's point. The message was that America was not going to fight back against China with everything at its military disposal, including nuclear weapons, because it made no political sense to do so. Instead, he excitedly told his staff that the Chiefs in Washington had 'finally overcome their illusions that fighting back against China would bring on global war." It was precisely the opposite of what Truman was attempting to tell him.

The nail in the coffin for MacArthur was the visit to Tokyo to deliver the Chiefs' memorandum of mid-January 1951. It was undertaken by Generals Lawton Collins and Hoyt Vandenberg. One of MacArthur's problems was that he didn't exploit Ridgway's success as the army commander in defeating the Chinese offensives and rolling them back to the 38th Parallel. Instead, he continued to fight a losing political battle with Washington, one which he did not have the sense to realise he could never win. When it became clear that Korea would be a limited war, and that Ridgway had won him a series of dramatic successes on the battlefield by halting the Chinese offensive, MacArthur would have been better advised to accept these victories as his own. Instead, he largely ignored them – even belittled them – in his struggle to expand the war into something much larger and bloodier than it ever needed to be. William Manchester described the 'formation of painful patterns' in the nature of the cable traffic between Tokyo and Washington. In the field, Ridgway was winning battles against the Chinese in Korea, while in Tokyo, MacArthur fought for permission to bomb this target in Manchuria, or that North Korean depot near the Soviet border. Anything that might escalate the war beyond the bounds of Korea was rejected, to MacArthur's increasing anger. The result was his growing irrelevance from the strategic conversations taking place at the highest levels in Washington, and New York. Like Icarus, inured to wise counsel, MacArthur flew too high to the sun and, his wings disintegrating, he fell to the earth. He was mortal after all.

––––––

*Quoted in William Manchester, *American Caesar* (Little Brown, 1978), 624.

Ridgway was thrown into Korea in the middle of an enemy offensive and an Eighth Army panicked into precipitate retreat. Much to MacArthur's surprise perhaps, Ridgway quickly transformed UN military fortunes and reversed a deteriorating operational – and ultimately strategic – situation. It was Ridgway's mastery of the battlefield that allowed President Truman and, after him, President Eisenhower to secure the conditions necessary to force China and North Korea to negotiate an armistice. He survived because, in the first place, he didn't rush to a panicked response and mount nugatory counterattacks. Instead, he planned a series of defensive backstops all the way down to Pyeongtaek, trading ground for time. He judged that with winter fully on them, he would stretch out the Chinese and exhaust them. His counteroffensives were careful and methodical and helped rebuild the confidence of the Eighth Army. Second, he gripped the senior leadership of the Eighth Army in a war that saw rapid results. He saw that leadership was deficient across the board and personally challenged commanders to lead their troops. Where they didn't, he removed them. He recognised morale to be low – and a contributory cause of defeat – and worked assiduously to improve it. When Ridgway stared at his face on the cover of *Newsweek* one day in April 1951, he knew that he had at least passed the first hurdle. The soldiers in Korea knew him, as did, now, their families back home. So too did the Chinese.

PART 3

Return to the *Status Quo Ante Bellum*

While we believe there were two distinct wars for Korea, an argument outlined in the preceding chapters, the second war for Korea comprised two equally distinct phases. The first involved the UN reaction to the various Chinese offensives launched between late October 1950 and July 1951. The second and final phase lasted for the remaining two years of the war, in which the UN deliberately sat on the defensive along a line approximating the 38th Parallel, fighting to secure an acceptable peace without attempting to challenge North Korean sovereignty nor to reunify the peninsula under a single government led by Seoul.

Prologue

The Imjin River Adventures of a National Service Subaltern

National Serviceman Lieutenant Denys Whatmore was commanding 11 Platoon, D Company, Gloucestershire Regiment when the battalion position was attacked by overwhelming numbers of Chinese soldiers of the 63rd Army on the night of 22/23 April 1951.

This prologue differs from the previous two, in that it is entirely in Denys Whatmore's own words and is offered here in its entirety. We hope readers appreciate the uniqueness of this first-hand view of the Imjin Battle from the pen of one of the very few survivors.*

A diary tells me that, in England, there was a full moon on Saturday 21 April 1951. The same was true in Korea, where we fought a battle in bright spring sunshine by day and under the huge, baleful moon by night. About mid-morning on Sunday 22 April, the Platoon Commanders were told by [Major] Mike Harvey [the commander of D Company] that intelligence had come down from above, indicating that the Chinese were advancing in strength towards the South. Much, much later, I learned that entire Chinese formations had escaped detection from the air by living in cunningly constructed camouflaged hides sited

---

*D. Whatmore, *One Road to Imjin* (Dew Line Publications, 1997), 67–84.

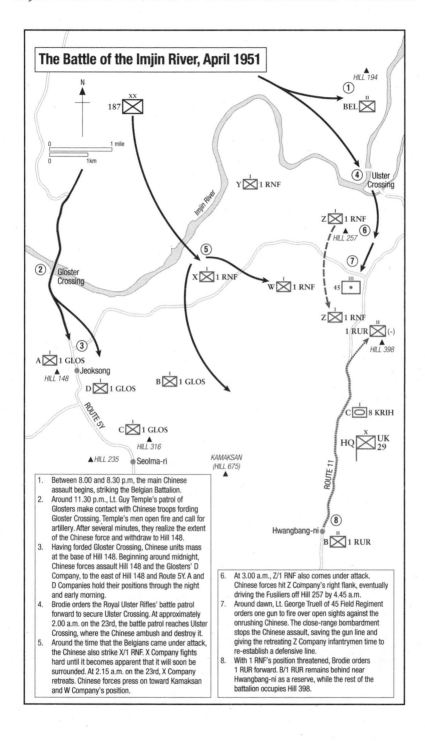

The Battle of the Imjin River, April 1951

N

0 ____ 1 mile
0 ____ 1km

187 ⊠ xx

HILL 194
①
BEL ⊠

Y ⊠ 1 RNF

④ Ulster Crossing

Z ⊠ 1 RNF
⑥
HILL 257

⑤

⑦

X ⊠ 1 RNF

W ⊠ 1 RNF   45 ⊡

Z ⊠ 1 RNF
1 RUR ⊠ (-)
HILL 398

② Gloster Crossing

③

A ⊠ 1 GLOS
HILL 148   ● Jeoksong
D ⊠ 1 GLOS   B ⊠ 1 GLOS

ROUTE 5Y

C ⊠ 1 GLOS
HILL 316

▲ HILL 235   ● Seolma-ri

KAMAKSAN (HILL 675)
▲

C ⊡ 8 KRIH

HQ ⊠ UK 29

ROUTE 11

⑧
Hwangbang-ni ●
B ⊠ 1 RUR

1. Between 8.00 and 8.30 p.m., the main Chinese assault begins, striking the Belgian Battalion.
2. Around 11.30 p.m., Lt. Guy Temple's patrol of Glosters make contact with Chinese troops fording Gloster Crossing. Temple's men open fire and call for artillery. After several minutes, they realize the extent of the Chinese force and withdraw to Hill 148.
3. Having forded Gloster Crossing, Chinese units mass at the base of Hill 148. Beginning around midnight, Chinese forces assault Hill 148 and the Glosters' D Company, to the east of Hill 148 and Route 5Y. A and D Companies hold their positions through the night and early morning.
4. Brodie orders the Royal Ulster Rifles' battle patrol forward to secure Ulster Crossing. At approximately 2.00 a.m. on the 23rd, the battle patrol reaches Ulster Crossing, where the Chinese ambush and destroy it.
5. Around the time that the Belgians came under attack, the Chinese also strike X/1 RNF. X Company fights hard until it becomes apparent that it will soon be surrounded. At 2.15 a.m. on the 23rd, X Company retreats. Chinese forces press on toward Kamaksan and W Company's position.
6. At 3.00 a.m., Z/1 RNF also comes under attack. Chinese forces hit Z Company's right flank, eventually driving the Fusiliers off Hill 257 by 4.45 a.m.
7. Around dawn, Lt. George Truell of 45 Field Regiment orders one gun to fire over open sights against the onrushing Chinese. The close-range bombardment stops the Chinese assault, saving the gun line and giving the retreating Z Company infantrymen time to re-establish a defensive line.
8. With 1 RNF's position threatened, Brodie orders 1 RUR forward. B/1 RUR remains behind near Hwangbang-ni as a reserve, while the rest of the battalion occupies Hill 398.

in re-entrants and valleys some 20 miles north of the river. On the chosen day, they simply had to march out towards their objectives, and it was only then that they were spotted. But at least in this case we had about 12 hours' tactical warning that action was imminent.

I had no real idea what to expect. I made sure, however, that the soldiers spent the day preparing for the worst, checking weapons and ammunition, filling magazines for the automatic weapons, making last minute attempts to improve the trenches, grabbing a meal and hot tea. We kept an eye on the north bank of the river as well, seeking sight of the enemy. I made a few minutes of time to use the field telephone network to get through to [Lieutenant] Phil Curtis in A Company, just to wish him luck in whatever was coming; he was away at an Orders Group and I asked that my message should be passed to him. Back on our hill, nothing happened to alarm us and the night fell just as on so many previous days, with the Platoon standing-to, though with rather more apprehension than usual. I kept half the Platoon on alert and allowed the others to sleep. Sergeant Dee and I arranged to share the night watch, he remaining awake for the first half of the night, myself to take the second half. I snatched a couple of hours' sleep.

Sergeant Dee woke me at about 2300 hours and reported the noise of firing to our left front, down near the river. He had already alerted the Platoon and we now all prepared ourselves for action, dressing to keep warm in the chill of the April night (I abandoned my beret for a cap comforter), and arming our weapons. I visited the Sections and they seemed to be as prepared as they could be. I reminded them to be vigilant in watching – so far as it was possible in the moon's light – the approaches to our positions.

While engaged in these visits, I realised that a battle had begun. The firing at the river's edge, where the road ran down to the ford, grew in intensity, the artillery joined in and the night came alive with flashes and noisy explosions all along the riverbanks to our front. I learned later that we had enjoyed a grandstand view of the opening phase of the battle, when an ambush patrol from C Company, led by Lieutenant Guy Temple, had successfully surprised the leading Chinese infantry wading across the river. The patrol did enormous damage and, calling on the artillery, created more and helped to delay the initial waves of Chinese at the river. The number of Chinese casualties, though uncountable of course, must have been very high, while the patrol, once its ammunition was used up, withdrew without loss.

David Holdsworth has his own tale to tell of this period. Sent out on another patrol down to the riverbank that evening, he found himself in the midst of the Chinese army which appeared to be coming across the river at several crossings. It was only with difficulty that he extricated himself and returned to the Company, there to lead his Platoon in what was becoming a fight on our own hill. In passing, I would mention, as a measure of the independence – not to say occasional isolation – of Platoon Commanders as I experienced them in this campaign, that I knew nothing of the intention to send out Guy Temple's and David Holdsworth's patrols mentioned above, nor the identity of those firing at the river's edge, until after the battle.

As the firing down at the river ceased and even the artillery fire slackened, the night took on an added darkness until our night vision was gradually restored. But the firing began again, over to our left, in the Castle Hill (A Company) area. It became intense and continuous, and it was possible roughly to gauge the rate of the enemy advance up the lower slopes of the hill by the flashes of their weapons. There was clearly a most tremendous fight going on. Then the Machine Gun Section sited immediately behind me joined in, sweeping fire towards the northeastern front of Castle Hill, the long, slow arcs of their fire beautiful in the night sky. I decided that the arching bullets seemed to travel so slowly because only one in every six or so was a visible tracer round, creating an illusion of a lazily moving firework display. Then return fire began to come in and nothing was lazy anymore.

It was obvious that we too were in for it. Soon – it must have been about 0230 hours on 23 April – we heard the enemy directly to our front. He was blowing a bugle, a strange and frightening sound on the night air, raucous and menacing, something I had not expected but which, I was told later, was a standard and simple Chinese device for keeping their soldiers in touch with the Headquarters and leaders when advancing at night. More bugles joined in, then whistles, and they were coming closer all the time. Then we heard the movement of men through the scrub, men advancing up the ridge, and I ordered the 2-inch mortar man (as it happened, it was Private Andman) to fire an illuminating parachute flare. The mortar banged, but no flare; it was a dud, one of the several we had that night. Sensibly not waiting for orders, Andman fired another and this one worked. And there, about forty yards away, were the attacking infantry, the shapes of men almost white in the combined glare of the magnesium flare and the moon. The leading sections needed no orders from me to open fire and enemy soldiers began to fall. Another flare or two were needed to continue the fire until that initial assault ran out of steam and the survivors went to ground. But they now knew precisely where we were.

So began a night and an early morning of repeated attacks, more parachute flares in the dark, fierce fire from the sections, minutes of calm as the Chinese reorganised themselves, then again their rushes forward. There seemed to be hundreds of them, concentrated onto the ridge at the top of which we formed a barrier to their advance and from which we kept up a constant fire. I soon learned that they had infiltrated around our flanks as well, as the rear Section and then 12 Platoon began firing. Later, there was firing from the B Company area, a thousand yards behind us, as infiltrators round our right flank reached it.

Early in the engagement, I thought it was time to call for the 3-inch Mortar Section's defensive fire I had been advised about. I had no instructions about using the Battalion's 3-inch mortars but, as the MFC [Mortar Fire Controller] was sitting in my trench with his radio, it seemed reasonable to make use of him; no one else could. The Corporal was all for it and made the necessary incantations into his radio mouthpiece. Soon, we heard the muffled thump in the rear which we took to be the mortars firing and down came the bombs – precisely on my Platoon position! The two bombs straddled us neatly, one near my left Section, one near my right. The concussion made my ears sing, but I heard the Corporal blaspheming and then, into his radio, speaking tersely, seeking to correct the range so that the next bombs would hit the enemy, not us. A cry from No. 2 Section informed me that the bomb there had injured one man, not seriously, but he was bleeding all over the place, our first casualty. I got him over to my slit trench and used the phone to contact Company HQ, where the Medical Sergeant agreed to come over and look at the wound. A few minutes later, he jumped into the trench, breathless, and declared the soldier – one of the latest National Service reinforcements, whose name I hardly knew – not badly hurt; a bomb fragment had sliced his ear and, like many ear wounds, the blood ran copiously but the actual cut was not too bad. The soldier returned to his position with a dressing on his ear but, just then, the Chinese made another frontal attack on the Platoon position, and kept it up so that it was impossible to get the Medical Sergeant back to Company HQ. He remained with me.

This attack brought a few of the Chinese into our midst but we shot them out again without resorting to hand-to-hand fighting. But when the Company Sergeant Major phoned through a few moments later asking about our situation, I was able to tell him 'They are right in among us, but we are coping.'

We began to run out of the precious parachute flares but, using the Company radio net this time – and, in the excitement, getting my wireless procedures wrong, for which I was severely rebuked by the broad Gloucestershire voice of the Private at the other end – I asked 10 Platoon to fire some in our direction and they helped no end. 10 Platoon was not seriously engaged in their location but 12 Platoon behind me was blazing away as the Chinese infantry outflanked me and pressed on towards the south, clearly with orders to make as much progress into the UN lines as they could. On our front, however, we began to be seriously plagued by a Chinese machine gun; I believe it was this gun that killed three or four of No. 1 Section and wounded others so that they had to be evacuated. I yelled to Private Andman, drawing his attention to the gun's location, about 100 yards out on the occasionally illuminated ridge, its muzzle flashes giving it away. I wanted some 2-inch mortar high-explosive bombs put down on it. Andman replied and within seconds had fired his mortar; it was the most amazing shot, for the bomb fell with a remarkably loud explosion exactly where the flashes had been seen, and the gun did not fire again. Fluke or skill, it did the job, and I yelled congratulations to Andman, into the din around us. It must have been soon after this that he was wounded.

The dawn came and we were so engaged in the fight that it was full daylight before we knew it. At about 0530 hours, the Chinese over-ran part of No. 1 Section, got into the slit trenches there and opened fire on the rest of us. I had a glimpse of a young Chinese in a steel helmet, mouth open, shouting, and then he threw a grenade at me. It flew towards my trench, the wooden handle gyrating in the air, and I just had time to yell 'Grenade' to warn the others, and to duck, when it fell on the breastwork on the lip of the trench. It teetered, dropped back outside the breastwork and exploded with an awful bang, showering us with stones; singing ears again but no injuries. I popped up and gave him a grenade in return; but mine was a [white] phosphorous [smoke] grenade, intended really to create an instantaneous smoke screen, but nasty because the ignited phosphorous burnt anything it touched. The grenade burst in the enemy soldier's face, he disappeared in a cloud of smoke and, when the air was clear, he had gone. So too had the others who had gained a toe hold.

Then disaster struck. A Chinese machine gun party had worked its way around to our right flank and began to spray us with very accurate fire. I put up my head to locate it and so did Private Binman, advancing his rifle at the same time to get a shot off. We were met by a burst of fire exactly at the height of our heads. Private Binman took a bullet in the eye, gave a gasp and fell over backwards at the feet of the crouching Medical Corporal. The remainder of the burst went over my right shoulder and I hit the deck fast. Another burst scattered the stones above us and hit the MFC's radio, cutting us off from the mortar section. My batman lay on his back breathing stentoriously but quite unconscious; the Medical Corporal, when I glanced at him, shook his head. And then the breathing stopped.

And still the attacks came on. We all fired our weapons – there were plenty of targets – until they were hot and uncomfortable to handle. Then my Sten gun jammed; that weapon had an infamous fault, in that occasionally it managed to feed two rounds into the chamber at once, causing an explosion which left jammed in the barrel the split brass casing of the first round. There was a clearing tool which could be used to get the casing out. In my case there was no time to fiddle with that, so I seized Private Binman's rifle and continued with that. I think someone else must have got the Chinese machine gun, for after a while it ceased to fire, at least in our direction.

By now it was about 0700 hours, broad daylight, sunny and warm. And we began to run out of ammunition. Even before dawn had broken, Corporal Norley had been calling for more ammunition and I had tossed over to him all the spare rounds we had. Now, from all sides, there were calls that ammunition was nearly exhausted. I myself ran out of rifle bullets and, soon after, pistol ammunition. In desperation, I loaded the Verey light pistol with a cartridge and aimed it at an advancing Chinese soldier who was firing a Burp gun; the searing red flare missed him, but he had a nasty fright; the next red and the last green missed too, but he fell eventually to someone else's shot. I had one grenade left and no other ammunition of any kind.

I now had to decide what to do. 11 Platoon had been sited in that position to prevent the enemy capturing it and I was reluctant to leave. But to stay without ammunition was impossible; we had fought to pretty well the last round – to fight to the last man seemed pointless. The field telephone line had been cut long since so whatever decision was to be taken, it had to be mine, and it had to be quick. I made the decision; we would go. I yelled at the top of my voice to the Sections, ordering them to retire as soon as they saw the last smoke grenade burst. Then I threw the grenade to screen us from the nearest enemy, yelled 'Go' and joined the rush towards 12 Platoon's position. As we went, I saw the Sergeant commanding the Machine Gun Section on the ridge wave and shout to us urgently, warning us of his fire; it seems that for some time his guns had been firing over open sights at the Chinese around the D Company hill, and we were in danger of running into a stream of bullets from the Vickers guns. He held his fire until we had passed through his position while, behind him, 12 Platoon continued to fire at the enemy on their right front. I noticed that only one Vickers was in action. The other was on its side and the Sergeant said it had been put out of action by enemy fire.

I looked back towards the position I had just evacuated but the enemy did not seem to be chasing us. So, we passed on through to Company HQ, where I informed [Major] Mike Harvey [the company commander] of the situation. He accepted the information calmly and showed what remained of the Platoon to a site along the ridge, behind 10 Platoon, to form a new reserve, however meagre. The Medical Corporal was able to rejoin Company HQ and the MFC went off to join his Mortar Section. I counted the men of 11 Platoon; only 13 of us had made it, none of us wounded. We learned, however, that several wounded men from the Platoon (much later I learned that Private Andman, with a bullet through the arm, was with them) had been evacuated during the night, so I was able to hope that the death toll had not been so very bad.

In our new position we had a good view of the terrain on the West side of D Company hill, though the township of Choksong was hidden by a spur of land. About 600 yards away I spotted a Chinese machine gun team – three men – moving forward, not engaged by any fire.

I directed a couple of soldiers to fire on them despite the extreme range, and it was sufficient to drive them to ground. But their reply was swift. A burst of their fire kicked up the dust at our feet, a most impressive display of marksmanship, but ineffectual in this case. We did not see them again and we were able to rest for a few moments as 12 Platoon continued in action. 10 Platoon did not seem to be under attack, but most of them were out of our view anyway. My head was still singing a bit and we were all very thirsty.

It can have been only half an hour later when Mike Harvey came up and said that D Company had been ordered to withdraw at 0830 hours, having first covered the withdrawal of the remnants of A and B Companies who had been ordered back to new positions on Hill 235 and the slopes of Kamak-san respectively. The Chinese no longer seemed to be pressing us and when the time came to leave the Company I was not aware of any pursuit or even of hostile fire directed against us. We descended the slopes southwards, down into a valley, west a few hundred yards, over a low hump in the ground and into the valley where lay Solma-ri village. On the way, we saw far away to our right members of A Company straggling back from Castle Hill and, for the first time, the explosions of enemy mortar bombs, some very close to the bent, slow moving men. An Oxford carrier was among them and it stopped at one point to pick up wounded men, then roared on into the relative safety provided by the hills around Battalion HQ in Solma-ri. Here I saw the CO and Adjutant and someone wearing the badges of a Warrant Officer Class 1 who must have been Jack Hobbs, the Regimental Sergeant Major, whom I had never seen before. He provided us with a small amount of ammunition; but, frankly, we were more concerned with the water and hard boiled eggs produced out of nowhere by some nameless miracle worker who, on his own, raised our morale enormously after the trying times we had just been through. We stayed in the valley for only a few minutes. Then Mike Harvey appeared again and told us that we were to join Support Company and the remains of A Company on Hill 235.

We looked at the hill and at one another. It was steep and scrub covered and the paths to the top appeared to be nearly vertical; but were we not used by now to vertical paths? So, we set off, grimy and unshaven, and reached the hilltop in a very tired state indeed. The Company was allocated a position on the East side of the ridge, a little below the summit and there, without further ado, we began to dig in the rock. We had evacuated no entrenching tools from the original position, so it was a question of using mess tins from packs and bare hands to prise into the rock and break off chunks in an effort to get into cover. We spent all day (Monday 23 April) at it and did manage to scrape shallow slits which gave protection more imaginary than real. We had little water and no food. With Sergeant Dee I tried to fit together a picture of the previous night and particularly to account for missing members of the Platoon. We came to very few conclusions; things had happened so fast and so furiously, it had been impossible to keep track of individuals, especially in the dark, and we could only hope that most of the missing had been evacuated, wounded.

The Chinese did not attack us that day. Indeed, the entire Battalion seemed to get off lightly during the daylight hours, suffering only occasionally from Chinese light weapons fire. We guessed, though I was not to learn for sure until after the battle, that the enemy had concentrated instead on penetrating round the flanks and into the rear areas, so that the Glosters were soon cut off. The other battalions of 29th Brigade to the East were themselves having a very hard time of it and, we learned later, were extricated only with great difficulty. Even Brigade HQ and the gun-lines behind us were not safe. Major Digby Grist who, as our Battalion Second in Command, was supposed to be left out of forward battle area (in order to take over the unit if something happened to the Commanding Officer – as it did in this case), avoided capture only by a high speed jeep drive on his way to Rear HQ, with a bullet through the wrist for his pains. He got to 29th Brigade HQ and spent his time helping to organise a force designed to relieve the Glosters. This force was to comprise No. 24 Battalion Combat Team of the Filipino Army, including some light tanks, and a squadron of the 8th Hussars. Bearing in mind the miles of narrow road they had to cover in a steep valley, this force had little hope of advancing other than as a column down the road, with the infantry sweeping the hills on either side.

As dusk fell on 23 April, the situation was relatively quiet. We stood-to, of course, and I then set sentries to watch while the rest of my little group of men, just one Section strong, settled to get some sleep. But none of us had any sleep, for in the darkness, perhaps about 2300 hours, the Chinese mounted a major attack on B and C Companies situated on the foothills of the Kamak-san feature below and about half a mile away from the D Company position and separated from us by the steep sided valley where the road ran. It was harrowing to watch that fight and the sporadic up-hill progress of the flashes from Chinese weapons as they made their way against tremendous defensive fire into the Glosters' positions. We could do nothing to help the outnumbered Companies, though 45 Field Artillery did sterling work in laying down a carpet of shells which must have inflicted heavy casualties on the Chinese infantry on the open sides and on the valley road below. We saw it all, and I observed after about four hours of it that the fire from the Glosters Companies was diminishing fast. The rattle of small arms, the 'poof' of No. 80 grenades, and the 'tungk' of No. 36 grenades faded out. At last, there came virtual silence and we knew that the tremendous fire fight had been won and lost. At some time or other the remains of C Company and Battalion HQ were pulled back to Hill 235, but it was not until the following morning, in the daylight, that the survivors of B Company were able to join us. Early on Tuesday morning, immediately to our right but, of course, about 600 feet below us, I saw a number of men suddenly dash across the valley floor from the Kamak-san side, towards 235. I thought at first that this was another Chinese attack but soon realised that the small group was British; they were, in fact, all that was left of B Company – about 20 men, commanded by Major Denis Harding. Some half hour later I saw them much closer as they toiled up the hill, some carrying a wounded man in a ground sheet. They were soon given anxious assistance and those who were fit went off to man another position. I met and spoke to Guy Temple (of the river ambush patrol) at this time and we voiced our concern about what was going to become of us. Soon afterwards some artillery men appeared; these were what remained of C Troop, 170 Mortar Battery, Royal Artillery, who had remained with the Battalion, supporting us with their 4.2-inch mortars. Now, they were carrying one of the huge mortar tubes on their backs, inching slowly up the hill to a new position. I do not think they had any ammunition, and I did not see a mortar base plate, needed to fire the weapon; I believe they brought the vital part of their weapon with them merely to keep it out of the hands of the enemy.

So, on the morning of Tuesday 24 April, what was left of the Battalion was concentrated on Hill 235, from where we still dominated use of the all-important road. Once again the Chinese failed to attack during daylight hours and everyone on the hill made the most of his time, resting, snatching a few minutes sleep, sipping such water as was available, watching, wondering what was going to happen next. We had not long to wait. First, in the early afternoon, we were told that the CO had received a radio message to say that the Filipino/8th Hussars relief force had failed in their attempt to get through to us and had turned back. It transpired that a Filipino light tank, miles away, had been knocked out at one of the narrowest points in the road and it was impossible to move it or to get past it. I do not remember feeling terribly worried at this news. By now we were all feeling rather jaded and worn down, though adrenalin to re-activate us was not wanting when the need arose. But I believe most of us now realised that we were in a desperate situation, and a bit more bad news really made little difference to our morale.

Then it was said that some American light aircraft of the Artillery Spotting type – like the old Auster – were going to try to drop some badly needed supplies to us. Several such sorties were flown, I believe, before the night came down, but I saw only one. He came in quite slowly and very low – about 30 feet up – and dropped a canvas wrapped package which I believe contained ammunition. It landed with a thump out of my sight; if the contents survived the fall, they were very welcome, I am sure. We heard that other drops had been made but these had landed outside the Battalion area and were lost. But there was the promise of proper parachuted re-supply by air the next day, using American 'Flying Box Cars', transport aircraft with a good carrying capacity.[*]

Before that, however, we had to survive the night. Colonel Carne closed up the remnants of the Battalion before darkness fell, so that our perimeter was tighter, more cohesive. This did not involve a move for 11 Platoon and we were able to scrape a few more inches into the ground to occupy the time, to share three small tins of food which appeared from somewhere – I had some American fruit cocktail, divided with Sergeant Dee and another – then to settle down and prepare for whatever the Chinese might do next. In fact, apart from a bit of probing which was fended off by small arms fire, they waited until well after midnight to mount their next major assault. Then, the bugles started

[*] Fairchild C-119.

again and massed Chinese infantry came up the spur at the northwest end of Hill 235 in the way we were now used to, non-stop, in waves, firing their weapons and guided by the bugles. The depleted A, B and C Companies were very hard pressed to keep the enemy out and only part of D Company was located with a field of fire suitable to join in the action and provide some enfilade fire. The 13 of us in 11 Platoon were sited to defend a different area, looking east, and we had no targets. The racket went on and on, gunfire and grenade explosions mixed with shouts, often interrupted by the crashes and flashes of 25-pounder shells being lobbed in with devastating accuracy by 45th Field Regiment. Two or three salvoes struck the ridges 25 to 30 yards below our trenches and we were torn between admiration for their accuracy and the hope that they would come no closer.

Still the Chinese could not break the ring and the fighting was going on as the darkness gave way to dawn and then to daylight. At about 0500 hours (it was now Wednesday, 25 April), without warning, a bugle blasted off immediately behind me, close. Chinese, so close! I swung round, Private Binman's rifle aimed, finger on trigger, and would immediately have shot the bugler had he been in sight. Luckily for him he was just over the crest of the ridge. Lucky for me, too, for after a few notes, I recognised the British Army bugle call with which we were being regaled by one of our own. I soon learned that Colonel Carne had ordered the Drum Major (Drum Major Buss) to play the Long Reveille in defiance of the Chinese bugles, and the gesture was well received. A small cheer went up and then the battle continued. But little did the Drum Major know what a near squeak he had had that morning, from 'friendly' fire!

With daylight came American aircraft, firing machine guns and dropping napalm along the edges of Hill 235 on groups of Chinese soldiers. I suppose they were Sabre jets, and devastatingly accurate. But I distinctly remember watching one which must have been a different type of aircraft. It flew very low up the road valley from the south, more or less on the same level as our heads, and dropped a napalm canister exactly on to a knoll lying below us and about 50 yards away where a Chinese machine gun team was beginning to bother us. The roar of the explosion and the Whoosh! of the subsequent oily flames was like the opening of a blast furnace door; the machine gun disappeared in a sea of fire. The aircraft had a rear turret, however, which sprayed bullets all over the place, including us, as it roared away from its target. No one was hit and we forgave him, for we did not hear from that Chinese machine gun again. Soon thereafter, the attacks lessened in their intensity and finally petered out completely.

We heard that a second attempt at relieving us by land had been abandoned. We looked out for the Flying Box Cars which were to help us from the air and I in fact saw them, but they were very high and dropped nothing. We were told after the battle that it had been impossible for them to identify the hill on which we were sited. The Battalion remained cut off, with many wounded, little ammunition, no food and water nearly exhausted. The unwounded were pretty worn down, but not yet quite exhausted. It was obvious, though, that we could not hold out much longer and soon, I was told that Colonel Carne had made this clear to Brigade HQ on the radio, now fading as the batteries ran down. It was on that radio that the message was finally received that the Glosters, having done the job they had been sent to do, could now retire from the position and extract themselves from their situation as best they could.

At 1030 hours on 25 April, Colonel Carne gathered his Company Commanders to give his final orders. Mike Harvey attended this meeting and soon returned to brief his Platoon Commanders. He told us that the Commanding Officer had received permission to abandon the position and that each Company was to try to make its own way out. He said that there were many wounded who could not be moved and that the Medical Officer, Bob Hickey, and his staff, and the Chaplain, Padre Sam Davies, intended to remain with them. He understood that the Commanding Officer, too, had decided to remain behind; this last point was later shown to be erroneous, for Colonel Carne made his way South, leading what remained of the Battalion towards safety.

Starkly, Mike Harvey put it to us that we had only two choices – to remain and surrender, or to fight our way out. If we chose to fight, we should have to move fast; there would be no stopping on the way for anyone wounded. We Platoon Commanders (and Lieutenant Bob Martin, the Machine Gun Platoon Commander, who had joined us) did not discuss the matter; we did not even glance at one another. We all said together 'We fight', and so the decision was made. Mike Harvey then told us his plan. He proposed to avoid the obvious shortest way out, that is, due south, where he thought it was probable the enemy lay in strength. He would take the Company due north to start with, into ground from which the enemy were likely to have moved on. He would then go west along the lower, north facing slopes of the hills and only then turn south towards friendly lines. It would be a long way round but, with luck, we should meet fewer Chinese that way. He advised us to pair off so that each man could help another, and then gave us a few minutes to brief and organise the Sections.

It took no time at all to tell my 12 soldiers what we were going to do and they prepared for the trek with a will. Sergeant Dee assembled them in pairs and made sure that each man had at least some ammunition. I discarded my battle dress blouse, for already it was warm and it was likely to get warmer, in more senses than one. And then we were off, D Company HQ, 10 and 12 Platoons which had received few casualties so far, the 13 of 11 Platoon, and a miscellany of Support Company soldiers, mainly Machine Gunners; a total, I believe, of about 90 men.

We went down the northern slopes of Hill 235, already named by some as Gloster Hill, at a fast walk, in good order and not a Chinaman in sight. At the bottom we followed Mike Harvey as he turned westwards and continued moving fast, my group somewhere in the middle of what became quite a long column, single file in places where the track demanded it. In one re-entrant, I saw a stagnant pool of muddy water into which a soldier was dipping a serrated ration tin and drinking. I said, 'Excuse me, but may I have a drink of your water, please?' He replied 'Certainly, Sir, so long as you let me have my tin back.' 'Of course,' said I, and swallowed water which tasted like wine. 'Thank you, Sir' he said as I returned his tin; I never saw the soldier again.

We continued west for about a mile and a half. At one point, there was a very brief burst of fire from the front of the line and I later passed a dead enemy soldier who clearly had had the misfortune to be in the way. Later, to the north about a hundred yards away, I saw three more Chinese on a crest; they looked at us but did nothing. Then we were swinging south into a valley, across a stream and, still moving quickly, beginning to hope. But the valley narrowed, the hills on either side rose steeper and steeper, and out of the topmost crags the Chinese began to machine gun us.

The situation very quickly deteriorated, so that we became the targets in a shooting gallery, with no hope of returning fire at our tormentors high above us even if we could have seen them. So it was a question of making use of every bit of cover we could find and going on. I was told later that many men went into the shallow stream which ran down the valley and crawled down that. At the time, I was quite unaware of that stream. I and many others, including my own few men, remained close to the foothills on our left (east), nipping in and out of re-entrants but continually moving south. I passed one soldier apparently lying quietly asleep against the grassy hill, the white ring of the Brigade sign on his tunic sleeve showing clean and bright. His face was calm, his eyes were closed and he seemed, somehow, comfortable and at peace. When I looked closer, I saw that he was dead.

Now we came to a muddy ditch, hardly more than a foot deep, probably some sort of drainage for the paddy fields terraced into the foothills. But it ran southwards and saved several lives, mine among them. We crawled down it, weapons as well as ourselves becoming covered in the mud. My right bootlace came undone again and the pressure of men behind me meant that I could not stop to tie it. The ditch levelled out at one point into a pool of water which, as I reached it, was being churned into mud by several men, one or two already wounded. I tried to encourage those who could move to keep on going, but they seemed exhausted and uncomprehending. Someone passing by said that the Chinese were after us, coming down the hillsides with knives. I hardly believed it and nor did the others. A couple moved from the pond but most were still there as I crawled on myself; I too was very worn down by this time.

Back in the welcoming ditch once more, I had the interesting experience of watching a tracer bullet burn. It was one of a burst of fire which entered the ditch just in front of my head, fired from high on my right. It half buried itself in the left side of the ditch about an inch from my eye, and there cheerfully hissed and glowed bright red until it burnt itself out. I moved on. The mud-covered bandolier of rifle bullets around my waist – one of those received from the RSM – dragged in the ditch bottom and slowed me down, so I abandoned it, but pulled the clogged rifle on with me.

This kind of progress went on for two or three miles. The bootlace came completely loose and I lost my boot and the sock with it, but

I was nearly past caring and almost exhausted. And then the few of us who had made it thus far had the misfortune to interrupt someone else's battle. The first I saw of it was a large, high built tank, 30 yards away and firing – at us! I could not make it out; no one had told us about Chinese tanks in the area and, somehow, it did not look Chinese, though what I knew about Chinese tanks at that stage was zero. Then, out of the blue, flying very low from the north down the valley we had just traversed, over us and over the tank, came a single engined aircraft – a Harvard, I believe – waggling its wings, trying to say something. The Chinese fire from above and behind had slackened a bit so I could raise my head to look at the plane and then the tank. Perhaps it was an American tank? At that moment, it fired its main armament at a couple of Glosters soldiers coming up five yards to my left and they fell like sacks, not hit, I believe, but knocked out or down by the shock wave of the shell passing within inches of them. The tank followed its shell with all-embracing machine-gun fire, the gun sticking out of its little armoured shield in the hull beside the driver's position moving in frantic circles as the gunner spewed his rounds in all directions. Then, quite slowly and I believed deliberately, the tank put its nearside track into the ditch and began to advance to crush me.

That, I felt, was enough. Chinese behind, a ruddy great hostile tank in front, a rifle, and exhaustion coming on, I stood up, put my hands up, and waved. A head appeared out of the tank turret and took a long look. The head was joined by a hand, which waved me forward. I limped on, bare foot sore on the paddy stubble. The head spoke with an American voice; 'Where the hell have you come from,' it said. Then the hand grasped the handle of the 50-calibre machine gun mounted on the turret, aimed the gun at the hills behind me, and loosed off a long burst. The owner of head, hand and voice then leaped out of his turret and had a few quick words before climbing back inside again. I think he wanted to check for himself that we were indeed United Nations troops, for by now we looked like a lot of scarecrows. Thus was I introduced to the 73rd Heavy Tank Battalion, US Army. I have wondered since if my appearance in front of the tank happened to coincide with the tank commander – a Lieutenant – receiving a radio message that what he had immediately in front of him was a bunch of friendly troops. The Harvard might have helped but, most importantly, Mike Harvey was somewhere forward, where, we learned later, he too had been fired on, had waved a beret and a white handkerchief to contact the tanks, and had explained the position.

Now more exhausted soldiers began to arrive from behind me and we all collected in the shelter of the tank while Chinese bullets began to rattle on the other side of it. I tried to get the men to link arms so that if one was hit he could be held by the others. Some obeyed but one or two were too worn out to understand me. The head had disappeared into the tank but every now and then the hand appeared and caused the turret machine gun to blaze away in a general northerly direction. Then the tank began to move back the way it had come, reversing, and we kept pace with it. I looked back and saw three or four bodies, quite still in the sunlight; there was no sign of anyone moving, attempting to join us, and no Chinese in pursuit, though heavy fire from the ridges above us had started again. The tank moved faster and covered two hundred yards before stopping. There, I saw that it had joined two more tanks, each with its little group of Glosters soldiers, and all the tanks were firing at the hills to our right rear. Peering round the south end of our shield I got the impression that I was witnessing the moment when a major infantry attack had failed and the troops involved were falling back in haste. It was a ROK infantry unit, and they were in retreat, covered by the fire of the tanks. They moved fast and the tanks went with them until, another couple of hundred yards on, we all turned a corner of the foothills on the eastern side of the broadening valley and were out of the line of Chinese fire. Here, the tanks stopped again and we were able to climb up onto the hulls, the two or three wounded with us, and then we moved south again, more quickly. Some of us were again in fear of our lives as the rotating tank turret threatened either to crush us or to knock us from our perches. We were spared the crack of the gun, however, for it now had nothing to fire at.

9

The Imjin River: The 'Korean Kohima'

As Denys Whatmore's description of the battle has so vividly described, if the Korean War is remembered at all in Britain today, it is so for the battle of the Imjin River, which began on St George's Day 1951 and continued for three subsequent days and nights. It was the place where, 25 miles north of Seoul, the 4,000 men of the 29th Infantry Brigade Group* received the full-frontal assault of as many as 50,000 troops of three Chinese divisions of General Yang Te-chih's *Sixty-Third Army*. From mid-April General Peng Te-Huai had 27 divisions at full strength, supported by considerable artillery and some armour. Withstanding the fearsome tide swirling against them, the soldiers of the brigade, about half of them conscripted National Servicemen, fought to the last round and the last man, before death, capture or enforced retirement to rebalance the UN line. It was the bloodiest battle a British formation has fought in the decades since the Second World War. A full quarter of the brigade was lost. But it was successful, for in the determined stand of stout-hearted soldiers the Chinese plan to envelop the advancing UN army failed. It is hard not to be mesmerised by the combat performance of the 29th Brigade, and especially of the 1st Battalion, Gloucestershire Regiment – soon to be called the 'Glorious Glosters', the old 'fore and afts'. Although the battalion was utterly destroyed in this battle, it blunted the Chinese offensive and denied to them the full fruits of a victory – the destruction

---

*Now reinforced by a 500-man-strong Belgian battalion.

of the Eighth Army and the capture of Seoul – they had confidently expected to secure.* For the Imjin River battle was the Kohima of Korea; a battle in which six years before a tiny group of superbly trained and confident Indian and British soldiers – the 4th Battalion, Royal West Kents, the Assam Regiment and Assam Rifles – fighting alongside each other in the common cause of the defence of India, sacrificed themselves as the defenders of a vitally strategic mountain pass, through which the enemy would only be allowed to progress over their dead bodies.† At Kohima 1,200 men held off 15,000, a ratio of 1 to 12.5. At Imjin, the ratio was exactly the same. At Kohima, as on the Imjin, there could be no contemplation of defeat, or failure. At Kohima in April 1944 the Japanese could not be allowed to fall into the Brahmaputra Valley and Bengal, for who knows what political damage would have been caused by an admission that the borders of India were not secure. In Korea, what lay beyond the Imjin was as equally needful for the Chinese to secure: the town of Uijongbu and, beyond that, the South Korean capital, Seoul. The see-sawing battles of the first three months of 1951 had come to an end, the stuffing removed from the Chinese rollercoaster offensives and the defensive line separating North from South beginning to firm up at long last. At Kohima some 1,200 unprepared though determined and experienced fighters held off the full weight of Lieutenant General Kōtoku Sato's 31st Division for an agonizing 16 days. It was long enough to enable the besiegers to hold on until at last they were relieved and the besiegers themselves became the besieged.

The battle of the Imjin River played a significant role in defeating the Chinese Fifth Phase Offensive, the final large-scale Chinese offensive of the war. It was important because, like Kohima, it demonstrated the efficacy of battle to achieve strategic objectives, a point intuitively understood by Ridgway, though seemingly forgotten by MacArthur, who had by now lost faith in the fighting prowess of his army.

---

*The Gloucestershire Regiment ('Glosters') had received the distinction of wearing two cap badges, each bearing a Sphinx, one fore (large) and one aft (small) on their headdress, in recognition of the battle of Alexandria in 1801, when men of the 28th Regiment fought in two ranks back-to-back against men of Napoleon's expeditionary force to Egypt.
†At Kohima all the Indian soldiers, who made up two-thirds of the defenders of Kohima Ridge, were volunteers. Most British soldiers were pre-war territorials or regular soldiers, with a smattering of wartime volunteers.

Embarrassingly for MacArthur, Ridgway's success in fighting the ground battle in Korea took place at a time when the C-in-C in Tokyo had given up on the power of conventional forces to stop the Chinese. The Imjin battle was a tactical defeat for the UN as it precipitated a short and temporary withdrawal, but by managing to contain the massive attack against it through successive short, subsequent withdrawals, by denying the Chinese their objectives, and by creating a further successful advance and realignment of the defensive positions along the 38th Parallel, the Eighth Army secured a strategic victory. The overwhelming numerical advantage enjoyed by the Chinese did not give them their desired victory. An ordinary battle, fought by perfectly ordinary infantry – many of whom were conscripted National Servicemen – armed with rifles, bayonets, grenades, accompanied by a good dose of professionalism, small unit leadership, personal courage, and lots of artillery – proved to have important strategic consequences for the UN. It demonstrated that they didn't need atomic bombs to stop the Chinese in their tracks. As the British Expeditionary Force in France fighting the 100-day battle from August 1918 demonstrates – along with the Commonwealth's Fourteenth Army in Eastern India and Burma in 1944 and 1945 (during which the battle of Kohima was fought), the Eighth Army in the Western Desert, Sicily and Italy, and the US Twelfth Army Group in northwest Europe during the 11 months between June 1944 and May 1945 – expertly fought battles brought about strategic success. So it was on the Imjin River in April 1951.

By early April Ridgway's army had achieved what only a few short months before had seemed impossible: it was holding temporary defensive positions astride the 38th Parallel. In the face of an array of difficulties, which included the dire initial state of American military morale and the scepticism of the C-in-C, Ridgway had planned and delivered a careful and systematic advance to the Han River and beyond, rolling up overstretched and exhausted Chinese formations with re-energised UN troops who fought because they were now executing a sensible and well-understood plan, and because they had tasted victory. The UN had finally seen the Chinese run, and it had been a comforting sight, especially after the shocks of the First, Second and Third Phase

Offensives the previous December and January. The line the Eighth Army held in mid-April was not intended to be permanent; rather a temporary phase line before a further advance would take place to establish the final defensive positions that would finally delineate North from South Korea and provide the physical basis for negotiations to talk about peace. A deliberately conceived policy of stalemate was now adopted by the UN. Their forces would fight to protect their defensive positions and even to improve them and to fight for local advantage where necessary, but they would not undertake any campaign of manoeuvre to upset the arbitrarily concocted defence line.

The Eighth Army, tails up, certainly expected a further Chinese counteroffensive: it had, after all, become something of a pattern in the see-saw nature of the fighting so far in Korea, but it is fair to say that the size and scale of the Chinese Fifth Phase Offensive was not expected. British troops along the Imjin, seeing little sign of the Chinese despite daily (and nightly) patrols into the northern hinterland across the river, saw nothing of note, and the men began to relax. The mail caught up, company cooks prepared hot food (rather than the individual or section feeding that took place in combat) and the men gathered for church services on Sunday morning. The weather was warm, balmy even. Morale was high. A battle was expected, sometime, but how bad could it be? For the Eighth Army a degree of complacency can also be said to have set in, perhaps allied to a long delay in establishing robust supply arrangements reaching back to Seoul. The situation was compounded by the fact that Ridgway, having replaced MacArthur following his sacking by the president, was now in Tokyo as C-in-C and his replacement, Lieutenant General James Van Fleet, was quickly getting his feet under the table in Korea.

The extreme west of the UN line was held by Milburn's I Corps, covering the lower Imjin, which sat astride the traditional attack route towards Seoul from the north. Ridgway and Milburn, however, suffered from the traditional curse of having insufficient troops to cover the entire line. Facing Milburn was the whole of the *19th Army Group*, the task of which was to smash his corps and open up the road to Seoul. On the left was the 1st ROK Division, with a frontage of over 20 miles. To their right was Major General Robert Soule's US 3rd Infantry Division, of which the British 29th Infantry Brigade Group was a part, sitting directly on the shortest route for the Chinese to reach Seoul. The 29th

Brigade's actual front, along the twisting turns of the river, running underneath heights that reached 2,000 feet, amounted to about 15 miles, far more than the nearly ten miles (17,000 yards) indicated on the map. As Brigadier Allan Mallinson suggests, this 'was considerably more than a brigade would expect to hold, except during an operational pause. Even in similar country in Italy in the Second World War, three miles at most would have been the rule.'* But needs must: there weren't any more troops available, and risks had to be taken. To the right of 29th Brigade was the US 65th Infantry Regiment sitting astride Route 33, which was the main road running south towards Seoul. Two rough tracks – the western one (known as Route 5Y) in fact not much more than a mountain path – ran south towards Seoul, only 25 miles further back; no bridges crossed the Imjin (they had been destroyed in the fighting), but at this time of year the river did not represent the obstacle it had been immediately after the spring thaw and the British Royal Engineers had built pontoons across the river to carry military traffic. It was also easily fordable in many places for infantry. The British dispositions were therefore widely scattered, so as to cover the main points of high ground covering the two tracks over an impossibly wide brigade position. This meant that the forward battalions were unable to provide mutual fire support to each other. In each battalion, companies could only support their own platoons, not other companies. Each company would have to fight, therefore, on its own. The alternative was to bring the companies together so that each battalion could fight as an integrated unit, although this would have meant very wide gaps being left between the three battalions in the brigade. Brigadier Tom Brodie, a vastly experienced combat veteran of the Burma campaign, was left with an option of difficulties. He was worried about how stretched his battalions were but had been told by Major General Robert Soule that there were simply no more men available. Soule's divisional reserve was a battalion of the 65th Regiment and a tank battalion, situated east of the Belgian position on Route 33.

Brodie would have to make do. There were no perfect solutions for the Imjin position; he chose a good option, which was to cover the wide expanse of his area of responsibility by spreading out his companies,

*Allan Mallinson, *The Shape of Battle* (Bantam Press, 2021), 293.

ensuring that the platoons in each could mutually support each other. From east to west, Brodie placed his Belgian battalion (which included a company of troops from Luxembourg) – all experienced veterans of the Second World War – on the right of the brigade on Hill 197, just north of the river; the Northumberland Fusiliers on Hill 257, south of the river; and the Gloucestershire Regiment a mile and a half to the left of the Fusiliers, forward of Hills 235 and 314. The dominating feature in the centre rear of the position was the towering 2,000-foot-high Kamak-san (Hill 675), around which the two tracks ran, but which separated the Glosters from the remainder of the brigade. The Gloster position dominated the rough track that ran from a ford across the Imjin, and thence back through the valley, the steep hills matted with thick scrub. For this reason, Brodie gave each battalion their own light artillery, a troop of six 4.2-inch mortars from 170 Battery, Royal Artillery. The Royal Ulster Rifles, the brigade's fourth battalion, weakened by the loss of over 200 men at Chunghung Dong in January, was in reserve to the rear on the main supply route to the right of Kamak-san. It was capable only of supporting the two battalions to its north, the Fusiliers and Belgian battalion. Further north of the Royal Ulster Rifles, on the same track (Route 11), behind the positions held by the Northumberland Fusiliers, was C Squadron, 8th King's Own Irish Hussars, with 16 Centurion tanks. The three 25-pounder gun batteries of 45th Field Regiment, Royal Artillery, were in the centre of the entire position, to the left of the tanks.* In addition to being widely dispersed, there was insufficient wire to protect the positions, and few anti-personnel mines had been laid, which might have impeded the overwhelming numbers of enemy infantry. Each battalion had four rifle companies, a support company with the battalion's 'heavy' weapons (3-inch mortars, Vickers medium machine guns, and the huge 17-pounder anti-tank guns towed by tracked carriers). With well-trained troops, able to fight when attacked and to rely on the 4.2-inch mortars and 25-pounders of their supporting artillery to help them destroy any assault, the only

---

*There were eight guns in each of three batteries. The regiment fired 24,000 rounds during the three-day battle, an average of 1,000 rounds per gun, much higher even than that fired at El Alamein in 1942, until then regarded as the most ever fired in a single battle by the Royal Artillery, in which 800 guns fired 600 rounds apiece.

challenge would be posed by running out of ammunition in a fight against very large numbers of enemy. This, essentially, is the story of the Imjin River battle. Brodie had observed, and Kohima had demonstrated, that there was no problem with being surrounded, so long as sufficient ammunition and water was available to the troops, and their fighting spirit remained undaunted. At Kohima the initial siege went on for 16 days, and successfully rebuffed Japanese attempts to capture this critical route into India. At the Imjin River the 29th Brigade was forced to withdraw after three days of intense fighting not because they had been defeated, but because the brigade had exhausted its ammunition and then had to conform with a general withdrawal.

———

Once the Kansas Line had been reached, Van Fleet's aim was to launch operations in the centre to disrupt Chinese counteroffensive potential south of an area between Chorwon, Pyonggang, and Kumhwa, an area known as the 'Iron Triangle'. These moves began on 21 April, while to the east X Corps prepared to launch its own offensive three days later. This attack was interrupted by General Peng Te-Huai's own offensive. From the outset there were no signs of an impending Chinese attack on 29th Brigade's front, as the Chinese had hidden themselves too well. Brigade patrols went up to 20 miles but found little of note. General Peng Te-Huai was repeating his earlier skilful tactics of hiding his army in the quiet folds of the distant hills, hidden in caves and tunnels, far from the scrutiny of nosy UN patrols or aircraft. But the first signs of renewed Chinese activity took place on Saturday 21 April, with reconnaissance patrols seeking out the British defensive positions along the river. The British had assumed, wrongly as it transpired, that any attack would come gradually, probing attacks building up over a period of days, sufficient to provide warning of the general location and size of any assault. On the late evening of 22 April, in brilliant moonlight, the Chinese-led army began what was to be its final attempt to smash UN forces in Korea and drive them into the sea.

The probing attacks on 21 April sounded the alarm across the front. During Saturday 22 April aerial reconnaissance revealed that the roads leading south from the village of Chorwon were crowded with vehicles and men. Peng was playing his hand. By 9 p.m. the Glosters,

Northumberland Fusiliers, and Belgians were all engaged with Chinese troops to their front, but not at that stage in large numbers. Within hours all that had changed, as shortly after 10 p.m. both the Northumberland Fusiliers and the Belgians received heavy attacks on their battalion fronts, while the Gloster platoon under Lieutenant Temple ambushed a large number of Chinese attempting to cross the ford over the Imjin in their sector, killing 70 for no loss. What shocked the men – including several who had fought the Japanese in Burma – was how many there were. They just kept on coming. Their ammunition finally exhausted, the Gloster patrol withdrew to A Company's position, the highest point of which was nicknamed Castle Hill from the remains of an ancient castle on the site. From the outset the 24 mortar tubes of 170th Battery (shared out between the battalions) and the 24 versatile 25-pounder gun howitzers of the 45th Field Regiment began a series of shoots ranging across the entire 12-mile frontage that were to last the entire three days of the battle. Three Chinese divisions advanced in column against the British position; each of the four Gloster companies (150 men each in A, B, C and D companies) initially faced a battalion each of between 800 and 1,000 men. The first attack on the 23rd was by the *187th Division* with three regiments, with perhaps 15,000 men. On the 24th the *188th* and *189th* crossed also, the *188th* joining attacks on the Fusiliers and the Royal Ulster Rifles, while the entirety of the fresh *189th* attacked the Glosters. Peng's aim was to swamp the defenders, whom he knew would be lightly stretched across difficult country, in which it would be impossible to control every crossing point on the shallow Imjin or protect every track through the hills. His operational directive was: 'we will mass our forces to wipe out the 6th Division of the Puppet Army,* the British 27th Brigade, the American 3rd Division, the Turkish Brigade, the British 29th Brigade and the 1st Division of the Puppet Army'. Once these formations had been smashed by the Chinese rollercoaster, the advance on Seoul would be undertaken. The offensive was deliberately designed to be a meat-grinder. Unfortunately for Peng, the meat that was ground in this battle was primarily Chinese.

Events moved quickly. Sudden shocking and mass assaults by Chinese infantry, blowing their ubiquitous horns, most firing sub-machine guns

*i.e., the ROK Army.

the UN troops called 'burp' guns after the sound they made firing, were made against A and D Companies of the Glosters in the southwest, the entire Belgian battalion position in the northeast and X and Y Companies of the Royal Northumberland Fusiliers in the centre.* By midnight the forward Gloster and Fusilier positions – all unwired – were under pressure from so many enemy assault troops the men had trouble loading their bolt-action 0.303-inch Lee Enfield rifles fast enough. Bren light machine gun barrels soon glowed red hot, and the wooden stocks of the rifles were too hot to hold. The British Army's continued strict insistence on what it still called 'musketry' could be seen to pay off handsomely, even the newest National Service recruits working their rifle bolts smoothly to achieve the required 15 aimed shots a minute. They needed to, because in that first night of battle the defenders' positions were swamped by a sea of enemy in places ten – sometimes 20 – times their own number. At the same time A Company of the Glosters came under heavy attack, with the two other forward companies, D and B, together with X Company of the Fusiliers, in an isolated position overlooking the river, also coming under strong attack. Too far from the other companies for support, X withdrew gradually closer into the centre of the battalion position, which made the position of the right forward (Y) company precarious, Chinese troops rushing past, left and right, in the darkness. The Belgian battalion on the north side of the river, which enjoyed the benefit of most of the brigade's supply of barbed wire, endured heavy attacks all night. An attempt by a platoon of the Royal Ulster Rifles in tracked Bren gun carriers to seize the crossing point behind the Belgians, securing their supply and potential withdrawal route, failed, with many casualties. The Chinese had got there first and ambushed the carriers as they approached. But the track to the south – 29th Brigade's main supply route, Route 11, which ran parallel with Route 33 – remained open during the night, the men of the Royal Ulster Rifles – the brigade reserve, committed from the beginning of the battle – fighting off attempts by Chinese troops to inveigle their way through to cut it off.

*The 'burp' gun was the PPSh-41 sub-machine gun, with a drum magazine holding up to 71 rounds. Five million were manufactured by the USSR during the war. The Chinese manufactured their own, calling it the Type 50. A North Korean version was called the Type 49.

Fighting continued during that first momentous night in a way that few veterans of the Second World War who found themselves fighting in this battle – and there were many who had fought in Burma, North Africa and Northwest Europe – had ever experienced. Companies fired disciplined engagements at close range all night, rapidly depleting their first-line stocks of ammunition, and still the Chinese came on, whooping, their commanders sounding bugles and the men firing their 'burp' guns as they ran uphill, through the thick scrub, into the relentless British fire. Hundreds of bodies piled up in front of each position, the British astonished at the Chinese profligacy. As the night went on the men in the various platoon and company positions counted seven, nine or 11 separate assaults each. This couldn't last forever: at some point they would either run out of ammunition and be overwhelmed, or the Chinese would run out of men to throw at them. But through that first night the 29th Brigade positions stood firm. Casualties, however, quickly mounted. By morning some Gloster platoons were down to fewer than ten men. A Company was reduced to 58 able-bodied men. On A Company's forward position, the highest point, Castle Hill, was taken by the Chinese, the defenders reduced to six men, the platoon commander and over 20 others killed. The company commander, Major Pat Angier, demanded that it be recovered, as with the dawn the Chinese would be able to fire on the remainder of A Company's position. The task was given to Lieutenant Philip Curtis, the young commander of No. 1 Platoon. Captain Tony Farrar-Hockley, the Glosters' adjutant, who had gone forward to A Company's position at dawn to ascertain for himself the state of the company, recorded what happened next:

Phil is called to the field telephone: Pat's voice sounds in his ear. 'Phil, at the present rate of casualties we can't hold on unless we get the Castle Site back. Their machine-guns up there completely dominate your platoon and most of Terry [Waters]. We shall never stop their advance until we hold that ground again.' Phil looks over the edge of the trench at the Castle Site, two hundred yards away, as Pat continues talking, giving him the instructions for the counterattack. They talk for a minute or so; there is not much more to be said when an instruction is given to assault with a handful of tired men across open ground. Everyone knows it is vital: everyone knows it is appallingly dangerous. The only details to be fixed are the arrangements for supporting fire; and, though A Company's machine-gunners are dead, D Company will support. Phil gathers his tiny assault party together. It is time; they rise from the ground and move forward to the barbed wire that once protected the rear of the forward platoon. Already two men are hit and Papworth, the Medical Corporal, is attending to them. They are through the wire safely – safely! – when the machine-gun in the bunker begins to fire. Phil is badly wounded: he drops to the ground. They drag him back through the wire somehow and seek what little cover there is as it creeps across their front. The machine-gun stops, content now it has driven them back – waiting for a better target when they move into the open again. 'It's all right, sir,' says someone to Phil. 'The Medical Corporal's been sent for. He'll be here any minute.' Phil raises himself from the ground, rests on a friendly shoulder, then climbs by a great effort on to one knee. 'We must take the Castle Site,' he says; and gets up to take it. The others beg him to wait until his wounds are tended. One man places a hand on his side. 'Just wait until Papworth has seen you, sir.'

But Phil has gone: gone to the wire, gone through the wire, gone towards the bunker. The others come out behind him, their eyes all on him. And suddenly it seems as if, for a few breathless moments, the whole of the remainder of that field of battle is still and silent, watching, amazed, the lone figure that runs so painfully forward to the bunker holding the approach to the Castle Site: one tiny figure, throwing grenades, firing a pistol, set to take Castle Hill. Perhaps he will make it – in spite of his wounds, in spite of the odds – perhaps this act of supreme gallantry may, by its sheer audacity, succeed. But the machine-gun in the bunker fires into him: he staggers, falls, and is dead instantly; the grenade he threw a second before his death explodes after it in the mouth of the bunker. The machine-gun does not fire on three of Phil's platoon who run forward to pick him up; it does not fire again through the battle: it is destroyed; the muzzle blown away, the crew dead.*

*Recounted in Anthony Farrar-Hockley, *The Edge of the Sword* (Frederick Muller Ltd, 1954), 27–28.

The 24-year-old Curtis was awarded a posthumous Victoria Cross for this exemplar of soldierly commitment to duty, regardless of the cost, even that of his own life. All three of the A Company platoon commanders became casualties that night, two of them killed and Lieutenant Terry Waters badly wounded, shot in the head. He was to die in Chinese captivity. A Company was now reducing rapidly. It was only a matter of time before it was overwhelmed. Major Pat Angier telephoned Lieutenant Colonel James 'Fred' Carne, the commanding officer, an experienced Burma veteran, to appraise him of the situation. Carne instructed him to remain 'at all costs'. 'Don't worry about us,' Angier replied. 'We'll be all right.' Within 15 minutes Angier himself was dead.

The early dawn of Sunday 23 April brought some respite in the northeast, but none in the southwest, as the two forward Gloster positions – A and D Companies – had now been under repeated attack for eight hours. D Company was in as bad a shape as A. It was proving difficult and dangerous to take up ammunition to the outlying companies, and it wouldn't be long before water was also exhausted. Lieutenant Colonel Carne decided to draw back what remained of these two companies to the site of the battalion command post, Hill 234, at Solma-ri. From about 8.30 a.m. the survivors came trickling back, bringing their wounded but leaving the dead, under cover from heavy, accurate and very welcome air attacks by USAF fighter ground attack aircraft. The Chinese attacks now switched to the B and C Company positions. Seeing the inevitability of them going the same way as A and D Companies, Carne ordered them to disengage between assaults and join the remainder of the battalion on Hill 234. The battalion would fight together on the patch of high ground, rapidly being denuded of its foliage, of what would in time become dubbed 'Gloster Hill'. The survivors of B Company, fighting for its life, weren't able to extricate themselves and join the rest of the battalion on Gloster Hill until the morning of 24 April. When it did so, it had been reduced to just two officers and 15 men. The Glosters' line had shrunk from four miles to 600 yards. The battalion now boasted just 300 men able to fight from 622 who had started the battle.

Likewise, in the darkness of the early morning of St George's Day, the regimental day, X Company of the Northumberland Fusiliers withdrew successfully from its exposed position overlooking the river, but an isolated platoon of Z Company, 1,000 yards to the rear of Y Company, found itself under attack from large numbers of Chinese who had infiltrated around the Belgian position. A grim struggle for the position, stretched out across two pinnacles, followed. By dawn on 25 April, following a night of non-stop attacks, an estimated 500 Chinese dead lay thickly carpeting the steep slopes to the position. The fighting had cost the Fusiliers 31 casualties. The vastly outnumbered Fusiliers, out of ammunition, were forced to withdraw, leaving Y Company in a precarious position, with Chinese to its front and rear, and the Belgians cut off. Y Company were withdrawn to assist the exhausted Z Company – out of ammunition – from the Pinnacle position. The Chinese quickly occupied the evacuated hill. Because the gun lines of the 45th Field Regiment Royal Artillery to the east of the hill were now directly threatened, the field batteries were withdrawn to secondary positions to the rear. This served to isolate the Belgians yet further on the northern side of the river, and the Glosters in the south, now fighting their own, desperate battles. By this stage of the battle every soldier in the brigade had picked up a weapon and was fighting as an infantryman, dug in and repelling massed Chinese assaults that were being pressed without much subtlety against the British and Belgian positions. American airstrikes supported the defenders.

By mid-afternoon the Glosters were under attack from the north, west and south, all weapons, including their 17-pounder anti-tank guns, being brought into action against groups of infantry massing against them. Y Company of the Fusiliers were safely extracted with the assistance of tanks of the 8th Hussars. The Fusiliers' Pinnacle position was not recovered, despite two attempted counterattacks, the first by the Fusiliers and the second by troops of the US 3rd Division later that evening. When asked to describe the opposition on the position, the subaltern who led the assault said that it was 'over-populated' by Chinese. By nightfall of the 23rd the Belgians succeeded in withdrawing back across the river, with the assistance of the tanks attached to the US 65th Infantry Regiment. But the situation was grave for the entire brigade. The Glosters were completely surrounded. The Chinese were swarming around each of the company positions, isolating them and attacking furiously. It was only a matter of time before each would run out of ammunition and be overwhelmed, unless they could be withdrawn to new positions. This – withdrawal in combat – was known by all to be a complicated and dangerous business, but unless the siege of the Glosters' position could be undertaken, this was the reality facing the survivors.

By nightfall on Sunday the 23rd, the Fusiliers successfully pulled back its W and Z Companies. X and Z Companies held positions on smaller hills near the floor of the valley to the left of the MSR. To the east were three companies of the Royal Ulster Rifles. As darkness fell on the second night of relentless battle, the moon shone brightly across a landscape illuminated by the slow-moving tracer from machine guns, mortar flares and artillery illumination rounds. But the enemy provided no let up. During the night that followed, one attack was quickly followed by another on positions across the entire brigade. The enemy was attempting to defeat each in detail but despite this had failed to exploit the wide-open gap between the Glosters and the Fusiliers. The Chinese appeared committed to surrounding and reducing each defensive position but were being rapidly weakened by the resistance they encountered.

As dawn broke on Monday the 24th, the smoke of battle hung heavily across the valleys and hilltops of the brigade position. On Gloster Hill, now entirely surrounded by enemy troops, some of the smoke drifting lazily into the sky was from burning scrub. The valley floor was shrouded in a dense early morning fog. B Company had been reduced to 15 men, and was withdrawn to support battalion headquarters, where men of the 17-pounder anti-tank platoon and the 4.2-inch and 3-inch mortar sections had also withdrawn. There was no food or water. Attempts were made to drop supplies on the position that day, and light bombers of the USAF provided repeated sorties – about 50 in all – against the attackers, sticks of bombs adding to the crazy cacophony of battle. The Chinese committed their second division to the fight during this morning, a company managing to drive its way through the gap between the Glosters and the Fusiliers and establish itself on Kamak-san, overlooking the MSR.

Soon after midday the Chinese bugles blew for a new assault on Gloster Hill, and the adjutant – Captain Anthony Farrar-Hockley, who many years later would write the Official British History of the war – ordered the regimental buglers to reply with a medley of regimental calls, excluding 'Retreat'. The Chinese did not manage to break in, but the first of several attempts to relieve the battalion failed.

Tanks supported by troops of the US 3rd Infantry Division – including a company of the Philippine Battalion Combat Team, sent by Major General Soule to reinforce 29th Brigade – attempted to make their way up the mountain path, but their three M-24 Chaffee tanks were put out of action and the infantry came under such a barrage of fire as to make the task impossible. In retrospect this was the point at which Lieutenant Colonel Carne should have been ordered to break out, but instead he was told to stick it out, as a second attempt to break through was to be made. It was a strange order. There was no way of anyone else in I Corps relieving the battalion, and the pressure of Peng's assault was now such that the entirety of Milburn's Corps would sooner rather than later be forced to withdraw to a new defensive position. It is more than possible that at this juncture of the battle the staff in Soule's divisional headquarters simply had no idea of how tenuous the hold of Brodie's brigade was on its scattered position. Milburn instructed Soule to withdraw the Glosters but, when asked for an update on 24 April, Brodie responded to Soule in a cricketing analogy that every Briton – but few Americans – would have instantly recognised: he explained that the situation was a trifle 'sticky'. The real meaning – that the situation was extremely difficult and required an immediate withdrawal to save the entire brigade – was lost. Thinking that nothing was amiss, Soule ordered the Glosters to stay put for the time being. 'I understand my position quite clearly,' responded Carne by radio when given the news. 'What I must make clear to you is that my command is no longer an effective fighting force. If it is required that we stay here, in spite of this, we shall continue to hold. But I wish to make clear the nature of my position.'

As darkness fell that night the Glosters drove off another assault, as the Fusiliers fought for their lives in the centre of the position. That morning the Fusiliers' position had been fatally weakened, with Y Company driven back, and only W Company left on the left flank. On the right the Royal Ulster Rifles reported that Chinese troops were attempting to drive a wedge between them and positions held by troops of the US 3rd Division (the 7th Regimental Combat Team) to their right. The Belgians, now evacuated from their original positions across the river, helped plug gaps in the centre of the brigade. In the evening, a heavy assault was made on Z Company, protecting the MSR against attack from the west from a steep ridge. The company was under attack for the entire night, from all directions. The company commander, Major John Winn, was wounded three times, but the company held on. Y Company was able to push through the attackers from the north to join up with Z Company, and together they held their ground. By the morning of Tuesday 25 April, the MSR remained open, though Chinese columns were moving through the gap left by the evacuation of the Belgians and pushing a wedge between them and the neighbouring American regiment. Meanwhile, to the right of the road, the Royal Ulster Rifles were also under constant attack. In the centre the tanks of the 8th Hussars held the road and the Belgians were fighting heavy enemy forces falling out of the valley from the Glosters' position, and from south of Kamak-san.

It was clear by now that the position was fatally compromised and would need to be evacuated. The remnants of the brigade would in time be crushed one by one in its company and battalion positions, as there was no relieving force or any sort of sustainable capability able to bring up (or drop from the air) food, water and ammunition. By the morning of the 25th it was clear that the Chinese, who had now launched the third division against the position, were attempting to cut off the entire brigade by striking directly at Uijongbu, doing perhaps what they should have done at the outset of the battle. Milburn accordingly ordered a general withdrawal to a new line north of Seoul. The 29th Brigade, with the remainder of the corps, was to withdraw. In contact, this is not an easy task, as troops have to move while continuing to engage the enemy. Brodie sent the Belgians to the south of the position to create a block on the road. The remaining Glosters and Fusiliers would withdrawal through this block, bringing all their equipment and wounded with them. The Royal Ulster Regiment and the tanks of the 8th Hussars would bring up the rear.

On Hill 234 on the morning of the 25th the Chinese assaults began for a third day, bugles sounding their discordant notes. Small-arms and machine-gun fire now played itself relentlessly from the surrounding hills. All attempts to relieve the battalion had failed. At 9.30 a.m. on 25 April Brodie called Carne and ordered him to break out in any way he could and attempt to meet up with the remainder of the brigade at the block. The medical officer and chaplain remained with the wounded, while the survivors departed through the scrub in company groups. Only a handful escaped – 39 men of D Company, including

Lieutenant Denys Whatmore – making it through to UN lines. The remainder were left to suffer the torments of communist captivity until the armistice was finally signed in July 1953. The battle of the Imjin River was a lesson 'in the duke of Wellington's old phrase, in how not to do it but for a shining example of how a battalion of 700 men can conduct themselves when they have been let down.'*

The withdrawal of 29th Brigade became a confusing, running battle, akin in nature to that experienced by the 2nd Division at Kunu-ri. The Chinese were across the road at several places and had to be ejected from each position in turn before the withdrawing troops could get through. The Centurion tanks of C Squadron, 8th Hussars, led the way but, with the hills swarming with Chinese, this was no easy matter, although most of the Fusiliers and the Royal Ulster Rifles succeeded in doing so, although the Fusiliers' commanding officer, Colonel Kingsley Foster, was killed. Those troops unable to extricate themselves from the position via the rearguard – B Company of the Royal Ulster Rifles – on the road made their way through the hills to the southeast. As they did so they came under repeated attacks from Chinese troops moving towards the road in large numbers from the west and down the slopes from Kanak-san: it was only a matter of time before the MSR would be irrevocably blocked. The tanks helped shepherd men of the Fusiliers and Royal Ulster Rifles through to the Belgian battalion's block, but in the fighting five were lost to anti-tank grenades and slipped tracks. Chinese infantry clambering onto the tanks were removed by the expedient of machine-gun fire from its neighbour. Thus it was that the 29th Brigade was bloodily extricated from its Imjin River position.

General Van Fleet's inquiry into the battle was submitted to General Ridgway on 26 May 1951:

> It is my opinion that all reasonable and possible courses of action open to the responsible commanders concerned were initiated in an effort to extricate the Gloucestershire battalion. Close and continuous liaison was maintained between commanders during this critical period and, as a result, maximum use was made of available resources, fire support and tactical air. The overwhelming strength

---

*Allan Mallinson, *The Making of the British Army* (Bantam Press, 2009), 393.

and determination of the enemy's attacks, together with his initial capability for early penetration by infiltration and enveloping tactics, taxed the corps, division and brigade commanders' limited reserve capabilities to the maximum. I believe that all decisions made were tactically sound and that subordinate commanders complied with orders to the maximum extent of their capabilities. The loss of this gallant fighting unit will continue to be felt with deep regret by myself and members of this command. Its magnificent stand in the face of overwhelming odds contributed immeasurably to the maintenance of the tactical integrity of the entire US I Corps.

The dominant feature of the fighting that erupted on 23 April was the *overwhelming force* of the Fifth Phase Offensive, which smashed against the scattered company positions of the British brigade – as they did across the entire UN line – in confident expectation that the defenders would fold under the sheer weight of Chinese manpower. This was Peng Te-Huai's intention. For all their prowess at infiltration, the Chinese objective on the Imjin was destruction rather than penetration, adopting the bludgeoning, crushing tactics of a Japanese-style assault. Clearly, Peng believed that the UN forces on this line would fold, as they had the previous year. Instead of bypassing Commonwealth positions and racing to the rear, there to capture logistical sites, block roads, destroy communications and generally sow confusion, Peng's battle plan was to fight it out this time on the Imjin River in a mass assault. It was, on reflection, a mistake, for in attempting to overwhelm the tiny British and Belgian garrison, the attacking divisions, acting like a battering ram, caused themselves unsustainable casualties, which was to prevent them from subsequently advancing far beyond the Imjin. It would have been more sensible to have infiltrated and outflanked the Imjin positions, allowing them to wither on the vine, rather than to have sought battle on such bloody and expensive terms as a mass human wave assault. The cohesion and fluidity of the Eighth Army's advance had surprised General Peng Te-Huai, who had made the mistake of believing, from his first experience of fighting, that Western troops were intrinsically weak. Underestimating one's enemy is a common failing in warfare; Peng Te-Huai fell into the same trap as the Imperial Japanese Army when it first encountered American and British Commonwealth troops in 1941 and 1942. They were to regret their complacency, as was Peng Te-Huai to regret his own hubris in far extending his own forces beyond the point at which they could fight for sustained periods.

The British suffered 1,091 casualties – including 140 killed, 109 wounded and in British hands and 842 captured, many of whom were wounded and now in Chinese hands – during the three-day battle of the Imjin River, 622 from the Glosters group, which suffered nearly 80 per cent casualties. The Glosters had started the battle with 798 men and suffered 622 casualties: 59 killed in action, 41 wounded but uncaptured and 522 taken prisoner, 180 of whom were also wounded. Thirty-four of these would die in captivity. A total of 217 paraded alive (176 unwounded) after the battle. This gallant brigade had held the extended line for a crucial period against three Chinese divisions. In the words of one American historian, it was because 'of British hearts and bayonets, the thrust at Seoul had failed ... the best their offensive could achieve was a realignment of UN lines.'* More importantly, it had demonstrated that hard, determined battle could achieve strategic results: Peng's exultant army had used the wrong tactics against the wrong enemy. By charging in feet first, hoping to excite a panicked withdrawal, the Chinese had thrown themselves against a very hard rock and suffered catastrophic casualties. China has never revealed its losses during these three days, but in this area of the Imjin it would have been around 10,000 dead and wounded, perhaps more. Fehrenbach suggests 15,000. The decision to fight, rather than to envelope or infiltrate, cost Peng the battle, because at the Imjin River the 29th Brigade was also determined to fight. As a result Peng failed to outflank I Corps and thus also failed to seize Seoul. The Fifth Phase Offensive was a failure, the *19th Army Group* fatally injured, large numbers of casualties caused for little gain. Indeed, within weeks the Eighth Army was pushing back towards the

*Fehrenbach, *This Kind of War*, 313.

38th Parallel and the conditions had been established for the Soviet Union to agree to establish peace talks. An American Presidential Citation was awarded to the Glosters on 8 May 1951:

The 1st BATTALION GLOUCESTERSHIRE REGIMENT, BRITISH ARMY and TROOP C, 170th INDEPENDENT MORTAR BATTERY, ROYAL ARTILLERY ... are cited for exceptionally outstanding performance of duty and extraordinary heroism in action against the armed enemy near Solma-ri, Korea on the 23rd, 24th and 25th of April 1951. The 1st BATTALION and TROOP C were defending a very critical sector of the battle front during a determined attack by the enemy. The defending units were overwhelmingly outnumbered. The 83rd Chinese Communist Army drove the full force of its savage assault at the positions held by the 1st BATTALION, GLOUCESTERSHIRE REGIMENT and attached unit. The route of supply ran Southeast from the battalion between two hills. The hills dominated the surrounding terrain northwest to the Imjin River. Enemy pressure built up on the battalion front during the day 23rd April. On 24th April the weight of the attack had driven the right flank of the battalion back. The pressure grew heavier and heavier and the battalion and attached unit were forced into a perimeter defence on Hill 235. During the night, heavy enemy forces had by-passed the staunch defenders and closed all avenues of escape. The courageous soldiers of the battalion and attached unit were holding the critical route selected by the enemy for one column of the general offensive designed to encircle and destroy 1st Corps. These gallant soldiers would not retreat. As they were compressed tighter and tighter in their perimeter defence, they called for close-in airstrikes to assist in holding firm. Completely surrounded by tremendous numbers, these indomitable, resolute, and tenacious soldiers fought back with unsurpassed fortitude and courage. As ammunition ran low and the advancing hordes moved closer and closer, these splendid soldiers fought back viciously to prevent the enemy from overrunning the position and moving rapidly to the south. Their heroic stand provided the critically needed time to regroup other 1st Corps units and block the southern advance of the enemy. Time and again efforts were made to reach the battalion, but the enemy strength blocked each effort. Without thought of defeat or surrender, this heroic force demonstrated superb battlefield courage and discipline. Every yard of ground they surrendered was covered with enemy dead until the last gallant soldier of the fighting battalion was over-powered by the final surge of the enemy masses. The 1st BATTALION, GLOUCESTERSHIRE REGIMENT and TROOP C, 170th INDEPENDENT MORTAR BATTERY displayed such gallantry, determination, and esprit de corps in accomplishing their mission under extremely difficult and hazardous conditions as to set them apart and above other units participating in the same battle. Their sustained brilliance in battle, their resoluteness, and extraordinary heroism are in keeping with the finest traditions of the renowned military forces of the British Commonwealth and reflect unsurpassed credit on these courageous soldiers and their homeland.

The truth is that the Imjin position was far too weak for the strength of the opposition arrayed against it. The Imjin was not an obstacle, and the position I Corps built was never able to withstand the full force of Peng's army. Brodie's brigade was far too spread out to allow its four battalions to provide each other with mutual fire support. Even if the battalions had been sited together rather than as disparate companies, the weight of enemy mass flung against it, with the opportunity for outflanking and infiltration available to it, the Chinese could easily have moved beyond the defences to Uijongbu. Brodie's decision to spread out his forces was probably the correct one, given that, although he, Major General Soule and Lieutenant General Milburn knew the Chinese would counterattack, they had no comprehension of the size of the onslaught to come, and that this deluge would be equally catastrophic for the brigade whether it was dispersed into company positions or concentrated together into battalions, as there was no reserve able to launch a rescue attempt when the entirety of the Eighth Army line was under attack by Peng's 29 divisions. Only soldierly fortitude would save it from the huge, violent tide about to wash over it.

Peng was convinced that mass human assault would be enough to overcome the UN's terrible superiority in weaponry – especially artillery and airpower – and that this use of mass manpower would serve again, as it had done so the previous year, to destroy UN morale and fighting spirit. He was partly right: some units did crumble, again. But sufficient did not, including the astonishing men of the 29th Infantry Brigade Group, who fought resolutely despite the huge odds, and refused to be intimidated by the vast forces arrayed against them.

While the 29th Brigade was battling it out on the Imjin, the entire UN line across the length and breadth of the Korean peninsula was under pressure from Peng's Fifth Phase Offensive. The brigade's compatriots in the 27th Brigade were undergoing a similar experience above the Kapyong River in the central sector, for which it was also to receive a Presidential Citation.* With the 6th ROK Division on the line giving way to the enormous pressure of the Chinese assault – it was green, and had no artillery or tank support – the 27th Brigade found itself acting as a block in a wide valley encased by steeply forested hills north of the village of Kapyong in the centre of the U. line – on a bend of the Pukhan River between Seoul and the Hwachon reservoir – against attack by two Chinese divisions. By this stage the King's Own Scottish Borderers had replaced the Argylls, who had returned to Hong Kong, and a Canadian battalion – the 2nd Battalion, Princess Patricia's Canadian Light Infantry, had arrived to join the brigade, as had the 16th New Zealand Field Artillery Regiment. Together with a company of American tanks from the 72nd Tank Battalion, the brigade successfully repelled these assaults between the night of 23 April and the morning of 25 April, ANZAC Day. The Chinese attacked each wing of the defensive position sequentially, the Australians on the right on the first night, and the Canadians on the left on the second. In both battles the defenders held off overwhelming attacks with the support of New Zealand artillery and American tank fire. The Australian battalion conducted a fighting withdrawal to a rear block around the brigade headquarters, supported again by the tanks and artillery. This was too much for the Chinese to bear and, suffering grievously,

*David Allison, *27th British Commonwealth Brigade Korea 1950–1951* (Pen and Sword, 2025).

they withdrew. A second attempt to achieve a breakthrough, this time against the Canadians the following night, also failed. The Chinese – brave, determined men, the historian of the Middlesex describing them as fighting 'extraordinarily well, and with great dash' – had got in among the Canadian trenches, but final protective fire called down by the Canadians on their own positions worked spectacularly. The Canadians, well dug in, suffered no loss, while the Chinese troops, in the open on the hill, were slaughtered in their scores. The battalion, surrounded but calm and confident in their ability to hold out come what may, received an airdrop of ammunition, food and water that day from C-119 Boxcars of the USAF, the old lessons of Burma being successfully and seamlessly adopted for this new war. In an innovation first practised in Burma in 1944, helicopters evacuated the wounded. Having lost what was estimated to be most of its strength, the Chinese divisions then withdrew. Their part in the Fifth Phase Offensive was now over and had ended in failure.

The Chinese had suffered grievously during this offensive. Combat casualties across the entire front between 22 and 29 April totalled up to 60,000, compared with the UN's 4,000. In one year of war the NKPA had lost perhaps 600,000 casualties, of whom 100,000 were prisoners. The Chinese had also lost in the region of 500,000 by this early stage of the war already, testament to Mao Tse Tung's morally bankrupt strategy of repeatedly deploying Chinese and North Korean manpower into the teeth of superior UN firepower. Mao was to demonstrate that communist tactics were exceptionally good at killing communist peasant soldiers and did so in their hundreds of thousands. These were devastating and ultimately unsustainable losses, and proved once again that vast Japanese-style 'banzai-type' attacks which Mao had adopted could only rarely overcome resolute defenders. Even as the communist armies grew in size – the combined Chinese/NKPA to 1.2 million – and as UN casualties also grew, at about 100,000 at the end of the first year of war, the UN strength in manpower and firepower was also increasing dramatically. UN land forces now numbered 1.5 million, a third of whom were ROK Army, while the size of the US Far Eastern Air Force had doubled to 1,400 aircraft in a mere seven months.

Attempts by the Chinese to withdraw from these astonishingly expensive engagements were interrupted by a further counterattack by

Eighth Army, seriously discomforting the Chinese in the process and forcing Peking and Moscow to recognise that they would never prevail militarily in Korea against the forces of the UN. In these operations Ridgway's troops recovered territory north of the 38th Parallel, with most forces stopping at what were called the Kansas and the Wyoming Lines. Very large numbers of Chinese and North Korean casualties were sustained in these offensives, the UN entirely gaining the upper hand in military operations. It was at the Kansas and Wyoming Lines that a north–south stalemate was then allowed to develop through to the armistice that was eventually signed in July 1953.

IO

How to End a War

The only thing more difficult than starting a war is ending it, especially in the absence of the prospect of an outright military victory. Such was the experience of Korea in the two years between July 1951 and July 1953. With Washington determining that the right thing to do was wind the conflict down to a close rather than seek ultimate victory in North Korea – by the conquest of North Korea – the challenge now was to persuade the communists likewise to seek a settlement. Settling on an end to the war with a still-divided Korea was not what either Kim Il-sung or Syngman Rhee wanted, but in Washington's view it was the only way to end the fighting in a war for which victory was now accepted by most Western policymakers as an illusory objective.

The war for the *status quo ante bellum* between July 1951 and July 1953 – the second and final phase of the second Korean War – took four forms.

1 A war for physical advantage along the Main Line of Resistance, one of the names given to the defensive line the United Nations built along the rough line of the 38th Parallel;
2 A propaganda war by the communists aimed at winning the hearts and minds of public opinion worldwide to the communist position, using what they described as US warmongering and war crimes as ammunition to fire at their enemy;
3 A war by the communists for the hearts and minds of the prisoners they held in North Korea, and the domination of

the US POW camps in the South that contained Chinese and
NKPA prisoners;

4 A continuing insurgent war by communist-led guerrillas across
rural swathes of the ROK designed to destabilise the ROK and
Rhee's hold on power.

The factor that more than anything else drove the Truman administration
into a process – both military and political – to end the war was the belated
realisation that the United States could never win a conventional war
with China – even if it wanted to fight one – without the expenditure of
vast human and material resources. Likewise, an ongoing war in Korea
could risk a war in Asia that might prejudice the security of Europe
where, it was commonly thought, the next communist blow – if it was
to come – would fall. There was simply no political commitment in
Washington at the time for a fight with China, despite the acceptance
in Washington that Communist China was an enemy of the USA. Nor
was there a desire to win the war by using any of America's arsenal of 369
atomic bombs. Truman for one was acutely conscious of the implications
for the world if nuclear weapons were used, especially if only to secure
a short-term political advantage or to rescue a failing conventional war.
They were weapons of last resort, and of deterrence. As early as 1946
he had written that 'The human animal … must change now, or he
faces absolute and complete destruction and maybe the insect age or
an atmosphere-less planet will succeed him.' Truman was determined
that the war in Korea would end like all wars that were not like the
Second World War, which demanded the unconditional surrender of
the aggressor: i.e., they would end by reasoned negotiation between
two sides that both wished to stop fighting, rather than a settlement –
such as Versailles in 1919 – imposed by the victor on the vanquished.
The war *could* be won earlier, Truman thought, by dropping atomic
bombs on China, but this would be akin to opening Pandora's Box.
If he had learned one thing already about the Korean War, it was the
bitter law of unintended consequences. Ironically, in 1953 it was the
threat by Eisenhower, Truman's successor as president, to use nuclear
weapons against China that eventually forced Mao to draw stumps on
his long campaign of prevarication and obfuscation at the 'peace talks'

(they would be better described as 'war talks', given that Mao didn't want the fighting to stop during the negotiations and only did so when the Politburo withdrew its support following the death of Stalin on 5 March 1953) and accept an armistice. But the situation in June and July 1951 was different from that which prevailed in 1953. The use of atomic weapons in 1951 would have entailed overreach of a kind for which the consequences – with Stalin still in control in Moscow – could not be guaranteed. Two years later, with Stalin dead, the *threat* of bombing Peking was precisely what President Dwight Eisenhower needed to force an obstinate Mao Tse Tung to end the fighting in Korea and to accept a divided Korea as an enduring political reality.

The UN's task in 1951 in pushing for a settlement was to persuade Mao Tse Tung and Joseph Stalin that it was also in China and the USSR's interests to do the same. The strategy worked, although it took time – two years in fact. The war only ended when the strategic ambitions of both sides were aligned. But how would China be persuaded that the USA no longer had any territorial ambitions in North Korea, and that the aim of unification was no longer a strategic objective for Washington? The answer was for UN forces to proceed no further forward than a defensive line, roughly approximating to the 38th Parallel, from which its forces could defend the territorial integrity of South Korea. This 155-mile line ran from the Yellow Sea in the West, about 20 miles north of Seoul, northeast towards the Imjin River valley – the Kansas Line. It then reached across to what was known as the 'Iron Triangle', bounded by the towns of Pyonggang, Kumhwa, and Chorwon. This area provided the terminus of a railway line from Manchuria. From here the line crossed the steep Taebaek mountains before falling south to a distinctive geographical feature called the Punchbowl, the rim of an extinct volcano, before crossing to the Sea of Japan on the east coast. It was along this line of contact that over the ensuing two years a positional war was fought in which the US – as leader of the UN coalition – deliberately eschewed the chance of securing an operational victory by defeating North Korea. In this act of deliberate self-limitation the US judged that while victory might be secured in North Korea, it would come at unacceptable costs in lives; it might provoke further unintended consequences, especially with regard to China, its huge army and its unpredictable leader; and it might lead to an unwanted nuclear war in a part of the world that had no long-term strategic interest for the USA. This decision and what followed was proof that fighting a limited war was possible within the context of a possible nuclear exchange. This period was before the era of Mutually Assured Destruction – known as MAD – when a large number of US weapons were matched against a similar number of Soviet ones, but the possibility of a dangerous nuclear exchange was nevertheless high. As General of the Army Omar Bradley said on 15 May 1951 to Congress, in the fall-out from MacArthur's removal:

> I am under no illusion that our present strategy of using means short of total war to achieve our ends and oppose communism is a guarantee that a world war will not be thrust upon us. But a policy of patience and determination without provoking a world war, while we improve our military power, is one which we believe we must continue to follow...
>
> Under present circumstances, we have recommended against enlarging the war from Korea to also include Red China. The course of action often described as a limited war with Red China would increase the risk we are taking by engaging too much of our power in an area that is not the critical strategic prize.
>
> Red China is not the powerful nation seeking to dominate the world. Frankly, in the opinion of the Joint Chiefs of Staff, this strategy would involve us in the wrong war, at the wrong place, at the wrong time, and with the wrong enemy.[*]

Withdrawing to a line of contact, subsequently defended at great cost in blood and treasure by soldiers of the UN coalition, was categorically not a surrender for the UN, though it was most certainly a risk. Would it work? Could the UN prevent communist troops breaking through? There was only one way to find out. The UN built up its forces along the line and defended it robustly. What was now dubbed the Jamestown Line consisted of an extensive range of defended positions stretching from one side of Korea to the other. Equally extensive communist positions sat in opposition, dug deep into the hills and mountains, boasting deep

---

[*]United States Congress. Hearings before the United States Senate Committee on Armed Services and the Committee on Foreign Relations, May 15, 1951 – Military Situation in the Far East, hearings, 82nd Congress, 1st session, part 2, 731–32.

bunkers and trench positions to a depth, in places, of 20 miles. Both Mao Tse Tung and Peng recognised that the ubiquity of UN airpower and the strength of its artillery meant that the Chinese needed to dig – and to dig deeper and more extensively than hitherto – to operate more at night than before, and to massively strengthen its own artillery arm to match the current overpowering advantage enjoyed by the UN. By the spring of 1952 the communists had 900,000 troops manning this line. A year later it was well over a million.

Withdrawal to the line was designed by the UN to provide for defensive operations only while both parties talked to reach a negotiated peace. It was a demonstration to Mao Tse Tung that the UN was serious about not launching offensive operations into North Korea. If the aim was a settlement of the war – as the UN insisted – the purpose of talks was to secure the best possible physical advantage along the existing line to ensure that South Korea was protected from any future aggression from the North. The US strategy to bring the war to an end entailed deliberately forcing China and North Korea to align their own objectives with those of the USA. This strategy of *strategic perseverance* would take time: there is no sense in 1951 that Washington guessed just how long. It was a strategy of pen *and* sword, the pen working simultaneously with the sword. It required Washington to service an increasingly attritional war for two long years, and to keep its allies conformed to this plan. By facing off against each other across the line of contact that divided the two Koreas, the North was forced, in time, to accept that a settlement would only come by accepting that the principle of a demarcation line was there to stay, that any aspiration to secure South Korea by force was no longer viable and that any form of peace would only come by way of a negotiated agreement. It is true that the North set out on the talks in July 1951 believing that it could bludgeon the UN into submission – fighting this war by other means – but the physical fighting on the Jamestown Line and the USA's resistance to the absurd theatre of the North's negotiating stance forced the communists – eventually – to come to terms. It came at a heavy price, but the alternative – escalation – offered a more expensive outcome.

———

The end of the Chinese Fifth Phase Offensive – which didn't conclude until late May 1951, with UN troops digging in along the main line of resistance, and on these positions began preparing extensive defensive structures to prevent any further Chinese breakthrough – wasn't the end of the Korean War, though it was certainly the end of the beginning. It was also – and deliberately, from the UN's perspective – the end of the war of movement.

It took some time for Mao Tse Tung to understand that the UN wanted to change the nature of the war, de-escalate the fighting and achieve a peace settlement with or without South Korean agreement (Rhee fought hard in fact to resist an agreement that disallowed him the right to unify the peninsula on the South's terms). There was a simple reason for the long delay. It was because neither the Soviet nor the Chinese side wanted *actual* peace in June 1951. They were very happy to talk about it, but both communist states wished to continue fighting for political and military advantage for just as long as they could. While he accepted that outright military victory could not be attained, Mao didn't consider the war *yet* to be over. Much could yet be attained by stretching out the talks to the greatest extent possible, not least of all in energising other communist and nationalist resistance movements elsewhere in Asia, such as in Malaya and Vietnam. This actually suited both Korean antagonists – North and South – neither of whom wanted a deal that did not entail unity under their chosen form of government. But control of the future of a united Korea was no longer in the hands of either Kim Il-sung or Syngman Rhee: after a year of bloody fighting, the process of securing a deal would be done to them, rather than by them. Accordingly, in this strategy of playing hardball, the communist side at the Kaesong talks sought from the outset (July 1951) to secure terms that were impossible for their enemy to accede. These included an immediate ceasefire along the actual line of the 38th Parallel (rather than the main line of resistance, or line of contact), the unilateral return of all prisoners of war and the departure of all foreign troops from the peninsula. The communists set out to use the talks as a propaganda tool against the Americans while they rearmed, rather than to secure, in good faith, agreed terms for a settlement. It appears that Mao in particular was not convinced that the UN was genuine in its desire to reach a settlement and withdraw from Korea. As a result, much of the two years of so-called negotiation were nothing of the kind. Prevarication and obfuscation became tools to obstruct and delay a settlement. The communists only agreed an armistice – strictly, an 'absence of war' – two years later when they had failed to secure any further military advantage from the positional struggle that characterised these 24 months of fighting across 155 miles of the neck of the Korean peninsula and were forced to accept an alignment of interests with those of the USA.

It took General Van Fleet some time, too, to understand Truman and Ridgway's strategy of locking the UN forces onto the line of conflict and deliberately eschewing the opportunity for fighting a new campaign for North Korea. He correctly thought that the communist forces in North Korea at the time had been defeated and wanted to capitalise on the defeat following the end of their Fifth Phase Offensive by striking hard for the Yalu again. His plan, suggested to Ridgway, was to launch amphibious attacks on the east coast while simultaneously attacking from the northeast of the line. 'At that time the east coast did not have a big build-up of defensive forces, and we could easily have made landings there,' he was later to explain. 'The Navy could have shot us ashore and kept us ashore as we built up. We had the Chinese whipped ... they were in awful shape ... they had no conception of fast moves ... they had no system of communication.' But Van Fleet, though he had read the memo from Truman, had not yet comprehended it. Truman's strategy was that the possibility of battlefield victory, though theoretically and practically achievable, had to be sacrificed in exchange for peace. A renewed offensive might be successful in the short term, but it would extend the war, conceivably make China feel vulnerable and might initiate a counter-response similar to the one which saw the first arrival of the Chinese in North Korea the previous October. Truman was also fearful that the domestic calls for the use of atomic bombs against China would be irresistible if in the next phase of fighting the tables were turned again, and American soldiers started dying on the Korean battlefield in large numbers. This simply wasn't a risk worth taking.

The political determination in Washington to go firm on a defensive line that secured the territorial integrity of both North and South Korea – effectively the *status quo ante bellum*, though the line did not represent the actual line of the 38th Parallel – came as something of a surprise to Mao Tse Tung, convinced that the UN would exploit its recent battlefield success by rushing again to the Yalu. Mao Tse Tung had not been watching Washington carefully enough to understand its desire to avoid what had begun in June 1950 as a local conflict becoming a global catastrophe. This suited the USSR, unwilling to continue to underwrite the North Korean military adventure in the South, which now encouraged all parties to seek a peaceful end to the war.

Talks began at Kaesong in mid-July 1951 but had collapsed by August. At the start, while reluctantly accepting the Soviet lead in seeking talks, the Chinese political strategy was to wear down the UN by making the process of talking as difficult as possible. For this reason, the so-called 'negotiations' were nothing of the kind. The North saw them simply as an opportunity to brow-beat their opponents, spread lies (such as that the USA was using biological weapons) and seek to score political points. To the bemused US negotiators, the shouting, posturing, arcane debates about trivialities and the long silences demonstrated simply that the North was unwilling to reach agreement. This was the classic strategy of fighting the war by other means. But this tactic failed: the only thing it did was prolong the war. The lack of good faith by Chinese and North Korean negotiators only became apparent to the US and UN over time, as the first set of discussions about bringing the war to an end stuttered and died in August, before being revived again in a repetitive cycle of behaviour, across the entire period of talks through to July 1953. Peng, advising Mao, suggested that advantage could be gained for China by fighting a war of attrition to wear down and demoralise their opponents, leaving them in a position where they would be happy to accept weaker terms than might otherwise have been the case. The chief stumbling block might have appeared to have been the status of the line of contact as the future demarcation line – the communists demanded that it be the actual physical *status quo ante bellum*, rather than the existing line of contact – but it was in fact the reality that the communists simply did not wish at this stage to secure a deal. Talking was something that had to be done while it rebuilt its strength and considered its options for the future. In 1952 and 1953 the communist side wished only to secure peace on its terms, not those which might bring a rapid end to the fighting.

The two years of positional warfare that accompanied the negotiations, first at Kaesong (until August 1951) and then at Panmunjom, were not – as is sometimes depicted – in any sense a stalemate. The war no

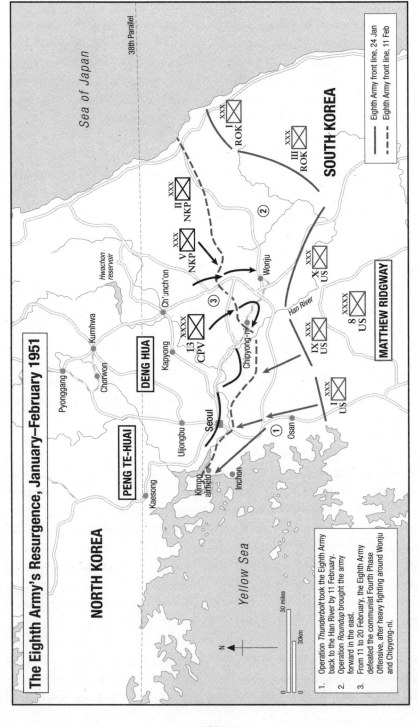

longer exhibited the crazy ebb and flow of the earlier battles but it was fought fiercely for positional and political advantage with the context of both sides recognising that the war would end on this line and nowhere else. Positional, because it was along the Jamestown Line that any final agreement would be based, and both sides worked hard to ensure that they maximised their side's advantage; and political, because although both sides had given up on the possibility of uniting the two Koreas, much remained at stake. The opportunity for the Chinese to make the most of the story that their proletarian armies had forced the USA to a military impasse was too good for Peking to ignore. For China, its status of the new communist kid-on-the-block in Asia, standing up to the Wall Street imperialists, was invaluable. From the UN perspective, both Ridgway in Tokyo and Van Fleet in Korea were agreed from the outset that they would have to fight to maintain the UN's defence of the geography they held.

The war thus became one of both sides attempting to secure respective physical, psychological and political advantage along the line of contact. Ridgway had been delighted with the performance of his troops during the final stages of the Chinese offensive in May, when the Eighth Army – including ROK and British and other UN contingent troops – rolled with the final Chinese punch and then pushed them back to dig in on the Jamestown Line. The men of Paik's ROK I Corps for example had fought well on the east coast, and as many as 17,000 Chinese troops lay dead.

In July 1951 Ridgway instructed Van Fleet to hold the existing defensive positions along the Kansas and Wyoming Lines but to do what he needed to improve the defences where this was tactically necessary, such as shortening and straightening sections of the line, improving positions and capturing terrain from the enemy that was directly advantageous to them. The term Ridgway used in his instructions to Van Fleet to build up the Jamestown Line was 'active defence'. This was where the war was to be fought to its conclusion. Accordingly, the Eighth Army undertook a series of offensives in autumn 1951, between late August and the onset of winter in November.

In the west, the task was to seize the high ground in the area where the Imjin River turns from flowing east–west to its turn towards the southwest and the Yellow Sea. The newly formed Commonwealth Division under Major General James Cassels undertook attacks in

September and October on the northern side of the Imjin to extend and strengthen this part of the line.* The first, Operation *Minden*, was successful and a second assault prepared for early October – Operation *Commando* – to seize the high ground of Kowang-san and Maryang-san, which provided dominating views over the Imjin and were strongly held by the Chinese. These positions were seized in a well-planned battle of exemplary professionalism conducted by first-class British and Australian infantry cooperating with British tanks and British, New Zealand and US artillery. Thrown off these hills, the Chinese counterattacked in overwhelming numbers a month later and regained Maryang-san in a battle in which a young soldier, Private Bill Speakman of the Black Watch, attached to the King's Own Scottish Borderers, though badly wounded, led repeated counterattacks against his attackers with bayonet and grenades. Speakman's battalion had been attacked by 6,000 Chinese. He was awarded the Victoria Cross.[†]

In the centre, a series of legendary battles were fought by X Corps to the west of the Punchbowl for Bloody Ridge, one of three interconnected hills to the southwest of the Punchbowl. Bloody Ridge had become something of a communist bastion, dominating the entirety of the centre-right of the line. Kim Il-sung had issued a 'stand or die' order to his troops, the NKPA *I, III*, and *VI Corps*, and they did as they were told. The ROK 7th Division managed to capture Bloody Ridge first but lost it again quickly to counterattack. The US 9th Infantry Regiment then attempted to secure the ridge in the face of fanatical NKPA opposition. Repeated, courageous assaults were made, all only to end in exhaustion at the culminating point, with Chinese and NKPA counterattacks ensuring that no attack succeeded in holding ground taken at great cost. The ridge was eventually seized on 5 September by the US Marines following ten days of intense fighting in a battle which saw 2,700 UN soldiers and perhaps 15,000 North Korean casualties. The focus in these summer battles around the Punchbowl now turned to Heartbreak Ridge, a seven-mile-long hill boasting formidable

---

*The 28th Commonwealth Brigade had inherited the mantle from 27th Brigade and was combined with the 25th Canadian Brigade and the 29th Brigade in the new 1st Commonwealth Division.
[†]His investiture was the first carried out by the new monarch, Queen Elizabeth II, shortly after she acceded to the throne in February 1952.

Chinese defences. The first attacks were mounted on 13 September and lasted for 40 days before the shattered ridge fell into the hands of the 25th Infantry Division in a battle in which American tanks helped turn the tide. The overall cost of the autumn campaign was an astonishing 60,000 casualties, 22,000 of them American. This was the price of fighting for peace. The two armies now stretched out facing each other on the line of confrontation, over 554,000 UN troops against over 459,000 communist troops, more than half of whom were Chinese.

A feature of these battles was a growing dependence by both sides on artillery. In the October battles for Maryang-san, for instance, the Chinese bombardment following the seizure of the ridge was described by all to be far greater than what they had experienced during the Second World War. The US 2nd Infantry Division fired an extraordinary 153,000 artillery rounds during August and September 1951. One of its artillery battalions fired a total of 14,425 rounds in only 24 hours from its 24 105mm field guns. Both Van Fleet and Ridgway recognised that artillery was the predominant weapon in the static warfare in which the UN was now engaged, with commensurately far greater ammunition requirements than the Second World War. The Chinese, likewise, reinforced their artillery arm substantially, though never coming close to the technical proficiency of British and American gunners. By the spring of 1952, however, they had deployed nearly 900 guns across the front. By mid-1952 the Chinese were firing 6,800 rounds a day. On 4 November it was estimated that 10,000 shells fell on the positions held by the 28th Commonwealth Brigade. In a period of 36 hours, the British responded with 30,829 rounds. As time progressed, the expenditure of artillery ammunition became prodigious, placing considerable pressure on both US manufacturing capability and logistical infrastructure. During June and July, the expenditure of artillery had become astonishing: in less than 60 days the communists fired over 700,000 rounds at the UN positions (nearly 12,000 per day), while the UN fired back over 4.7 million (nearly 80,000 per day). Not much seemed to have changed in positional warfare since 1916.

Far to the rear of the main line of resistance, insurgents loyal to Pyongyang undertook a guerrilla campaign across the ROK. Some of these were stay-behinds from the 1950 offensive; some were left-leaning Southerners recruited to the communist cause, and yet others were Northern commandos infiltrated into the South. Their targets were UN lines of communication and ROK state structures, such as the police, courts and local civic authorities. Their aim was to sow division and discord. They did this spectacularly but were ruthlessly eliminated using means that provided no quarter. The violence and murder perpetrated by the North was matched in equal ferocity by the ROK security forces: that they were fighting an existential struggle for survival against a totalitarian foe was no excuse for the scale of the barbarity exercised on occasions against communist supporters in the country. The Korean War, in the struggle against the NKPA and Northern sympathisers in the civilian population far behind the front lines, became a watchword in state-sponsored violence in both North Korea and the ROK, an exercise in over-reach which shocked those who saw it and which has left such a legacy of bitterness that a Truth and Reconciliation Commission was established in 2005 to investigate state violence during the Korean War. The Commission was expected to produce a final report in 2010 but at the time of writing in 2024 its remit had been extended to 2025. Much occurred in plain sight of foreign journalists and soldiers. In the four months between December 1951 and March 1952, for example, 11,090 guerrillas were killed and 9,916 captured, a proportion that suggests that questions were often not asked first. Atrocities were widespread, on both sides. One, at Kochang in February 1951, involved the execution of up to 1,000 villagers by South Korean security forces. The withdrawal of the NKPA from areas they occupied following the UN counteroffensive in September and October 1950 revealed the scale of these atrocities. Major General Paik, for instance, visited Pyongyang Prison on 19 October 1950. He described the scene he witnessed as 'hellish':

The enemy had murdered the inmates, throwing their bodies into every well on the compound in an attempt to hide the deed. By the time they finished, bodies lay in numberless profusion throughout the compound. Evidence indicated that many had been sealed in cells and suffocated. Before they fled, the enemy forces butchered every single person they had kidnapped from South Korea as well as those the regime characterized as 'reactionary elements'. The entire prison was pervaded with an odour so foul it took my breath away. The silent, wretched prison seemed to serve as a mausoleum for the spirits of the men and women who had died so unjustly within its confines.

My party and I trembled in anger as we viewed with our own eyes the inhumane consequences of the true communist character.

But the ROK was equally involved in such methods. When Pyongyang was recaptured in October 1950 a 30,000-strong police force was established, aimed at hunting down communist sympathisers. Within a month some 55,000 had been rounded up, many of them 'vicious red-hot collaborators and traitors'. What happened to truckloads of bound prisoners was observed by horrified troops of the British 27th Brigade, who saw convoys taking them to the countryside to be shot. London heard of these atrocities and complained to Washington, but despite protests it seems that little was done to rein in these excesses. The challenge for the UN at the time lay in fighting the NKPA and China on the battlefield, while simultaneously encouraging and supporting the growth of responsible civil government in the ROK. The moral foundation of UN action against the predatory North lay in preserving the difference between combatants and non-combatants and in enabling and nurturing the rule of law in civil society. This principle was not always defended as it ought. The indiscriminate killings of civilians removed part of the moral foundation of the UN's purpose, which was to protect the lives and freedoms of the innocent from depredation from the North. The South Korean Truth and Reconciliation Commission has subsequently estimated that as many as 160,000 civilians were killed during the Korean War by the NKPA, the ROK Army and Security Forces, UN troops and the US Armed Forces.

At the same time as building up the Jamestown Line in 1951, the USAF launched Operation *Strangle*, an attempt to destroy Chinese and NKPA supply and transport infrastructure in North Korea, not least the railway network. Plenty of influential voices in the administration in Washington believed that unrestricted aerial bombing of the kind would destroy North Korea's will to resist. The purpose of the operation was to reduce the ability of the Chinese and NKPA to stockpile ammunition in preparation for use along the line. While *Strangle* did help to limit the creation of stockpiles, it – as was the experience in Germany during the Second World War – did nothing to persuade the

North Koreans not to fight. Bombing of railway targets simply made the North Koreans adept at instigating rapid repairs, the ever-growing workforce adapting quickly to this bludgeoning from the air. In time the North Koreans had over half a million men and women working round the clock on railway line repair. This unsophisticated though resilient civilian population proved adept at countering the massive technical superiority of American airpower, and dramatically limited its advantages. Trains and carriages would hide in mountain tunnels during the day. At the same time B-29 attacks on cities such as Pyongyang raised alarm in London, given the inevitable killing of large numbers of innocent civilians these would entail. While the purpose of *Strangle* was military, the fact that it would inevitably cause considerable numbers of civilian casualties raised the question of *proportionality*. Washington's view was that collateral damage – to use that dreadful phrase in an era before it was first used – was an acceptable price to pay for forcing the Chinese and North Korean negotiators to take discussions about achieving a peaceful end to the war. The best that could be said about *Strangle* and operations like it was that it served to limit the North's ability to bring forward and stockpile ammunition and stores that would be used for offensive purposes against the Eighth Army. An eventual lifting of attacks on the railways saw a shift by the USAF to other industrial and strategic targets, such as airfields, railway systems, supply and communication centres and the hydro-electric systems in the north of the country, attacks which continued relentlessly for the duration of the war.

But *Strangle* wasn't the only use of airpower in Korea. It is hard not to agree with historian Bruce Cumings' assertion that 'we carpet-bombed the North for three years with next to no concern for civilian casualties.' The air assaults against North Korean cities extended from the widespread use of firebombing to the destruction of huge North Korean dams in the final stages of the war. The USAF air campaign against North Korea was dramatic. Much of it was directed against industrial targets in civilian areas with commensurate civilian casualties. Precision bombing was as elusive in Korea in 1950 and 1951 as it had been in Japan in 1944 and 1945, so the default setting for attacks on strategic and industrial targets across North Korea was area bombing, with the consequential impact on civilian lives that left North Korean towns and cities in ruin. Curtis LeMay, the architect of the area bombing campaign against Japan, observed that in Korea, 'We burned down every town in North Korea and South Korea, too…'* One example was the attack on Pyongyang on 11 July 1952 in which 1,254 B-29 sorties were launched during the day and 54 by night. Attacks on a further 30 towns and cities followed. During the war 75 per cent of the city was levelled by aerial bombing. Every other North Korean town was smashed to varying degrees.

Cumings' comparison of the relative tonnages of bombs dropped on Germany and those on North Korea – a maximum of nine years separated these events – is remarkable. He compares the 657,000 tons of bombs dropped by the RAF on Germany from 1942 to 1945, and the 543,000 by the USAAF. By comparison, the United States dropped 667,557 tons of high explosive and napalm in Korea, nearly 20 per cent more than it dropped on Germany. Likewise, the USAAF dropped 503,000 tons in the entire Pacific theatre in the Second World War; it dropped 25 per cent more on Korea during three years of war. The key difference was that in Korea the strategy followed that of area destruction against Japan from March 1945, when precision bombing had been ditched because it had failed to degrade the enemy's war effort to the extent the airpower theorists had boasted. This enables Cumings' comparison of destructiveness to be understood. 'Whereas sixty Japanese cities were destroyed to an average of 43 percent,' he notes, 'estimates of the destruction of towns and cities in North Korea … at least 50 per cent of eighteen out of the North's twenty-two major cities were obliterated.' The list includes Pyongyang (75 per cent), Chongjin (65 per cent), Hamhung (80 per cent), Hungnam (85 per cent), Sariwon (95 per cent), Sinanju (100 per cent) and Wonsan (80 per cent).

War in areas of high civilian populations always involve the tragic deaths of innocent men, women and children as a result of ground combat. The challenge in Korea was that the fighting began in 1950 in areas with relatively high centres of population. This is bad enough. What is worse is when civilians become 'collateral damage' by design. A consequence of the advent of airpower in the 1920s was that civilians, innocent of bearing arms or being directly involved in the fighting,

*Princeton University, J. F. Dulles Papers, Curtis LeMay oral history, April 28, 1966, cited in Bruce Cumings, *The Korean War: A History* (Modern Library, 2010), 151–52.

could nevertheless find themselves targets of aerial bombardment. This was in fact one of the features of airpower doctrine that developed at this time. As the Second World War progressed, the inability by air forces of all combatants to hit precise targets with the technology available at the time, at a height forced on the bombers by anti-aircraft weapons, meant that increasingly area targets were engaged, even by the USAAF, which had long propounded the virtues of precision bombing.* By 1945 whole Japanese cities were targeted for destruction – 66, in fact – and, in the eyes of the Allies, the primary victims of both Hiroshima and Nagasaki were the 'civilian enemy'; those people who, while not fighting directly, were nevertheless supporting the war effort by giving moral and practical encouragement and support to war fighters. The same tortuous logic leapt the years between 1945 and 1950 and was applied by military strategists in Korea. It seemed entirely logical to visit on the civilian component of the enemy state the same indiscriminate model of bombing that had brought death and destruction to hundreds of thousands of German and Japanese civilians during the Second World War.

The principle that has long driven Western warmaking is that it is ethically illogical to fight a righteous war by unethical means. 'The two traditional criteria of justice in the course of war – and insurgency – are discrimination and proportionality', writes Professor Nigel Biggar, a foremost ethicist on the subject of morality and war. 'The first requires that the belligerents do not intentionally kill or harm non-combatants, and that they strive to avoid killing them incidentally. The second requires that military operations cause no more evil than is necessary – that is, that wounding, killing, and wider destruction be governed and constrained by the just end of rectifying injustice.'† Using this definition as a yardstick, it is clear that for both sides the Korean War broke these injunctions. The war saw the bloody destruction of life and property by both sides. Where the USA exceeded both the North Koreans and the Chinese in the scale of the destruction enacted was in the application of airpower against unprotected North Korean towns and cities.

*James Scott, *Black Snow: Curtis LeMay, the Firebombing of Tokyo, and the Road to the Atomic Bomb* (W. W. Norton and Co., 2022).
†Nigel Biggar, *In Defence of War* (Oxford University Press, 2013), 311.

It appears that when the decision was made to bomb North Korea, no case was made for anything other than the full expression of total war as evidenced during the period of aerial bombing between 1943 and 1945.[*] It seemed that massive and indiscriminate aerial attacks on anything that moved in North Korea were justified. This was war, so the argument went, and the war had to be won. North Korea was the enemy. The fact that its people, innocent or otherwise, were caught up in the conflict was simply a hard fact of life. War was tough, and it couldn't be hamstrung by moral challenges about who was an enemy combatant or who simply lived in an enemy country but who might otherwise be a civilian sustainer of the war. Using this logic there are no innocent civilians in war. To the authors of this book, however, it seems axiomatic that the Korean War was not a total war, and did not require the unconditional surrender of the enemy. What was required was the achievement of a strictly limited objective, the recovery of the *status quo ante bellum*. Using techniques and approaches to war that reflected the nature of the previous war (which can best be described in its post-1943 incarnation as a total war, in which the destruction of the nation state was a war aim) to engineer the surrender of the enemy through the collapse of its society was morally repugnant, politically unnecessary and militarily wasteful. This lack of clarity in Washington in particular about what the war was for, what it had to achieve and how best to carry it out, was the primary reason why so many civilians ended up dying unnecessarily during the three long years of war.

The result was mass civilian casualties of a kind that far outstripped those even of the Second World War, on both quantitative and relative grounds. Part of the problem of course was that precision bombing was not technically feasible until the 1970s, so as a weapon of war mass bombing had to be indiscriminate. It was simply not possible to remove the railway station at Dresden, for instance, without wiping out swathes of the surrounding city. As historian Richard Overy[†] suggests, over a long war it became easier and easier to justify the killing

[*]The key difference was that German towns and cities were protected by comprehensive anti-aircraft defences. North Korean ones were not.
[†]Richard Overy, *The Bombers and The Bombed* (Viking, 2013), 361–428.

of civilians. It was bad luck that the Korean War came so quickly after the end of the Second World War, as these ingrained attitudes to civilian casualties were simply transferred from one war to the other. A lack of concern for large numbers of civilian casualties is an essential element in allowing for the idea that millions of people would inevitably die in a nuclear exchange. It is certainly possible to argue that the USA fell victim to a widespread moral anaesthesia in respect of fighting and winning in Korea, seemingly treating North Korean civilians as valueless moral units in the mathematics of destruction. They were killed from the air in astonishingly large numbers, seemingly without moral qualms in Washington. Few people in the West were prepared to stand up for the people at the receiving end of these bombs in respect of a discussion about military utility and moral necessity, the *ends* and *means* of war, perhaps for fear of being labelled a 'commie' themselves. The American view in Korea was akin to that which developed over the issue of Japan in 1945: the loss of Korean lives was justified so long as it saved American lives.

Was this slaughter understood at the time? Certainly. Cumings quotes an early account of the war, published in 1952, which put it like this: 'So, we killed civilians, friendly civilians, and bombed their homes; fired whole villages with the occupants – women and children and ten times as many hidden Communist soldiers – under showers of napalm, and the pilots came back to their ships stinking of vomit twisted from their vitals by the shock of what they had to do.'*

As they had done in the Second World War, many airpower professionals and theorists convinced themselves that aerial bombing was the decisive factor in bringing the North to the negotiating table. It was nothing of the kind. It was, however, very, very good at killing large numbers of people.

The winter of 1951 to April 1952 saw a dramatic reduction in offensive activity by both sides as the vicious Korean winter took hold, and

*Walter Karig, Malcolm W. Cagle and Frank A. Manson, *Battle Report: The War in Korea* (Rinehart, 1952) quoted in Cumings, *The Korean War: A History*, 160–61.

discussions took place at a new site, a tented encampment in a field at Panmunjom, six miles east of the first site at Kaesong. During the spring, summer and autumn of 1952, most of the efforts of the combatants were expended on the battlefield rather than the negotiating table. 1952 was a year of battle. During the year the Chinese launched their Sixth Phase Offensive, designed to push the allies off the line of contact and back to the 38th Parallel. It was a war of hilltop names to become famous in the lexicon of battle. One can trace its violence, beginning in mid-1951, along the artery of war which was the main line of resistance: White Horse Mountain, Bunker Hill, Old Baldy, Sniper Ridge, Capitol Hill, Triangle Hill, Pike's Peak, Jackson Heights, Betty Grable and Jane Russell Hill, the latter two so named by the troops by virtue of their distinctive anatomical-like features. By the time fighting faded in mid-November 1952, the Eighth Army had lost 10,000 men, the Chinese 15,000. A description of one such will need to suffice for a long, angry series of see-saw battles for which the object was dominance at Panmunjom. The platoon action by men of 179th Infantry Regiment at Outpost Erie in March 1952 was one of many thousands of such actions that characterised this new stage of the war. It is remembered to history because Russell Gugeler included it in his compilation of representative combat actions in 1954 for the US Army Historical Series.

On the night of 21 March 1952 26 men of 3 Platoon, Company K, 179th Infantry Regiment, under the command of Lieutenant Omer Manley trudged out in single file to occupy a bald pimple a mile north of the Main Line of Resistance ten miles west of Chorwon. It was one of hundreds of separate actions being undertaken that day and every day along the Main Line of Resistance. It was part of the routine tedium of retaining an offensive spirit while maintaining a static defensive position over a long period of time. The pimple was Outpost Eerie, a patrol base designed to serve as a permanent listening patrol to provide warning in front of the 179th Infantry's positions of an impending Chinese attack, as well as to mount patrols against the Chinese line of resistance, which lay a mile and a half to the north. Outpost Eerie occupied the northern end of a long ridge sitting about 120 feet above the padi fields below. The position included nine inter-locking bunkers providing all-round defence of the position, wrapped about with three separate layers of barbed wire. The platoon would stay there for five days before being replaced. The platoon comprised four groups of men who would occupy the two and three-man bunkers: two rifle sections, a 60mm mortar section of five men; and a light machine gun section of three men equipped with .30 calibre machine gun. Forward of all but two of the bunkers – which were designed for sleeping only – was a fire or communication trench that ran around the full extent of the position. It was from this that the men would fight, if necessary, for the defence of the outpost. The platoon Command Post (CP) bunker with three men – Manley and two others – was connected to the Company K positions back on the MLR by radio and telephone line. It was from here that artillery and mortar support would come in case it was required. Each bunker was connected by an internal telephone system. A sound-powered telephone system connected the nine bunkers.

Unknown to Lieutenant Manley and his men, that same night a Chinese company commander from the positions to the north began preparing 60 of his own men for a raid on Outpost Eerie. Their task was to attack the position and capture two prisoners.

The battle for Outpost Eerie that night would reflect one of many thousands of similar platoon level actions that defined this period of trench warfare.

On taking over the position that rainy afternoon Lieutenant Manley allocated his troops to their firing positions. The three northern most bunkers were allocated to the light machine gun section on the left, and two other bunkers, each with three men. Not unreasonably Lieutenant Manley wanted to place his firepower at the most vulnerable spot and where it could do the most damage to an attacker, assuming that he came from the north. His own platoon CP was immediately to the rear of these forward bunkers. To the rear, the south-eastern five-man bunker was occupied by the platoon's 60mm mortar section. The remaining four bunkers held two or three men armed with Browning Automatic Rifles and M1 semi-automatic carbines.

In addition to the 26 men on Eerie that night, the battalion deployed two separate patrols, taking up ambush positions to the west and east of Outpost Eerie. These were designed to further protect the outpost from a surprise attack. Both left Eerie that night at 7 p.m. The first patrol was to occupy an ambush position on the track 600 yards to the north while the second patrol comprised nine men who were to occupy Hill 191

about 600 yards to the north west. The Hill 191 patrol was to return to
Eerie about 2 a.m. while the ambush patrol was due to return directly
to the MLR at the same time.

The rain stopped by 8 p.m. but it was cold and misty. This was
an active area of the front and Lieutenant Manley and his men fully
expected some action. The first sign of enemy activity was a report
from the Hill 191 patrol at 11 p.m. that a party of six Chinese had been
spotted a hundred yards to their front setting up a machine gun. About
the same time the ambush party on the track to the north reported
a platoon of enemy heading south, at a distance of about 150 yards.
They opened fire in the darkness but the enemy appeared to ignore the
firing and kept going. Lieutenant Manley immediately reported this to
his company commander on the MLR: 'The patrol has broken contact
and is withdrawing to the MLR. We're cocked and primed and ready
for anything.'

Fifteen minutes the troops on Eerie, tensed for action, heard sounds
in front of forward bunkers but no one could determine whether these
were from the returning patrol or the Chinese. A few minutes after
this, at 11.30 p.m., two trip flares went off beyond the barbed wire to
the front of the position. An attack was imminent. Sergeant Calvin
Jones and the other men at the northern end of the outpost opened fire
with automatic weapons and small arms. Chinese voices could now be
clearly heard beyond the wire.

At this point two enemy machine guns began spraying the positions
from the north east and north west. At least one of these had been
spotted by the patrol on Hill 191. Grazing fire fell across the entire
Eerie position. Corporal Nick Masiello, commanding the .30 calibre
machine gun, alternated his bursts between these weapons and the
Chinese who were attempting to breach the wire below him. The enemy
gunners replied by concentrating fire on Masiello's gun. Meanwhile, on
receiving the report from Lieutenant Manley, his company commander
on Hill 418 to the rear, Captain Clark, began to provide in-depth fire
to support the defenders of Eerie, using his company mortars and a
.50-calibre machine gun on Hill 418. Clark could see the machine gun
duel lighting up the sky in a bright technicolour display to his front.
When the mortar shells began landing around the position Lieutenant
Manley telephoned the necessary adjustments back to Captain Clark.

'They're giving us a hell of a battle out here, but we're O.K. so far' Manley reported. 'Bring the mortars in closer. No, that's too close! Now, leave them right where they are.'

Chinese machine gun rounds were now ripping through the unprotected shelter covers over the bunkers, forcing Manley and the forward defenders to crouch down in the firing trench. It was from here he realised that the battle for Outpost Eerie would have to be fought.

Fifteen minutes after the Chinese covering fire began, blanketing the position, a burst from one of the enemy heavy machine guns hit and killed Corporal Nick Masiello. His crewmen got the machine gun going again. A battle of machine guns continued for the next 45 minutes. Lieutenant Manley attempted to remove one of them on the Hill 191 ridge by calling in artillery fire on the Chinese positions, though it was impossible in the dark to get an accurate fix on the enemy machine gun. During a telephone report at 12.30 a.m. Private Winans, the platoon runner, reported to Captain Clark: 'Everything's OK, sir; they're not through the wire yet.'

Winans' assumption that this was what the Chinese were doing was correct. Two enemy assault groups were, under cover of their supporting machine gun fire, attempting to blow gaps in the circle of protective wire around the position. The only counter Manley could deploy, so close to his position, was artillery fire which he called in repeatedly. Attempts to provide illumination rounds from a supporting 155mm artillery battery failed, most of the shells inexplicably bursting too close to the ground to provide effective light.

Meanwhile, Chinese machine gun fire wounded Private Robert Fiscus, a Browning Automatic Rifleman in the northernmost bunker. Almost immediately afterwards Private Hugh Menzies was wounded by grenade fragments.

It was at about 1 a.m. that it became apparent that the enemy had succeeded in breaching the wire in two places. Lieutenant Manley yelled to his men, 'Get up and fight or we'll be wiped out! This isn't any movie!' Chinese assault parties were now crawling up onto the position, throwing grenades as they went, not standing up to present themselves as easy targets. The 3 Platoon medic, who until then had been doing sterling work on others, was hit in both legs by burp-gun fire, and in the arm and head by shell fragments. Of the nine men initially occupying the three bunkers facing the enemy attack only five remained unharmed.

The struggle for Eerie now became one of individual life and death. BARs and rifles were fired until ammunition was exhausted. Corporal Godwin, who had moved up into the centre bunker from the CP, realising that there were no more grenades, picked up a rifle and began firing into the advancing Chinese from a position in the fire trench until his ammunition was gone, before throwing his rifle at the nearest Chinese. He saw the butt hit the man in the face, knocking him back down the hill.

The time was now about 1.15 a.m. The machine gun trench was under direct assault. Soon after, Godwin's position was also attacked; Chinese troops were spotted on the roof. It was now a fight between man and man.

Corporal Godwin spotted a Chinese soldier coming along the trench toward him. He stepped back against the bunker, waited until the Chinese was within point-blank range, and shot him in the head with his pistol. An enemy soldier standing on the edge of the trench fired a burst at him from his burp gun, but then moved on without determining whether he had hit Godwin, doing no more harm that denting his helmet. Moments later an enemy soldier threw a concussion grenade at him and knocked him unconscious.

While this assault was taking place the Chinese were making a simultaneous breach from the west. Sergeant Kenneth Ehlers, who was the section commander ('squad leader') for the four rear left bunkers was joined in his trench area by Lieutenant Manley, Corporal Robert Hill and Corporal Joel Ybarra, fighting off the incursion with their automatic rifles, M1 rifles, and grenades. Both Ehlers and Hill were killed. At a critical moment Lieutenant Manley ran out of ammunition for his carbine, so he threw it at the Chinese and then started throwing grenades at them. After only a few moments, however, all resistance from this side ended; the platoon leader and Corporal Ybarra disappeared. At about the same time a shell destroyed the CP bunkers, killing its remaining occupants.

The three remaining bunkers in the south west of the perimeter continued to hold, despite it being obvious to them that the Chinese had occupied the centre of the Outpost in force and that the forward bunker positions had fallen. The time was about 1.20 a.m. Realising that this must be the situation, having not heard from the CP or Lieutenant Manley for some time, back on Hill 418 Captain Clark

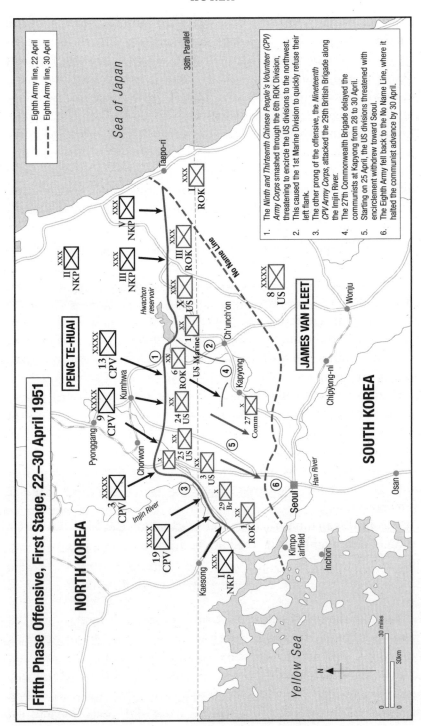

Fifth Phase Offensive, First Stage, 22–30 April 1951

Eighth Army line, 22 April
Eighth Army line, 30 April

1. The *Ninth* and *Thirteenth Chinese People's Volunteer (CPV) Army Corps* smashed through the 6th ROK Division, threatening to encircle the US divisions to the northwest.
2. This caused the 1st Marine Division to quickly refuse their left flank.
3. The other prong of the offensive, the *Nineteenth CPV Army Corps*, attacked the 29th British Brigade along the Imjin River.
4. The 27th Commonwealth Brigade delayed the communists at Kapyong from 28 to 30 April.
5. Starting on 25 April, the US divisions threatened with encirclement withdrew toward Seoul.
6. The Eighth Army fell back to the No Name Line, where it halted the communist advance by 30 April.

Sea of Japan

38th Parallel

PENG TE-HUAI

JAMES VAN FLEET

NORTH KOREA

SOUTH KOREA

No Name Line

Yellow Sea

ordered his artillery to fire a final defensive fire onto the top of the Outpost Eerie position. In a few minutes, 105 mm rounds began bursting over the position. There followed the sound of a horn blown three times, and within a few minutes enemy activity ceased and firing died down. The Chinese now withdrew from the shattered position. At 2 a.m. Captain Clark had gathered his company together on the MLR and began moving out to relieve the outpost. On the way they met the ambush patrol, all members of which were safe. The patrol had been caught in the open when the fighting commenced and had been unable to take an effective part in the action. Company K reached Eerie at 4 a.m., about two hours after leaving the main line. After an hour's search, Captain Clark had accounted for all men except Lieutenant Manley and Corporal Ybarra, both of whom had disappeared from the same bunker.

Of the 26 men who had defended Outpost Eerie, eight were dead, four wounded, and two were missing in action, a casualty rate of more than 50 per cent. Captain Clark considered that it was the final artillery fire which fell on the outpost that had prevented further casualties and forced the Chinese to withdraw. They had, after all, achieved their objective, dragging Lieutenant Manley and Corporal Ybarra with them into a captivity that would end over a year later with the armistice.

A single night's platoon action on a remote and isolated hill forward of the MLR accounted for the expenditure of 2,614 rounds of artillery ammunition. In addition the regimental mortar company and the 3rd Battalion's heavy weapons company fired 914 mortar shells. The bodies of 31 enemy dead were recovered, and a wounded prisoner taken captive.

It was in this manner that the war raged along the MLR, day after day, night after night during the long period of static warfare.

The Battle of the Hook between October 1952 and May 1953 was the last major offensive in which British forces were engaged in Korea. It involved five separate engagements. Among those taking part were 1st Battalion Black Watch and 1st Battalion Duke of Wellington's Regiment, comprising 80 per cent National Servicemen. The 7th Marines had first captured the Hook, though it fell back into Chinese hands on

27 October 1952. After one of the biggest artillery concentrations of the Korean War, they got it back that afternoon. The Black Watch took it over from the 7th Marines on 14 November. The Second Battle of the Hook began on 18 November and fighting continued through the winter. Between January and April 1953, the Hook changed hands about 20 times.

Chinese commanders hoped that they had persuaded president-elect Eisenhower to abandon any ambitious plans for a major offensive in 1953. The folly of this thinking was that Eisenhower had been elected to end the war, not to continue it. He replaced Truman in January 1953. Accordingly, the Chinese offensive was flawed in conception and achieved nothing in actuality, except for a high butcher's bill for both sides. But China did not appear to be concerned about its mounting casualties, though Mao was now fighting not for a strategic or political objective but to secure glory and renown for his communist revolution. It was an awful waste of blood for such a puerile outcome. But the communists did not appear to value the lives of the proletariat over grandiose expressions of socialist greatness.

Beyond the issue of the precise location of the demarcation line (which was resolved at Panmunjom in November 1951), the principal impediment to a rapid alignment between the communists and the UN was that the communists were terrified of being humiliated on the global stage by the very large number of their own POWs who might choose not to return home, either to China or to North Korea. They fought tooth and nail for the principle that all of their prisoners were to be returned to them regardless of the personal views of the men concerned.

The US, naively perhaps, began with the assumption that all prisoners in their hands would simply be handed back to their originating countries in accordance with the 1949 Geneva Conventions. South Korea, however, opposed this policy. In addition, many scores of thousands of individual POWs were unwilling simply to be sent home. As many as 40,000 POWs were in fact South Korean citizens forcibly conscripted by the conquering NKPA in 1950 and recaptured during the UN advances in September 1950. Non-return was, of course, anathema for North Korea and China as it directly challenged communist propaganda about the communist utopia in which their fighters supposedly lived and for which they fought. Why on earth would anyone *not* want to return? The political and propaganda battle on this subject was fought out at Panmunjom and in the world's press up until the armistice in July 1953.

Truman determined in January 1952 that the USA would respect the individual wishes of each POW and would not repatriate those unwilling to return to their country of origin. He was perhaps mindful of the imprisonment by Stalin of returning Russians who had been captured by the Axis forces and who were therefore politically suspect in the eyes of the regime in Moscow, and those Russians who had served in the Axis armies during the war and who had been forcibly repatriated to the USSR, there to face the gulag, or worse.

The POW camps in South Korea became a new battleground in the Korean War. For those in North Korean or Chinese captivity, the challenge of imprisonment had both physical and psychological aspects. For most, captivity required surviving a poor diet, non-existent healthcare and routine brutality. For a few, it also included harsh treatment, solitary confinement – sometimes for months – and torture. For all, it included relentless propaganda and attempts to indoctrinate POWs into the virtues of communism. For some, a tiny few, this indoctrination worked. The story of psychological deprivation and indoctrination of UN troops was of a kind never previously experienced in the West. It was entirely different than the experience suffered by Allied POWs in Japanese hands during the Second World War. The North experimented with alarming mind games against UN POWs designed to force them to believe in the moral virtue of communism, the ultimate weakness of the capitalist West and its eventual demise into the dustbin of history. This was a subject the West was right to be concerned about as the extent of Soviet propaganda against Western captives was relentless. The Secret Intelligence Service agent George Blake is one example of a man who was turned during his time in captivity.[*]

[*]Roger Hermiston, *The Greatest Traitor: The Secret Lives of Agent George Blake* (Aurum, 2013), 85–138.

The North deliberately infiltrated agitators into their camps who organised them on strict anti-capitalist lines and sought actively to become a new front in the war. Beginning in December 1951, a series of rebellions took place which entailed the extraordinary capture by the ruthlessly organised prisoners of the senior American officer responsible for one of the UN's largest POW camps on Koje-do Island, Brigadier General Francis Dodd. This was as much a humiliation for the USA as it was a belated realisation that the North had mobilised their own men in these camps to fight on a new front against their captors. These rebellions took six months to crush.

Eventually a solution to the principle of voluntary repatriation proposed by India was adopted following Stalin's death, albeit reluctantly by China, in which those unwilling to return home had the opportunity to be persuaded to change their minds. Few did so. In accordance with the final armistice agreement, both sides directly exchanged all prisoners who wanted to return to their homelands. In total, 75,823 communist and 12,773 UN personnel (including 3,597 Americans) returned home from captivity under this arrangement. A total of 347 UN soldiers (including one Briton) elected to remain in North Korea or China, while 21,000 Chinese and North Koreans elected to remain in South Korea or Taiwan. On 18–19 June 1953, unilaterally and without US knowledge, Syngman Rhee put the cat among the pigeons at Panmunjom by releasing 27,000 Korean POWs (decreed by the ROK as 'internees' because they had been forcibly recruited by the NKPA). The Chinese side raged. In fact, the North benefited by this legerdemain, as it resulted in many fewer of their POWs voting to remain in the South when the eventual exchanges took place. In the end over 46,000 communist soldiers refused repatriation.

Was continued adherence to this principle worth it? Assuming that a peace deal could have been agreed in December 1951 if the UN had not insisted on the principle of repatriation based on individual choice – the issue of the location for the physical barrier between North and South Korea had been agreed in November 1951 – the cost of continuing to fight in the 19 months that followed (375,000 casualties, two-thirds of them communist) was considerable. Some principles are worth fighting for. Was this one of them? China certainly thought so, and continued to battle on, throwing the lives of its benighted troops at UN defences along the line of contact with the consummate profligacy of states that value their people only for their blood. Indeed, the final Chinese offensive of the war began on 6 July 1953, with attacks on UN positions at Pork Chop Hill and the Kumsong River. In the later, the ROK II Corps fell back several miles under the pressure of the Chinese assault. What was the point of such sacrifice? The North never lost sight of the reality that they could stomach the loss of large numbers of men; the West could not. Despite this, the war had to end for the North as much as it did for the UN. On 20 July an armistice agreement – the absence of war, but not a formal peace – was agreed. In silence, the negotiators, who were not even on speaking terms, finally signed the instruments at Panmunjom on 27 July. At 10 p.m. the guns quietened across the line of contact. Men on both sides, aware of the impending moment, came out of their foxholes and celebrated the unusual silence in the starry Korean night. For the time being at least, the Korean War was over.

Reflections

Did the ending of the war in the way it did end in July 1953 represent a failure of diplomacy and of the negotiations necessary to bring about an enduring peace? In a sense it did: no peace deal was signed in July 1953 – merely an armistice that drew the fighting to a close – and the region and the world has been forced to put up with the sabre-rattling legacy of war ever since. The negotiations were not conducted in good faith by the communist side, and it was a final threat by the new Republican administration in Washington to deploy B-29s over China that, with the absence of Stalin from the power-equation following his death in March, forced an agreement on North Korea and its Chinese ally. But this view – that a negotiated end to the war was a failure – is perhaps too binary. How much has the extent of regional tension since 1953 been the result of the Kim family's desperate attempt to hold onto power in North Korea, rather than the absence of a peace deal? There has been no general war on the peninsula since 1953, and this must be regarded as a success. Indeed, a peace deal alone would not necessarily have guaranteed 72 years of peaceful coexistence on the peninsula: Versailles only lasted 17 years, for instance, and the legacy of that peace could not be described as good.

We think there is another way of looking at the outcome of July 1953. This is that the UN refused to be drawn into a wider war, de-escalating both the fighting in Korea and the rhetoric of war expansion coming from some quarters in the USA and the Supreme Commander in Tokyo. Rather than bomb China, the UN and USA forced the North to come to terms with the result of battle in Korea and refused to be intimidated at the negotiating table. This has, in fact, stood the test of time. If ending the war and preventing its uncontrolled expansion was one of Truman's goals in 1951, it can be said that he succeeded. Much to Mao Tse Tung's surprise, Truman made the deliberate (and by no means widely agreed, in the USA at least) decision that he would limit the war to the *status quo ante bellum*, and both he and his successor, Dwight Eisenhower, stuck to this strategy through the long years of attritional fighting that followed – after the failure of the race to the Yalu – conducting a war along the line of contact that restricted the fighting to this place, and this place alone. Peace-making does not mean that both parties come to the table in a ready-made political or psychological state to agree a deal. (Indeed, for much of the period in question, the negotiations were conducted in an atmosphere of ill-disguised animosity and acrimony.) It requires, rather, at least one of the parties to *make* the peace; to force the pace and the process on the other party until an agreement to desist from fighting has been reached. This is precisely what happened in Korea and must therefore be considered a success for the USA and UN despite the reality that no Versailles deal was struck. Perhaps it is just as well. Similarly, Kyiv's strategy in 2024 and 2025 to change the nature of a heretofore attritional battlefield was undertaken to force its opponent to seek terms to end the fighting, an open acknowledgement that, for both parties, sacrifices in some ambitions would be required if the fighting was to end. At the time of writing, this initiative had been at the behest of Ukrainian strategy, not Russian, which continued to apply much of the attritional, one-dimensional playbook undertaken hitherto.

Was there a winner from the Korean War? Both sides say they won, but it is easy to see through the propaganda to recognise that the clear winner was *the rule of law*. Despite all the errors and excesses of the conduct of the war, such as an aerial bombing campaign that achieved little of strategic value and generated vast numbers of civilian dead, the principle of the sovereignty of the state was upheld. The challenge to national sovereignty – namely, the sacrosanct impermeability of national borders, attacked so egregiously by Adolf Hitler in the Sudetenland in 1938 and ignored by the international community at the time – was protected. This is a founding principle of international order, without which anarchy reigns. It was essential for the ordered conduct of global affairs that the United Nations acted so decisively, under US aegis, and rapidly inserted Task Force Smith to Osan within days of Kim Il-sung's attempted smash-and-grab in June 1950. This is not to say, however, that the war was conducted well. The war showed up the fallacies inherent in the post-war march to a peaceful nirvana wished by many in the United States after 1945, as the country rapidly demilitarised in an atmosphere of pacific stupefaction. Then, strategically, the mad rush to the Yalu – endorsed by Truman, MacArthur and the UN in October 1950 – illustrated the temporary madness that afflicted Washington and Tokyo in the flush of excitement that followed the success of the Inchon landings. It demonstrated more than anything the importance of keeping alive the political conversation about the strategic ends and means of war *during* conflict: the disastrous absence of acute thinking about the purpose and outcome of strategy, especially of confusing strategy with operational decision-making after Inchon, led to the disaster that was the second Korean War.

Was the reaction of the USA in securing a military push-back to the invasion in June 1950 the right thing to do? Undoubtedly. The reaction to the North's invasion was the solidarity of the free world, led by the USA, determined not merely to uphold the sanctity of sovereignty but to provide protection for a friend that had been attacked by a predator. As an aside, a continuing or unconstrained war in one territory can sometimes cause spillover into another, because of the failure to take effective action to end the fighting. Appeasing gangsterism (or allowing it to flourish by inaction) has the effect – sometimes – of allowing instability to flare up elsewhere because the costs of war are not considered too onerous by those willing to embark on it. The willingness of Russia to embark on a war against Ukraine in 2022 had its origins in the failure of other parties – Europe in particular – to persuade Russia by diplomatic or military counteraction as early as the invasion of Georgia in 2008 that this behaviour was not acceptable. In reality, for too long, the opposite message was sent to Moscow. It acted in 2022 as it did precisely because it believed that it had been given carte blanche to do so, just as North Korea considered that it had been given in 1950.

The war in Korea articulated the intent of the USA specifically, and the West more generally, to deploy military force to resist communist aggrandisement wherever it occurred. The first was important in the context of the newly formed UN, the second in terms of the trust friends must have in the sanctity of their defence agreements, especially minnows in a sea of sharks. It was this principle upon which the UK and France declared war on Germany on 3 September 1939, in defence of its security pact with Poland. As this book has argued, the opportunism of both the

US administration and of the UN in widening the war to invade North Korea over the 38th Parallel in October 1950 was a mistake of enormous proportions, killing many more people, achieving nothing of material or political substance as a result, and doing more than anything else to bring the world even closer to the potentiality for a cataclysmic war. Our belief, therefore, is that though the war could be described as limited, it could easily have been more limited still, and over far quicker, with far fewer casualties and at far less cost in blood and treasure, having achieved all its objectives, had the USA maintained a sense of realism and proportionality in its military strategic ambitions in October 1950 when victory over the North Korean Army in the South had first been achieved.

Who was to blame for the cataclysm that tore such a devastating swathe through the lives of millions and brought the world so close to a Third World War? Many accounts attempt to blame the Cold War itself, as if the developing hostility between the East and West during the last half of the 1940s was itself responsible for lighting the fires of war. But this confuses the *result* of confrontation with its *cause*. Those who take this line seem to suggest that, because there is apparently no smoke without fire, both sides were equally guilty; equally responsible for the war that saw the first conflagration of the Cold War between the superpowers. This is, to us, an unsatisfactory explanation. The USA did not, for instance, have any colonial ambitions in Korea in the late 1940s, and did not see South Korea as a bastion in Asia against the threat of communism, an inference that this argument – that the Korean War was itself caused by the Cold War – makes. Few accounts place the blame firmly where it should be; namely the deliberate aggrandisement of North Korea and its Moscow-appointed leader, Kim Il-sung. Like Vladimir Putin's egregious attack on Ukraine in February 2022, Kim Il-sung, recognising that he would be unable to secure the unification of the entire Korean peninsula on his terms by consensus – or at least by political means – decided that it was easier to avoid all that diplomatic botheration by doing it by force. The cause of the war and therefore the blame for its compound miseries sits squarely at the feet of this man, an ideologically driven megalomaniac. Without his desire for a forced reunification of Korea, the deaths of millions, perhaps as many as 3 million people, would not have occurred.

If ever a plan backfired, it was Kim Il-sung's ill-considered war. Korea demonstrates the limitations, as well as the utility, of military force in attempting to secure one's political ends. Kim Il-sung used his invasion of the ROK as a substitute for politics, precisely because he knew that he could never hope to achieve his objectives – the unification with the South, on his terms – peacefully. Some have suggested, on a par with those passive-aggressive arguments that suggest the victim of violence has brought it on themselves by some form of provocative behaviour, that the South was in large part to blame for the North's actions, because it sabre-rattled as noisily as did the North in the months leading up to war, and indeed undertook military raids against the North. Certainly, both North Korea and the ROK carried out attacks on one another in the years before 1950. The North in particular launched many operations short of war to destabilise the South, fomenting rebellion and supporting civil unrest, as well as undertaking direct raids and guerrilla activity in pursuit of an overall political strategy that sought unification on its own terms. But it was never possible for the South to be able to achieve such unification by military means, as the USA deliberately starved it of the resources to do so. Not so the North, where military resources and planning capabilities were provided by the USSR.

Likewise, some have attempted to blame the USA for the war, because America failed to indulge the left-leaning 'people's committees' established in the early post-Japanese days to align the country with an increasingly strident communist separatism based in the North. One line of argument goes so far as to assert that the 'popular effort to create a unified and sovereign Korea was suffocated by the US occupation in 1945 and a revanchist state and strongman installed in the south in 1948, one dedicated to unification by force.'* The one-sidedness of this claim is breathtaking. It is akin to blaming the doomed efforts by democrats in Hungary, Poland, the Baltic states and Czechoslovakia for the resulting Soviet subjugation, and its accompanying Stalinist terror, during the same period. The truth is that it was a determinedly separatist communist regime in the North, appointed and sustained by the USSR, in the face of every effort by the UN to achieve peaceful unification of the country by means of the ballot box, which was the direct cause of the separation of the peninsula, and the coming of war.

---

*John Tirman, *The Deaths of Others: The Fate of Civilians in America's Wars* (Oxford University Press, 2011), 91.

The USA can be blamed for many things, including its excessive reliance on force and its unthinking failure to discriminate between combatants and non-combatants on occasions as well as its seeming reluctance to challenge ROK atrocities against leftist sympathisers; but its desire at this time to resist the death-grasp of Moscow-engineered communist imperialism in Korea is not one of them. The attack by the North in 1950 was thus a deliberate attempt to unify the peninsula by force, and in respect of who was responsible, North Korea was clearly the instigator. But if the blame for Kim Il-sung's war can be apportioned further afield, consideration should be given to levelling the blame at Moscow, for it was in the construction of a client state in the north that the USSR forcibly separated North from South and engineered a regime in Pyongyang that was ideologically hostile to the idea of unification on the basis of a popular vote. By refusing to allow Korea to reunify under a single democratically elected process, overseen by a UN-appointed commission, the USSR deliberately sowed the seeds of discord and, in allowing for the construction of a client-state in the north that was resolutely set on obeying Moscow, or at the very least setting up a strictly communist state, created the conditions for conflict.

It is in this context that the Korean War can be regarded as the last military campaign of the Second World War. It was also the first campaign of the new Cold War, but it needs to be understood, at least in part, as being the residue of a war in which Stalin jockeyed for post-ceasefire advantage and allowed his proxy in Pyongyang to use force to achieve his political ends. The buffer states Moscow deliberately created around itself in Europe were replicated on the landmass of Asia by means of the client state based in Pyongyang. This artificial re-engineering of post-colonial Korean statehood directly created the conditions for conflict, given that the truly democratic means of uniting the country and forging a new future after the departure of the Japanese were denied to Koreans by the USSR's insistence that the country remained divided, and that the North remained in its pocket.

Apart from the fact that the Korean War still continues today, bubbling away quietly in the background, if only in legal fact rather than in physical actuality – at least as fighting between the belligerents is concerned (as we've noted, the stand-off between the governments of North Korea and the ROK remains) – are there any other reasons why Korea should be remembered? After all, it took place a long time ago. Seventy-five years, the same distance in time from a person living at the start of the war in 1950 to 1875 – the year in which Alexander Graham Bell made the first sound transmission, setting the conditions for the invention of the telephone – a distance in time that seems as remote today as modernity is from the horse and cart. The Korean War feels a little like ancient history, or at least something that happened in an entirely different age. But it would be a mistake to dismiss the Korean War merely as 'old' history. Why? It was not just one of the bloodiest wars of modern history – proportionately bloodier (per head of population) than even the Second World War – but the world continues to live within the set of global strategic relationships established by this conflict. Indeed, it wasn't the Second World War that made the security structures which frame our modern world, but the Korean War. The war left an indelible imprint on the way in which the world manages the balance of power left following the cessation of the Second World War. The war served to pull the USA out of its dangerous post-war political lethargy, forcing it to recommit to the defence of the free world, not least to NATO. It rebuilt the defence industries that had reverted to producing ploughshares rather than tanks and made permanent the establishment of garrisons and naval bases across the globe that had not existed before, or that had been abandoned after 1945. American defence expenditure quadrupled during the Korean War. That Kim Il-sung had not envisaged that his precipitate actions in June 1950 would awaken a sleeping giant, and place it front and centre of global security concerns to the current day, was another example of the unintended consequences of ill-thought-out strategy. The balance of global power was now an explicit feature of US foreign policy. War was no longer fought on the basis of crusades against evildoers, but to ensure that friends were protected and enemies contained. It was an old style of power-based pragmatism, based on the need to enforce a new set of common international agreements and to prevent the disaster of the 1930s. As historian T. R. Fehrenbach memorably remarked:

Harry Truman had ordered troops into action on the far frontier. This was the kind of order Disraeli might have given, sending Her Majesty's regiments against the disturbers of Her Majesty's peace. Or the emperor in Rome might have given such a command to the legions when his governor in Britain sent word the Picts were over the border.

This was the kind of war that had bleached the bones of countless legionnaires on the marches of the empire, and had dug the graves of numberless Britons, wherever the sun shone. In 1950 there was only one power and one people in the world who could prevent chaos and a new, barbarian tyranny from sweeping the earth. The United States had become a vast world power, like it or not. And liking it or not, Americans would find that if a nation desires to remain a great and moral power there is a game it must play, and some of its people must pay the price. Truman, sending the divisions into Korea, was trying to emulate the Roman legions and Her Majesty's regiments [and gunboats] – for whether the American people have accepted it or not, there have always been tigers in the world, which can only be contained by force. You might believe that it was America's duty to contain those tigers or not, but the overwhelming political consensus of 1950 was that Korea presaged a new world, one in which military intervention to contain and restrain a rampant enemy – the tiger – was overwhelmingly virtuous. This was an imperialism of virtue; of standing up for friends, to preserve the right; to uphold international law; to ensure that US power wasn't challenged where it was needed to preserve the security of a region. And it was this war, in Korea, which saw the expansion of American power globally on a proactive basis, for the first time. It wasn't 1941 or 1945, but 1950, which was the year in which America sought not to rule the world, but to contain it within the context of its own national interest.

Did the war fuel the confrontation between East and West? No: it merely illuminated it. The confrontation had begun with Stalin's efforts in 1943 and 1944 to rebuild and protect the Soviet empire; the Korean War allowed the USA to see this with clarity for the first time. Dean Acheson was later to comment that the Korean War 'saved us', i.e., it fully justified US fears about the threat of communist hegemonic ambitions (even those wrapped up in a nationalist veneer) that had first led to the writing of NSC-68. The Korean War thus validated US and Western fears that Moscow-engineered communism was a growing threat to the world, entirely supporting the assumptions that framed Truman's policy of containment and of NSC-68. The strategy of containing communist expansion was initially primarily a diplomatic and political task, not a military one. Korea changed all that. The war against Moscow-inspired communism had become all too real. Thus, the Korean War formed, for the West at least, an elegant superstructure to frame the doctrine of containment of the communist menace. By offering war as 'politics by other means' in Korea, the West became immediately alarmed that Moscow would do something similar in Europe. The future of NATO was secured *because* of North Korea's aggression against South Korea and confirmed by China's crusading counteroffensive in October 1950. In other words, Korea frightened Europe so much that NATO was the natural place within which to hide in respect of the threat to the reconstruction of the world following the end of the Second World War.

Likewise, the Korean War has much to teach us, as both historians and practitioners of war, not merely about the conduct of war but about its evolution in the modern world and in particular its utility as a tool of international politics. Throughout the writing of this book the shadow of Ukraine loomed large. The parallels between the two conflicts are strong, both in respect of the aspirations and assumptions of the aggressor, and in the response of the wider world to the war. The Korean War thus offers intriguing insights into the nature of modern war, including the result of miscalculation, of cause and effect, and of unintended consequence. It demonstrates that the path of war is never straightforward, and it exposes fundamental issues with how liberal democracies fight wars in terms of proportionality and moral effect. It also demonstrates the absolute utility of effective tools of collective defence. When Putin's Russia invaded Ukraine in February 2022, in spite of all its pledges (and treaties) not to do so, Ukraine sat within no communal defence structure that offered mutual support. Indeed one of the guarantors of Ukraine's future, having given up its nuclear weapons, namely Russia, was itself the aggressor. However, 1950 South Korea was more fortunate. It had signed a defence agreement with the USA guaranteeing military support in response to an attack from any known predator. All at the time knew that the only real predator was North Korea, militantly determined to unite the Korean peninsula under its brand of familial hegemony. The best example of a collective defence treaty – or at least the most well-known, a product of the modern age – is the North Atlantic Treaty Organisation. Article V of this treaty commits all members to the collective defence of each other. Ukraine in 2022 did not benefit from any such protection. It was alone and was gobbled up (or attempted to be) by an unscrupulous predator for whom 'might is right' remains the fundamental reality of international intercourse. Collective security gives the best hope against the depredations of men like Kim Il-sung and Vladimir Putin. In 1950 the ROK was not part of the UN but it did have a mutual defence agreement with the USA. This is what Kim foolishly ignored in his decision to head south. In the few years since 2022 considerable military aid has been provided to Ukraine; however, much of it is conditional, based on self-interest, not on treaty commitment.

The real problem in 1950 was that the USA was not ready for war. It had limited means by which it could execute its commitment to the new imperialism defined by NSC-68. It possessed only a total of ten divisions (by contrast, the Wehrmacht had fielded 400 during the Second World War), but these were weak, as each regiment had only two battalions and each division had only two regiments. Worse, the army had negligible trained manpower. Neither men nor units nor larger formations had undertaken any form of systematic combat training since the Second World War. As the US Army was to discover when it went to war, the training, professionalism and technical competence of soldiers, NCOs and officers is a much-underrated virtue and requires hard and dedicated training and preparation to get right. Neither was available in sufficient quantities when battle was joined in early July 1950. A fundamental requirement of achieving America's newly sought policy objectives was to have a sufficiently large and capable professional army, adequately equipped and trained and ready for the tasks given to it. Relying on the draft for emergency actions meant throwing poorly prepared and inadequately trained citizen soldiers into the fray. The results, against a tough and determined foe, are obvious. Korea was always going to be a land war, because land forces were required to occupy ground. For the USA to play in this game, it too needed effective land forces able to defeat a land enemy attempting to capture ground, and to then secure it against counterattack. One of the many challenges for American thinking in 1950 was that it had failed to consider the requirement to build a modern, deployable, relevant, professional and well-trained and well-equipped army once the boys had come home from the Second World War. It was widely considered that the next war would be fought, and won, by long-range bombers and atomic bombs. There would be no need for a deployable army able to execute American foreign policy where and when it might be needed. Now, when such an army was required, the USA was found wanting.

The war demonstrated repeatedly that military competence is an underrated virtue in the management of armies and the prosecution of war. Professional armies need to do all they can to nurture, develop and sustain the combat proficiency of their best leaders – NCOs and officers – *before* war is enjoined. This entails thorough preparation for war during times of peace. Leaders must be able to respond instinctively to threat and challenge; this is the result of hard training and professional competence developed during years of peace. The war was a reminder of just how critical it is for a country to be prepared for any military eventuality in defence of national interest. Not only was South Korea unprepared for war, but nor too were the USA or the UK. Neither had a readily available 'fire brigade' of troops ready to fight. Armies are no good if they are not available when required. Nor are they any good if they don't possess the requisite capabilities to deal with challenges when these occur. Korea demonstrated just how weak Western armies had become in the drive to secure a peace dividend following the end of the Second World War. British involvement in support of the United Nations' request for troops to repel the invader exposed all the old problems of a people tired of war and unprepared for a new one. In 1950 the British Army, hard at war in Malaya and busy across a range of global commitments, still had no deployable or expeditionary capability.

Korea showed that 'victory' need not be zero-sum. Success for one side does not need to mean total defeat for the loser. Negotiated settlements, even those without peace deals, can and do work if the political will exists to make them.

The Korean War reminded the world that war was bloodily destructive. By the time the armistice agreement was signed on 27 July 1953, British casualties had totalled 793 killed and 2,878 wounded and missing: American totals were 36,940 killed, 92,134 wounded and 8,176 missing or taken prisoner. But these figures pale into insignificance for those suffered by the two Koreas, especially by civilian casualties of the war. South Korea suffered 415,000 dead (of whom 140,000 were military), and a further 897,832 casualties of various kinds: a total of 1.3 million. It is hard to estimate North Korean casualties, but a consensus rests on about 2 million, of whom 520,000 were fighting soldiers. The Chinese lost just short of a million troops. Civilian casualties of the fighting were astronomical and outstrip in relative terms any previous war of recent memory. North Korea, with a pre-war population of about 9 million, lost 16.5 per cent of its population during the war. This was extraordinary. In terms of context, the war that had just ended in Europe had cost the lives of perhaps 5 million Germans – from a pre-war population of 70 million – or 7 per cent of its total. In Japan the cost was 2 million dead from a population of 60 million, or 3 per cent. In Korea, in only three bloody years, a loss of 3 million lives from a pre-war population of 29 million (across both North and South), was a total of just over 10 per cent of the entire population. The loss suffered by North Korea was greater even than that of the estimated 10 per cent of Soviet citizens (20 million from a population of 200 million) during the Great Patriotic War. The only country with a worse statistic was benighted Poland, which lost over 17 per cent of its entire population (6 million men, women and children from an original population of 30 million) during the war. In other words, this short, savage war caused proportionately a greater level of destruction to the people of a country than that suffered by the USSR, Germany and Japan, and nearly as great as Poland, in the most destructive wars in human history that had just ended.* If countries outside Korea ever knew this, they've certainly forgotten it. It's certainly grounds for remembrance, if only for the mathematics of death.

Was the war worth all the expenditure it entailed in blood and treasure? The first thing to say is that this war of political aggrandisement by North Korea was entirely unjustified. It began as a land grab by a puppet of Moscow. It is in the response by the international community that the answer to this question must be unequivocally positive. For all its grotesque loss of life, the war was an essential counter to the challenge of anarchy. Blatant aggression by North Korea did not receive its hoped-for reward. Indeed, North Korea ended the war with a net loss of territory over that with which it had started, with the almost complete trashing of the country and, in relative terms, suffering the greatest loss of its soldiers and civilians of any country in any war in modern history. If the UN had

*This terrible number includes 66 per cent of European Jewry. Approximately 9.5 million Jews lived in Europe in 1933, representing 1.7 per cent of Europe's total population and more than 60 per cent of the world's Jewish population. By 1945, 6.3 million Jews – two out of every three – had been killed.

not pushed back against this untrammelled aggression, it is not difficult to see what message this would have given to those around the world who are dependent for their security on the sanctity of sovereignty.

The biggest problem with starting war is knowing how to end it. We have criticised the USA in this book for failing to end the war when it had the opportunity to, chasing instead an illusory vision of total victory that entirely ignored what was staring them in the face: the possibility of Chinese intervention. While responding with alacrity to blatant DPRK aggression, the US-led UN coalition spectacularly failed to end it quickly when it had the opportunity to do so. What should have happened? Simply, military force should have restored the *status quo ante bellum* without any attempt to utterly destroy the North Koreans, as this, as proved to be the case, would only destabilise the region by encouraging the Chinese to intervene. MacArthur's campaign naively believed that a new world could be made by means of military force, as it had done in 1945. The Korean War was not, as many have supposed it to be, a triumph of containment. It was the opposite. By ignoring the threat of Chinese retaliation, the US recklessly threw away its military advantage in 1950 by inadvertently forcing an escalation. MacArthur was pleased at this, as it gave him the opportunity for more war – possibly this time with nuclear weapons – against a China that had ungratefully turned its back on American salvation and had opted instead for communism. It would serve them right. At the time President Truman saw Communist China in terms of a satellite of the USSR and rejected Attlee's suggestion that a more emollient line be taken with China. He retorted: 'The only way to meet communism is to eliminate it.' After Korea would follow Hong Kong, Indochina and Malaya, the latter already in turmoil as the result of a communist insurgency that had begun in 1948. Equally, there didn't seem much point in pushing back hard against the communists in Europe, while being soft on them in Asia. Geopolitical perspectives ruled the attitudes of both men. Negotiations with China were a non-starter. On the subject of the use of atomic weapons, Truman reserved for the USA the right to use them if US interests demanded it, though its allies would be consulted in advance. In exchange, Attlee promised Truman that the UK would remain firmly by its side, through thick and thin, in Korea. For Attlee the principle was simple. As he told the British people in a broadcast from Canada following the visit to Truman, Britain had to fight alongside the Americans in Korea to uphold the authority of the United Nations. History was at stake. Britain was not going to make the mistake of Munich again, at least not on Attlee's watch.

If the Korean War was therefore a war that had its roots in the relentless post-war meddling of the Soviet Union, it was also a war that lay at the heart of Kim Il-sung's personal desire to run a pro-Soviet, communist state across the entirety of the Korean peninsula. But war rarely runs a course as the progenitor determines or wishes it. For this reason, the Korean War can only be truly understood in terms of its being not a single war, but two. We suggest that there were, in effect, two wars for Korea, one running into the other. In the first place there was the war between North and South Korea in 1950. The North invaded the South in an attempt to force the unification of the country on the North's terms. In this respect the war was, at heart, a domestic squabble in which push was used by one side (the North) in order to force through a political settlement it didn't believe – correctly – that it could achieve by peaceful means. In this sense it can be described as a civil war. The historian Bruce Cumings also posits the argument that North Korea was fighting to resist what it considered to be the renewed 'Japanisation' of Korea. This argument was that Kim Il-sung saw the ROK to be the successor of the Japanese colonial state, supported and endorsed by the USA, its leaders rehabilitated collaborators with the Japanese.[*] This might or might not be true: either way, it is an *explanation* (possibly also an excuse) for invasion, not a legal basis or reason for war.[†]

To see the Korean War exclusively in terms of civil war (or, more correctly perhaps, an *uncivil* war) is to fail to understand that by 1950 Korea was no longer united in a legal sense, or indeed in a political and perhaps even a social one either; it hadn't been united since the Japanese surrendered and the 38th Parallel was established as a means of ensuring

[*] Cumings, *The Korean War*, 209.
[†] The evidence from the subsequent seven decades of single-family rule in North Korea since the war suggests that it was this and its own brand of totalitarianism that motivated the North to attack the South, not the hoped-for prospect of utterly erasing the influence of Japan from its history, polity and control. Japan may indeed have loomed large in the consciousness of the North and indeed that of the South, but to suggest that this was its primary motivating factor in attempting to unify Korea by force ignores the very real and very obvious political motivation of Kim Il-sung and his regime for power across the entire peninsula.

that the Allies undertook the surrender of the ruling Japanese in August 1945. Because of this, the war was a clear case of aggression between an illegal state (the North was only recognised by the USSR and its friends) and the UN-recognised state of Korea, the Republic of Korea. The war initiated by Kim Il-sung on Sunday 25 June 1950 was one between a *de facto* state – the North – and a *de jure* one, the ROK. Even though it was a war between Koreans, it does not solely fit the criteria for being a civil war. This was not a case of a once-united state fighting among its communities for military and political supremacy, but two separate states on the peninsula vying between themselves to unite the country under a single government. The Korean War was more a state-on-state conflict brought about by the refusal of the USSR to allow a peaceful and democratic means to unify in 1945 or 1946, than it was ever a civil war, although, as we have shown, it possessed elements of both. In this war, the members of the newly established United Nations determined unanimously that it would fight to prevent the North profiting from its unwarranted aggression. Unwarranted? Certainly. The world had determined, following the end of the Second World War, that wars of sovereign aggression were illegal, given that recourse to the alternative forms of mediation, in the form of the new body of the United Nations, were available. Despite the fact that life was not to work out exactly as the idealists had hoped, there was enough determination in Western capitals still, in 1950, to ensure that, where it could, the free world no longer appeased aggression of this kind and would see no repeat of Munich.

In its second (and unplanned phase), with the North Korean 'People's Army' defeated by mid-October following the amphibious landings at Inchon and the breakout by the Eighth Army from the Pusan perimeter, the Korean War changed fundamentally in character. The war as it had first started was one in which the United Nations agreed to intervene to restore the balance of power in the region, following North Korea's invasion of the ROK. It was now transformed into something quite different, in which the United States, without any effective political or diplomatic challenge, decided to expand the war into one of *conquest*. It wasn't sufficient for the North Koreans to be defeated on the battlefield and for the *status quo ante bellum* to be restored. In a significant escalation of the war, the USA decided to occupy and destroy North Korea, effectively handing the country to the ROK for the purposes of forcible unification. While this decision, taken quickly and without much thought for the consequences, may well have appeared the rational thing to do militarily at the time (and was strongly advocated for by President Syngman Rhee), both politically and pragmatically it was on much shakier ground. It turned out to be the trigger for a massive counter-intervention by 'Red' China in late October 1950. The USA entirely miscalculated the Chinese response to North Korean defeat and humiliation. For Peking, the North Korean defeat was one thing. It is highly likely that China would have supported a return to the *status quo ante bellum* if UN troops had not proceeded beyond the 38th Parallel in mid-October 1950. However, the humiliation of North Korea, and an American presence on the Yalu, only 500 miles from Peking, was unacceptable to the new Chinese leadership. China's intervention was quite deliberately a Chinese war against America, brought about by hubris and miscalculation in Washington.

In the same way that the Second World War did not start on 3 September 1939, with the British and French declaration of war against Germany in response to the invasion of Poland, but sometime in 1937, when Japan launched its general invasion of China, the Second World War did not end in 1945 but on 27 July 1953, with an armistice closing the Korean War. The war in Korea in 1950 came about as a direct result of the USSR deliberately establishing a client state in North Korea in 1945, refusing the UN's calls to unify the peninsula using democratic means and sponsoring the DPRK's invasion in June 1950. The Korean War was a re-lit ember from the dying fire of global war caused by the policy determination of the USSR to surround itself with a buffer of client states, and to proselytise communism where it could. In this case the wartime allies turned on themselves, and fought each other, evidencing the essential fragility of the wartime coalition. We fought together against the Nazis because we had to: they were the enemy at the gate, but other enemies existed too, on our own side. The moment that the USSR began to assert its totalitarian and repressive prerogatives against those of the group of allies who had defeated Nazism, a new war – a Cold War with hotspots – began. The war that began in 1937 – or 1931, if Japan's adventure in Manchuria is included – is a war that continues today: a war without end.

Order of Battle, US Eighth Army

The Orders of Battle are confusing, as US, UK, and ROK formations moved between the three Corps (I, IX and X) at various points in the fighting. Some divisions, therefore, spent time in one corps before moving to another, and then returning. The dates are to the end of the war, unless otherwise specified.

- US I Corps – from 13 September 1950
  - US 2nd Infantry Division   23 July 1950–22 September 1950
  - US 1st Cavalry Division   13 September 1950–January 1951; April 1951–December 1951
  - US 24th Infantry Division   13 September 1950–January 1951; January 1953
  - ROK 1st Infantry Division   13 September 1950–April 1951; March 1952
  - UK 27th Infantry Brigade   13 September 1950–January 1951
  - UK 1st Commonwealth Division   March 1952–January 1953
  - US 3rd Infantry Division   January 1951; 11 July 1952; January 1953
  - US 25th Infantry Division   January 1951–March 1952; January 1953
  - US 45th Infantry Division   December 1951–January 1953
  - ROK 8th Infantry Division   March 1952–January 1953
  - ROK 9th Infantry Division   March 1952–January 1953
  - US 7th Infantry Division   January 1953
  - US 1st Marine Division   January 1953
  - ROK 2nd Infantry Division   January 1953
  - ROK 25th Infantry Division   January 1953

- US IX Corps – from 23 September 1950
  - US 2nd Infantry Division   23 September 1950–January 1951; March 1952–January 1953
  - US 25th Infantry Division   23 September 1950–January 1951
  - US 187th Regimental Combat Team   January 1951–March 1951
  - US 24th Infantry Division   January 1951–January 1952
  - US 1st Cavalry Division   January 1951–January 1952
  - US 1st Marine Division   January 1951–March 1951
  - ROK 6th Infantry Division   January 1951–January 1952
  - UK 27th Infantry Brigade   17 February 1951
  - US 7th Infantry Division   March 1951–January 1953
  - ROK 2nd Infantry Division   March 1951–January 1952; March 1952–January 1953
  - US 5th Regimental Combat Team   January 1952
  - US 45th Infantry Division   January 1952–March 1952
  - US 40 Infantry Division   March 1952–January 1953
  - ROK Capital Division   March 1952
  - ROK 3rd Infantry Division   March 1952–January 1953
  - ROK 9th Infantry Division   January 1953

- US X Corps – 15 September 1950
  - US 7th Infantry Division   15 September 1950–April 1951
  - US 1st Marine Division   15 September 1950 –December 1950; January 1953
  - ROK 2nd Infantry Division   October 1950–March 1952
  - ROK 5th Infantry Division   October 1950–April 1951
  - ROK 8th Infantry Division   October 1950–April 1951; March 1952
  - US 3rd Infantry Division   24 December 1950–April 1951
  - US 2nd Infantry Division   April 1951–March 1952
  - ROK 7th Infantry Division   April 1951
  - US 25th Infantry Division   March 1952–January 1953
  - ROK 6th Infantry Division   March 1952–January 1953
  - US 40th Infantry Division   January 1953
  - US 45th Infantry Division   January 1953
  - ROK 12th Infantry Division   January 1953
  - ROK 20th Infantry Division   January 1953

Acknowledgements

The authors are indebted to all those who have contributed to bringing this book – our third collaboration – to fruition. It was prompted by the Russian invasion of Ukraine in February 2022, which provided the rationale to rescue this forgotten, misunderstood and unnecessary war from the relative obscurity in which it continues to languish in the history of the United Kingdom. It has much to teach politicians and soldiers today about the use and misuse of political and military power and remains a cautionary tale for politicians and soldiers of all stamps, but only if they read their history.

We wish first to thank a number of libraries and manuscript repositories in the United Kingdom and the United States, without which this book would not have been possible. In the United Kingdom we extend our thanks inter alia to the Keeper of the National Archives at Kew; the British Library; the Trustees of the Liddell Hart Centre for Military Archives at King's College, London; the Controller of Her Majesty's Stationery Office and the Imperial War Museum, for access to material and for permission to quote from the documents and manuscripts in their charge. In the United States the digital archives in the Harry S. Truman Presidential Library and Museum and the National Archives are national treasures and have been indispensable to the writing of this book. The wholesale digitisation of archives has been a phenomenon that has made the work of historians both better, and yet harder. Better, because previously hard copies of documents are now accessible without the need to travel to view them; harder, because at a stroke a vast array of new and variegated sources are now available which authors have to consider and assess when researching and writing their books. This requires a new type of discipline in writing: a relentless focus on the sources that are best able to support the author's narrative, and the discarding of vast amounts of excellent though distracting material. The authors could have spent many more years on this project than we were allocated by our publisher, simply in sifting through the full extent of the archival material available to us. The vast amount of material in the US archives in particular has at times been daunting. There can by definition, therefore, never be a 'final' or 'complete' account of the Korean War, or any other war for that matter. This is ours, written for a particular purpose in the years between 2023 and 2025. We hope that you, the reader, feel that it achieves our aim of interpreting this war of yesteryear through the prism of today.

Many people assisted us in various ways as we tracked our way through the issues and arguments developed in these pages, some directly and others indirectly. Those who helped us indirectly did so by their writings, of which the full extent of our indebtedness can be found in the bibliography. We started by reading a carefully curated selection of British and American assessments of the war published close to the time of the war, as well as the Official Histories of South Korea, the United States and the United Kingdom, and ended by doing the same with contemporary assessments, including many Korean. We are especially grateful to friends who have gone the extra mile by reading parts or all of the manuscript. Our thanks go to General David Petraeus, Lord Andrew Roberts, David Allison, Brigadier Ben Barry, Professor Jeremy Black, Dr Su-Kyoung Hwang, Fergal Keane, Dr Stephen Prince, Michael Shipster, Dr Hugo Slim and Brigadier Allan Mallinson. It goes without saying that any errors of judgement or fact are, of course, entirely our own. We are grateful to Michael Shipster for permission to quote from his father's *Mist Over the Rice Fields* and to Professor Dame Sarah Whatmore for permission to quote from her father's remarkable memoirs, *One Road to Imjin*.

We wish also to thank our agent, Charlie Viney, for steering this project to its conclusion, together with the advice, encouragement and skilful pen of our editor, Kate Moore; the managing editor, Gemma White; the senior marketing executive, Elle Chilvers and the senior head of publicity, Rachel Nicholson, all of Osprey Publishing. And many thanks to Gilly Goldsmid who has sorted out many of Richard's and Rob's diary issues.

Finally, we wish to acknowledge the steadfast support of our respective families during this endeavour. To our wives, Philippa and Hannah, both authors offer their grateful thanks, and love.

Bibliography

PRIMARY SOURCES

Official Histories
Farrar-Hockley, General Sir Anthony. *The British Part in the Korean War.*
2 vols. London, 1990–95.
Suk Lee-hyung, ed. *History of the United Nations Forces in the Korean War.*
5 vols. Seoul, 1972–77.
United States Army in the Korean War. Various volumes, including:
Appleman, R. *South to the Naktong, North to the Yalu.* Washington DC:
Center of Military History, United States Army, 1961; Mossman, B. *Ebb
and Flow: November 1950–July 1951.* Washington DC: Center of Military
History, United States Army, 1990.

British Government Publications
- Cmd 7631, February 1949: Statement on Defence.
- Cmd 7633, February 1949: Memorandum of Secretary of
State for War on Army Estimates 1949–50.
- Cmd 7895, March 1950: Statement on Defence.
- Cmd 8078, March 1950: Summary of Events leading to
Korea.
- Cmd 8475, February 1952: Summary of Events.
- Cmd 8477, February 1952: Memorandum of Secretary of
State for War on Defence
- Estimates 1952/3.
- Cmd 8716, December 1952: Summary of the Indian
proposals for resolution of the prisoners-of-war problem.
- Cmd 8768, February 1953: Statement on Defence 1953.

- Cmd 9072, February 1954: Memorandum of Secretary of State on Defence Estimates 1954/5.

The National Archives, Kew
The files listed below have extensive components, which are too lengthy to list here. They can be easily viewed in detail at https://discovery .nationalarchives.gov.uk

- CAB 21
- WO 216
- WO 32
- WO 281
- WO 308

Harry S. Truman Library – Truman Office Files (microfiche)
- Reels MF 427–423.
- J. C. S. Series: Microfiches 68, 76, 79.
- S–XA – Military History in Korea: events in South Korea 25 June–1 July 1950.
- S–XB
- MFF 8

Imperial War Museum – Documents
- 18379 Major-General B. A. Coad CB CBE DSO
- 4482 Colonel A. M. Man DSO OBE
- 3163 Brigadier G. Taylor CBE DSO
- 11300 General Sir M. A. R. West GCB DSO

Imperial War Museum – Audio
- 18262 Francis Carter
- 15256 Douglas Charlton
- 9537 Andrew Man
- 15338 Byron Murphy

SECONDARY SOURCES

Acheson, Dean. *The Korean War*. W. W. Norton & Co., 1971.
Alexander, Bevin. *Korea: The First War We Lost*. Hippocrene, 1986.

Allison, David. *27th British Commonwealth Brigade Korea 1950–1951*. Pen and Sword, 2025.

Appleman, Roy E. *Disaster in Korea*. Texas A & M University Press, 1989.

Appleman, Roy E. *Ridgway Duels for Korea*. Texas A & M University Press, 2005.

Attlee, C. R. *As It Happened*. Heinemann, 1954.

Baik, Tae-Ung. 'A War Crime against an Ally's Civilians: The No Gun Ri Massacre'. *Notre Dame Journal of Law, Ethics and Public Policy* 15:2 (2012): 455–505.

Barth, George. 'The First Days in Korea'. *Combat Forces Journal* (March 1951): 28–31.

Bew, John. *Citizen Clem, A Biography of Attlee*. Riverrun, 2016.

Biggar, Nigel. *In Defence of War*. Oxford University Press, 2013.

Blair, Clay. *The Forgotten War: America in Korea 1950–1953*. Doubleday, 1987.

Brune, Lester H., ed. *The Korean War: Handbook of the Literature and Research*. Greenwood Press, 1996.

Carew, Tim. *The Korean War: The Story of the Fighting Commonwealth Regiments 1950–1953*. Pan Books, 1970.

Chen Jian. *China's Road to the Korean War: The Making of the Sino-American Confrontation*. Columbia University Press, 1994.

Cotterell, A. *East Asia: From Chinese Predominance to the Rise of the Pacific Rim*. Oxford University Press, 1993.

Crane, Conrad. *American Airpower Strategy in Korea 1950–1953*. University Press of Kansas, 2000.

Cumings, Bruce. *The Korean War: A History*. Modern Library, 2010.

Cumings, Bruce. *The Origins of the Korean War*. Vol. II: *The Roaring of the Cataract*. Princeton University Press, 1992.

Cumings, Bruce and J. Halliday. *The Unknown War: Korea*. Penguin, 1988.

Cunningham-Booth, A. and P. Farrar, eds. *British Forces in the Korean War*. British Korean Veterans' Association, 1988.

Cutforth, René, *Korean Reporter*. Allan Wingate, 1952.

Davies, S. J. *In Spite of Dungeons*. Hodder and Stoughton, 1954.

Deane, Hugh. *The Korean War: 1945–1953*. China Books and Periodicals, 1999.

Dixon, Pierson. *Korea: Britain and the Korean War, 1950–51*. Foreign and Commonwealth Office Library and Records Department, Historical Branch, second edition: revised 1995.

Edwards, Paul M. *The Korean War: An Annotated Bibliography*. Greenwood Press, 1998.

Edwards, Paul M. *General Matthew B. Ridgway: An Annotated Bibliography.* Greenwood Press, 1993.

Farrar-Hockley, A. *The Edge of the Sword.* Frederick Muller Ltd, 1954.

Fehrenbach, T. R. *This Kind of War.* Macmillan, 1963.

Foot, Rosemary. *The Wrong War: American Policy and the Dimensions of the Korean Conflict, 1950–1953.* Cornell University Press, 1985.

Gaddis, John Lewis. *Strategies of Containment: A Critical Appraisal of American National Security Policy during the Cold War.* Oxford University Press, 1982.

Gaston, P. *Thirty-Eighth Parallel: The British in Korea.* A. D. Hamilton, 1976.

George, A. L. *The Chinese Army in Action: The Korean War and its Aftermath.* Columbia University Press, 1967.

Goldstein, Donald M. and Harry James Maihafer. *The Korean War: The Story and Photographs.* Potomac Books, 2000.

Goulden, Joseph C. *Korea: The Untold Story of the War.* McGraw-Hill Books, 1982.

Grey, Jeffrey. *The Commonwealth Armies and the Korean War.* Manchester University Press, 1988.

Gugeler, Russell, *Combat Actions in Korea.* Washington DC: Office of the Chief of Military History, 1970.

Guttmann, Allen. *Korea: Cold War and Limited War.* Heath Company, 1967.

Hackworth, David. *About Face.* Sidgwick & Jackson, 1989.

Halberstam, David. *The Coldest Winter: America and the Korean War.* Hyperion, 2007.

Hanley, Charles. *Ghost Flames: Life & Death in a Hidden War, Korea 1950–1953.* Hachette, 2021.

Hanson, Victor Davis. *The Savior Generals.* Bloomsbury, 2013.

Hastings, Max. *The Korean War.* Simon and Schuster, 1987.

Hee-Kyung, Suh. 'Atrocities Before and During the Korean War: Mass Civilian Killings by South Korean and U.S. Forces'. *Critical Asian Studies* 42, no. 4 (2010): 553–88.

Heinl, Robert Debs. *Victory at High Tide. The Inchon Seoul Campaign.* Leo Cooper, 1972.

Hennessey, Thomas. *Britain's Korean War: Cold War Diplomacy, Strategy and Security.* Manchester University Press, 2013.

Hermes, Walter G. *Truce Tent and Fighting Front. United States Army in the Korean War.* (Washington, DC: US Army Center of Military History, 1988.

Hermiston, Roger. *The Greatest Traitor: The Secret Lives of Agent George Blake.* Aurum, 2013.

Hickey, Michael. *The Korean War: The West Confronts Communism.* Overstock Press, 2000.

Higgins, Marguerite. *War in Korea: The Report of a Woman Combat Correspondent.* Doubleday and Company, 1951.

Higgins, Trumbull. *Korea and the Fall of MacArthur.* Oxford University Press, 1960.

Hinshaw, Arned. *Heartbreak Ridge: Korea, 1951.* Praeger, 1989.

Hua, Qingzao. *From Yalta to Panmunjom: Truman's Diplomacy and the Four Powers, 1945–1953.* Cornell University, 1993.

Hwang, Su-kyoung. *Korea's Grievous War.* University of Pennsylvania Press, 2016.

Jackson, W. G. F. and E. N. W. Bramall. *The Chiefs.* Brassey's, 1995.

Korea Institute of Military History. *The Korean War.* First published 1997; Bison Books ed., 2000.

Kim, Chae-dong. *Foreign Intervention in Korea.* Dartmouth Publishing, 1993.

Kim, Dong Choon. 'Forgotten War, Forgotten Massacres – the Korean War (1950–1953) as Licensed Mass Killings', *Journal of Genocide Research* 6, no. 4 (2004): 523–44.

Leary, William, ed. *MacArthur and the American Century.* University of Nebraska Press, 2001.

Leckie, Robert. *Conflict: The History of the Korean War, 1950–53.* Putnam, 1962.

Lee, Steven Hugh. *The Korean War.* Routledge, 2013.

Li, X., A. Millet and B. Yu. *Mao's Generals Remember Korea.* University Press of Kansas, 2001.

Linklater, E. *Our Men in Korea.* HMSO, 1951.

Lyman, Robert. *The Generals.* Constable, 2008.

MacArthur, Douglas. *Reminiscences.* McGraw Hill, 1964.

MacDonald, C. '"So terrible a liberation" – The UN Occupation of North Korea', *Bulletin of Concerned Asian Scholars*, 23(2) (1991), 3–19.

Mallinson, Allan. *The Shape of Battle.* Bantam Press, 2021.

Mallinson, Allan. *The Making of the British Army.* Bantam Press, 2009.

Manchester, William. *American Caesar: Douglas MacArthur 1880–1964.* Dell Publishing, 1978.

Marshall, S. L. A. *The River and the Gauntlet: Defeat of the Eighth Army by the Chinese Communist Forces, November 1950 in the Battle of Chongchon River, Korea.* Battery Press, 1987.

Marshall, S. L. A. *Pork Chop Hill.* Permabooks, 1959.

McCullough, David. *Truman.* Simon & Schuster, 1992.

Millet, Allan R. 'Korean War', https://www.britannica.com/event/Korean -War

Millett, Allan R. *The War for Korea 1950–1951, They Came from the North.* University Press of Kansas, 2010.

Mitchell, George Charles. *Matthew B. Ridgway: Soldier, Statesman, Scholar, Citizen.* Stackpole Books, 2002.

Osborne, John. 'Men at War: The Ugly War', *Time* magazine, 21 August 1950, https://time.com/archive/6615304/men-at-war-the-ugly-war/

Overy, Richard. *The Bombers and The Bombed.* Viking, 2013.

Paik, Sun Yup. *From Pusan to Panmunjom.* Brassey's, 1992.

Perret, Geoffrey. *Old Soldiers Never Die: The Life of Douglas MacArthur.* Adams, 1996.

Petraeus, General David and Andrew Roberts. *Conflict: The Evolution of Warfare from 1945 to Ukraine.* William Collins, 2023.

Rees, David. *Korea: The Limited War.* Macmillan, 1964.

Ridgway, Matthew B. *The Korean War.* Doubleday, 1967.

Russ, Martin. *Breakout: The Chosin Reservoir Campaign, Korea, 1950.* Penguin, 1999.

Salmon, Andrew. *Scorched Earth, Black Snow. Britain and Australia in the Korean War, 1950.* Aurum, 2011.

Salmon, Andrew. *To The Last Round: The Epic British Stand on the Imjin River, 1951.* Aurum, 2009.

Schnabel, James F. *Policy and Direction: The First Year.* Washington, DC: Center of Military History, 1992.

Scott, James. *Black Snow: Curtis Le May, the Firebombing of Tokyo and the Road to the Atomic Bomb.* W. W. Norton and Co., 2022.

Shipster, John, ed. *The Diehards in Korea.* Privately published, 1975.

Shipster, John. *Mist over the Rice Fields.* Leo Cooper, 2000.

Spanier, John W. *The Truman–MacArthur Controversy and the Korean War.* W. W. Norton and Co., 1965.

Spurr, Russell. *Enter the Dragon: China's undeclared war against the U.S. in Korea, 1950–51.* Newmarket Press, 1988.

Stueck, William. *Rethinking the Korean War: A New Diplomatic and Strategic History.* Princeton University Press, 2002.

Stueck, William. *The Korean War: An International History.* Princeton University Press, 1995.

Taaffe, Stephen R. *MacArthur's Korean War Generals.* University Press of Kansas, 2016.

Thompson, Julian. *The Lifeblood of War: Logistics in Armed Conflict.* Brassey's, 1991.

Thompson, Reginald. *Cry Korea*. MacDonald and Co., 1951.

Tirman, John. *The Deaths of Others: The Fate of Civilians in America's Wars*. Oxford University Press, 2011.

Truman, Harry S. *Memoirs, Year of Decisions*, Vol. I and *Memoirs, Years of Trial and Hope 1946–1952*, Vol. II. Doubleday, 1955.

Walker, A., ed. *A Barren Place: National Servicemen in Korea, 1950–54*. Pen and Sword, 1994.

Weathersby, K. 'New Russian Documents on the Korean War', *Cold War International History Project Bulletin*, issues 6–7 (winter 1995–96).

Weintrub, Stanley. *Macarthur's War: Korea and the Undoing of an American Hero*. Prentice Hall, 2000.

Whatmore, D. *One Road to Imjin*. Dew Line Publications, 1997.

Wiest, Andrew, Mary Kathryn Barbier and Glenn Robins. *America and the Vietnam War: Re-examining the Culture and History of a Generation*. Routledge, 2009.

Wittington, Alan, *Breakfast with Mao: Memoirs of a Foreign Correspondent* (Lawrence and Wishart, 1986)

Xiaobing, Li. *China's Battle for Korea: The 1951 Spring Offensive*. Indiana University Press, 2014.

Index

References to maps are in **bold**.